THE PERILOUS PUBLIC SQUARE

ABOUT THE KNIGHT FIRST AMENDMENT INSTITUTE

The Knight First Amendment Institute was established in 2016 by Columbia University and the John S. and James L. Knight Foundation to safeguard free expression in the shifting landscape of the digital age. The Institute's litigation, research, and public education efforts focus on new manifestations of longstanding threats to freedom of speech and the press, and the many novel challenges arising from evolving technologies.

THE PERILOUS PUBLIC SQUARE

STRUCTURAL THREATS TO FREE EXPRESSION TODAY

Edited by David E. Pozen

COLUMBIA UNIVERSITY PRESS   NEW YORK

COLUMBIA UNIVERSITY PRESS
Publishers Since 1893
New York   Chichester, West Sussex
cup.columbia.edu
Compilation copyright © 2020 Columbia University Press
All rights reserved

Library of Congress Cataloging-in-Publication Data
Names: Pozen, David E, editor, author. | Knight First Amendment Institute at
    Columbia University.
Title: The perilous public square : structural threats to free expression today /
    edited by David E Pozen.
Description: New York : Columbia University Press, 2020. | This volume grew out
    of, and includes, a series of papers entitled "Emerging threats" published from
    September 2017 to October 18 at the website of the Knight First Amendment Institute at
    Columbia University—ECIP Introduction. | Includes bibliographical references and index.
Identifiers: LCCN 2019048989 (print) | LCCN 2019048990 (ebook) |
    ISBN 9780231197120 (cloth) | ISBN 9780231197137 (paperback) |
    ISBN 9780231551991 (ebook)
Subjects: LCSH: Freedom of expression—United States.
Classification: LCC KF4770 .P47 2020 (print) | LCC KF4770 (ebook) |
    DDC 342.7308/53—dc23
LC record available at https://lccn.loc.gov/2019048989
LC ebook record available at https://lccn.loc.gov/2019048990

Cover design: Julia Kushnirsky
Cover Image: © istockphoto

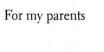

CONTENTS

THE PERILOUS PUBLIC SQUARE

INTRODUCTION

David E. Pozen

EVERYONE SEEMS TO AGREE: we live "at a time when free speech is under attack."[1] But under attack from what?

Justice Samuel Alito declined to elaborate on that claim in his June 2019 concurring opinion in *Iancu v. Brunetti*. Presumably he did not have in mind the 73-year-old trademark registration statute that was at issue in the case. More likely, he was alluding to what many critics, especially though not exclusively on the political right, describe as a culture of close-mindedness on university campuses and in elite media circles. According to this account, American students, professors, and pundits are increasingly challenging the value of open inquiry and resorting to tactics—from obstreperous protests to speaker disinvitations to demands for trigger warnings and safe spaces—that stifle debate and enforce the prevailing intellectual and ideological orthodoxy.[2]

Meanwhile, many other critics, especially though not exclusively on the political left, offer a very different vision of what imperils free speech today. According to this account, the Supreme Court's conservative majority has "weaponized" or "Lochnerized" the Constitution's free speech guarantee over a series of rulings to undermine the First Amendment interests of ordinary workers, voters, and consumers while protecting the privileges of well-heeled corporations and donors (to say nothing of pornographers, neo-Nazis, and other controversial beneficiaries of prior precedents).[3] The result is an ever more plutocratic expressive order that elected officials can do little to fix. Justice Alito's lament is highly ironic on this view, for he is not so much the victim of an attack on free speech as a leading perpetrator.

Both of these critiques raise important issues. They draw on different strands of liberal theory as well as different sources of evidence, and they have generated passionate debate. Nevertheless, they capture only a slice of the threats currently facing our system of free expression.

Well beyond America's campuses and courthouses, a set of political, economic, social, and technological developments have been raising profound challenges for this system in recent years. These developments range from the rise of authoritarian nationalism, "fake news," and national security secrecy; to the decline of print journalism and of trust in experts; to increasingly subtle forms of governmental and nongovernmental surveillance and speech control made possible by digital platforms. We might call these threats "structural" insofar as they arise not only or primarily from discrete decisions or events but also from broad changes in the means and forms of mass communication, collective organization, and capitalist production.

The First Amendment literature has confronted structural problems before. Although much of the literature has focused on defining and defending the rights of specific speakers, a distinguished line of authors have widened the analytic lens and asked "how to engineer a fairer, fuller, 'freer' expressive environment for everyone"[4]—or at least, how to prevent the expressive environment from tilting too far in the opposite direction. In this vein, jurists such as Justice Stephen Breyer, Justice John Paul Stevens, and Judge J. Skelly Wright have defended the constitutionality of campaign spending limits on the ground that these limits can promote "the truth-producing capacity of the marketplace of ideas"[5] and "the integrity, competitiveness, and democratic responsiveness of the electoral process."[6] Scholars such as Jack Balkin, Yochai Benkler, Owen Fiss, and Cass Sunstein have similarly defended policies meant to promote corresponding values in the media[7]: for instance, a "fairness doctrine" requiring broadcasters to cover topics of public importance in a balanced manner,[8] "must-carry" rules for cable providers,[9] and "net neutrality"[10] and "open access"[11] rules for internet carriers. These proposals differ in many particulars. They are united in the belief that, as Balkin puts it, a well-functioning "system of free speech depends not only on the mere absence of state censorship but also on an infrastructure of free expression."[12]

The question of how to secure such an infrastructure has become more complicated in the twenty-first century. The United States' ongoing transformation from an industrial to an informational mode of capitalism has made it harder to separate commercial speech from noncommercial speech and economic activity from expressive activity—and thus to maintain some of the distinctions at the heart of modern free speech law.[13]

A small number of digital companies exercise enormous power over a virtual public square that is short on privacy, civility, and local news coverage and long on conspiracy theories, sensationalistic content, and worse.[14] Although the companies themselves are generally assumed to be unconstrained by the First Amendment, because they are not "state actors," they are quick to invoke the Free Speech Clause against unwanted litigation and legislation.[15] Both online and offline, rising levels of socioeconomic inequality have exacerbated concerns about the distribution of access to educational and expressive resources.[16] Rising levels of polarization in politics and the media, in conjunction with the internet "echo chambers,"[17] "filter bubbles,"[18] and "information cocoons"[19] that are their partial cause and consequence, have exacerbated concerns about the coherence of public discourse and its capacity to sort fact from fiction, much less to foster good-faith deliberation.

All of these developments, and more, have contributed to a "powerful collective anxiety"[20] about the state of free expression. Even as the legal rights of Americans to speak their minds have arguably never been stronger, and overt government censorship never been weaker, the fear that there is nonetheless something deeply amiss with our speech system continues to mount.

ORIGINS AND GOALS OF THIS VOLUME

This volume responds to that fear and tries to throw some light on it. It does so by bringing together leading legal thinkers to help identify and investigate newly arising or intensifying structural threats to the system of free expression. Although the contributors are mostly based in the United States and mostly concentrate on U.S. laws and institutions—a parochialism endemic to First Amendment scholarship—almost all of the threats they address have global implications, as their pieces make clear.

Substantively, this volume grows out of a conviction that the structural dimensions of free speech deserve ongoing solicitude and study, inasmuch as truly free speech requires a mix of legal, material, and cultural ingredients that collectively enable effective voice and participation throughout society. These ingredients, moreover, may change over time as society changes. Safeguarding the system of free expression is a dynamic challenge. The overarching goal of the volume is to call attention to a number of particularly important structural threats to the current system and, in so doing, to begin to move these matters from the periphery toward the center of the free speech conversation.

Campus PC-ism and First Amendment Lochnerism have been explored at length in academic articles and in the popular press.[21] Other, more diffuse phenomena with the potential to destabilize the speech system have received less attention from legal scholars, many of whom are accustomed to taking their cues from the courts and their immediate professional surroundings. To the best of my knowledge, structural threats to the speech system—threats to the channels and institutions that make interpersonal communication and democratic self-governance possible—have never before been considered as a group across the disciplinary boundaries of First Amendment law, internet law, media law, legal history, and legal theory.

Organizationally, this volume grows out of the efforts of the Knight First Amendment Institute at Columbia University to establish a research program in support of its mission to defend the freedoms of speech and the press in the digital age. The Knight Institute was created in 2016 by Columbia University and the John S. and James L. Knight Foundation. A nonpartisan nonprofit, the Institute has close ties to Columbia's law school and journalism school, among other departments. Throughout all its work, the Institute aims "to promote a system of free expression that is open and inclusive, that broadens and elevates public discourse, and that fosters creativity, accountability, and effective self-government."[22]

I served as the inaugural visiting scholar at the Knight Institute in 2017–2018. One of the main projects that I undertook in this role was commissioning and editing a series of papers on emerging threats to the system of free expression titled, rather unimaginatively, *Emerging Threats*. The series ran from September 2017 to October 2018. It featured seven substantial papers, which were published on the Knight Institute's website together with commentaries by distinguished respondents.

Emerging Threats struck a chord with readers anxious to make sense of an expressive environment that, in the age of Trump and Twitter,[23] appears almost unrecognizable in numerous respects from its mid- and late twentieth-century predecessors. Each of the seven installments received an enthusiastic response from students, scholars, practitioners, journalists, and others who follow the Knight Institute's work. A senior editor at Columbia University Press, Philip Leventhal, took notice. After the series closed, Leventhal invited the Institute to collaborate with the press on turning the series into an edited volume.

The result is the book you now have in your hands. All of the pieces from the *Emerging Threats* series are collected here, in lightly edited and updated form. In addition to giving the series a permanent, physical home, the hope is that assembling the pieces in one volume will help expand the audience for their arguments and allow readers to draw fruitful connections and contrasts across the full set.

THEMES AND THROUGHLINES

At any given time, there are apt to be dozens of structural challenges facing any given system of free expression. Reasonable minds may disagree on what exactly constitutes a "structural challenge" in this context and what exactly constitutes a "system of free expression." Where some might see a threat to speech interests, others might see instead a conflict between free speech and other values, such as equality or dignity. People may likewise disagree as to the novelty or severity of particular threats and, *a fortiori*, as to the overall health of the system. Regardless, the basic point holds. The public square is always imperiled, to a greater or lesser degree. Structural challenges are everywhere.

The essays in this volume, accordingly, do not and could not explore all of the threats to the speech system today. For instance, none of the essays examines the economic plight of investigative journalism, the dwindling prospects for campaign finance reform, or the growing use of criminal probes and penalties for suspected leakers of classified information. Each of those topics has spawned a great deal of scholarly study.[24] In part, the selection of topics for this volume reflects the Knight Institute's desire to tackle relatively underexplored problems. In part, it reflects a desire to defer consideration of issues that the Institute has taken up or will soon be taking up in other venues, such as the Institute's March 2018 symposium on equality and the First Amendment,[25] its November 2018 event on the "chilling effects" of surveillance,[26] its November 2019 convening on the potential use of anti-monopoly tools to address the tech giants' influence over public discourse,[27] and its pending constitutional challenge to the federal executive branch's system of "prepublication review" for former employees.[28] And in part, the selection of topics simply reflects the preferences of the contributors, who were invited to address particular areas of concern but were given wide latitude within those parameters.

While this volume is therefore selective in multiple senses, and far from comprehensive, it provides a wide-ranging survey of some of the most pressing challenges facing the system of free expression today. Put another way, it provides a kind of heat map to those parts of the contemporary expressive environment of greatest concern to structurally oriented legal scholars. Moreover, because the essays are paired with multiple commentaries, some of them quite critical, the volume offers a multifaceted perspective not only on the speech system writ large but also on each part of the system that it spotlights.

Multifaceted does not mean cacophonous. Across the essays and commentaries in the volume, a number of high-level anxieties and diagnoses continually resurface. Among the most notable, it seems to me, are the following:

- **Platform power.** Threaded throughout many of the pieces is a concern that the dominance of a few privately owned communications platforms, different from one another in various ways but joined in their insatiable appetite for user data, has been warping democratic deliberation and degrading the public sphere. The generally grim portrait of cyberspace that emerges from these pages stands in stark contrast to the benevolent narratives promoted by social media executives (as described in the chapters by Kate Klonick, Olivier Sylvain, and Heather Whitney), not to mention the utopian visions promoted by U.S. government officials at the internet's founding (see the chapter by Jack Goldsmith).
- **Limits of laissez-faire.** Several of the chapters (by Goldsmith, Sylvain, and Tim Wu) implicitly resist the inevitability of such concentrated, and corrosive, platform power by emphasizing legal choices made and not made over the past two decades. The United States' generally light-touch, industry-friendly approach to regulating online service providers, their analyses suggest, has played a large role in constructing the dominance of a small set of firms and in enabling the business practices that now compromise the virtual marketplace of ideas.
- **Tragic tradeoffs.** To note the limits of laissez-faire is not to imply that regulating the speech system is easy. On the contrary, nearly all of the chapters underscore that, online as well as offline, government officials and social media executives who seek to safeguard this system confront vexing tradeoffs—for example, between deterring hecklers and encouraging inflammatory speakers (see the chapter by Frederick Schauer);

between protecting against malicious cyber intrusions and minimizing government involvement in domestic networks (see the chapter by Goldsmith); and between maintaining content "neutrality" and enforcing minimal standards of accuracy, quality, or civility (see the chapters by Klonick and Whitney).

- **Amplification of analog problems.** Not only has the advent of the digital age failed to solve stubborn expressive tradeoffs, many of the chapters further contend, but it has also magnified preexisting problems. For instance, if government archivists have long struggled with meager budgets and recalcitrant national security agencies, the exponential growth in electronic records has made the job of preserving the historical record almost impossible under current conditions (see the chapter by Matthew Connelly). And if women and racial minorities have long faced abuse in public and quasi-public forums, the "unforgiving ecology" of cyberspace, in which vitriolic content spreads with unprecedented speed and scale, "raises the stakes" (see the chapter by Sylvain).

- **Strained legal and intellectual paradigms.** In the face of such dramatic technological developments, as well as new academic learning, all of the chapters raise hard questions about whether traditional legal and intellectual frameworks for promoting free expression have become outmoded or even perverse. This theme is most pronounced in the chapter by Wu, which asks the reader (in a manner cautiously commended by Goldsmith) "to imagine how First Amendment doctrine might adapt to the kinds of speech manipulation" that currently pervade the internet. But a readiness to rethink prevailing paradigms can also be seen in Connelly's call for Congress to impose a cap on the ratio of classification to declassification actions and to create a new independent agency "with a mandate to control official secrecy"; in Klonick's call to "dispatch . . . altogether" with the concepts of voluntariness and involuntariness in determining who counts as a public figure online; in Schauer's call to enlist the tools of cognitive psychology to assess which forms of audience behavior interfere with public presentations; in Sylvain's call to realign the law of intermediary liability with "the political economy of contemporary online information flows"; and in Whitney's call to move beyond the hoary analogies that have guided much of the First Amendment conversation about Facebook, Google, and Twitter.[29]

These are broad themes. They do not amount to a unified theory of free speech or speech regulation. Taken together, however, they limn some of the key contours of the key threats facing the expressive environment today. In the process, they demonstrate just how much creativity and commitment will be needed to address these threats to any meaningful degree.

PLAN OF THE BOOK

The chapters in this volume are organized as dialogues. With the exception of the first chapter, to which I will turn shortly, each chapter starts with a brief introduction by me. Then comes the principal essay, followed by two to four commentaries on the essay. This organization allows readers to dip in and out of specific chapters, while preserving a coherent narrative flow for those who wish to engage with all of them.

The chapters appear in the order in which they appeared in the original *Emerging Threats* series. In my introductions to each chapter, I try to set the stage for the principal essay and the commentaries that respond to it. Because these introductions provide a preview of every piece in every chapter, it would be redundant to offer another preview here.

To give a more appetizing taste of what is to come, however, we can go directly to the source. The following passages from the principal essays strike me as capturing, especially succinctly, some of their core claims.

> **WU:** "The most important change in the expressive environment can be boiled down to one idea: it is no longer speech itself that is scarce, but the attention of listeners. Emerging threats to public discourse take advantage of this change. . . . The apparent flurry of First Amendment activity masks the fact that the Amendment has become increasingly irrelevant in its area of historic concern: the coercive control of political speech."

> **SCHAUER:** "It is now widely believed that restricting the speaker on account of the actual or predicted hostile and potentially violent reaction of the audience gets our First Amendment priorities backwards. But it is hardly clear that this belief was ever correct, and even if it were, it is even less clear that it is sufficient to deal with the constitutional and policy complexities of many of the contemporary encounters."

WHITNEY: "In debates over tech companies and free speech coverage, neither the gravity of the policy stakes nor the complexity of the things being compared has dampened the willingness of courts and scholars to use tenuous analogies in charting the way forward. . . . But the point of this paper is that casual analogical methods . . . do not tell us whether or to what extent [search engines and social media platforms should be covered by principles of a free press]."

SYLVAIN: "Section 230 [of the Communications Decency Act of 1996] is no longer serving all the purposes it was meant to serve. The statute was intended at least in part to ensure the vitality and diversity, as well as the volume, of speech on new communications platforms. By allowing intermediaries to design their platforms without internalizing the costs of the illegal speech and conduct they facilitate, however, the statute is having the opposite effect."

GOLDSMITH: "The U.S. internet freedom project deserves significant credit for the remarkable growth of the global internet, and especially global commerce, in the last two decades. But on every other dimension, the project is failing, and many of its elements lie in tatters. . . . The relatively unregulated internet in the United States is being used for ill to a point that threatens basic American institutions."

CONNELLY: "While politicians will continue to appeal to history when convenient, they have so neglected the National Archives and so failed to control official secrecy that future historians will have a hard time proving anything at all. . . . How will history judge a generation of government officials who not only insist on working in secrecy but also fail to protect, or even destroy, the record of their actions?"

KLONICK: "The internet has eroded some of the traditional reasons for specially protecting speech concerning public figures, based on the assumption that people become public figures by choice and that, as public figures, they have greater access to channels of rebuttal. These assumptions are becoming increasingly outdated in the digital age, given the dynamics of online virality and notoriety and given the ubiquity of channels for engaging in counterspeech."

These claims are bold, and they seem likely to unsettle readers of almost any ideological stripe. But the claims are also grounded, in all cases, in careful analysis, diligent research, and deep subject-matter expertise. Free speech advocates ignore them at their own peril.

FIRST (AMENDMENT) THINGS FIRST

The volume opens with an essay by Tim Wu, a leading scholar of communications law and my colleague at Columbia Law School. Wu observes that some of the forces that undermine the integrity and the humanity (sometimes quite literally) of political discourse today—forces such as "troll armies" and propaganda robots that aim to distort or drown out disfavored speech—may be beyond the reach of the First Amendment as it has been traditionally construed. To help secure the expressive environment against these menaces, Wu considers a range of possible responses. For instance, courts could invigorate the "accomplice liability" and "captive audience" doctrines under the First Amendment, and Congress could enact new criminal sanctions for online intimidation of members of the press.

Two eminent constitutional thinkers offer very different reflections on these arguments. Noting historical parallels to some of the threats that Wu recounts, Geoffrey Stone of the University of Chicago Law School suggests that Wu is too quick to discount the benefits of existing First Amendment law and too eager to empower prosecutors to combat socially harmful speech. Rebecca Tushnet of Harvard Law School, on the other hand, echoes Wu's pessimistic descriptive account and considers possible extensions of his reform ideas in areas such as compelled speech and public education.

As explained above, subsequent chapters will lead off with introductions by me. But Wu's bracing essay does not need any further setup. I can think of no better way to begin a book by legal scholars on challenges to the contemporary speech system than with the question it poses: is the First Amendment obsolete?

NOTES

1. *Iancu v. Brunetti*, 139 S. Ct. 2294, 2302–03 (2019) (Alito, J., concurring) (capitalization altered).
2. Among the most significant statements of this critique are Greg Lukianoff & Jonathan Haidt, *The Coddling of the American Mind: How Good Intentions and Bad Ideas Are Setting Up a Generation for Failure* (2018); and Keith E. Whittington, *Speak Freely: Why Universities Must Defend Free Speech* (2018). For an illuminating study of the backlash to perceived "political correctness" (or "PC-ism") on college campuses from 1989 to 2016, see Heidi Kitrosser, *Free Speech, Higher Education, and the PC Narrative*, 101 Minn. L. Rev. 1987 (2017).

3. *See, e.g., Janus v. Am. Fed'n of State, Cty., & Mun. Emps., Council 31,* 138 S. Ct. 2448, 2501 (2018) (Kagan, J., dissenting) (asserting that, "not [for] the first time," the Roberts Court was "weaponizing the First Amendment, in a way that unleashes judges . . . to intervene in economic and regulatory policy"); Jeremy K. Kessler & David E. Pozen, *The Search for an Egalitarian First Amendment,* 118 Colum. L. Rev. 1953, 1959–64 (2018) (reviewing recent works advancing this account). Although they have become much more prominent since 2010, concerns about "First Amendment Lochnerism" have been around for decades. *See* Jeremy K. Kessler, *The Early Years of First Amendment Lochnerism,* 116 Colum. L. Rev. 1915, 1917 n.4 (2016) (collecting older sources, beginning with Thomas H. Jackson & John Calvin Jeffries, Jr., *Commercial Speech: Economic Due Process and the First Amendment,* 65 Va. L. Rev. 1, 30–32 (1979)). The charge of Lochnerism in this context refers to the anticanonical case *Lochner v. New York,* 198 U.S. 45 (1905), and to a First Amendment jurisprudence that, much like the original *Lochner* decision did through the Due Process Clause, "disables redistributive regulation and exacerbates socioeconomic inequality." Kessler & Pozen, *supra,* at 2007.

4. Kessler & Pozen, *supra* note 3, at 2002.

5. J. Skelly Wright, *Money and the Pollution of Politics: Is the First Amendment an Obstacle to Political Equality?,* 82 Colum. L. Rev. 609, 636 (1982).

6. *Citizens United v. FEC,* 558 U.S. 310, 472 (2010) (Stevens, J., concurring in part and dissenting in part); *see also* Stephen Breyer, *Active Liberty: Interpreting Our Democratic Constitution* 47 (2005) ("Ultimately, [campaign finance laws] seek . . . to maintain the integrity of the political process—a process that itself translates political speech into governmental action.").

7. For an overview of these arguments, see Kessler & Pozen, *supra* note 3, at 2002–04.

8. *See, e.g.,* Owen M. Fiss, *The Irony of Free Speech* 56–60 (1996).

9. *See, e.g.,* Cass R. Sunstein, *A New Deal for Speech,* 17 Hastings Comm. & Ent. L.J. 137, 138–40, 154–59 (1994).

10. *See, e.g.,* Jack M. Balkin, *The Future of Free Expression in a Digital Age,* 36 Pepp. L. Rev. 427, 428–33 (2009).

11. *See, e.g.,* Yochai Benkler, *Ending the Internet's Trench Warfare,* N.Y. Times (Mar. 20, 2010), http://www.nytimes.com/2010/03/21/opinion/21Benkler.html.

12. Balkin, *supra* note 10, at 432 (punctuation omitted).

13. *See generally* Julie E. Cohen, *The Regulatory State in the Information Age,* 17 Theoretical Inquiries L. 369 (2016); Kessler & Pozen, *supra* note 3, at 1970–77; Amanda Shanor, *The New Lochner,* 2016 Wis. L. Rev. 133.

14. *See generally, e.g.,* Shoshana Zuboff, *The Age of Surveillance Capitalism: The Fight for a Human Future at the New Frontier of Power* (2019); Emily Bell & Taylor Owen, *The Platform Press: How Silicon Valley Reengineered Journalism,* Tow Ctr. for Digital Journalism (Mar. 29, 2017), https://www.cjr.org/tow_center_reports /platform-press-how-silicon-valley-reengineered-journalism.php. On the idea that the internet in general, and social media sites in particular, are "the modern public square," see *Packingham v. North Carolina,* 137 S. Ct. 1730, 1737 (2017).

15. *See, e.g.,* Lina M. Khan & David E. Pozen, *A Skeptical View of Information Fiduciaries,* 133 Harv. L. Rev. 497, 530 (2019) ("First Amendment law, at least

in its current 'Lochnerian' form, works almost exclusively to the advantage of the online platforms. Instead of empowering users to challenge their policies, the First Amendment empowers the companies themselves to challenge statutes and regulations intended to promote antidiscrimination norms or users' speech and privacy, among other values." (internal citation and quotation marks omitted)).

16. *See* Kessler & Pozen, *supra* note 3, at 1954–60.

17. *See, e.g.*, David Robert Grimes, *Echo Chambers Are Dangerous—We Must Try to Break Free of Our Online Bubbles*, Guardian (Dec. 4, 2017), https://www .theguardian.com/science/blog/2017/dec/04/echo-chambers-are-dangerous -we-must-try-to-break-free-of-our-online-bubbles.

18. *See, e.g.*, Eli Pariser, *The Filter Bubble: How the New Personalized Web Is Changing What We Read and How We Think* (2012).

19. *See, e.g.*, Jonathan Chait, *The Great Epistemic Closure Debate*, New Republic (Apr. 9, 2010), https://newrepublic.com/article/74356/the-great-epistemic -closure-debate.

20. Marc O. DeGirolami, *The Sickness unto Death of the First Amendment*, 42 Harv. J.L. & Pub. Pol'y 751, 754 (2019); *see also* Peter M. Shane, *"The Expanding First Amendment" in an Age of Free Speech Paradox*, 78 Ohio St. L.J. 773, 773 (2017) ("[T]he Supreme Court in recent years has broadened the domain of commu- nicative activity covered by the First Amendment's 'speech' protection and has limited in other ways the capacity of government to regulate communication based on content. . . . But in terms of felt experience, many Americans perceive that their capacity to speak freely is increasingly being imperiled in ways for which they have no legal recourse.").

21. *See supra* notes 2–3 and accompanying text.

22. *About the Knight Institute*, Knight First Amendment Inst., https://knightcolumbia. org/content/about-knight-institute (last visited July 18, 2019).

23. I borrow this phrase from Christian Fuchs, *Digital Demagogue: Authoritarian Capitalism in the Age of Trump and Twitter* (2018).

24. Within the larger literature about the economic plight of the news media, for example, there is a substantial subliterature on the specific (and highly conten- tious) question of whether and how the government should subsidize investiga- tive reporting. For a sampling of such proposals, see Geoffrey Cowan & David Westphal, USC Annenberg Ctr. on Commc'n Leadership & Pol'y, *Public Policy and Funding the News* (2010); Leonard Downie, Jr. & Michael Schudson, *The Reconstruction of American Journalism*, Colum. Journalism Rev., Nov./ Dec. 2009, at 28, 45–50; and Brad A. Greenberg, Comment, *A Public Press? Evaluating the Viability of Government Subsidies for the Newspaper Industry*, 19 UCLA Ent. L. Rev. 189, 197–98 (2012).

25. *See A First Amendment for All? Free Expression in an Age of Inequality*, Knight First Amendment Inst. (Mar. 23, 2018), https://knightcolumbia.org /content/3232018-first-amendment-all-free-expression-age-inequality.

26. *See Freedom of Expression in an Age of Surveillance: Measuring the "Chilling Effect,"* Knight First Amendment Inst. (Nov. 14, 2018), https://knightcolumbia .org/content/111418-freedom-expression-age-surveillance-measuring-chilling -effect.

27. *See The Tech Giants, Monopoly Power, and Public Discourse*, Knight First Amendment Inst. (Nov. 14, 2019), https://knightcolumbia.org/content/the-tech-giants-monopoly-power-and-public-discourse-1.

28. *See Edgar v. Maguire*, Knight First Amendment Inst., https://knightcolumbia.org/cases/edgar-v-maguire (last visited Dec. 12, 2019).

29. For a complementary argument about the limits of analogies in this area, see Julie E. Cohen, *Scaling Trust and Other Fictions*, Law & Pol. Econ. (May 29, 2019), https://lpeblog.org/2019/05/29/scaling-trust-and-other-fictions ("Analogies to the past are instructive . . ., but they cannot teach us how to devise governance mechanisms optimized for data-driven algorithmic processes and oriented toward the problems of speed, scale, immanence, and automaticity that such processes present.").

1

IS THE FIRST AMENDMENT OBSOLETE?

Tim Wu*

THE FIRST AMENDMENT was a dead letter for much of American history. Unfortunately, there is reason to fear it is entering a new period of political irrelevance. We live in a golden age of efforts by governments and other actors to control speech, discredit and harass the press, and manipulate public debate. Yet as these efforts mount, and the expressive environment deteriorates, the First Amendment has been confined to a narrow and frequently irrelevant role. Hence the question—when it comes to political speech in the twenty-first century, is the First Amendment obsolete?

The most important change in the expressive environment can be boiled down to one idea: it is no longer speech itself that is scarce, but the attention of listeners. Emerging threats to public discourse take advantage of this change. As Zeynep Tufekci puts it, "censorship during the Internet era does not operate under the same logic [as] it did under the heyday of print or even broadcast television."[1] Instead of targeting speakers directly, it targets listeners or it undermines speakers indirectly. More precisely, emerging techniques of speech control depend on (1) a range of new punishments, like unleashing "troll armies" to abuse the press and other critics, and (2) flooding tactics (sometimes called reverse censorship) that distort or drown out disfavored speech through the creation and dissemination of fake news, the payment of fake commentators, and the deployment of propaganda robots.[2] As journalist Peter Pomerantsev writes, these techniques employ "information . . . in weaponized terms, as a tool to confuse, blackmail, demoralize, subvert and paralyze."[3]

The First Amendment first came to life in the early twentieth century, when the main threat to the nation's political speech environment was state suppression of dissidents. The jurisprudence of the First Amendment was shaped by that era. It presupposes an information-poor world, and it focuses exclusively on the protection of speakers from government, as if they were rare and delicate butterflies threatened by one terrible monster.

But today, speakers are more like moths—their supply is apparently endless. The massive decline in barriers to publishing makes information abundant, especially when speakers congregate on brightly lit matters of public controversy. The low costs of speaking have, paradoxically, made it easier to weaponize speech as a tool of speech control. The unfortunate truth is that cheap speech may be used to attack, harass, and silence as much as it is used to illuminate or debate. And the use of speech as a tool to suppress speech is, by its nature, something very challenging for the First Amendment to deal with. In the face of such challenges, First Amendment doctrine seems at best unprepared. It is a body of law that waits for a pamphleteer to be arrested before it will recognize a problem. Even worse, the doctrine may actually block efforts to deal with some of the problems described here.

It may sound odd to say that the First Amendment is growing obsolete when the Supreme Court has an active First Amendment docket and there remain plenty of First Amendment cases in litigation. So that I am not misunderstood, I hasten to add that the First Amendment's protection of the press and political speakers against government suppression is hardly useless or undesirable.[4] With the important exception of cases related to campaign finance,[5] however, the big free speech decisions of the last few decades have centered not on political speech but on economic matters like the right to resell patient data[6] or the right to register offensive trademarks.[7] The safeguarding of political speech is widely understood to be the core function of the First Amendment. Many of the recent cases are not merely at the periphery of this project; they are off exploring some other continent.[8] The apparent flurry of First Amendment activity masks the fact that the amendment has become increasingly irrelevant in its area of historic concern: the coercive control of political speech.

What might be done in response is a question without an easy answer. One possibility is simply to concede that the First Amendment, built in another era, is not suited to today's challenges. Instead, any answer must lie in the development of better social norms, adoption of journalistic ethics by private speech platforms, or action by the political branches. Perhaps constitutional law has reached its natural limit.

On the other hand, in the 1920s Justices Oliver Wendell Holmes and Louis Brandeis and Judge Learned Hand also faced forms of speech control that did not seem to be matters of plausible constitutional concern by the standards of their time. If, following their lead, we take the bolder view that the First Amendment should be adapted to contemporary speech conditions, I suggest it may force us to confront buried doctrinal and theoretical questions, mainly related to state action, government speech, and listener interests. We might, for instance, explore "accomplice liability" under the First Amendment. That is, we might ask when the state or political leaders may be held constitutionally responsible for encouraging private parties to punish critics. I suggest here that if the president or other officials direct, encourage, fund, or covertly command attacks on their critics by private mobs or foreign powers, the First Amendment should be implicated.

Second, given that many of the new speech control techniques target listener attention, it may be worth reassessing how the First Amendment handles efforts to promote healthy speech environments and protect listener interests. Many of the problems described here might be subject to legislative or regulatory remedies that would themselves raise First Amendment questions. For example, consider a law that would bar major speech platforms and networks from accepting money from foreign governments for materials designed to influence American elections. Or a law that broadened criminal liability for online intimidation of members of the press. Such laws would likely be challenged under the First Amendment, which suggests that the needed evolution may lie in the jurisprudence of what the amendment permits.

These tentative suggestions and explorations should not distract from the main point of this essay, which is to demonstrate that a range of speech control techniques have arisen from which the First Amendment, at present, provides little or no protection. In the pages that follow, the essay first identifies the core assumptions that proceeded from the founding era of First Amendment jurisprudence. It then argues that many of those assumptions no longer hold, and it details a series of techniques that are used by governmental and nongovernmental actors to censor and degrade speech. The essay concludes with a few ideas about what might be done.

CORE ASSUMPTIONS OF THE POLITICAL FIRST AMENDMENT

As scholars and historians know well, but the public is sometimes surprised to learn, the First Amendment sat dormant for much of American history, despite its absolute language ("Congress shall make no law . . .")

and its placement in the Bill of Rights.[9] It is an American "tradition" in the sense that the Super Bowl is an American tradition—one that is relatively new, even if it has come to be defining. To understand the basic paradigm by which the law provides protection, we therefore look not to the Constitution's founding era but to the First Amendment's founding era, in the early 1900s.

As the story goes, the First Amendment remained inert well into the 1920s. The trigger that gave it life was the federal government's extensive speech control program during the First World War. The program was composed of two parts. First, following the passage of new Espionage and Sedition Acts,[10] men and women voicing opposition to the war, or holding other unpopular positions, were charged with crimes directly related to their speech. Eugene V. Debs, the presidential candidate for the Socialist Party, was arrested and imprisoned for a speech that questioned the war effort, in which he memorably told the crowd that they were "fit for something better than slavery and cannon fodder."[11]

Second, the federal government operated an extensive domestic propaganda campaign.[12] The Committee on Public Information, created by Executive Order 2594, was a massive federal organization of over 150,000 employees. Its efforts were comprehensive and unrelenting. As George Creel put it: "The printed word, the spoken word, the motion picture, the telegraph, the cable, the wireless, the poster, the sign-board—all these were used in our campaign to make our own people and all other peoples understand the causes that compelled America to take arms."[13] The Committee on Public Information's division of news supplied the press with content guidelines, "appropriate" materials, and pressure to run them. All told, the American propaganda effort reached a scope and level of organization that would be matched only by totalitarian states in the 1930s.[14]

The story of the judiciary's reaction to these new speech controls has by now attained the status of legend. The federal courts, including the Supreme Court, widely condoned the government's heavy-handed arrests and other censorial practices as necessary to the war effort. But as time passed, some of the most influential jurists—including Hand, followed by Brandeis and Holmes—found themselves unable to stomach what they saw, despite the fact that each was notably reluctant to use the Constitution for anti-majoritarian purposes.[15] Judge Hand was the only one of the three to act during wartime,[16] but eventually the thoughts of these great judges (mostly expressed in dissent or in concurrence) became the founding jurisprudence of the modern First Amendment.[17] To be sure, their views remained in the minority into the 1950s and 1960s, but eventually the dissenting and concurring opinions would become majority holdings,[18] and by the 1970s the core political protections of the First Amendment had become fully active, achieving more or less the basic structure we see today.

Left out of this well-known story is a detail quite important for our purposes. The Court's scrutiny extended only to part of the government's speech control program: its censorship and punishment of dissidents. Left untouched and unquestioned was the Wilson administration's unprecedented domestic propaganda campaign. This was not a deliberate choice, so far as I can tell (although it does seem surprising, in retrospect, that there was no serious challenge brought contesting the president's power to create a major propaganda agency on the basis of a single executive order).[19] Yet as a practical matter, it was probably the propaganda campaign that had the greater influence over wartime speech, and almost certainly a stronger limiting effect on the freedom of the mainstream press.

I should also add, for completeness, that the story just told only covers the First Amendment's protection of political speech, or what we might call the story of the "political First Amendment."[20] Later, beginning in the 1950s, the Court also developed constitutional protections for nonpolitical speech, such as indecency, commercial advertising, and cultural expression, in landmark cases like *Roth v. United States*[21] and *Virginia State Board of Pharmacy v. Virginia Citizens Consumer Council, Inc.*[22] The Court also expanded upon both who counted as a speaker[23] and what counted as speech[24]—trends that have continued into this decade.[25] I mention this only for making the boundaries of this essay clear: it is focused on the kind of political and press activities that were the original concern of those who brought the First Amendment to life.[26]

Let us return to the founding jurisprudence of the 1920s. In its time, for the conditions faced, it was as imaginative, convincing, and thoughtful as judicial writing can be. The jurisprudence of the 1920s has the unusual distinction of actually living up to the hype. Rereading the canonical opinions is an exciting and stirring experience not unlike rewatching *The Godfather* or *Gone with the Wind*. But that is also the problem. The paradigm established in the 1920s and fleshed out in the 1960s and 1970s was so convincing that it is simply hard to admit that it has grown obsolete for some of the major political speech challenges of the twenty-first century.

Consider three main assumptions that the law grew up with. The first is an underlying premise of informational scarcity. For years, it was taken for granted that few people would be willing to invest in speaking publicly. Relatedly, it was assumed that with respect to any given issue—say, the war—only a limited number of important speakers could compete in the "marketplace of ideas."[27] The second notable assumption arises from the first: listeners are assumed not to be overwhelmed with information, but rather to have abundant time and interest to be influenced by publicly presented views. Finally, the government is assumed to be the main threat to the marketplace of ideas through its use of criminal law or other coercive instruments to target speakers (as opposed to listeners) with punishment or bans on publication.[28] Without government intervention, this assumption goes, the marketplace of ideas operates well by itself.

Each of these assumptions has, one way or another, become obsolete in the twenty-first century, due to the rise in importance of attention markets and changes in communications technologies. It is to those phenomena that we now turn.

ATTENTIONAL SCARCITY AND THE ECONOMICS OF FILTER BUBBLES

As early as 1971, Herbert Simon predicted the trend that drives this essay. As he wrote:

> In an information-rich world, the wealth of information means a dearth of something else: a scarcity of whatever it is that information consumes. What information consumes is rather obvious: it consumes the attention of its recipients. Hence a wealth of information creates a poverty of attention and a need to allocate that attention efficiently among the overabundance of information sources that might consume it.[29]

In other words, if it was once hard to speak, it is now hard to be heard. Stated differently, it is no longer speech or information that is scarce, but the attention of listeners. Unlike in the 1920s, information is abundant and speaking is easy, while listener time and attention have become highly valued commodities. It follows that one important means of controlling speech is targeting the bottleneck of listener attention, instead of speech itself.[30]

Several major technological and economic developments over the last two decades have transformed the relative scarcity of speech and listener attention. The first is associated with the popularization of the internet: the massive decrease since the 1990s in the costs of being an online speaker, otherwise known (in Eugene Volokh's phrase) as "cheap speech," or what James Gleick calls the "information flood."[31] Using blogs, micro-blogs, or platforms like Twitter or Facebook, just about anyone, potentially, can disseminate speech into the digital public sphere. This has had several important implications. As Jack Balkin, Jeffrey Rosen, and I myself have argued, it gives the main platforms—which do not consider themselves to be part of the press—an extremely important role in the construction of public discourse.[32] Cheap speech also makes it easier for mobs to harass or abuse other speakers with whom they disagree.

The second, more long-term, development has been the rise of an "attention industry"—that is, a set of actors whose business model is the resale of human attention.[33] Traditionally, these were outfits like broadcasters or newspapers; they have been joined by the major internet platforms and publishers, all of which seek to maximize the amount of time and attention that people spend with them. The rise and centrality of advertising to their business models has the broad effect of making listener attention ever more valuable.

The third development is the rise of the "filter bubble."[34] This phrase refers to the tendency of attention merchants or brokers to maximize revenue by offering audiences a highly tailored, filtered package of information designed to match their preexisting interests. Andrew Shapiro and Cass Sunstein were among the first legal writers to express concern about filter bubbles (which Sunstein nicknamed "the Daily Me").[35] Over the 2010s, filter bubbles became more important as they became linked to the attention-resale business model just described. A platform like Facebook primarily profits from the resale of its users' time and attention: hence its efforts to maximize "time on site."[36] That, in turn, leads the company to provide content that maximizes "engagement," which is information tailored to the interests of each user. While this sounds relatively innocuous (giving users what they want), it has the secondary effect of exercising strong control over what the listener is exposed to, and blocking content that is unlikely to engage.

The combined consequence of these three developments is to make listener attention scarce and highly fought for. As the commercial and political value of attention has grown, much of that time and attention has become subject to furious competition, so much so that even institutions like the family or traditional religious communities find it difficult to compete. Additionally, some form of celebrity, even micro-celebrity, has become increasingly necessary to gain any attention at all.[37] Every hour, indeed every second, of our time has commercial actors seeking to occupy it one way or another.

Hopefully the reader (if she hasn't already disappeared to check her Facebook page) now understands what it means to say that listener attention has become a major speech bottleneck. With so much alluring, individually tailored content being produced—and so much talent devoted to keeping people clicking away on various platforms—speakers face ever greater challenges in reaching an audience of any meaningful size or political relevance. I want to stress that these developments matter not just to the hypothetical dissident sitting in her basement, who fared no better in previous times, but to the press as well. Gone are the days when the CBS evening news might reach the nation automatically, or whatever made the front cover of the *New York Times* was known to all. The challenge, paradoxically, has only increased in an age when the president himself consumes so much of the media's attention.[38] The population is distracted and scattered, making it difficult even for those with substantial resources to reach an audience.

The revolutionary changes just described have hardly gone unnoticed by First Amendment or internet scholars. By the mid-1990s, Volokh, Kathleen Sullivan, and others had prophesied the coming era of cheaper speech and suggested it would transform much of what the First Amendment had taken for granted. (Sullivan memorably described the reaction to the internet's arrival as "First Amendment manna from heaven."[39]) Lawrence Lessig's brilliant "code is law" formulation suggested that much of the future of censorship and speech control would reside in the design of the network and its major applications.[40] Rosen, Jack Goldsmith, Jonathan Zittrain, Christopher Yoo, and others, including myself, wrote of the censorial potential that lay either in the network infrastructure itself (hence "net neutrality" as a counterweight) or in the main platforms (search engines, hosting sites, and later social media).[41] The use of infrastructure and platforms as a tool of censorship has been extensively documented overseas[42] and now also in the United States, especially by Balkin.[43] Finally, the democratic implications of filter bubbles and similar technologies have become their own cottage industries.[44]

Yet despite the scholarly attention, no one quite anticipated that speech itself might become a censorial weapon, or that scarcity of attention would become such a target of flooding and similar tactics.[45] While the major changes described here have been decades in the making, we are nonetheless still in the midst of understanding their implications for classic questions of political speech control. We can now turn to the ways these changes have rendered basic assumptions about the First Amendment outmoded.

OBSOLETE ASSUMPTIONS

Much can be understood by asking what evil any law is designed to combat. The founding First Amendment jurisprudence presumed that the evil of government speech control would be primarily accomplished by criminal punishment of publishers or speakers (or the threat thereof) and by the direct censorship of disfavored presses. These were, of course, the devices used by the Espionage and Sedition Acts in the 1790s and variations from the 1910s through the 1960s.[46] On the censor's part, the technique is intuitive: it has the effect of silencing the speaker herself, while also chilling those who might fear similar treatment. Nowadays, however, it is increasingly *not* the case that the relevant means of censorship is direct punishment by the state, or that the state itself is the primary censor.

THE WANING OF DIRECT CENSORSHIP

Despite its historic effectiveness, direct and overt government punishment of speakers has fallen out of favor in the twenty-first-century media environment, even in nations without strong free speech traditions. This fact is harder to see in the United States because the First Amendment itself has been read to impose a strong bar on viewpoint-based censorship. The point comes through most clearly when observing the techniques of governments that are unconstrained by similar constitutional protections. Such observation reveals that multiple governments have increasingly turned away from high-profile suppression of speech or arrest of dissidents, in favor of techniques that target listeners or enlist government accomplices.[47]

The study of Chinese speech control provides some of the strongest evidence that a regime with full powers to directly censor nonetheless usually avoids doing so. In a fascinating ongoing study of Chinese censorship, Gary King, Jennifer Pan, and Margaret Roberts have conducted several massive investigations into the government's evolving approach to social media and other internet-based speech.[48] What they have discovered is a regime less intent on stamping out forbidden content, but instead focused on distraction, cheerleading, and preventing meaningful collective action. For the most part, they conclude, the state's agents "do not censor posts criticizing the regime, its leaders, or their policies" and "do not engage on controversial issues."[49] The authors suggest that the reasons are as follows:

> Letting an argument die, or changing the subject, usually works much better than picking an argument and getting someone's back up. . . . Since censorship alone seems to anger people, the [Chinese] program has the additional advantage of enabling the government to actively control opinion without having to censor as much as they might otherwise.[50]

A related reason for avoiding direct speech suppression is that under conditions of attentional scarcity, high-profile government censorship or the imprisonment of speakers runs the risk of backfiring. The government is, effectively, a kind of celebrity whose actions draw disproportionate attention. And such attention may help overcome the greatest barrier facing a disfavored speaker: that of getting heard at all. In certain instances, the attention showered on an arrested speaker may even, counterintuitively, yield financial or reputational rewards—the opposite of chill.

In internet lore, one term for this backlash potential is the Streisand effect.[51] Named after celebrity Barbra Streisand, whose lawyer's efforts to suppress aerial photos of her beachfront resort attracted hundreds of thousands of downloads of those photos, the term stands for the proposition that "the simple act of trying to repress something . . . online is likely to make it . . . seen by many more people."[52] To be sure, the concept's general applicability might be questioned, especially with regard to viral dissemination, which is highly unpredictable and rarer than one might imagine.[53] Even still, the possibility of creating attention for the original speaker makes direct censorship less attractive, given the proliferation of cheaper—and often more effective—alternatives.

As suggested in the introduction, those alternatives can be placed in several categories: (1) online harassment and attacks, (2) distorting and flooding, or so-called reverse censorship, and (3) control of the main speech platforms. (The third topic is included for completeness, but it has already received extensive scholarly attention.[54]) These techniques are practiced to different degrees by different governments abroad. Yet given that they could be used by U.S. officials as well[55]—and that they pose a major threat to the speech environment whether or not one's own government is using them—all are worth exploring in our consideration of whether the First Amendment, in its political aspects, is obsolete.

TROLL ARMIES

Among the newer emerging threats is the rise of abusive online mobs who seek to wear down targeted speakers and have them think twice about writing critical content, thus making political journalism less attractive. Whether directly employed by, loosely associated with, or merely aligned with the goals of the government or particular politicians, the technique relies on the low cost of speech to punish speakers.

While there have long been internet trolls, in the early 2000s the Russian government pioneered their use as a systematic speech control technique with the establishment of a "web brigade" (Веб-бригады), often called a "troll army." Its methods, discovered through leaks and the undercover work of investigative reporters,[56] range from mere encouragement of loyalists to funding groups that pay commentators piecemeal to employing full-time staff to engage in around-the-clock propagation of pro-government views and attacks on critics.[57]

There are three hallmarks of the Russian approach. The first is obscuring the government's influence. The hand of the Kremlin is not explicit; funding comes from pro-Kremlin groups or nonprofits, and those involved usually disclaim any formal association with the Russian state.[58] In addition, individuals sympathetic to the cause often join as de facto volunteers. The second is the use of vicious, swarm-like attacks over email, telephone, or social media to harass and humiliate critics of Russian policies or President Putin. While the online hate mob is certainly not a Russian invention,[59] its deployment for such political objectives seems to be a novel development. The third hallmark is its international scope. Although these techniques have mainly been used domestically in Russia, they have also been employed against political opponents elsewhere in the world, including in Ukraine and in countries like Finland, where trolls savagely attacked journalists who favored joining NATO (or questioned Russian efforts to influence that decision).[60] Likewise, these tactics have been deployed in the United States, where paid Russian trolls targeted the 2016 presidential campaign.[61]

Soviet-born British journalist Peter Pomerantsev, who was among the first to document the evolving Russian approach to speech control, has presented the operative questions this way:

> What happens when a powerful actor systematically abuses freedom of information to spread disinformation? Uses freedom of speech in such a way as to subvert the very possibility of a debate? And does so not merely inside a country, as part of vicious election campaigns, but as part of a transnational military campaign? Since at least 2008, Kremlin military and intelligence thinkers have been talking about information not in the familiar terms of "persuasion," "public diplomacy" or even "propaganda," but in weaponized terms, as a tool to confuse, blackmail, demoralize, subvert and paralyze.[62]

Over the last several years, the basic elements of the Russian approach have spread to the United States. As in Russia, journalists of all stripes have been targeted by virtual mobs when they criticize the American president or his policies. While some of the attacks appear to have originated from independent actors who borrowed Russian techniques, others have come from the (paid) Russian force itself; members of the Senate Select Committee on Intelligence have said that over 1,000 people on that force were assigned to influence the U.S. election in 2016.[63] For certain journalists in particular, such harassment has become a regular occurrence, an ongoing assault. As David French of the *National Review* puts it: "The formula is simple: Criticize Trump—especially his connection to the alt-right—and the backlash will come."[64]

Ironically, while sometimes the president himself attacks, insults, or abuses journalists, this behavior has not necessarily had censorial consequences in itself, as it tends to draw attention to the speech in question. In fact, the improved fortunes of media outlets like CNN might serve as a demonstration that there often is a measurable Streisand effect.[65] We are speaking here of a form of censorial punishment practiced by the government's *allies*, which is much less newsworthy but potentially just as punitive, especially over the long term.

Consider, for example, French's description of the response to his criticisms of the president:

> I saw images of my daughter's face in gas chambers, with a smiling Trump in a Nazi uniform preparing to press a button and kill her. I saw her face photoshopped into images of slaves. She was called a "niglet" and a "dindu." The alt-right unleashed on my wife, Nancy, claiming that she had slept with black men while I was deployed to Iraq, and that I loved to watch while she had sex with "black bucks." People sent her pornographic images of black men having sex with white women, with someone photoshopped to look like me, watching.[66]

A similar story is told by Rosa Brooks, a law professor and popular commentator, who wrote a column in late January of 2017 that was critical of President Trump and speculated about whether the military might decline to follow plainly irrational orders, despite the tradition of deference to the commander-in-chief. After the piece was picked up by Breitbart News, where it was described as a call for a military coup, Brooks experienced the following. Her account is worth quoting at length:

> By mid-afternoon, I was getting death threats. "I AM GOING TO CUT YOUR HEAD OFF . . . . BITCH!" screamed one email. Other correspondents threatened to hang me, shoot me, deport me, imprison me, and/or get me fired (this last one seemed a bit anti-climactic). The dean of Georgetown Law, where I teach, got nasty emails about me. The Georgetown University president's office received a voicemail from someone threatening to shoot me. New America, the think tank where I am a fellow, got a similar influx of nasty calls and messages. "You're a fucking cunt! Piece of shit whore!" read a typical missive. My correspondents were united on the matter of my crimes (treason, sedition, inciting insurrection, etc.). The only issue that appeared to confound and divide them was the vexing question of just what kind of undesirable I was. Several decided, based presumably on my first name, that I was Latina and proposed that I be forcibly sent to the other side of the soon-to-be-built Trump border wall.

Others, presumably conflating me with African-American civil rights heroine Rosa Parks, asserted that I would never have gotten hired if it weren't for race-based affirmative action. The anti-Semitic rants flowed in, too: A website called the Daily Stormer noted darkly that I am "the daughter of the infamous communist Barbara Ehrenreich and the Jew John Ehrenreich," and I got an anonymous phone call from someone who informed me, in a chillingly pleasant tone, that he supported a military coup "to kill all the Jews."[67]

The angry, censorial online mob is not merely a tool of neo-fascists or the political right, although the association of such mobs with the current administration merits special attention. Without assuming any moral equivalence, it is worth noting that there seems to be a growing, parallel tendency of leftist mobs to harass and shut down disfavored speakers as well.[68]

Some suppression of speech is disturbing enough to make one wonder if the First Amendment and its state action doctrine (which holds that the amendment only applies to actions by the state, not by private parties) are hopelessly limited in an era when harassment is so easy. Consider the story of Lindy West, a comedian and writer who has authored controversial columns, generally on feminist topics. By virtue of her writing talent and her association with the Guardian, she does not, like other speakers, face difficulties getting heard. However, she does face near-constant harassment and abuse. Every time she publishes a controversial piece, West recounts, "the harassment comes in a deluge. It floods my Twitter feed, my Facebook page, my email, so fast that I can't even keep up (not that I want to)." In a standard example, after West wrote a column about rape, she received the following messages: "She won't ever have to worry about rape"; "No one would want to rape that fat, disgusting mess"; and many more.[69] As West observes: "It's a silencing tactic. The message is: you are outnumbered. The message is: we'll stop when you're gone."[70] Eventually, West quit Twitter and other social media entirely.

It is not terribly new to suggest that private suppression of speech may matter as much as state suppression. For example, John Stuart Mill's On Liberty seemed to take Victorian sensibilities as a greater threat to freedom than anything the government might do.[71] But what has increased is the ability of nominally private forms of punishment—which may be directed or encouraged by government officials—to operate through the very channels meant to facilitate public speech.

REVERSE CENSORSHIP, FLOODING, AND PROPAGANDA ROBOTS

Reverse censorship, which is also called flooding, is another contemporary technique of speech control. With roots in so-called astroturfing,[72] it relies on counterprogramming with a sufficient volume of information to drown out disfavored speech or at least distort the information environment. Politically motivated reverse censorship often involves the dissemination of fake news (or atrocity propaganda) in order to distract and discredit. Whatever form it takes, this technique clearly qualifies as listener-targeted speech control.

The Chinese and Russian governments have led the way in developing methods of flooding and reverse censorship.[73] China in particular stands out for its control of domestic speech. China has not, like North Korea, sought to avoid twenty-first-century communications technologies. Its embrace of the internet has been enthusiastic and thorough. Yet the Communist Party has nonetheless managed to survive—and even enhance—its control over politics, defying the predictions of many in the West who forecast that the arrival of the internet would soon lead to the government's overthrow.[74] Among the Chinese methods uncovered by researchers are the efforts of as many as 2 million people who are paid to post on behalf of the party. As King, Pan, and Roberts have found:

> The [Chinese] government fabricates and posts about 448 million social media comments a year. In contrast to prior claims, we show that the Chinese regime's strategy is to avoid arguing with skeptics of the party and the government, and to not even discuss controversial issues. We show that the goal of this massive secretive operation is instead to distract the public and change the subject, as most of these posts involve cheer-leading for China, the revolutionary history of the Communist Party, or other symbols of the regime.[75]

In an attention-scarce world, these kinds of methods are more effective than they might have been in previous decades. When listeners have highly limited bandwidth to devote to any given issue, they will rarely dig deeply, and they are less likely to hear dissenting opinions. In such an environment, flooding can be just as effective as more traditional forms of censorship.

Related to techniques of flooding is the intentional dissemination of so-called fake news and the discrediting of mainstream media sources. In modern times, this technique seems, once again, to be a key tool of political influence used by the Russian government. In addition to its attacks on regime critics, the Russian web brigade also spreads massive numbers of false stories, often alleging atrocities committed by its targets.[76] While this technique can be accomplished by humans, it is aided and amplified by the increasing use of human-impersonating robots, or "bots," which relay the messages through millions of fake accounts on social media sites like Twitter.

Tufekci has documented similar strategies employed by the Turkish government in its efforts to control opposition. The Turkish government, in her account, relies most heavily on discrediting nongovernmental sources of information. As she writes, critics of the state found "an enormous increase in challenges to their credibility, ranging from reasonable questions to outrageous and clearly false accusations. These took place using the same channels, and even the same methods, that a social movement might have used to challenge false claims by authorities."[77] The goal, she writes, was to create "an ever-bigger glut of mashed-up truth and falsehood to foment confusion and distraction" and "to overwhelm people with so many pieces of bad and disturbing information that they become confused and give up trying to figure out what the truth might be — or even the possibility of finding out what is true."[78]

While the technique was pioneered overseas, it is clear that flooding has come to the United States. Here, the most important variant has been the development and mass dissemination of so-called fake news. Consider in this regard the work of Philip Howard, who runs the Computational Propaganda Project at Oxford University. As Howard points out, voters are strongly influenced by what they think their neighbors are thinking; hence fake crowds, deployed at crucial moments, can create a false sense of solidarity and support. Howard and his collaborators studied the linking and sharing of news on Twitter in the week before the November 2016 U.S. presidential vote. Their research produced a startling revelation: "junk news was shared just as widely as professional news in the days leading up to the election."[79]

Howard's group believes that bots were used to help achieve this effect. These bots pose as humans on Facebook, Twitter, and other social media, and they transmit messages as directed. Researchers have estimated that Twitter has as many as 48 million bot users,[80] and Facebook has previously estimated that it has between 67.65 million and 137.76 million fake users.[81] Some percentage of these, according to Howard and his team, are harnessed en masse to help spread fake news before and after important events.

Robots have even been employed to attack the "open" processes of the administrative state. In the spring of 2017, the Federal Communications Commission (FCC) put its proposed revocation of net neutrality up for public comment. In previous years, such proceedings attracted vigorous argument by (human) commentators. This time, someone directed robots to impersonate—via stolen identities—hundreds of thousands of people, flooding the system with fake comments, all of which were purportedly against federal net neutrality rules.[82]

* * *

As it stands, the First Amendment has little to say about any of these tools and techniques. The mobilization of online vitriol or the dissemination of fake news by private parties or foreign states, even if in coordination with the U.S. government, has been considered a matter of journalistic ethics or foreign policy, not constitutional law. And it has long been assumed (though rarely tested) that the U.S. government's own use of domestic propaganda is not a contestable First Amendment concern, on the premise that propaganda is "government speech."[83] The closest thing to a constitutional limit on propagandizing is the premise that the state cannot compel citizens to voice messages on its behalf (under the doctrine of compelled speech)[84] or to engage in patriotic acts like saluting the flag or reciting the pledge of allegiance.[85] But under the existing jurisprudence, it seems that little—other than political norms that are fast eroding—stands in the way of a full-blown campaign designed to manipulate the political speech environment to the advantage of current officeholders.

WHAT MIGHT BE DONE

What I have written suggests that the First Amendment and its jurisprudence is a bystander in an age of aggressive efforts to propagandize and control online speech. While it does wall off the most coercive technique of the government—directly punishing disfavored speakers or the press—that's just one part of the problem.

If it seems that the First Amendment's main presumptions are obsolete, what might be done? There are two basic answers to this question. The first is to admit defeat and suggest that the role of the political First Amendment will be confined to harms that fall within the original 1920s paradigm. There remains important work to be done here, as protecting the press and other speakers from explicit government censorship will continue to be essential. And perhaps this is all that might be expected from the Constitution (and the judiciary). The second—and more ambitious—answer is to imagine how First Amendment doctrine might adapt to the kinds of speech manipulation described above. In some cases, this could mean that the First Amendment must broaden its own reach to encompass new techniques of speech control. In other cases, it could mean that the First Amendment must step slightly to the side and allow different legal tools—like the enforcement of existing or as-yet-to-be-created criminal statutes—to do the lion's share of the work needed to promote a healthy speech environment.

ACCEPTING A LIMITED FIRST AMENDMENT

If we accept the premise that the First Amendment cannot itself address the issues here discussed, reform initiatives must center on the behaviors of major private parties that are, in practice, the most important speech brokers of our times. What naturally emerges is a debate over the public duties of both the media, traditionally understood, and of major internet speech platforms like Facebook, Twitter, and Google. At its essence, the debate boils down to asking whether these platforms should adopt (or be forced to adopt) norms and policies traditionally associated with twentieth-century journalism.[86]

We often take for granted the press's role as a bulwark against the speech control techniques described in this essay. Ever since the rise of objectivity and independence norms in the 1920s, along with the adoption of formal journalism codes of ethics, the press has tried to avoid printing mere rumors or false claims, knowingly serving as an arm of government propaganda efforts, or succumbing to the influence of business interests.[87] It has also guaranteed reporters some security from attacks and abuse. The press may not have performed these duties perfectly, and there have been the usual debates about what constitutes a fact or objectivity. But the aspiration exists, and it succeeds in filtering out many obvious distortions.

In contrast, the major speech platforms, born as tech firms, have become players in the media world almost by accident. By design, they have none of the filters or safeguards that the press historically has employed. There are advantages to this design: it yields the appealing idea that anyone, and not only professionals, might have her say. In practice, it has precipitated a great flourishing of speech in various new forms, from blogging to user-created encyclopedias to social media.[88] As Volokh prophesized in 1995: "Cheap speech will mean that far more speakers—rich and poor, popular and not, banal and avant garde—will be able to make their work available to all."[89] But it has also meant, as we've seen, that the platforms have been vulnerable to tactics that weaponize speech and use the openness of the internet as ammunition. The question now before us is whether the platforms need to do more to combat these problems for the sake of political culture in the United States.

We might, for example, fairly focus on Twitter, which has served as a tool for computational propaganda (through millions of fake users), dissemination of fake news, and harassment of speakers. Twitter does little about any of these problems. It has adopted policies that are meant, supposedly, to curb abuse. But the policies are widely viewed as ineffective, in no small part because they put the burden of action on the person being harassed. West, for example, describes her attempt to report as abusive a user who threatened to rape her with an "anthropomorphic train."[90] Twitter staff responded that the comment was not sufficiently abusive and was "currently not violating the Twitter Rules."[91] When Twitter's CEO recently asked, "What's the most important thing you want to see Twitter improve or create in 2017?" one user responded: a "comprehensive plan for getting rid of the Nazis."[92] To suggest that private platforms could—and should—be doing more to prevent speakers from harassment and abuse is perhaps the clearest remedy for the emerging threats identified above, even if it is not clear at this time exactly what such remedies ought to look like.

The troll problem is among the online world's oldest problems and a fixture of early cyberspace debates.[93] Anonymous commentators and mobs have long shown their capacity to poison any environment and, through their vicious and demeaning attacks, chill expression. That old debate also revealed that design can mitigate some of these concerns. For example, consider that Wikipedia does not have a widespread fake news problem.[94] But even if the debate remains similar, the stakes and consequences have changed. In the 1990s, trolls would abuse avatars, scare people off AOL chatrooms, or wreck virtual worlds.[95] Today, we are witnessing efforts to destroy the reputations of real people for political purposes, to tip elections, and to influence foreign policy. It is hard to resist the conclusion that the law must be enlisted to fight such scourges.

FIRST AMENDMENT POSSIBILITIES

Could the First Amendment find a way to adapt to twenty-first-century speech challenges? How this might be accomplished is far from obvious, and I will freely admit that this essay is of the variety that is intended to ask the question rather than answer it. The most basic stumbling block is well known to lawyers. The First Amendment, like other guarantees in the Bill of Rights, has been understood primarily as a negative right against coercive government action—not as a right against the conduct of nongovernmental actors, or as a right that obliges the government to ensure a pristine speech environment. Tactics such as flooding and purposeful generation of fake news are, by our current ways of thinking, either private action or, at most, the government's own protected speech.

A few possible adaptations present themselves, and they can be placed in three groups. The first concerns the "state action" doctrine, which is the limit that most obviously constrains the First Amendment from serving as a check on many of the emerging threats to the political speech environment. If a private mob attacks and silences critics of the government, purely of its own volition, under a basic theory of state action there is no role for the First Amendment—even if the mob replicates punishments that the government itself might have wanted to inflict. But what about when the mob is not quite as independent as it first appears? The First Amendment's underdiscussed "accomplice liability" doctrine may become of increasing importance if, in practice, governmental units or politicians have a hand in encouraging, coordinating, or otherwise providing direction to what might seem like private parties.

A second possibility is expanding the category of "state action" itself to encompass the conduct of major speech platforms like Facebook or Twitter. However, as discussed below, I view this as an unpromising and potentially counterproductive solution.

Third, the project of realizing a healthier speech environment may depend more on what the First Amendment permits, rather than what it prevents or requires. Indeed, some of the most important remedies for the challenges described in this essay may consist of new laws or more aggressive enforcement of existing laws. The federal cyberstalking statute,[96] for example, has already been used to protect the press from egregious trolling and harassment.[97] New laws might target foreign efforts to manipulate American elections or provide better and faster protections for members of the press. Assuming such laws are challenged as unconstitutional, the necessary doctrinal evolution may involve the First Amendment accommodating robust efforts to fight the new tools of speech control.

Let us look a little more closely at each of these possibilities.

STATE ACTION—ACCOMPLICE LIABILITY   The state action doctrine, once again, limits constitutional scrutiny to (as the name suggests) actions taken by the state. However, in the troll army model, punishment of the press and political critics is conducted by ostensibly private parties or foreign governments. Hence, at a first look, such conduct seems unreachable by the Constitution.

Yet as many have observed, the current American president has seemingly directed online mobs to go after his critics and opponents, particularly members of the press.[98] Even members of the president's party have reportedly been nervous to speak their minds, not based on threats of ordinary political reactions but for fear of attack by online mobs.[99] And while the directed-mob technique may have been pioneered by Russia and employed by Trump, it is not hard to imagine a future in which other presidents and powerful leaders sic their loyal mobs on critics, confident that in so doing they may avoid the limits imposed by the First Amendment.

But the state action doctrine may not be as much of a hindrance as this end-run supposes. The First Amendment already has a nascent accomplice liability doctrine that makes state actors, under some circumstances, "liable for the actions of private parties."[100] In *Blum v. Yaretsky*, the Supreme Court explained that the state can be held responsible for private action "when it has exercised coercive power or has provided such significant encouragement, either overt or covert, that the choice must in law be deemed to be that of the State."[101] The *Blum* formulation echoes common-law accomplice liability principles: a principal is ordinarily liable for the illegal actions of another party when it both shares the underlying *mens rea*, or purpose, and when it acts to encourage, command, support, or otherwise provide aid to that party.[102] *Blum* itself was not a First Amendment case, and it left open the question of what might constitute "significant encouragement" in various settings.[103] But in subsequent cases, the lower courts have provided a greater sense of what factual scenarios might suffice for state accomplice liability in the First Amendment context.

For example, the Sixth Circuit has a line of First Amendment employment retaliation cases that suggest when public actors may be held liable for nominally private conduct. In the 2010 case *Paige v. Coyner*, the Sixth Circuit addressed the constitutional claims of a woman who was fired by her employer at the behest of a state official (Coyner) after she spoke out at a public meeting in opposition to a new highway development.[104] Unlike a typical retaliation-termination case, the plaintiff presented evidence that she was fired because the state official complained to her employer and sought to have her terminated.[105] The Sixth Circuit held that the lawsuit properly alleged state action because Coyner encouraged the firing, even though it was the employer who actually inflicted the punishment.[106] Moreover, the court suggested an even broader liability standard than *Blum*, holding that the private punishment of a speaker could be attributed to a state official "if that result was a reasonably foreseeable consequence."[107] More recently, the Sixth Circuit reaffirmed *Coyner* where a police officer, after a dispute with a private individual, went to her workplace to complain about her with the "reasonably foreseeable" result of having her fired.[108] Similar cases can be found in other circuits.[109]

In the political "attack mob" context, it seems that some official encouragement of attacks on the press or other speakers should trigger First Amendment scrutiny. Naturally, those who attack critics of the state merely because they feel inspired to do so by an official's example do not present a case of state action. (If burdensome enough, however, the original attack might be a matter of First Amendment concern.) But more direct encouragement may yield a First Amendment constraint. Consider, for example, the following scenarios:

- If the president or other government officials name individual members of the press and suggest they should be punished, yielding a foreseeable attack;
- If the president or other officials call upon media companies to fire or otherwise discipline their critics, and the companies do so;
- If the government is found to be directly funding third-party efforts to attack or flood critics of the government, or organizing or coordinating with those who provide such funding; or

■ If the president or other officials order private individuals or organizations to attack or punish critics of the government.

Based on the standards enumerated in *Blum* and other cases, these scenarios might support a finding of state action and a First Amendment violation. In other words, an official who spurs private censorial mobs to attack a disfavored speaker might—in an appropriately brought lawsuit, contingent on the usual questions of standing and immunity—be subject to a court injunction or even damages, just as if she performed the attack herself.

STATE ACTION—PLATFORMS The central role played by major speech platforms like Twitter, Google, and Facebook might prompt another question: should the platforms themselves be treated as state actors for First Amendment purposes? Perhaps, like the company town in *Marsh v. Alabama*,[110] these companies have assumed sufficiently public duties or importance that they stand "in the shoes of the State."[111] While some have argued that this is appropriate,[112] there are a number of reasons why treating these platforms as state actors strikes me as an unpromising and undesirable avenue.

First, there are real differences between the *Marsh* company town and today's speech platforms. *Marsh* was a case where the firm had effectively taken over the full spectrum of municipal government duties, including ownership of the sidewalk, roads, sewer systems, and policing.[113] The company town was, in most respects, indistinguishable from a traditional government-run locality—it just happened to be private. The residents of Chickasaw had no way of escaping the reach of the company's power, as the Gulf Shipbuilding Corporation claimed, in Max Weber's terms, a "monopoly of the legitimate use of physical force."[114] To exempt such a company town from constitutional scrutiny therefore produced the prospect of easy constitutional evasion by privatization.

However important Facebook or Google may be to our speech environment, it seems much harder to say that they are acting like the government all but in name. It is true that one's life may be heavily influenced by these and other large companies, but influence alone cannot be the criterion for what makes something a state actor; in that case, every employer would be a state actor, and perhaps so would nearly every family. If the major speech platforms (including the major television networks) ought to be classified as state actors based not on the assumption of specific state-like duties but merely on their influence, it is hard to know where the category ends.

This is not to deny that the leading speech platforms have an important public function. In fact, I have argued in other work that regulation of communications carriers plays a critical role in facilitating speech, comprising a de facto First Amendment tradition.[115] Yet if these platforms are treated as state actors under the First Amendment in all that they do, their ability to handle some of the problems presented here may well be curtailed. This danger is made clear by *Cyber Promotions, Inc. v. America Online*, a 1996 case against AOL, the major online platform at the time.[116] In *Cyber Promotions*, a mass-email marketing firm alleged that AOL's new spam filters were violations of the First Amendment as, effectively, a form of state censorship. The court distinguished *Marsh* on factual grounds, but what if it hadn't? Holding AOL—or today's major platforms—to be a state actor could have severely limited its ability to fight not only spam but also trolling, flooding, abuse, and myriad other unpleasantries. From the perspective of listeners, it would likely be counterproductive.

STATUTORY OR LAW ENFORCEMENT PROTECTION OF SPEECH ENVIRONMENTS AND THE PRESS

Many of the efforts to control speech described in this essay may be best countered not by the judiciary using the First Amendment, but rather by law enforcement using already existing or newly enacted laws. Consider several possibilities, some of which target trolling and others of which focus on flooding:

- Extensive enforcement of existing federal or state anti-cyberstalking laws to protect journalists or other speakers from individual abuse;
- The introduction of anti-trolling laws designed to better combat the specific problem of troll army–style attacks on journalists or other public figures;
- New statutory or regulatory restrictions on the ability of major media and internet speech platforms to knowingly accept money from foreign governments attempting to influence American elections; and
- New laws or regulations requiring that major speech platforms behave as public trustees, with general duties to police fake users, remove propaganda robots, and promote a robust speech environment surrounding matters of public concern.

The enactment and vigorous enforcement of these laws would yield a range of challenging constitutional questions that this essay cannot address in their entirety. But the important doctrinal question held in common is whether the First Amendment would give sufficient room for such measures. To handle the political speech challenges of our time, I suggest that the First Amendment must be interpreted to give wide latitude for new measures to advance listener interests, including measures that protect some speakers from others.

As a doctrinal matter, such new laws would bring renewed attention to classic doctrines that accommodate the interests of listeners—such as the doctrines of "true threats" and "captive audiences"—as well as to the latitude that courts have traditionally given efforts to protect the electoral process from manipulation. Such laws might also redirect attention to a question originally raised by the FCC's fairness doctrine and the *Red Lion Broadcasting Co. v. FCC* decision: how far the government may go solely to promote a better speech environment.[117]

We might begin with the prosecution of trolls, which could be addressed criminally as a form of harassment or threat. Current case law is relatively receptive to such efforts, for it allows the government to protect listeners from speech designed to intimidate them by creating a fear of violence.[118] The death threat and burning cross serve as archetypical examples. As we have seen, trolls frequently operate by describing horrific acts, and not in a manner suggesting good humor or artistic self-expression.[119] In the Supreme Court's most recent statement on the matter, it advised that "intimidation in the constitutionally proscribable sense of the word is a type of true threat, where a speaker directs a threat to a person or group of persons with the intent of placing the victim in fear of bodily harm or death."[120] The fact that threats are often not carried out is immaterial; the intent to create a fear of violence is sufficient.[121] Given this doctrinal backdrop, there is reason to believe that the First Amendment can already accommodate increased prosecution of those who try to intimidate journalists or other critics.

This belief is supported by the outcome of *United States v. Moreland*, the first lower court decision to consider the use of the federal cyberstalking statute to protect a journalist from an aggressive troll.[122] Jason Moreland, the defendant, directed hundreds of aggressive emails, social media comments, and physical mailings at a journalist living and reporting in Washington, D.C. Many of his messages referenced violence and "a fight to the death." In the face of a multifaceted First Amendment challenge, the court wrote:

> His communications directly referenced violence, indicated frustration that CP would not respond to his hundreds of emails, reflected concern that CP or someone on her behalf wanted to kill Moreland, stated that it was time to "eliminate things" and "fight to the death," informed plaintiff that he knew where her brother was, and repeatedly conveyed that he expected a confrontation with CP or others on her behalf. . . . The Court concludes that the statute is not unconstitutional as applied, as the words are in the nature of a true threat and speech integral to criminal conduct.[123]

Cases like *Moreland* suggest that while efforts to reduce trolling might present a serious enforcement challenge, the Constitution will not stand in the way so long as the trolling at issue looks more like threats and not just strongly expressed political views.

The constitutional questions raised by government efforts to fight flooding are more difficult. Much depends on the extent to which these efforts are seen as serving important societal interests beyond the quality or integrity of public discourse, such as the protection of privacy or the protection of the electoral process.

Of particular relevance, as more and more of our lives are lived online—for many Americans today, nearly every waking moment is spent in close proximity to a screen—we may be captive audiences far more often than in previous decades. The captive audience doctrine, first developed in the 1940s, describes situations in which one is left with no practical means of avoiding unwanted speech. It was developed in cases like *Kovacs v. Cooper*,[124] which concerned a city ban on sound trucks that drove around broadcasting various messages at a loud volume so as to reach both pedestrians and people within their homes. The Court wrote that "the unwilling listener is not like the passer-by who may be offered a pamphlet in the street but cannot be made to take it. In his home or on the street he is practically helpless to escape this interference with his privacy by loud speakers except through the protection of the municipality."[125] It is worth pondering the extent to which we are now captive audiences in somewhat subtler scenarios, and whether we have developed virtual equivalents to the home—like our various devices or our email inboxes—where it is effectively impossible to avoid certain messages. The idea that one might simply "avert the eyes"[126] as a means to deal with offensive messages seems increasingly implausible in many digital contexts. Relying on cases like *Kovacs*, the government might seek to develop and enforce anti-captivity measures that are designed to protect our privacy or autonomy online.

Other government interests may be implicated by efforts to fight flooding in the form of foreign propaganda. Consider, for instance, a ban on political advertising—including payments to social media firms—by foreign governments or even foreigners in general. Such a ban, if challenged as censorship, might be justified by the state's compelling interest in defending the electoral process and the national political community, in the same manner that the government has justified laws banning foreign campaign contributions. As a three-judge panel of the D.C. district court explained in a recent ruling: "the United States has a compelling interest for purposes of First Amendment analysis in limiting the participation of foreign citizens in activities of American democratic self-government, and in thereby preventing foreign influence over the U.S. political process."[127] It should not be any great step to assert that the United States may also have a compelling interest in preventing foreign interests from manipulating American elections through propaganda campaigns conducted through social media platforms.

I have left for last the question presented by potential new laws premised solely on an interest in improving the political speech environment. These laws would be inspired by the indelible dictum of Alexander Meiklejohn: "What is essential is not that everyone shall speak, but that everything worth saying shall be said"[128]—and, to some meaningful degree, heard. Imagine, for instance, a law that makes any social media platform with significant market power a kind of trustee operating in the public interest, and requires that it actively take steps to promote a healthy speech environment. This could, in effect, be akin to a fairness doctrine for social media.

For those not familiar with it, for decades the fairness doctrine obligated broadcasters to use their power over spectrum to improve the conditions of political speech in the United States.[129] It required that broadcasters affirmatively cover matters of public concern and do so in a "fair" manner. Furthermore, it created a right for anyone to demand the opportunity to respond to opposing views using the broadcaster's facilities.[130] At the time of the doctrine's first adoption in 1949, the First Amendment remained largely inert; by the 1960s, a constitutional challenge to the regulations became inevitable. In the 1969 *Red Lion* decision, the Supreme Court upheld the doctrine and in doing so described the First Amendment's goals as follows:

> It is the right of the viewers and listeners, not the right of the broadcasters, which is paramount. It is the purpose of the First Amendment to preserve an uninhibited marketplace of ideas in which truth will ultimately prevail, rather than to countenance monopolization of that market, whether it be by the Government itself or a private licensee.[131]

While *Red Lion* has never been explicitly overruled, it has been limited by subsequent cases, and it is now usually said to be dependent on the scarcity of spectrum suitable for broadcasting.[132] The FCC withdrew the fairness doctrine in 1987, opining that it was unconstitutional,[133] and *Red Lion* has been presumed dead or overruled by a variety of government officials and scholars.[134] Nonetheless, in the law, no doctrine is ever truly dead. All things have their season, and the major changes in our media environment seem to have strengthened the constitutional case for laws explicitly intended to improve political discourse.

To make my own preferences clear, I personally would not favor the creation of a fairness doctrine for social media or other parts of the web. That kind of law, I think, would be too hard to administer, too prone to manipulation, and too apt to flatten what has made the internet interesting and innovative. But I could be overestimating those risks, and my own preferences do not bear on the question of whether Congress has the power to pass such a law. Given the problems discussed in this essay, among others, Congress might conclude that our political discourse has been deeply damaged, threatening not just coherent governance but the survival of the republic. On that basis, I think the elected branches should be allowed, within reasonable limits, to try returning the country to the kind of media environment that prevailed in the 1950s. Stated differently, it seems implausible that the First Amendment cannot allow Congress to cultivate more bipartisanship or nonpartisanship online. The justification for such a law would turn on the trends described above: the increasing scarcity of human attention, the rise to dominance of a few major platforms, and the pervasive evidence of negative effects on our democratic life.

CONCLUSION

It is obvious that changes in communications technologies will present new challenges for the First Amendment. For nearly twenty years now, scholars have been debating how the rise of the popular internet might unsettle what the First Amendment takes for granted. Yet the future retains its capacity to surprise, for the emerging threats to our political speech environment are different from what many predicted. Few forecast that speech itself would become a weapon of censorship. In fact, some might say that celebrants of open and unfettered channels of internet expression (myself included) are being hoisted on their own petard, as those very same channels are today used as ammunition against disfavored speakers. As such, the emerging methods of speech control present a particularly difficult set of challenges for those who share the commitment to free speech articulated so powerfully in the founding—and increasingly obsolete—generation of First Amendment jurisprudence.

Reflections on Whether the First Amendment Is Obsolete

Geoffrey R. Stone

TIM WU'S remarkable essay raises profound questions about the future of free expression in a world of ever-changing technology. Wu identifies a number of potentially serious threats to our capacity to maintain the robust public discourse that is essential to a well-functioning democracy. Before offering a few thoughts on those challenges, though, let me first take issue with the central question raised in the essay: "Is the First Amendment Obsolete?"

In raising this question, and arguing that in large part the First Amendment—as currently understood—is, in fact, obsolete, Wu misses a fundamental reality. The issues he rightly identifies in his essay are critical to our democratic future only because the First Amendment, as interpreted and applied by the Supreme Court, has been extraordinarily successful at constraining the primary evil at which the First Amendment was directed— government censorship of unwelcome ideas and criticism.

If the Supreme Court had not done such a good job of enforcing the central meaning of the First Amendment, then all of the issues that concern Wu would be largely unimportant. If, as was once the case, government could constitutionally imprison anyone whose ideas it sought to suppress, then none of the issues that concern Wu would matter all that much. These issues are critical only because the First Amendment has, on balance, been remarkably successful in constraining the fundamental evil at which it was directed. It is important to give credit where credit is due!

None of that is to suggest, however, that the concerns that Wu raises are not deeply troubling. They do, indeed, pose serious threats to the future functioning of our democracy. There are at least two ways in which the First Amendment might be relevant to these issues. First, the First Amendment might be interpreted in such a way as to forbid some of these activities.

Second, the First Amendment might be interpreted in such a way as to allow government to forbid some of these activities.

The primary constraint on the first approach is, as Wu notes, the state action doctrine. Most of the concerns he raises involve speech by private actors—for example, those who flood the marketplace of ideas with fake news or who threaten those who express views they want to stifle. Under well-settled principles of constitutional interpretation, the actions of those individuals, even if they act in concert with one another, do not constitute state action and thus do not trigger the First Amendment.

There have been occasional instances, however, in which the Court has played rather fast and loose with the state action doctrine in order to bring essentially private action within the sphere of constitutional law. This was so in cases like *Shelley v. Kraemer*[135] and *Marsh v. Alabama*,[136] and it is at least possible that the Court would once again move in that direction in the face of what it might perceive as profound private threats to our system of free expression. For example, one could imagine the Court holding that extraordinary powerful internet sites, like Facebook, Twitter, and Google, are so powerful that they are in effect government actors and must therefore be deemed the equivalent of public forums. *Marsh*, which dealt with company towns, might be a good jumping-off point for such an analysis.

The more likely expansion in the scope of First Amendment restrictions, as Wu notes, is in the realm of government speech. This is still a relatively novel concept in First Amendment jurisprudence, and recognition that the government is permitted to express points of view does not imply that government has unlimited authority to exercise its power to speak when doing so violates the Constitution. For example, if a state government, in which all three branches are controlled by the same political party, authorizes the expenditure of public funds to support the election of only Republican Party candidates, that would surely violate the First Amendment. Some government speech, in other words, is itself unconstitutional.

The more difficult question, as Wu observes, is whether the government's use of public resources to advocate a particular political position can ever go so far as to violate the First Amendment. The World War I example poses a useful illustration of the problem. The challenge, of course, is figuring out when too much is too much. A similar issue arises when the government encourages private speakers to advance a particular partisan or political position. The Supreme Court has not yet begun to grapple with these questions, but as Wu notes they might well come before the Court in the future, and one can imagine situations in which the Court would in fact hold that such conduct violates the First Amendment, although the line-drawing issues would be daunting.

The second way in which the First Amendment might be relevant to the concerns described by Wu is by permitting greater government regulation of the marketplace of ideas. That is, the government might attempt to address some of these concerns by legislation or regulation, and the Supreme Court might then interpret the First Amendment in a way that permits such intervention, even though the intervention itself raises potentially serious First Amendment questions.

It is worth recalling that there was a time in our history when technological advances in the communications market caused similar angst. This occurred with the advent of radio, when citizens feared that, in light of the small number of available frequencies, a handful of wealthy individuals could take control of those frequencies and thus dominate public discourse. Faced with that concern, Congress created the Federal Radio Commission in 1926 and then the Federal Communications Commission (FCC) in 1934 and gave them the authority to regulate radio in "the public interest, convenience, or necessity."

Under the authority of this legislation, the FCC licensed those who could use radio (and later television) frequencies, and in 1946 it adopted the Fairness Doctrine, which required the holders of broadcast licenses both to present controversial issues of public importance and to do so in a manner that was fair and balanced. Although such a regulation of newspapers would clearly have violated the First Amendment, the Supreme Court in *Red Lion Broadcasting Co. v. FCC*[137] held that the Fairness Doctrine was consistent with the First Amendment, in part because of the distinctive power wielded by these means of communication. One can imagine a scenario in which similar legislation might someday be enacted and upheld with respect to such internet sites as Facebook, Twitter, and Google in order to address some of the challenges described by Wu.

Other issues identified by Wu, like threats and mass harassment designed to deter people from expressing their views on the internet, might also be addressed by legislation, although that would require careful analysis of how to define precisely what speech should be forbidden. While this problem is certainly magnified on the internet, it is worth noting that it has always existed in society. Individuals who take positions that offend others in their community have always been vulnerable to condemnation by others, and such personal condemnation by neighbors, friends, employers, and coworkers might be far more daunting than mass condemnation by strangers, especially once people get used to such behavior. And, yet, we lived with it.

One of the most vexing issues concerns the proliferation of intentionally false information on the internet. On the one hand, it seems easy to say that government should have the authority to punish intentionally false statements that are designed to mislead others. Although the Supreme Court has rejected the idea that intentionally false statements are automatically unprotected by the First Amendment, and that such speech can be restricted only if it can be shown to cause significant harm—as would be true, for example, with defamation, perjury, and fraud[138]—one might readily argue that widespread lies that are intended to distort public discourse rise to that level of harm. Even if that is so, however, there may be good reasons not to make such speech actionable. After all, putting the power to prosecute such statements in the hands of public officials is a recipe for potential disaster, because those officials will likely prosecute only those false statements that harm their own positions.

In the end, the primary response to most of the dangers identified by Wu must rest in the people themselves. The First Amendment assumes the existence of a populace that is reasonably educated, thoughtful, responsible, and intelligent. Most of the dangers Wu identifies can be addressed by the people themselves, if they take the time to understand the contemporary distortions in the marketplace of ideas and figure out how to compensate for them.

This has, of course, always been true. If citizens are too lazy, too ignorant, and too indifferent to learn how to cope with these risks of distortion, then democracy is doomed anyway. If we rely on the people themselves to figure out whether or not to go to war, whom to elect as president, and whether to support candidates who want tax reform, health care reform, or environmental reform, then surely they can figure out how to deal with distortions in the marketplace of ideas—once those distortions are brought to their attention. Right?

Not Waving but Drowning: Saving the Audience from the Floods

Rebecca Tushnet

TIM WU'S challenging essay explores what has gone wrong with First Amendment law in recent decades—how it has become detached from key threats to the freedom of speech, and in fact has been twisted to support some of those threats. I am highly sympathetic to his arguments, so I will offer a few riffs on them, including some suggestions for integrating them more closely with existing First Amendment doctrines and forms of argument.

The pro-corporate, anti-regulatory thrust of much modern First Amendment doctrine is an example of what Jack Balkin has called "ideological drift," but I also see in Wu's essay elements of "naming, blaming, and claiming"—that is to say, identifying phenomena in the world and then arguing that they have normative weight, and specifically that they are *legal* problems rather than social or moral problems.[139] Reframing government speech as something that ought to be limited by the First Amendment, because of its potential effects on private speech, is a key example. The deliberate destruction of public discourse by state and nonstate actors has not previously been one of the dangers we think of the First Amendment as addressing, at least not at this scale, though we can find some analogies in the past, for example in Southern officials' attempts to use defamation law to suppress reporting on the civil rights movement. Because Southern officials used the law itself as their weapon of disruption, changing First Amendment doctrine to preclude such claims was sufficient to beat back the threat. As Wu persuasively explains, however, the use of troll armies and information flooding can't be fought with the same tools that protected the *New York Times* in the 1960s.

Furthermore, as Wu observes, "the use of speech as a tool to suppress speech is, by its nature, something very challenging for the First Amendment to deal with." We've seen speech-versus-speech arguments before, in fields from copyright to pornography to campaign finance, but in general there has been an identifiable government intervention that could be challenged or defended as promoting some speech to the detriment of other speech. In copyright, for example, the government grants authors rights in some speech, and they can use those rights in court to suppress other speech. Yet today's flooding and trolling doesn't bother with invoking government processes. Pamphleteers are buried in the crowd, not arrested.

Wu argues that, rather than responding to these new threats to political speech and democratic governance, First Amendment jurisprudence has been off on a "frolic and detour" of its own, expanding the domain of commercial speech and threatening the scope of economic regulations—a new Lochnerism. Instead, he wants the jurisprudence to focus on newly salient threats to robust public debate, which he suggests would lead to more attention to structural components of "speech environments," as well as to listeners' interests. These are not new ideas, even if there are new reasons that they are important; they've appeared in defenses (and critiques) of copyright law, as well as in justifications for limited but significant protection for truthful commercial speech and for the constitutionality of campaign finance laws. Balkin presciently argued that, in the internet age, structural and regulatory issues would be more important for the robustness of free speech than traditional areas of First Amendment interest such as libel.[140] Wu's contribution is to urge that these new issues should themselves be understood as First Amendment concerns. Whether it's possible to overcome the strong negative-rights bias of American constitutional law is a larger question.

One fruitful avenue of comparison to existing First Amendment doctrines might come from the law of mandated disclosures, a subset of the law of compelled speech. There is a robust debate over when (and even whether) mandatory disclosures of various risks or facts help consumers. One significant aspect of this debate involves the problem of information overload. As Wu says, attention is inherently limited. Audiences generally take in only a small number of key messages from any given communication; this can also be true of any given communicative encounter, no matter how many different people are participating. Courts recognize that one of the relevant considerations in evaluating the constitutionality of a mandatory disclosure is the effect it will have on other messages the speaker wants to communicate. Government drowning out of other discourse by flooding the environment could therefore be seen as a variant of an already known First Amendment problem, by analogy to unduly burdensome mandatory disclosures. This analogy also takes advantage of Wu's suggestion to focus on particular methods of government speech, rather than on the existence of propaganda. (The tools courts have for assessing whether a message is factual or propaganda are, as the mandatory disclosure debates show, very limited—in fact a message can easily be both, though a requirement that the government not engage in false speech is also, sadly, important.)

Compelled speech doctrine more generally also recognizes the importance of identifying the government as the source of speech, rather than attributing it to nongovernmental sources. Anonymity may be a First Amendment right for private speakers under many circumstances, but there is little reason to allow the government the same kind of freedom in pretending to be something it's not. Compelled speech doctrine has identified one particular harm—the harm to the speaker of a false attribution to it of a position that actually comes from the government. But even when there is no real speaker, the false attribution harms the audience, and that ought to be enough to create a First Amendment problem where the speaker is in fact a government entity.

Wu proposes a similar doctrinal reorientation in the understanding of a captive audience, a situation in which the Supreme Court has allowed more government regulation of third-party speech. He argues that changing technologies make us captive audiences in more situations, and his suggestion finds support in the recent Supreme Court case invalidating a ban on social media for registered sex offenders.[141] The Court wrote eloquently about the centrality of social media to ordinary American life and the possibly devastating, certainly isolating, consequences of being excluded from Facebook, LinkedIn, Twitter, and numerous other new communications tools. Although some people may choose to self-exclude and self-silence to protect themselves from exposure to messages from such services, the importance of these communications channels means that it is not reasonable to ask audience members to do this, any more than it is reasonable to tell people that they shouldn't take public transportation if they want to avoid discriminatory messages. This is the very definition of a captive audience: one that has no realistic choice but to listen, for whom turning away will come too late.

One friendly amendment I'd add is that, along with the measures Wu discusses, it might be useful to reexamine education as a First Amendment issue.

Understanding the new information environment may be the most important tool citizens have to participate in democracy, which is a core First Amendment aim.[142] Education has always been important, of course, and learning how to think has long been at the center of the Western educational mission. Education specifically in how to evaluate information, however, has a shorter history. The growing field of media education has many ideas about how to do this, but it is not yet a standard part of the curriculum—a "reality" to be added to reading, writing, and arithmetic. If we see government as responsible for the speech environment, and particularly for structuring markets in which some groups get to silence other groups, then the government's obligation to assist in media education is another First Amendment issue.

Finally, it's worth considering that constitutional expansion in one direction (protecting corporate speech about commercial matters and unrestricted election spending) has led Wu to advocate, not contraction, but expansion in a different direction. I'm not sure about the strategic implications of that response. On the one hand, it could be that articulating a coherent, larger-in-some-ways version of the First Amendment could help explain where the First Amendment should *not* extend. On the other hand, because the interests the First Amendment serves have long been multivalent and at times incoherent, not least because of competing theories among the justices of the Supreme Court, projects such as Wu's might push us further in the direction of making everything a First Amendment issue.[143] Because Wu's arguments do not focus, as some previous interventions in this vein have done, on the way that helping some speech is hurting other speech, they may be more likely to have the latter effect: more First Amendment constraints on government speech alongside more First Amendment protections for corporate speech. But that is speculation. I raise the issue merely to note that a full conception of the First Amendment should include a theory of what speech is not protected.

NOTES

IS THE FIRST AMENDMENT OBSOLETE?

These ideas were first formulated at the Knight Institute's opening event, "DISRUPTED: Speech and Democracy in the Digital Age," during a panel discussion with Zeynep Tufekci. I am grateful to David Pozen for extensive help; to Jeffrey Stein for research assistance; and to Tufekci, who pioneered the recognition of new forms of censorship.

1. Zeynep Tufekci, *Twitter and Tear Gas: The Power and Fragility of Networked Protest* 226 (2017).
2. A third, slightly older technique—control of speech platforms—is also used to regulate speech, but it is not the subject of this essay. *See, e.g.,* Lawrence Lessig, *What Things Regulate Speech: CDA 2.0 vs. Filtering,* Berkman Klein Ctr. for Internet & Soc'y (May 12, 1998), https://cyber.harvard.edu/works/lessig/what _things.pdf; Jack Goldsmith & Tim Wu, *Who Controls the Internet? Illusions of a Borderless World* (2006); Jack M. Balkin, *Old-School/New-School Speech Regulation,* 127 Harv. L. Rev. 2296 (2014). One reason is that these techniques have already been subject to extensive scholarly attention. The other is that laws that require speech platforms to control speech are usually subject to First Amendment scrutiny. *See, e.g., Reno v. American Civil Liberties Union,* 521 U.S. 844 (1997).
3. Peter Pomerantsev, *The Menace of Unreality: How the Kremlin Weaponizes Information, Culture and Money,* Interpreter (Nov. 22, 2014), http://www .interpretermag.com/the-menace-of-unreality-how-the-kremlin-weaponizes -information-culture-and-money.
4. There may, moreover, be more work to be done now in areas such as libel law. Given the raft of libel-trolling suits that burden small presses, stronger and faster First Amendment protection has arguably become necessary.
5. *See, e.g., Citizens United v. FEC,* 558 U.S. 310 (2010).
6. *Sorrell v. IMS Health Inc.,* 564 U.S. 552 (2011).
7. *Matal v. Tam,* 137 S. Ct. 1744 (2017).
8. The merits of the recent economic-rights case law are not the subject of this essay. Suffice it to say that these rulings have some academic supporters and many detractors. *See, e.g.,* Amanda Shanor, *The New* Lochner, 2016 Wis. L. Rev. 133 (2016); Jeremy K. Kessler, *The Early Years of First Amendment Lochnerism,* 116 Colum. L. Rev. 1915 (2016); Samuel R. Bagenstos, *The Unrelenting Libertarian Challenge to Public Accommodations Law,* 66 Stan. L. Rev. 1205 (2014); Leslie Kendrick, *First Amendment Expansionism,* 56 Wm. & Mary L. Rev. 1199 (2015).
9. The First Amendment was even silent when Congress passed its first laws restricting speech in 1798, not long after the adoption of the Bill of Rights and with the approval of many of the framers. This fact, among others, has long been slightly embarrassing to would-be "originalists" who by disposition would like to believe in a strong First Amendment. Robert Bork was rare among the first wave of originalists in calling attention to the amendment's unpromising early history. *See* Robert H. Bork, *Neutral Principles and Some First Amendment Problems,* 47 Ind. L.J. 1, 22 (1971).
10. Sedition Act of 1918, Pub. L. No. 65–150 (1918); Espionage Act of 1917, Pub. L. No. 65–24 (1917).
11. *Debs v. United States,* 249 U.S. 211, 214 (1919).
12. *See, e.g.,* Alan Axelrod, *Selling the Great War: The Making of American Propaganda* (2009); James R. Mock & Cedric Larson, *Words That Won the War: The Story of the Committee on Public Information, 1917–1919* (1968).
13. George Creel, *The First Telling of the Amazing Story of the Committee on Public Information That Carried the Gospel of Americanism to Every Corner of the Globe* 3–9 (1920).

14. As described in Tim Wu, *The Attention Merchants* (2016), and sources cited therein.

15. On this tension, see Vincent A. Blasi, *Rights Skepticism and Majority Rule at the Birth of the Modern First Amendment*, in *The Free Speech Century* 13 (Lee C. Bollinger & Geoffrey R. Stone, eds., 2019).

16. *See Masses Pub. Co. v. Patten*, 244 F. 535, 543 (S.D.N.Y.), rev'd, 246 F. 24 (2d Cir. 1917) (granting a preliminary injunction to the publisher of *The Masses*, a revolutionary journal that the Postmaster General intended to withhold from the mails because it featured cartoons and text critical of the draft); *see also* Vincent Blasi, *Learned Hand and the Self-Government Theory of the First Amendment: Masses Publishing Co. v. Patten*, 61 U. Colo. L. Rev. 1 (1990).

17. *See, e.g., Whitney v. California*, 274 U.S. 357, 372 (1927) (Brandeis, J., concurring); *Abrams v. United States*, 250 U.S. 616, 624 (1919) (Holmes, J., dissenting).

18. In cases like *Dennis v. United States*, 341 U.S. 494 (1951), and *Brandenburg v. Ohio*, 395 U.S. 444 (1969).

19. *See, e.g., Encyclopedia of the American Constitution: Supplement I* 585 (Leonard W. Levy, Kenneth L. Karst & Adam Winkler, eds., 1992) (describing the absence of a constitutional challenge to the Committee on Public Information).

20. *Cf.* Alexander Meiklejohn, *The First Amendment Is an Absolute*, 1961 Sup. Ct. Rev. 245, 255 (arguing that the First Amendment "protects the freedom of those activities of thought and communication by which we 'govern'"); Bork, *supra*, note 9, at 27–28 (defining political speech as "speech concerned with governmental behavior, policy or personnel, whether the governmental unit involved is executive, legislative, judicial, or administrative").

21. 354 U.S. 476 (1957).

22. 425 U.S. 748 (1976).

23. *See, e.g., First Nat'l Bank of Boston v. Bellotti*, 435 U.S. 765 (1978).

24. *See, e.g., Buckley v. Valeo*, 424 U.S. 1 (1976).

25. The trend is summarized well in Morgan N. Weiland, *Expanding the Periphery and Threatening the Core: The Ascendant Libertarian Speech Tradition*, 69 Stan. L. Rev. 1389 (2017).

26. In other words, this is an essay about speech and reporting concerned with how we are governed, which includes political criticism, campaigning, and public debates over policy or specific regulatory or legislative initiatives. By focusing on the political First Amendment, I am not taking the position that other domains of the First Amendment are unimportant. *Cf.* Robert Post, *Meiklejohn's Mistake: Individual Autonomy and the Reform of Public Discourse*, 64 U. Colo. L. Rev. 1109 (1993).

27. A metaphor suggested, though not actually used, by Justice Holmes. *See* Vincent Blasi, *Holmes and the Marketplace of Ideas*, 2004 Sup. Ct. Rev. 1, 4.

28. This corresponds to Balkin's "old-school" speech regulation techniques. *See* Balkin, *supra* note 2, at 2298.

29. Herbert A. Simon, *Designing Organizations for an Information-Rich World*, in *Computers, Communications, and the Public Interest* 37, 40–41 (Martin Greenberger, ed., 1971).

30. Consider that information—including speech—is not actually received or processed unless it attracts the fickle attention of the listener. As William James

first pointed out in the 1890s, and as neuroscientists have confirmed, the brain ignores nearly everything, paying attention to a very limited stream of information. William James, *The Principles of Psychology* 403–04 (1890). At a minimum, the total capacity for attention is limited by time—168 hours a week—which becomes of particular relevance when the listeners in question are members of Congress, regulators, or others who are the supposed customers in the marketplace for good policy ideas.

31. *See, e.g.,* James Gleick, *The Information: A History, a Theory, a Flood* (2011); Eugene Volokh, *Cheap Speech and What It Will Do,* 104 Yale L.J. 1805 (1995).

32. *See, e.g.,* Balkin, *supra* note 2; Jeffrey Rosen, *The Deciders: The Future of Privacy and Free Speech in the Age of Facebook and Google,* 80 Fordham L. Rev. 1525 (2012); Tim Wu, *Is Filtering Censorship? The Second Free Speech Tradition,* Brookings Inst. (Dec. 27, 2010), https://www.brookings.edu/research/is-filtering -censorship-the-second-free-speech-tradition.

33. *See generally* Wu, *supra* note 14.

34. *See* Eli Pariser, *The Filter Bubbles: What the Internet Is Hiding from You* (2011). Scholarly consideration of filtering came earlier. *See, e.g.,* Cass Sunstein, *Republic.com* (2001); Dan Hunter, *Philippic.com,* 90 Calif. L. Rev. 611 (2002) (reviewing Sunstein's *Republic.com*); Elizabeth Garrett, *Political Intermediaries and the Internet "Revolution,"* 34 Loy. L.A. L. Rev. 1055 (2001).

35. Borrowing a term popularized by Nicholas Negroponte, the founder of MIT's Media Lab. *See* Nicholas Kristof, *The Daily Me,* N.Y. Times (Mar. 18, 2009), http://www.nytimes.com/2009/03/19/opinion/19kristof.html.

36. *See* Lauren Drell, *Why "Time Spent" Is One of Marketing's Favorite Metrics,* Mashable (Dec. 13, 2013), http://mashable.com/2013/12/13/time-spent-metrics/.

37. *See* Wu, *supra* note 14, at 303.

38. *See* Tim Wu, *How Donald Trump Wins by Losing,* N.Y. Times (Mar. 3, 2017), https://www.nytimes.com/2017/03/03/opinion/sunday/how-donald-trump-wins-by -losing.html.

39. Kathleen M. Sullivan, *First Amendment Intermediaries in the Age of Cyberspace,* 45 UCLA L. Rev. 1653, 1669 (1998).

40. Lessig, *supra* note 2; *see also* Lawrence Lessig, *Code and Other Laws of Cyberspace* (1999).

41. *See* Jonathan Zittrain, *Internet Points of Control,* 44 B.C. L. Rev. 653 (2003); Christopher S. Yoo, *Free Speech and the Myth of the Internet as an Unintermediated Experience,* 78 Geo. Wash. L. Rev. 697 (2010); Jeffrey Rosen, *Google's Gatekeepers,* N.Y. Times (Nov. 28, 2008), http://www.nytimes .com/2008/11/30/magazine/30google-t.html; Goldsmith & Wu, *supra* note 2.

42. The Open Net Initiative, launched as a collaboration among several universities in 2004, was and is perhaps the most ambitious documentation of online censorship around the world. *See* Evan M. Vittor, *HLS Team to Study Internet Censorship,* Harv. Crimson (Apr. 28, 2004), http://www.thecrimson.com /article/2004/4/28/hls-team-to-study-internet-censorship.

43. *See generally* Balkin, *supra* note 2 (describing "new school" speech control).

44. *See, e.g.,* R. Kelly Garrett, *Echo Chambers Online?: Politically Motivated Selective Exposure Among Internet News Users,* 14 J. Computer-Mediated Comm. 265 (2009); W. Lance Bennet & Shanto Iyengar, *A New Era of Minimal Effects?*

The Changing Foundations of Political Communication, 58 J. Comm. 707 (2008); Sofia Grafanaki, *Autonomy Challenges in the Age of Big Data*, 27 Fordham Intel. Prop. Media & Ent. L.J. 803 (2017).

45. For a notable partial exception, *see* Danielle Keats Citron, *Cyber Civil Rights*, 89 B.U. L. Rev. 61 (2009) (discussing online hate-mob attacks on women and other vulnerable groups).

46. For a full account of the speech-restrictive measures taken by the U.S. government during wartime, see Geoffrey R. Stone, *Perilous Times: Free Speech in Wartime, From the Sedition Act of 1798 to the War on Terrorism* (2004).

47. *See generally* Tufekci, *supra* note 1.

48. Gary King, Jennifer Pan & Margaret E. Roberts, *How Censorship in China Allows Government Criticism but Silences Collective Expression*, 107 Am. Pol. Sci. Rev. 326 (2013); Gary King, Jennifer Pan & Margaret E. Roberts, *How the Chinese Government Fabricates Social Media Posts for Strategic Distraction, Not Engaged Argument*, 111 Am. Pol. Sci. Rev. 484 (2017) [hereinafter King et al., 2017 APSR].

49. King et al., 2017 APSR, *supra* note 48, at 496 (emphasis omitted).

50. *Id.* at 497.

51. The term was coined in an article about a cease-and-desist letter sent by Marco Beach Ocean Resort to Urinal.net—a "site [that] has hundreds of fans who regularly submit pictures of urinals they take from locations all over the world"—threatening legal action unless the website stopped mentioning the resort's name alongside photos from its bathroom. The cease-and-desist letter prompted more attention than the original posts on Urinal.net. Mike Masnick, *Since When Is It Illegal to Just Mention a Trademark Online?*, Techdirt (Jan. 5, 2005), https://www .techdirt.com/articles/20050105/0132239.shtml.

52. *Id.* However, the Streisand example may be obscuring that many other cease-and-desist letters—even issued by celebrities—never attract much attention.

53. *See* Sharad Goel et al., *The Structural Virality of Online Diffusion*, 62 Mgmt. Sci. 180 (2016).

54. *See supra* note 2. The potential for requiring internet intermediaries to control speech was something a number of people noticed early in the internet's history. As Lessig observed in 1998, we had already begun to live in an era in which it was clear that networks might be designed to filter some speech and leave others untouched, or make intermediaries liable for carrying "forbidden" content. *See generally* Lessig, *supra* note 2. Around that same time, Congress undertook what Balkin later called "collateral censorship" techniques: requiring search engines and others to block copyrighted materials on request and requiring hosts to prevent minors from accessing indecent content. *See, e.g.,* Online Copyright Infringement Liability Limitation Act, Pub. L. No. 105–304 (1998); Communications Decency Act of 1996, Pub. L. No. 104–104 (1996). The potential for foreign governments to rely on targeting search engines, ISPs, and major hosting sites as a technique of control was also recognized. *See generally* Goldsmith & Wu, *supra* note 2. By now, it has become common knowledge that platforms like Google and Facebook exert a major influence on the speech environment, and the techniques of targeting intermediaries have evolved considerably. For a comprehensive survey of such techniques, see Balkin, *supra* note 2; *see also* Seth F. Kreimer, *Censorship by Proxy: The First Amendment, Internet*

Intermediaries, and the Problem of the Weakest Link, 155 U. Pa. L. Rev. 11 (2006).

55. In fact, recent reports suggest that President Trump and his associates may have already engaged in the distraction and cheerleading techniques described above. *See, e.g.*, Oliver Darcy, *Lawsuit: Fox News Concocted Seth Rich Story with Oversight from White House*, CNN (Aug. 2, 2017), http://money.cnn .com/2017/08/01/media/rod-wheeler-seth-rich-fox-news-lawsuit; Taylor Link, *President Trump Gave a Shout Out to an Apparent Twitter Bot, Hasn't Removed the Retweet*, Salon (Aug. 6, 2017), http://www.salon.com/2017/08/06/president -trump-gave-a-shout-out-to-an-apparent-twitter-bot-hasnt-removed-the-retweet.

56. Max Seddon, *Documents Show How Russia's Troll Army Hit America*, BuzzFeed (June 2, 2014), https://www.buzzfeed.com/maxseddon/documents -show-how-russias-troll-army-hit-america; Pomerantsev, *supra* note 3; *Russia Update: Questions About Putin's Health After Canceled Meetings & Vague Answers*, Interpreter (Mar. 12, 2015), http://www.interpretermag.com/russia -update-march-12-2015/#7432.

57. Peter Pomerantsev, *Inside the Kremlin's Hall of Mirrors*, Guardian (Apr. 9, 2015), https://www.theguardian.com/news/2015/apr/09/kremlin-hall-of-mirrors -military-information-psychology.

58. Pomerantsev, *supra* note 3.

59. *Cf.* Citron, *supra* note 45.

60. Andrew Higgins, *Effort to Expose Russia's "Troll Army" Draws Vicious Retaliation*, N.Y. Times (May 30, 2016), https://www.nytimes.com/2016/05/31/world/europe /russia-finland-nato-trolls.html.

61. *See* Rachel Roberts, *Russia Hired 1,000 People to Create Anti-Clinton "Fake News" in Key US States During Election, Trump-Russia Hearings Leader Reveals*, Independent (Mar. 30, 2017), https://www.independent.co.uk/news /world/americas/us-politics/russian-trolls-hilary-clinton-fake-news-election -democrat-mark-warner-intelligence-committee-a7657641.html; Natasha Bertrand, *It Looks like Russia Hired Internet Trolls to Pose as Pro-Trump Americans*, Bus. Insider (July 27, 2016), http://www.businessinsider.com/russia -internet-trolls-and-donald-trump-2016-7.

62. Pomerantsev, *supra* note 3; *see also* Pomerantsev, *supra* note 57.

63. *See* Roberts, *supra* note 61. The degree to which trolls operating in the United States are funded by or otherwise coordinated with the Russian state is a topic of wide speculation. However, based on leaked documents and whistleblower accounts, it is clear that at least some of the attacks on Trump critics in 2016 and 2017 were launched by Russia itself. *See, e.g.*, Alexey Kovalev, *Russia's Infamous "Troll Factory" Is Now Posing as a Media Empire*, Moscow Times (Mar. 24, 2017), https://themoscowtimes.com/articles/russias-infamous-troll-factory-is-now-posing -as-a-media-empire-57534.

64. David French, *The Price I've Paid for Opposing Donald Trump*, Nat'l Rev. (Oct. 21, 2016), http://www.nationalreview.com/article/441319/donald-trump-alt-right -internet-abuse-never-trump-movement.

65. Stephen Battaglio, *Trump's Attacks On CNN Aren't Hurting It One Bit*, L.A. Times (Feb. 16, 2017), http://www.latimes.com/business/hollywood/la-fi-ct-cnn -zucker-20170216-story.html.

66. French, *supra* note 64.

67. Rosa Brooks, *And Then the Breitbart Lynch Mob Came for Me*, Foreign Pol'y (Feb. 6, 2017), http://foreignpolicy.com/2017/02/06/and-then-the-breitbart-lynch -mob-came-for-me-bannon-trolls-trump.

68. *See. e.g.*, Katharine Q. Seelye, *Protesters Disrupt Speech by "Bell Curve" Author at Vermont College*, N.Y. Times (Mar. 3, 2017), https://www.nytimes .com/2017/03/03/us/middlebury-college-charles-murray-bell-curve-protest.html.

69. But even more cruelly:

> Someone—bored, apparently, with the usual angles of harassment—had made a fake Twitter account purporting to be my dead dad, featuring a stolen, beloved photo of him, for no reason other than to hurt me. The name on the account was "PawWestDonezo," because my father's name was Paul West, and a difficult battle with prostate cancer had rendered him "donezo" (goofy slang for "done") just 18 months earlier. "Embarrassed father of an idiot," the bio read. "Other two kids are fine, though." His location was "Dirt hole in Seattle."

> The fake father then proceeded to harass and abuse her every day. Lindy West, *What Happened When I Confronted My Cruelest Troll*, Guardian (Feb. 2, 2015), https://www.theguardian.com/society/2015/feb/02/what-happened-confronted -cruellest-troll-lindy-west.

70. *Id.*

71. John Stuart Mill, *On Liberty and Other Writings* 69 (Stefan Collini, ed., Cambridge University Press 1989) (1859) ("These tendencies of the times cause the public to be more disposed than at most former periods to prescribe general rules of conduct, and endeavour to make every one conform to the approved standard.").

72. *See generally* Adam Bienkov, *Astroturfing: What Is It and Why Does It Matter?*, Guardian (Feb. 8, 2012), https://www.theguardian.com/commentisfree/2012 /feb/08/what-is-astroturfing.

73. *See* Goldsmith & Wu, *supra* note 2 (including an earlier investigation into Chinese censorship innovations).

74. Predictions of the Communist Party's downfall at the hands of the internet are surveyed in Chapter 6 of *id.*

75. King et al., 2017 APSR, *supra* note 48, at 497.

76. *See* Pomerantsev, *supra* note 57.

77. Tufekci, *supra* note 1, at 246.

78. *Id.* at 231, 241.

79. Philip N. Howard et al., *Junk News and Bots During the U.S. Election: What Were Michigan Voters Sharing over Twitter?*, Computational Propaganda Project (Mar. 26, 2017), http://comprop.oii.ox.ac.uk/wp-content/uploads/sites /89/2017/03/What-Were-Michigan-Voters-Sharing-Over-Twitter-v2.pdf.

80. Onur Varol et al., *Online Human-Bot Interactions: Detection, Estimation, and Characterization*, Int'l AAAI Conf. Web & Social Media (Mar. 27, 2017), https:// arxiv.org/pdf/1703.03107.pdf.

81. Rebecca Grant, *Facebook Has No Idea How Many Fake Accounts It Has— But It Could Be Nearly 140M*, VentureBeat (Feb. 3, 2014), https://venturebeat .com/2014/02/03/facebook-has-no-idea-how-many-fake-accounts-it-has-but-it-could -nearly-140m.

82. Patrick Kulp, *Bots Flood the FCC with Fake Anti-Net Neutrality Comments*, Mashable (May 10, 2017), http://mashable.com/2017/05/10/bots-net-neutrality-comments-fcc.

83. The Supreme Court reaffirmed last spring that U.S. government propaganda is outside the reach of the First Amendment. *See Matal v. Tam*, 137 S. Ct. 1744, 1758 (2017) (noting, in dicta, that "the First Amendment did not demand that the Government balance the message of [pro–World War II] posters by producing and distributing posters encouraging Americans to refrain from engaging in these activities"). For an argument that such propaganda ought be subject to First Amendment controls, see William W. Van Alstyne, *The First Amendment and the Suppression of Warmongering Propaganda in the United States: Comments and Footnotes*, 31 Law & Contemp. Probs. 530 (1966).

84. *See Wooley v. Maynard*, 430 U.S. 705 (1977).

85. *See, e.g., West Virginia State Board of Education v. Barnette*, 319 U.S. 624 (1943); *see also Linmark Assocs., Inc. v. Willingboro Twp.*, 431 U.S. 85 (1977). Other constraints are surveyed in Mark G. Yudof, *When Governments Speak: Toward a Theory of Government Expression and the First Amendment*, 57 Tex. L. Rev. 863 (1979).

86. For a sample of the debate, see Robyn Caplan, *Like It or Not, Facebook Is Now a Media Company*, N.Y. Times (May 17, 2016), https://www.nytimes.com/roomfordebate/2016/05/17/is-facebook-saving-journalism-or-ruining-it/like-it-or-not-facebook-is-now-a-media-company.

87. *See* Stephen J.A. Ward, *The Invention of Journalism Ethics, First Edition: The Path to Objectivity and Beyond* (2006); David T.Z. Mindich, *Just the Facts: How "Objectivity" Came to Define American Journalism* (2000).

88. *See* Clay Shirky, *Here Comes Everybody: The Power of Organizing Without Organizations* (2008); *cf.* William W. Fisher III, *Theories of Intellectual Property*, in *New Essays in the Legal and Political Theory of Property* 168, 193 (Stephen R. Munzer, ed., 2001) (describing semiotic democracy).

89. Volokh, *supra* note 31, at 1807.

90. Lindy West, *Twitter Doesn't Think These Rape and Death Threats Are Harassment*, Daily Dot (Dec. 23, 2014), https://www.dailydot.com/via/twitter-harassment-rape-death-threat-report.

91. *Id.*

92. Lindy West, *I've Left Twitter. It Is Unusable for Anyone but Trolls, Robots and Dictators*, Guardian (Jan. 3, 2017), https://www.theguardian.com/commentisfree/2017/jan/03/ive-left-twitter-unusable-anyone-but-trolls-robots-dictators-lindy-west.

93. *See, e.g.*, Julian Dibbel, *A Rape in Cyberspace: How an Evil Clown, a Haitian Trickster Spirit, Two Wizards, and a Cast of Dozens Turned a Database into a Society*, Village Voice (Dec. 23, 1993), http://www.juliandibbell.com/texts/bungle_vv.html.

94. *See* Cade Metz, *At 15, Wikipedia Is Finally Finding Its Way to the Truth*, Wired (Jan. 15, 2016), https://www.wired.com/2016/01/at-15-wikipedia-is-finally-finding-its-way-to-the-truth.

95. *See* Wu, *supra* note 14, at 292.

96. This statute proscribes conduct that is intended to "harass" or "intimidate," is carried out using "any interactive computer service or electronic communication

service or electronic communication system of interstate commerce," and can "reasonably expected to cause substantial emotional distress." 18 U.S.C. § 2261A(2)(B) (2012).

97. *See, e.g.*, *United States v. Moreland*, 207 F. Supp. 3d 1222, 1229 (N.D. Okla. 2016) (holding that the cyberstalking statute's application to a defendant who repeatedly sent bizarre and threatening messages to a journalist on social media websites is not barred by the First Amendment).

98. *See, e.g.*, Martin Pengelly & Joanna Walters, *Trump Accused of Encouraging Attacks on Journalists with CNN Body-Slam Tweet*, Guardian (July 2, 2017), https://www.theguardian.com/us-news/2017/jul/02/trump-body-slam-cnn -tweet-violence-reporters-wrestlemania.

99. *See* French, *supra* note 64.

100. *Blum v. Yaretsky*, 457 U.S. 991, 1003 (1982).

101. *Id.* at 1004. The Fourth Circuit puts it slightly differently: the state is acting when it "has coerced the private actor" or when it "has sought to evade a clear constitutional duty through delegation to a private actor." *German v. Fox*, 267 F. App'x 231, 234 (4th Cir. 2008).

102. *See, e.g.*, N.Y. Penal Law § 20.00 (McKinney); Model Penal Code § 2.06 (Am. Law Inst. 2016).

103. In *Blum* itself, the Supreme Court stated that the medical decisions made by the nursing home were insufficiently directed by the state to be deemed state action. *Blum*, 457 U.S. at 1012.

104. 614 F.3d 273 (6th Cir. 2010).

105. *Id.* at 276.

106. *Id.* at 284.

107. *Id.* at 280.

108. *Wells ex rel. Bankr. Estate of Arnone-Doran v. City of Grosse Pointe Farms*, 581 F. App'x 469 (6th Cir. 2014).

109. In a district court case in New Jersey, the court refused to dismiss an action brought by a woman who was fired by her nonprofit after local government officials extensively criticized her for comments she made about law enforcement. *Downey v. Coal. Against Rape & Abuse, Inc.*, 143 F. Supp. 2d 423 (D.N.J. 2001); *see also Lynch v. Southampton Animal Shelter Found. Inc.*, 278 F.R.D. 55 (E.D.N.Y. 2011) (denying summary judgment where a privatized animal shelter that fired a volunteer who was an animal rights activist was alleged to be a state actor); *Ciacciarella v. Bronko*, 534 F. Supp. 2d 276 (D. Conn. 2008); *Pendleton v. St. Louis County*, 178 F.3d 1007 (8th Cir. 1999).

110. 326 U.S. 501 (1946).

111. *Lloyd Corp., Ltd. v. Tanner*, 407 U.S. 551, 569 (1972).

112. *See, e.g.*, Trevor Puetz, Note, *Facebook: The New Town Square*, 44 Sw. L. Rev. 385, 387–88 (2014) (arguing that "Facebook should be analyzed under the quasi-municipality doctrine, which allows for the application of freedom of speech protection on certain private property").

113. *Marsh*, 326 U.S. at 502–03.

114. Max Weber, *Politics as a Vocation*, in *From Max Weber: Essays in Sociology* 77, 78 (H.H. Gerth & C. Wright Mills, eds. & trans., 1946). Even the town's policeman was paid by the corporation. *Marsh*, 326 U.S. at 502.

115. Wu, *supra* note 32.
116. 948 F. Supp. 436 (E.D. Pa. 1996).
117. 395 U.S. 367 (1969).
118. *See, e.g.*, *Virginia v. Black*, 538 U.S. 343 (2003) (describing the true threat doctrine).
119. *See Watts v. United States*, 394 U.S. 705 (1969) (barring the prosecution of a defendant when a threat was obviously made in jest); *see also Elonis v. United States*, 135 S. Ct. 2001 (2015) (reversing a conviction where the defendant maintained that his threats were self-expressive rap lyrics).
120. *Black*, 538 U.S. at 360.
121. *Id.*
122. 207 F. Supp. 3d 1222 (N.D. Okla. 2016).
123. *Id.* at 1230–31.
124. 336 U.S. 77 (1949).
125. *Id.* at 86; *see also Frisby v. Schultz*, 487 U.S. 474 (1988) (upholding a municipal ordinance that prohibited focused picketing in front of residential homes).
126. *Erznoznik v. City of Jacksonville*, 422 U.S. 205, 210 (1975) (quoting *Cohen v. California*, 403 U.S. 15, 21 (1971)).
127. *Bluman v. FEC*, 800 F. Supp. 2d 281, 288 (D.D.C. 2011), *aff'd*, 565 U.S. 1104 (2012). A related interest—protecting elections—has been called on to justify "campaign-free zones" near polling stations. *See Burson v. Freeman*, 504 U.S. 191, 211 (1992).
128. Alexander Meiklejohn, *Free Speech and Its Relation to Self-Government* 25 (1948).
129. *See Report on Editorializing by Broadcast Licensees*, 13 F.C.C. 1246 (1949).
130. Applicability of the Fairness Doctrine in the Handling of Controversial Issues of Public Importance, 29 Fed. Reg. 10,426 (July 25, 1964).
131. *Red Lion Broad. Co. v. FCC*, 395 U.S. 367, 390 (1969).
132. *See, e.g.*, *Miami Herald Pub. Co. v. Tornillo*, 418 U.S. 241 (1974) (striking down a state "right of reply" statute as applied to a newspaper).
133. *Syracuse Peace Council*, 2 F.C.C. Rcd. 5043, 5047 (1987).
134. *See, e.g.*, Thomas W. Hazlett et. al., *The Overly Active Corpse of* Red Lion, 9 Nw. J. Tech. & Intell. Prop. 51 (2010).

REFLECTIONS ON WHETHER THE FIRST AMENDMENT IS OBSOLETE

135. 334 U.S. 1 (1948).
136. 326 U.S. 501 (1946).
137. 395 U.S. 367 (1969).
138. *See United States v. Alvarez*, 567 U.S. 709 (2012).

NOT WAVING BUT DROWNING: SAVING THE AUDIENCE FROM THE FLOODS

139. J.M. Balkin, *Ideological Drift and the Struggle over Meaning*, 25 Conn. L. Rev. 869 (1993); William Felstiner, Richard Abel & Austin Sarat, *The Emergence and Transformation of Disputes: Naming, Blaming, and Claiming* . . ., 15 Law & Soc'y Rev. 631 (1980–1981).

140. *See, e.g.*, Jack M. Balkin, *The Future of Free Expression in a Digital Age*, 36 Pepp. L. Rev. 427 (2009).

141. *Packingham v. North Carolina*, 137 S. Ct. 1730 (2017).

142. *See, e.g.*, David Weinberger, *Pointing at the Wrong Villain: Cass Sunstein and Echo Chambers*, L.A. Rev. Books (July 20, 2017), https://lareviewofbooks.org /article/pointing-at-the-wrong-villain-cass-sunstein-and-echo-chambers ("Our educational systems need to do a better job of teaching us not just what we should know, but how to know in the age of the internet. How can we assess the worthiness of what we have just read?").

143. *See* Frederick Schauer, *Categories and the First Amendment: A Play in Three Acts*, 34 Vand. L. Rev. 265, 267–82 (1981); *see also* Mark V. Tushnet, Alan K. Chen & Joseph Blocher, *Free Speech Beyond Words: The Surprising Reach of the First Amendment* (2017).

2

FROM THE HECKLER'S VETO TO THE PROVOCATEUR'S PRIVILEGE

David E. Pozen

"IT IS NOW widely believed," Frederick Schauer observes in this chapter's principal essay, "that restricting the speaker on account of the actual or predicted hostile and potentially violent reaction of the audience gets our First Amendment priorities backwards." To restrict speakers on this basis would be to grant the so-called heckler's veto. Angry audiences would have, in effect, a right to enlist the state to suppress speech they don't like. The more mayhem they threaten, the more potent this right would become.

Over the past fifty years or so, the U.S. Supreme Court has become less and less willing to countenance the heckler's veto. Its First Amendment case law turned decisively against the proposition that a speaker may be punished for provoking a hostile audience, or inciting a sympathetic one, in a series of cases from the 1960s involving civil rights demonstrators. By the time the Court decided *Forsyth County v. Nationalist Movement* in 1992,[1] it was not clear there were any justices who would allow a government body to impose higher fees on speakers, such as the white supremacists of the Nationalist Movement, whose messages were likely to create higher expenses for police or related services because of their inflammatory content.

Lower courts have applied *Forsyth County* with vigor.[2] By now, constitutional law scholar Dan Coenen recently opined, "the heckler's-veto-based, hostile-audience-speech concept" appears "all but constitutionally extinct."[3] The basic First Amendment question that a city like Charlottesville faces today when white supremacists seek to hold a rally is not whether it can force them to internalize the resulting law enforcement costs, much less ban them altogether. The question Charlottesville faces is just how much money and effort must be allocated to protecting the white supremacists.

In place of the heckler's veto, the Court has thus created what we might call the provocateur's privilege. Extreme speakers have become entitled not only to use public forums in the face of actual or anticipated hostility but also to commandeer public resources to try to keep that hostility within bounds. And the more extreme a speaker is, the more hostility will need to be managed and so the more resources will need to be commandeered: as Schauer writes, "the greater the provocation, the greater the reallocation." Modern First Amendment doctrine, in other words, does not simply prevent neo-Nazis, neo-Confederates, and the like from being silenced by disapproving communities. It forces those communities to pay extra to enable their speech.

Schauer's essay explores this dilemma in light of recent confrontations between speakers and protesters in Charlottesville, Berkeley, Boston, and beyond. The essay does not offer any comprehensive constitutional solutions. Short of rethinking a half century of judicial resistance to content discrimination, it is hard to see how First Amendment doctrine could supply one. But with characteristic insight, Schauer helps us think through the dilemma by specifying its contours and by placing it in historical, conceptual, and comparative context.

Four commentators pick up where Schauer leaves off. Jelani Cobb draws a distinction between a *movement* and a *mob* and submits that the Unite the Right rallygoers in Charlottesville were the latter, which implies that the "hostile audience" paradigm gives a misleading impression of where the true threat to public safety came from in that case—namely, from the speakers.

Mark Edmundson suggests that the incidence of extreme audience hostility might be reduced through "resourceful use of technology and . . . resourceful policy-making," including systematic surveillance of demonstration sites. For some readers, this suggestion may be yet more evidence of a kind of law of conservation of perversity, or the way in which solutions to the problem of the heckler's veto always seem to produce their own democratic and deliberative harms.

Suzanne Goldberg examines different types of "costs"—pecuniary, pedagogic, psychological—that speakers can impose on colleges and universities, and lays out a series of approaches that a private institution might employ in determining whether to allow certain especially offensive or disruptive speakers on campus.

Finally, Rachel Harmon calls attention both to the central role of the police in managing large-scale protests and to the broad discretion that police officers continue to enjoy in this role, notwithstanding the First Amendment restrictions that have been heaped on permitters and prosecutors. Whatever the best view of the First Amendment, Harmon explains, "it is largely the police department rather than the law that determines what constitutes permissible protest and what instead represents a sufficient threat to public order to justify a forceful response."

I suspect that few, if any, readers will agree with all of these commentaries. Taken together, they offer a rich and unsettling portrait of complexities raised by the hostile audience problem.

The Hostile Audience Revisited

Frederick Schauer*

IN MY OWN newly famous city of Charlottesville, Virginia, as well as in Berkeley, Boston, Middlebury, and an increasing number of other locations, individuals and groups engaging in constitutionally protected acts of speaking, parading, protesting, rallying, and demonstrating have become targets for often-large groups of often-disruptive counterprotesters.[4] And although most of the contemporary events have involved neo-Nazi, Ku Klux Klan, and other white supremacist speakers who are met with opposition from audiences on the political left, it has not always been so. Indeed, what we now identify as the problem of the *hostile audience*[5] has often involved more sympathetic speakers confronted by less sympathetic crowds.[6] Yet though the issue is hardly of recent vintage, contemporary events have highlighted the importance of reviewing the relevant constitutional doctrine and thinking again and anew about how, if at all, government and law should respond to disruptive audiences.

The value of returning to the question of the hostile audience is heightened by the fact that existing legal doctrine on the question is, at best, murky. It is now widely believed that restricting the speaker on account of the actual or predicted hostile and potentially violent reaction of the audience gets our First Amendment priorities backwards.[7] But it is hardly clear that this belief was ever correct, and even if it were, it is even less clear that it is sufficient to deal with the constitutional and policy complexities of many of the contemporary encounters. The point of revisiting the problem of the hostile audience is therefore not so much to urge a change in existing understandings and legal doctrine as it is to emphasize how many open questions still remain, and how current events might bear on possible answers to these questions.

THE FORGOTTEN DENOUEMENT OF A REMEMBERED EVENT

As has been extensively documented,[8] in 1977 a group called the National Socialist Party of America, self-described as Nazis and led by a man named Frank Collin, proposed to conduct a march in Skokie, Illinois. The neo-Nazi marchers chose Skokie as their venue because of its substantial Jewish population,[9] a population that at the time contained an especially large number of Holocaust survivors. And in order to inflict the maximum amount of mental distress on Skokie's residents, the marchers were planning to carry Nazi flags, display the swastika, and wear Nazi uniforms, jackboots and all.

Despite the efforts of the Village of Skokie[10] to prohibit the event, the Nazis' First Amendment right to hold the march was upheld by both the Supreme Court of Illinois[11] and the United States Court of Appeals for the Seventh Circuit.[12] And although the United States Supreme Court's refusal to give the case full plenary consideration[13] was technically not a decision on the merits of the controversy, the events were so broadly publicized that the Court's refusal to hear the case with full briefing and argument was widely understood by the public, and presumably by the members of the Court as well, as firmly announcing that the Nazis' right to march was by then clearly established in constitutional doctrine.[14]

Although the Nazis prevailed in several courts and thus won their right to march when, where, and how they had proposed, what is often forgotten is that the march never happened. The Nazis wrapped themselves in their legal victory but at no time actually exercised the right that they had won in court, at least in Skokie itself. They did hold similar but small events in Chicago on June 24 and July 9, 1978, both without benefit of permit, but the permit they were eventually granted to march in Skokie on June 25 went unused.

We remain unsure why. Perhaps the Nazis disbelieved Skokie's representation that the town would make "every effort to protect the demonstrators . . . from responsive violence."[15] Perhaps they viewed their legal victory as more important than the march itself. Or perhaps the publicity surrounding the event made it seem more desirable to the Nazis to march in front of what they hoped would be a larger audience in Chicago. But whatever the reason, the Nazis never marched in Skokie.

Because the Skokie march never happened, we can only speculate about the answers to questions that may have arisen had it taken place. Some of those questions relate to law enforcement. Assuming that there would have been far more objectors than Nazis, and that at least some of those objectors would have been inclined to physically confront or assault the marchers, would the Skokie police department have attempted to prevent the physical encounters, and if so, how, with what size force, and with what degree of aggressiveness? And if Skokie's police department, even assuming its best efforts, was not up to the task because of the sheer size of the hostile audience, would the Illinois State Police have stepped in? The Cook County Sheriff's Office? The Illinois National Guard? Would Illinois state authorities have requested federal assistance to protect the exercise of a federal constitutional right? Even absent a request from the state, would federal forces have been deployed to secure compliance with a constitutional right and a judicial order, as when President Dwight Eisenhower sent troops to Little Rock, Arkansas, in 1957?[16] These are factual and historical questions rather than normative or doctrinal ones, but they suggest a number of issues that are indeed normative or doctrinal, or both, about which the current doctrine provides few answers.

The overarching legal question that would have been presented had the Nazis marched in Skokie, and the question presented by so many of the contemporary events, is the question of the hostile audience. Assuming the existence of a group or of individuals otherwise constitutionally entitled to say what they want to say where they want to say it, how does the existence of an actually or potentially hostile audience change, if at all, the nature of the speakers' rights or change, if at all, the obligation, if any, of official responsibility to protect the speakers and their speech?

THE DOCTRINAL FOUNDATION—HOLES AND ALL

One motivation for this essay, even apart from the way in which current events have highlighted the problem of the hostile audience, is that there is less settled law on the questions raised at the close of the previous section than we might have supposed. But what law there is dates to 1940 and the case of *Cantwell v. Connecticut*.[17] Jesse Cantwell, like so many of the individuals who helped forge the modern First Amendment tradition, was a Jehovah's Witness.[18] He, along with his brother and father, traveled to a street in New Haven, where he attempted to sell books and pamphlets in a neighborhood that was approximately 90 percent Catholic, in the process playing a phonograph record vehemently attacking the Catholic Church. The content of the record angered several onlookers, some of whom testified that they "felt like hitting" Cantwell if he did not leave immediately. In fact he did leave when confronted, but Cantwell, his brother, and his father were nevertheless charged with "breach of the peace" under Connecticut law. The convictions of the brother and father were reversed by the Supreme Court of Connecticut,[19] but Jesse's was upheld. On appeal to the U.S. Supreme Court, however, Jesse's conviction was found to be a violation of the First Amendment, with Justice Owen Roberts writing the unanimous opinion. The Court held out the possibility that a conviction might be sustained were a speaker to use profane words, indecent language, epithets, or personal abuse directed specifically at particular listeners or were a statute to have been aimed precisely at conduct such as Cantwell's and to have incorporated a legislative finding that such conduct constituted a clear and present danger.[20] But because Cantwell was prosecuted only under the general common law notion of breach of the peace, and because there had been no profane or indecent direct personal abuse, the Court concluded that Cantwell's conviction could not stand.

Even though the *Cantwell* Court suggested that the reactions of listeners could justify punishing a speaker under certain circumstances, the opinion still says next to nothing about what a legislature would need to do in order to craft a constitutionally permissible statute. And because the audience in *Cantwell* consisted of only a few people to whom Cantwell had generally addressed his words and his recording, the decision in its entirety is at best a precursor to the hostile audience problem and appears to be more of an angered listener case than a hostile audience one.[21] The first true hostile audience case was yet to come, and it arrived nine years after *Cantwell* in *Terminiello v. Chicago*,[22] a decision worthy of more extended discussion.

Arthur Terminiello, a suspended Catholic priest, was invited to Chicago from his Birmingham, Alabama, base to deliver a well-publicized and virulent anti-Communist and anti-Semitic speech, in which he referred to "atheistic, communistic . . . Zionistic Jews" as "slimy scum," accused former Secretary of the Treasury Henry Morgenthau of plotting to cut off the limbs of German babies, charged Franklin and Eleanor Roosevelt and the Supreme Court with being part of the same Jewish Communist conspiracy, and announced that the New Deal itself was among the prominent manifestations of this conspiracy. Terminiello's audience in a rented hall consisted of somewhere between 800 and 1,000 people, most of them sympathetic but some hostile. Outside there were gathered another 200 to 300 people who had been turned away for reasons of space, an additional several hundred members of a picket line, and more than 1,000 other protesters, all of whom were being monitored by 70 police officers. The police presence turned out to be nowhere near sufficient to prevent the pushing, milling, fighting, and rioting that broke out both inside and outside the hall, and the disorder was marked by the throwing of stones, sticks, bricks, bottles, and other makeshift weapons. As a result of this tumult, Terminiello was arrested, tried, convicted for breach of the peace, and fined one hundred dollars.

On appeal to the Supreme Court, Justice William Douglas wrote for a 5–4 majority. Relying heavily on *Stromberg v. California*,[23] the Court reversed Terminiello's conviction, largely because the ordinance under which Terminiello had been convicted made it an "offense merely to invite dispute or to bring about a condition of unrest."[24] Chief Justice Fred Vinson and Justice Felix Frankfurter dissented, but it was Justice Robert Jackson's dissent, joined by Justice Harold Burton, that focused most closely both on what Terminiello had said and on the disorder that had ensued. On his reading of the events, Justice Jackson concluded that the existence of a "riot and . . . a speech that provoked a hostile mob and incited a friendly one"[25] justified Terminiello's conviction. Justice Jackson did not, however, draw much of a distinction between the hostile and the friendly mobs, and so did not distinguish Terminiello's responsibility for the actions of the supporters he incited from his responsibility for the reactions of the opponents he angered. And, thus, although the question of the hostile audience was clearly on the table in *Terminiello*, the case still produced little guidance about the extent to which a speaker might be responsible not for what he urged others to do but instead for what his words might prompt others to do to him and his supporters.

The *Terminiello* scenario was repeated, albeit on a smaller scale, several years later in *Feiner v. New York*,[26] noteworthy in part for giving rise to the first actual judicial use of the term *hostile audience*.[27] But again the facts made the conclusions to be drawn from the case less than crystal clear. Irving Feiner had given a speech in Syracuse criticizing President Harry Truman, the mayor of Syracuse, the American Legion, and others, but the chief import of his open-air address to a racially mixed crowd of about eighty was "to arouse the Negro people against the whites."[28] Believing the crowd to be on the verge of erupting into a number of racially charged fights, the police first requested and then demanded that Feiner stop talking, but he refused to do so and was accordingly arrested for disorderly conduct. His conviction was affirmed by the New York Court of Appeals and then by the U.S. Supreme Court, the latter, in an opinion written by Chief Justice Vinson, observing that "it is one thing to say that the police cannot be used as an instrument for the suppression of unpopular views, and another to say that, when as here the speaker passes the bounds of argument or persuasion and undertakes incitement to riot, they are powerless to prevent a breach of the peace."[29] Justice Hugo Black dissented, as did Justice Douglas, joined by Justice Sherman Minton, all of them relying heavily on *Cantwell* and on their belief that the real problem was the presence of police who saw their job more as siding with the hostile portion of the audience than as protecting the speaker.

Feiner is commonly taken to represent the extreme case of allowing the hostile audience to exercise the so-called heckler's veto,[30] but a close reading of the opinion makes that conclusion not nearly so obvious. Was Feiner charged with provoking a hostile audience or with inciting a sympathetic one? Was his wrong in giving his speech or in disobeying the plausible orders of the police? Could he, as a lone speaker, have been physically removed rather than arrested?[31] Should he have been?

Although *Feiner* is hazy in just these ways, the decisions that mark *Feiner's* burial contain fewer uncertainties. In three different 1960s cases dealing with civil rights demonstrators confronted by unambiguously hostile audiences, the Supreme Court appears to have eviscerated *Feiner* of whatever authority it may have had. In *Edwards v. South Carolina*,[32] an 8–1 Supreme Court reversed the breach of the peace conviction of 187 black civil rights demonstrators who were marching and singing in Columbia, South Carolina. The police, fearing impending violence by the hostile audience, threatened the demonstrators with arrest if they did not disperse, and the arrest, trial, and conviction of the demonstrators followed their refusal of the police demand. For Justice Potter Stewart, this case was "a far cry from the situation in *Feiner*"[33] and seemed to him to involve "no more than that the opinions which [the demonstrators] were peaceably expressing were sufficiently opposed to the views of the majority of the community to attract a crowd and necessitate police protection."[34] Quoting *Terminiello*, Justice Stewart concluded that criminal convictions of the speakers would be permitted only if there was a "clear and present danger . . . that rises far above inconvenience, annoyance, or unrest."[35]

Facts similar to those in *Edwards* were presented in *Cox v. Louisiana*,[36] where again the leader of a civil rights demonstration, the Reverend Elton Cox, was arrested for, among other things, disturbing the peace in Baton Rouge, Louisiana. As a result of his arrest, Cox was sentenced to a cumulative one year and nine months in jail for leading a group of about 2,000 singing, cheering, and clapping demonstrators. In response to the city's claim that action was taken against the demonstration because "violence was about to erupt,"[37] Justice Arthur Goldberg again distinguished *Feiner*, pointing out that no actual violence had ensued, that the presence of local and state police appeared sufficient to prevent any violence, and that "constitutional rights may not be denied simply because of hostility to their assertion or exercise."[38] And thus by the time similar facts were once again presented in 1969 by a case involving a Chicago demonstration led by the comedian and civil rights activist Dick Gregory,[39] Chief Justice Earl Warren was able to begin his majority opinion, an opinion that followed *Edwards* and *Cox* in all material respects, with the observation: "This is a simple case."[40]

Although some might suspect that the results in *Edwards*, *Cox*, and *Gregory* were heavily influenced by the Warren Court's sympathy with the civil rights demonstrators and the causes they were espousing,[41] that conclusion is belied[42] by subsequent developments, most directly the Supreme Court's 1992 decision in *Forsyth County v. Nationalist Movement*.[43] Here the demonstrators were members of a white supremacist organization who proposed to conduct a demonstration in opposition to the federal holiday commemorating the birth of Martin Luther King Jr. But because the county sought to impose a fee under a county ordinance allowing the amount of the fee to vary with the expected costs of law enforcement for the particular demonstration, the demonstrators refused to pay the fee and instead challenged the constitutionality of the ordinance.

Much of Justice Harry Blackmun's majority opinion dealt with the question of whether a facial challenge was appropriate, but the most important aspect of *Forsyth County* for present purposes is the Court's conclusion that imposing a fee based on the expected costs of police protection and other security constituted impermissible content regulation, given that the amount of security required would plainly vary with the content of the speech.[44] And although Chief Justice William Rehnquist dissented, joined by Justices Byron White, Antonin Scalia, and Clarence Thomas, the thrust of the dissent was that no such content-based fee had been imposed in this case, or even in previous demonstrations under the ordinance. And so although we do not know how the dissenters would have voted had such a fee been imposed here, it is at least plausible to speculate that in 1992 all nine members of the Supreme Court believed it a violation of the First Amendment to impose upon demonstrators the cost of police protection and related security to control a hostile audience whose hostility was in response to the content of an otherwise constitutionally protected speech, protest, march, demonstration, parade, or rally.[45]

On the surface, it appears that we now have a considerable amount of law on the problem of the hostile audience, a body of doctrine going back at least to the 1930s and continuing through a collection of modern lower-court cases applying what seems to be Supreme Court doctrine through *Forsyth County*.[46] But appearances can be deceiving. In important respects, the doctrine leaves substantial and increasingly salient questions unanswered. For example, almost all of the Supreme Court decisions described above rely heavily or at times exclusively on the vagueness of the relevant governing standards and thus on the consequent worry that such vagueness will allow excess official discretion, a discretion that would create an undue risk of impermissible content-based (and especially viewpoint-based) discrimination among different types of demonstrators.[47] But a vagueness determination is often the path of least resistance, allowing courts to skirt the direct question of which kinds of non-vague restrictions are permissible and which are not.[48] As a consequence, we know less than we might—here and elsewhere—about just what kinds of specific (non-vague) standards would be permissible or just how specific the standard must be to avoid invalidation on vagueness grounds.

Other "holes" in the existing doctrine are equally apparent. We know that law enforcement must take all reasonable steps before shutting down a speaker whose words have created a dangerous situation, but we know little about what counts as reasonable, what degree of deployment a police department is required to use, and whether a local police department is required to call upon county law enforcement, state law enforcement, or state military (i.e., the National Guard) forces before taking action against the speaker. Relatedly, if law enforcement fails to protect the speaker, what state and federal remedies, if any, are available to the speaker against the relevant officials and agencies? What follows is an attempt to explore these and other questions now arising in the context of a growing number of increasingly hostile confrontations between speakers and those who would protest and demonstrate against them.

HOW MUCH LAW ENFORCEMENT IS ENOUGH?

As recent events make clear, the modern problem arising from demonstrations, rallies, and even individual inflammatory speakers is rarely that speakers will urge their listeners to take unlawful actions against third parties, as was the case in *Brandenburg v. Ohio*.[49] Nor is it that listeners may be offended, disgusted, or shocked, as in *Cohen v. California*,[50] although that is surely often the case. Rather, the problem, and especially the First Amendment problem, is that offended, shocked, disgusted, angry, or strongly disagreeing listeners (or viewers) will threaten or take violent action against the initial speakers and disorder will ensue, as occurred in the cases described above, and as probably would have occurred had the Nazis actually marched in Skokie in 1977. Often the accounts of such events are unclear and conflicting, so it is probably wise to include those events in which audience reactions eventually lead to violence and disorder,[51] even as it is sometimes unclear exactly who, literally or figuratively, has thrown the first punch. Still, the basic idea is that a speaker's words or images are sometimes viewed as highly controversial, offensive, or harmful by some portion of an audience, and genuine physical violence or the imminent threat of it ensues.

One thing that is now settled, if anything is settled, and that the post-*Feiner* cases make reasonably clear, is that law enforcement may not initially or prematurely arrest the speaker. It also appears settled that the state may not prosecute on grounds of incitement the speakers whose speech has prompted the reactions. To do so would be to create what we now call the heckler's veto, allowing those who would protest against a speech the right, in effect, to stop the speaker from speaking. And it is probably settled as well that even if getting the speaker to stop speaking would be genuinely necessary to prevent violence, punitive actions against the speaker may not take place until after the speaker has been given the opportunity to leave the venue on his or her own and, perhaps, absent the speaker's willingness to depart, until after there has been an attempt at a nonpunitive removal of the speaker.[52]

But again, although this much seems more or less clear, what is importantly not clear is just how much the authorities must do before taking some sort of action against the speaker or before bringing the entire event to a halt. In some past cases, as in the civil rights demonstration cases,[53] the authorities have done little, often because of greater police sympathy with the objectors than with the initial speaker. But even assuming good faith and the best intentions on the part of a municipality, how much must that municipality do? Must it deploy all or most of its police force, even if doing so would create other dangers to safety and security?[54] Must it call on nonlocal authorities, such as county police, state police, or even the National Guard?

These problems come to us now with real numbers and real dollars attached to them. The University of California at Berkeley estimates a cost in the vicinity of $2 million to provide law enforcement and related services for the actual or planned speeches by only three individuals—Ann Coulter, Ben Shapiro, and Milo Yiannopoulos.[55] The city of Charlottesville spent $70,000 on the widely publicized Unite the Right rally on August 12, 2017, as well as $30,000 for providing extra police and other services for a July 8 march by the Ku Klux Klan.[56] It might once have been said that claims about the expense of providing protection for speakers likely to cause[57] a violent confrontation with a hostile audience were prone to exaggeration by state and local officials eager to prevent the speech in the first place, but today such suspicions rest on a flimsier basis. Now, with the benefit of actual events and hard numbers, we can understand that officials who are worried about monetary costs, as well as about physical danger and psychological distress, will be concerned that every dollar spent on protecting unpopular or even hateful speakers will be a dollar unavailable to seemingly—at least to them—more worthy purposes.

The question "How much must the authorities do?" in such situations involves a complex intersection of financial, logistical, personnel, and jurisdictional considerations. In the typical hostile audience scenario, the size of the hostile audience is substantially greater than the size of the group of "primary" speakers.[58] And often the size of the hostile audience dwarfs the size of the local police force. In such cases, local law enforcement appears to have a series of choices, and it will be useful to explore several alternatives.

One possibility, when faced with the prospect of a large and potentially violent counterdemonstration, is simply for local law enforcement to do the best it can with its existing resources and personnel. If violence breaks out during the event or is about to break out imminently, the police could then, but not earlier, use whatever local mechanisms are available—in Charlottesville it was the declaration of an "unlawful assembly"[59]—to bring the event to a halt and to restrict or apprehend those who do not obey lawful orders to disperse. Assuming that the police do not selectively single out the initial speaker (or speaking group) for apprehension or restriction, and assuming that any anticipatory halting of the event requires genuine immediate prospects of violence, there appears to be no First Amendment problem with such an approach. The police do, after all, break up fights all the time, and no one has even suggested that this creates a First Amendment problem, even if, as is so often the case, the fight was ignited by an exchange of what would be, in other contexts, constitutionally protected speech.

For admirable reasons, however, law enforcement officials would generally prefer preventing fights to breaking them up, and here matters become more difficult. Assuming, realistically, that officials anticipate disorder prior to some event, and assuming, more and more realistically these days, that local law enforcement believes that it is unlikely, with existing personnel and resources, to be able to control the violence once it erupts, what should the officials do? What *must* they do? As we know from the cases described above, the government cannot, under existing First Amendment doctrine, simply sanction the speaker or refuse to grant a permit or otherwise refuse to allow the event to take place.[60] And as we know from actual events, local law enforcement will typically request support from regional and state law enforcement, such requests being commonly granted if reasonable. But the costs of this extra-jurisdictional or cross-jurisdictional support are considerable, and at some point a city, county, or state will not have the available personnel or funds (however "available" is defined). When this point is reached, can a city then deny a permit or otherwise prohibit the event? And assuming that such decisions will eventually come before the courts, can a city, county, or state argue that providing more than some amount of law enforcement would take funds away from school lunches? From emergency medical services? From public housing? From low-income welfare assistance? From providing services that themselves have a constitutional aspect, such as providing a certain quality of unpaid legal assistance for defendants in criminal cases or, in earlier times, providing police protection for black children seeking to attend previously segregated schools? Now that we know the actual costs involved in places such as Berkeley and Charlottesville, we cannot avoid confronting the fact that protecting certain speakers exercising their First Amendment rights will come at a cost to other worthy municipal goals, including, at times, protecting or enforcing other constitutional rights.

These problems are exacerbated by the fact that more extreme speakers are likely to require more protection from hostile audiences. And thus, perhaps perversely, the more extreme a group's views are, the greater will be its ability to call upon public resources for its protection, and the greater the amount of the resources it will require for its protection. And thus, even more ironically, it may turn out that difficult decisions of allocation of state and local resources are being made not by legislatures, and not by courts, but by those who are least representative of the public whose resources are being expended.

Alternatively, law enforcement might at some point simply say to prospective demonstrators that it can provide only so much protection and that any injuries caused by disruption beyond the ability of the police to control the audience will simply have to be borne by those who have suffered them. But although local police may on occasion stand back and let a small number of combatants in a bar fight simply fight it out, such an approach seems morally, politically, and perhaps constitutionally unacceptable both for bar fights and for larger events.[61] And as long as that is so, then there is no avoiding the problem occasioned by the fact that providing security for the exercise of First Amendment rights will draw resources away from other uses.

Faced with this inevitability, the entity responsible for the additional costs might attempt to pass them on to others. The University of California or the University of Virginia could raise tuition, presumably following the lead of the car rental companies and the airlines with their fuel price fees, by calling the tuition increase a "First Amendment security fee" or something like that. But universities operate in competitive and price-elastic markets[62] and, thus, attempting to pass costs on to students—or on to faculty by cutting salaries, for example, or on to a university's athletics fan base by raising ticket prices or reducing the number of football and basketball scholarships—will involve other sacrifices.[63] So too with cities and towns, especially ones that seek to attract business by offering lower taxes or special tax breaks or rebates. Here again the incentives are almost all in the direction of municipalities attempting to reduce the costs of what the courts have said they must do in the name of the First Amendment, and as long as it remains generally constitutionally impermissible for federal courts to order state and local governments to raise taxes,[64] the problem appears ever more intractable.[65]

These problems of allocation and prioritization are beyond easy solution, but they have arisen in analogous contexts. Most relevantly, the problem of constitutionally mandated and potentially unpopular allocation and reallocation of scarce resources has been widely discussed in the context of judicially enforced social welfare rights.[66] Such rights—to housing, education, welfare, and health care, for example—are not much part of the American constitutional landscape, but they have a larger presence elsewhere. And thus when the Constitutional Court of South Africa mandated greater governmental expenditures on housing,[67] it forced the South African Parliament to allocate scarce resources among, say, housing, education, food, and health in a way other than that which might have been chosen by a judicially unconstrained Parliament. And when the same court required the government to provide anti-retrovirals to those suffering from AIDS,[68] it inevitably drew resources away from those suffering from other illnesses. This is not the place to replay the many debates already existing on the subject, but it is a reminder that the constitutionalization of an interest will produce resource reallocations, and when constitutionalization is accompanied by judicial enforcement, the consequence, sometimes wise and sometimes not, is judicial determination of social resource allocations.[69] Of course existing First Amendment doctrine itself involves judicially mandated reallocation of resources in the direction of speech protection, as compared to how most legislatures would allocate resources absent First Amendment constraints. But even if we take some considerable amount of American-style free speech protection as the baseline, it is worth noting the incremental resource allocation decisions that courts are making when they require substantial protections of speakers in the face of increasingly hostile audiences.

More precisely, therefore, the basic normative tension produced by the hostile audience scenario arises from the way in which requiring protection for those who would exercise their First Amendment rights requires a government to spend more than it would have spent had it possessed the ability simply to prohibit the speech—and requires the government either to secure additional resources for such protection or to reallocate resources toward protecting highly provocative speakers and away from other potentially worthy goals. Moreover, as noted above, the problem is not that this reallocation is at the direction of a less popularly responsive court.[70] Rather, it is that under existing doctrine, such First Amendment–driven reallocations of governmental resources turn out to be substantially in the control of the speaking groups themselves, and so the greater the provocation, the greater the reallocation. Provocative speakers have the ability to capitalize on this phenomenon by forcing the government to spend money for their protection, money that might otherwise be spent in ways the provocative speaker disfavors.

Part of the dilemma of the hostile audience, and part of the dilemma of the resource reallocation that dealing with a hostile audience occasions, is created by the reluctance of officials to impose very much in the way of serious penalties when actual violence breaks out at a rally or demonstration. The possible causes for this reluctance are multiple. Some might stem from a general unwillingness of law enforcement to employ arrest and prosecution as a remedy for street disturbances, regardless of their nature. Some might be attributable to law enforcement sympathy with counterprotesters and hostility to the speakers whose words and symbols have caused outrage in others. And some might arise from the difficulty in identifying actual perpetrators under circumstances in which angry words and then angry gestures and then physical contact appear to come from both sides. But whatever the cause, it is impossible to completely discount the possibility that the actual or impending violence that creates the need for an expensive law enforcement presence is related to the fact that for many members of a hostile audience the initiation of physical contact, often by throwing various projectiles or wielding sticks and poles, seems to them to be a relatively risk-free act, legally if not physically. And thus, perhaps again ironically, a hostile audience may at times draw resources away from governmental goals of which members of the hostile audience might very well approve.

ON THE RESPONSIBILITIES—LEGAL AND OTHERWISE— OF THE HOSTILE AUDIENCE

Although actual physical violence has, tragically, ensued from rallies and demonstrations in Charlottesville and elsewhere, far more often a hostile audience manifests its hostility in physically nonviolent ways. Sometimes such tactics include impeding speakers' access to the designated location for the demonstration, as happened in Charlottesville when a group of religious leaders locked arms to block the white supremacists from reaching the park where the rally was to occur.

This type of obstruction raises few conceptual difficulties. Such blocking or obstructing is typically unlawful,[71] and the reluctance to sanction the obstructers is often a combination of law enforcement sympathy for their cause and law enforcement fear of embarrassing publicity if the obstructers must be carried away or otherwise physically removed, a fear heightened in an age when everything is photographed by someone with a smartphone. But there is little doubt that blocking can be subject to sanctions of some variety, and we would scarcely hesitate before concluding that the police and the legal system may intervene to punish or restrict those who would keep people from getting to their home, their place of business, or the bus stop. There should be even less doubt about the impermissibility of the police responding to the blocking by sanctioning or moving the speakers who are being blocked. If speakers are prevented by others from getting to where they have a legal and constitutional right to be, the remedy cannot, at least in theory, be to tell the speakers that they must go elsewhere.

There remains an interesting question as to what private remedies are available against those who would obstruct others in the exercise of their constitutional rights. If the obstruction is physical, presumably an injunction would be available, but the typical demonstration scenario involves little notice in advance and takes place in time periods shorter than the ability of formal legal processes to respond. There could still, however, be after-the-fact common law or statutory remedies that might, depending on the circumstances, undergird an action for false imprisonment, assault, creating a public nuisance, or possibly interference with advantageous relations, even though some or all of these, in most circumstances, might be somewhat of a stretch as a matter of tort law. Initially plausible might be some variety of civil rights action, given that blockers are preventing the exercise of a constitutional right. And we might think that the most likely civil rights action would be based on, ironically, Section 1985(3) of Title 42 of the United States Code,[72] which creates a private cause of action against those who would conspire to deprive others of their civil rights.[73] But Section 1985(3) does not on its face apply to those who would deprive others of all or any of their civil rights, only to those who would conspire to deprive others of the "equal protection of the laws" or of their "equal privileges and immunities under the laws." Although the latter phrase might be argued to apply, especially if we conveniently ignore the word "equal," the far more likely textual conclusion, and one supported by the cases,[74] is that neither Section 1985(3) nor any other federal statute makes it a crime or creates a private cause of action when private persons interfere with the free speech rights of others.

The unavailability of a federal civil rights action does not mean that a state could not create such an action, or that a community could not enact an ordinance prohibiting such interference, or that a police officer could not issue a lawful order to counterprotesters to stop interfering, the violation of which would constitute the independent offense of disobedience of a lawful order of a police officer. But although some number of universities have or are now creating rules forbidding students from interfering with speakers at public university events, there do not yet seem to exist parallel state or local laws explicitly prohibiting obstructing the exercise of free speech rights. At the present time, therefore, those who would wish for sanctions against interference must rely on controversial and expansive interpretations of existing criminal law or tort law. None of this is to say that enactment or use of such laws would necessarily be wise as a matter of policy. The risks of such laws may well outweigh their potential benefits, and their misuse might well overwhelm their apt uses. But even if such laws—at least on the state or national level, as opposed to, say, university regulations regulating members of the university community—are in the final analysis unwise, it is worth thinking carefully and critically about the consequences of not providing speakers with remedies, apart from those available under general criminal and tort law, against those who would interfere with the exercise of their constitutional rights.

An even greater problem, even assuming the existence of some sort of rule prohibiting interference or disruption, concerns how we would define the interfering or disrupting behavior. Until now we have been considering only physical interference, where the application of various existing criminal, civil, and regulatory laws might be plausible, but what of the counterprotesters who bang on drums, engage in loud yelling, or create deafening noises with air horns? The use of such aural obstruction is these days as common as it is effective, but again a question arises about whether there is (or should be) a remedy for this kind of obstruction. Presumably a venue might impose a content-neutral noise regulation, along the lines of the regulation upheld for the public streets in *Kovacs v. Cooper*,[75] but such a regulation would be most plainly constitutional only if it restricted the original speakers as well as those who are trying to keep them from being heard. The more difficult question is whether a content-neutral restriction on those who would, with noise or signs or otherwise, interfere with the lawful speech of a speaker can be sustained against the claim that the objectors have no fewer free speech rights than does the original speaker. We worry about the so-called heckler's veto, but the First Amendment, after all, presumably protects the hecklers as well as the hecklees.[76]

Although it is plain that hecklers have free speech rights, specifying just what those rights are presents more difficult issues. If a protester has a free speech right to post signs, does a counterprotester have the free speech right to remove the signs or paint over them? If a protester has a right to speak, does a counterprotester have a free speech right to drown out the original speaker with horns or drums? In the clear cases of sign removal or plain drowning out, the argument that hecklers or counterprotesters have free speech rights to prevent a speaker's (or writer's) message from being heard or seen seems strained. As long as reasonable and content-neutral time, place, and manner restrictions are permissible, then some sort of first-come, first-served regulations would seem constitutionally permissible as well. But that which is constitutionally permissible may remain politically or morally problematic, and we might wonder whether privileging those who get there first, or apply for a permit first, will reward those who have the resources to be, figuratively and occasionally literally, first in line. As a constitutional matter, however, such objections seem less powerful than the argument for at least the reasonableness of regulations aimed at making the right to free speech meaningful and designed to restrict those who would make its exercise ineffective.[77]

Short of actual drowning out by sound or by obstruction or destruction of a written message, however, the question of how to deal with other forms of interference by hecklers or counterprotesters is more problematic. If there is a public concert on July 4 featuring the community band playing John Philip Sousa marches, may audience members bring their own instruments (or CD players) to play peace songs by Peter, Paul and Mary at the same time and at the same volume? If the community orchestra is playing an overture from a Wagner opera, may members of an audience offended by Wagner's anti-Semitic associations play annoying popular music — "The Little Drummer Boy," for example — at the same time, even if at lower volume? And if we suppose that restricting such interference is permissible, can we distinguish these examples from someone playing "God Bless America" while a speaker is delivering an antiwar speech or from someone who holds up the graphic homoerotic photographs of Robert Mapplethorpe during a public lecture about pretty much anything?

In such cases, restriction of the counterspeaker seems often inappropriate and sometimes unconstitutional, but non-restriction may amount to the heckler's veto in different clothing.

In dealing with such issues, much appears to depend on the nature of the forum, in the nontechnical sense of that term. And thus restrictions on non-drowning-out interference that might be impermissible for public speeches might be permissible for public concerts, and sign restrictions that would be permissible for lectures in a lecture hall might not be permissible in a public park. But even when restrictions on disruption of or interference with speakers lawfully entitled to speak in a given venue are permissible, questions about what forms of behavior actually amount to interference will persist, although they may be questions of cognitive psychology more than questions of law. Consider, for example, the experiences of many of us when the person next to us at the theater, at a concert, or at the movies is loudly chewing gum. And what if, instead, those people were holding blocks of smelly Limburger cheese? Or pieces of dog poop? Or nibbling on the carcass of an uncooked dead bat? These increasingly disgusting examples are designed to suggest that interference need not come only from greater decibels produced by the audience, or from someone who literally obliterates someone else's sign, but from a large number of other behaviors that some would consider only mildly annoying and easily ignored, but others would find as obstructing of their ability actually to hear and appreciate the speaker as the distractions caused by drums and loud horns. And the same is true of visual distractions: it is hard to imagine a prochoice speaker[78] not feeling interfered with were a large number of audience members to hold up signs portraying aborted fetuses.[79]

The question of how much interference with free speech should be permitted is thus not only a question of *physical* interference, although such interferences appear to be the ones most amenable to legal remedies. It is also a question of which forms of nonphysical interference are likely to be more or less disruptive, which should be sanctioned in some way, which should be encouraged, and which should be discouraged. But to answer those questions we would need to confront directly the largest issues of just what it is that a free speech regime—legal and otherwise—is designed to accomplish, a task that obviously transcends the hostile audience issues on which this essay has focused.

CONCLUSION: THE LIMITS OF THE LAW

There is more that can and should be said about the law on interference with or disruption of demonstrations, such as it is, but as is so often the case, the behavior that takes place in the world is often more or less than what the law permits or requires. Although this essay began with the hard law of the First Amendment as that law has in the past applied and does now apply to the problem of the hostile audience, the analysis has exposed some larger issues about speaker and listener behavior beyond the law. Under all but the self-expression justifications for freedom of speech, and thus under the arguments from truth-finding and from democratic deliberation, among others, free speech is about a certain kind of environment in which we learn from each other, deliberate with each other, and engage in various forms of collective communicative activity. In important respects, the actively hostile audience challenges not only the speaker but also the particular free speech–inspired legal and social rules according to which the speaker is protected in the first place. But whether *that* challenge, in the age of the neo-Nazis, in the age of the resurgence of the Klan, and in the age of the rise of other white supremacist speakers, is fundamentally sound or fundamentally misguided is a question that can hardly be answered in the context of this more limited inquiry.

Unsafe Spaces

Jelani Cobb

A GREAT DEAL of the debate around contemporary free speech centers upon "safe spaces," often derided by critics as dissent-free zones where people can comfortably presume the righteousness of their own worldviews. But Frederick Schauer's essay points to the centrality of safety, in the more physical sense of the term, in our conceptions of free speech. It is worth considering the point that the parameters of free speech are set not just by the limits of public tolerance but also by the practical budgetary concerns of ensuring a safe forum in which ideas—even repugnant, morally disreputable ones—can be expressed.[80]

There are inherent dangers to allowing the limits of free speech to be determined by the tolerance of angry listeners, not the least of which is the fact that throughout history demagogues and visionaries have often encountered similarly hostile reactions to their ideas. The long view of history has sorted the differing social value between the rhetoric of Martin Luther King Jr. and that of George Lincoln Rockwell. But at the time, an uninformed viewer might simply have seen them as two men whose views aroused a great deal of outrage among those who disagreed. Viewed another way, this is a question of democracy and minority rights. What, as Salman Rushdie asked when the fatwa was issued against him, can be smaller than a minority of one?

On the other side of the equation, the fact that such criminal offenses as "incitement to riot" exist points to contradictions within the idea that the "marketplace of ideas" will ultimately give speech its appropriate valuation absent outside interference. Why, in a perfect world full of rational actors, would we need laws to impede the likelihood that a single speaker can inspire an audience of presumably rational individuals toward ends that are calamitous, disruptive, violent, and damaging to the broader municipal interests? What dark power does a single individual possess that might push people past their rational inclinations and into bedlam?

These are interesting questions but in reality not entirely germane to what happened in Charlottesville on August 12, 2017. There was good reason to believe that the Unite the Right rallygoers were not there simply to exercise their rights of free speech—Nazi ideology is not big on personal liberty in the first place—but rather to intimidate and threaten. It wasn't a coincidence that the demonstrators arrived like an army amassing on the border of a warring nation, equipped with shields, batons, and firearms. Nor should it be at all surprising that they eventually found their way over to the church where the interracial group of counterdemonstrators was praying and surrounded it while carrying torches. Even a passing familiarity with the history of arson and racial terrorism in the American South would register the broader connotations of that act. The central question is less whether the audience was hostile than whether the audience was to be the target of hostility all along. There was a single fatality in Charlottesville: a counterdemonstrator named Heather Heyer who was run down by a vehicle driven by a man with white nationalist sympathies as he plowed into a crowd of pedestrians. Thus the reasonable question is whether the city of Charlottesville possessed the resources to protect the public *from* the demonstrators.

By couching their movement as a matter of constitutional principle, the Unite the Right rallygoers recalled the Cold War truism that hostile forces who wish to subvert democracy will often use the very institutions of democracy to achieve that goal. Nor should it be particularly surprising that race is an arena in which democratic ideals can be utilized to such antidemocratic ends. The Fifth Amendment protections of due process were once notably deployed to argue that emancipation of enslaved black people was unconstitutional. In 1915, requests that the film *The Birth of a Nation* be banned in the city of Boston were rejected on First Amendment grounds. The film was central to the rebirth of the Ku Klux Klan and to reinvigorating the fervor to lynch Southern blacks and intimidate them from participating in the political process.

The distinguishing element between a mob and a movement is the purpose for which their members have gathered. A movement seeks the realization of some idea, even an odious one. A mob is a gathering devoted to the gratification of primal instinct. One wishes to express a sentiment, while the other communicates in the language of fist, stick, knife, and gun. We have cause to be concerned about the rights of the former; the latter is simply a cause for concern. Charlottesville pointed to the reality that there are often deadly costs when people of good sense and presumably noble intentions fail in noticing the difference.

Heading Off the Hostile Audience

Mark Edmundson

I'M PLEASED and grateful to have had the chance to read Frederick Schauer's thoughts on the hostile audience issue. Although Professor Schauer and I are colleagues at the University of Virginia, we have not to my knowledge met. I'm in the English department, he's in the law school, which means we're separated by about a mile of terrain and whatever differences of assumption and approach our disciplines possess. I'm very happy to make his acquaintance, if only virtually: the clarity of mind and worthiness of purpose on display in his essay are praiseworthy indeed.

The legal questions that arise from the hostile audience issue are obviously complex, and it seems to me that the essay does an excellent job of delineating them. I read with fascination about the legal history of the issue and rapidly concurred with the author that some solution is needed. How much are states and municipalities supposed to spend on providing security for controversial speakers? At what point is enough expenditure truly enough? Public budgets are finite, and what's given over to protect a provocative speaker may come out of worthy endeavors: education, public safety, assistance to the poor. If I understand it correctly, the implications of this essay tend toward the pragmatic: what is the best way to allocate existing resources to get the best results?

If you think, as I do, that free speech is one of our highest ideals, perhaps the highest ideal in a democracy, then the implications of a pragmatic approach chafe a bit. Democracy lives or dies, on this view, by virtue of its power to allow all sorts of speech and let its citizens sort the truth out for themselves. One can be—I am inclined to be—rather passionate about this. Every time someone's legitimate right to free speech is undermined, the experiment that is democracy dies a little.

But there are those costs to consider, are there not?

I can contribute nothing of value on the legal question of the hostile audience. I'm void of qualifications. But I do think that in this case an issue that is being considered in legal terms might also be considered in other ways. The terms I'll propose are radically unglamorous, but they may be effective.

I think that some resourceful use of technology and some resourceful policy-making might go a long way toward solving this problem, and saving some money to boot.

It may be that today's counterprotesters are persuaded that they can act with impunity against speakers who are legally entitled to speak in a given venue. They can throw rocks and bottles; they can kick and punch. "It is impossible to completely discount the possibility," Schauer observes, "that the actual or impending violence that creates the need for an expensive law enforcement presence is related to the fact that for many members of a hostile audience the initiation of physical contact, often by throwing various projectiles or wielding sticks and poles, seems to them to be a relatively risk-free act, legally if not physically." We shouldn't let initiating physical contact remain legally risk-free.

We might, for example, sow every rally and demonstration site with surveillance cameras. We should make it clear that after the events of the day, the film will be carefully and expertly reviewed and those who commit serious crimes will answer for them. We should make identification easier by prohibiting the wearing of masks at public demonstrations. Masks are already against the law in Virginia—although not in California and some other states. They should be. Word would get around very quickly among demonstrators and counterdemonstrators, including the Antifa, that there would be a price exacted for resorting to violence at a demonstration. Most Antifa, in my experience, are personally timid and are brave only in the group or under the mask. The prospect of jail time would probably deter most of them from the most extreme forms of hostility.

We should be able to prepare for controversial rallies and speakers better than we do. Every state might have a task force of manageable size that is expert in keeping controversial rallies peaceful. These task forces should know the latest methods for controlling a counterprotesting crowd. How much space between rallygoers and protesters is best? What kind of barricades, if any, should be used? What venues are most conducive to relatively peaceful expression of ideas? When a controversial speaker is scheduled, these task forces should repair to the district in question and offer all the help they can. The police I saw in Charlottesville on August 12 seemed to have no clue about how to handle demonstrators. They needed some schooling and some support. With cameras and expert planning, cities could do more than they currently do, probably with the need of fewer resources.

As to the right to heckle a controversial speaker—that's obviously a complex legal question and beyond an English professor's remit. Aren't those hecklers also exercising their right to free speech? But I think it a reasonable idea to check in with the most likely-to-be-offended groups and invite them to propose a speaker to respond to and if possible rebut the invitee. The price for that rebuttal ought to be enough silence on the part of the audience to allow the initial speaker to say his or her piece.

There's another sort of response available when the hecklers not only scream and clap but also come with noisemakers and musical instruments that they intend to use in anything but a musical way. The last word will always belong to the biggest battalions, Napoleon said. In this case, the last word must belong to the one with the biggest sound system. As a former rock-and-roll stagehand and security guy, I can tell you that rigging up a big sound system—more booming than anything a hall full of protesters can match—is not hard to do.

In his famous Albert Hall concert, Bob Dylan took a lot of heckling from crowd members who were enraged at him for breaking away from the folkie tradition and playing hard-core electric rock and roll. "Judas!" one guy cried. "I don't believe you," said Dylan. "You're a liar." Then as the band broke into "Like a Rolling Stone," the future Nobel laureate turned to the band and said, "Play fucking loud."

Costing Out Campus Speaker Restrictions

Suzanne B. Goldberg*

WE FIND OURSELVES TODAY in a challenging, and arguably absurd, situation, where a commitment to free expression has enabled provocateurs not only to spew hostile messages into our communities but also to divert extraordinary levels of resources to protect their messaging.

This is not new, of course. Governments and courts have long wrestled with speakers dropping into communities where they are not wanted, generating significant tension and upset, and requiring outsized expenditures in efforts to ensure public safety.

But the challenges have grown exponentially of late, particularly on college campuses. From the time that Donald Trump's candidacy gained traction until now, the quasi-celebrity status of white supremacists, anti-Muslim activists, and misogynists available to speak on campuses has surged. Distinct from the era in which most First Amendment jurisprudence emerged, these speakers have a quick path to national notoriety via Twitter and blogs, which in turn prompts invitations from students, some of whom appear to be more interested in provoking controversy than in bringing meaningful discussion and debate to campus.

Although the psychological costs these speakers impose may be difficult to measure,[81] the financial costs are increasingly clear—and increasingly high in an era when firearms are widely available and open carry is claimed by some as an expressive act. Even on campuses and in cities that forbid firearms at protests, the costs associated with safety management along with the attention required by dozens and sometimes hundreds of staff are beyond substantial.[82]

So we might read Frederick Schauer's essay in this collection as requiring that, at a minimum, we engage in the thought experiment of what restrictions on speakers on college campuses might look like. Few if any colleges and universities would claim to have an overabundance of resources, and most or all have substantial needs to hire essential faculty, enhance student services and supports, and maintain their infrastructure. While every dollar spent is arguably an investment in the First Amendment, it is also a diversion of funds from these other uses. Further still, as Schauer observes, the diversion is often away from resources that might benefit the very groups the speaker derides.

In fact, there are certainly schools that simply lack the funds to protect yet another vituperative speaker. What then? The remainder of this commentary will pick up where Schauer leaves off and explore, preliminarily and tentatively, several options. To be clear, I do not offer or endorse any of these as a policy recommendation.[83] Each option presents serious difficulties, as I note below. Each may also be, in some respects, in tension with modern First Amendment jurisprudence and the free expression commitments made by many higher education institutions to which the First Amendment does not apply. And yet, as Schauer suggests, we may do ourselves a disservice if we do not take this conversation some steps further. These ideas are intended as a prompt for such conversation.[84]

* * *

Since cost is the impetus for reconsidering an all-speakers approach, I offer here three cost-based approaches a college or university might consider when it believes it lacks the resources to manage a contentious situation safely. Each reflects a distinct understanding of how to ascertain the costs that may be imposed by a hostile speaker. Before turning to them, it bears noting Schauer's observation that a public institution could not likely bar a speaker based on expected cost or other concerns unless it had a viewpoint-neutral and content-neutral standard in place. Consequently, these approaches may be more directly relevant to private institutions, though in the spirit of this thought experiment, they might be worthy of reflection more broadly.

First is an approach that looks to past events to predict future costs. Here, a school might exclude speakers whose recent events have been accompanied by violence or severe disruption or perhaps by protests that are large, vigorous, and nonviolent.

Second is an approach that seeks to predict event-management costs based on the risks posed by a speaker's message. Here, the focus would be on the extent to which a speaker's usual message encourages violence and harassment either generally or toward specific groups within the community, even though the message has not previously prompted violence or large, unruly protests.

Third is an approach that focuses on costs *over time* from messages that community members experience as threatening, not necessarily of imminent violence but of longer-term harm. More particularly, this approach would potentially exclude speakers who are known to express derogatory messages that leave certain community members feeling threatened and exposed to increased risk as a result.

* * *

One might argue that the first approach is the most rational and feasible cost-management measure in that it relies on past experience to predict the extent of institutional resources required to ensure safety at an upcoming event.[85] But as discussed below, this approach fails to distinguish between the costs associated with securing a campus for self-promoting provocateurs and for speakers—particularly those in government—who have drawn conflict because of their political positions or acts.

Alternately, one might also argue that the second approach—taking account of a speaker's encouragement of violence, either generally or toward specific groups—is actually more relevant to assessing costs than protests in the past. Here, the institution would be on notice that the speaker could be expected to encourage conduct, either by supporters or protesters, that would prove to be unmanageable. On this view, the institution could not responsibly let an event occur without devoting resources for protection against that possible violence. Recent battles in Charlottesville and Berkeley might be illustrative in that, even without past events as predictors, violent messages contributed to an environment that arguably abetted the violence that subsequently occurred.

Yet it might be even more sensible, arguably, to take seriously the third approach: exclusion of speakers whose messages are perceived by students and others as threatening. Here the argument is that these threats will have an enduring—and costly—effect on the campus community with respect to future physical safety risks and increased need for resources to support community members' sense of well-being, which in turn contributes to academic and workplace success.

In short, cost predictions do not provide much in the way of definitive guidance for schools trying to identify principles by which they might exclude certain provocative speakers from campus.[86] Each approach discussed above rests on a theoretically sound rationale: relying on the past to predict the future, linking messaging to outcomes, and recognizing the diffusion of harms as a consequence of targeted hostile messages. Yet because the different approaches focus on a distinct aspect of the relationship between a speaker's message and audience, each is also likely to identify different speakers for exclusion. Citing "cost," in other words, does not itself answer the question of how a school might approach this task.

* * *

Perhaps another layer of analysis will help. One might consider which of these approaches would be "least harmful" to the underlying goals of the First Amendment's expressive freedom protections.

Taking Schauer's view first, the question could be framed as whether any of the cost-focused approaches better protects speech that enables the search for truth or engagement in democratic decision-making. Unfortunately, this does not seem to provide much guidance as applied. It is possible, at least in theory, that messages arousing passionate protests, encouraging certain forms of violence, or expressing ideas that leave some listeners feeling threatened are consistent with truth-seeking and reasoned deliberation.

The self-expression arguments for free speech, of which Schauer is skeptical, also do not provide much assistance in determining which speakers to exclude. Perhaps this assessment would lead to the adoption of whichever rule would restrict the fewest speakers. But it would be unduly simplistic to assume that more speakers necessarily means more self-expression, both because speakers might engage in self-expression to differing extents and because the commentary of some speakers might disproportionately stifle self-expression of others in the community.

Of course, each approach must also contend with the more conventional arguments against restrictions on speech—including that the line-drawing necessary to decide which threat levels are unacceptable raises serious risks that unpopular speech, including the speech of vulnerable minorities, will be swept into these restrictions. Put another way, messages that one group perceives as stirring up hatred may be experienced by another as a necessary articulation of basic truths or rights.[87] At institutions that value academic freedom, these risks are likely to be particularly troubling.

* * *

But recall that our thought experiment assumes the institution is truly unable to afford security and must explicitly or effectively disallow some speakers—so that the question is not whether but how to make such determinations.

In this situation, it may be that the least imperfect from among imperfect choices is to create a two-step process. The first step would be to make all reasonable efforts to predict costs, perhaps based on some combination of the approaches set out above or others that might do better work. Among these approaches, the third—which involves assessing the increased sense of community members' vulnerability and related costs of addressing the effects that can be attributed to the speaker—may be most popular with those on campus who object to the harm flowing from certain types of hostile or offensive messages. But it will almost certainly also be the most difficult to measure effectively.[88]

Yet even if each of these approaches could produce a reliable number, cost prediction is too blunt an instrument on its own. It misses the difference between speakers who are primarily hostile provocateurs and speakers whose messages advance discussion and debate in the educational environment, even if their ideas are deeply unpopular.

For this reason, an additional step would be needed as a check against overzealous or unnuanced cost assessment that elides important academic values. This second step would ask, in essence, whether the proposed speaker contributes, undermines, or is neutral vis-à-vis the school's commitments to teaching, research, service, or any other core aims. We might think of this as a "mission screen."[89] This, too, is clearly subject to the content-based value judgments that First Amendment jurisprudence generally abhors.

Yet, if a proposed speaker will require security or generate other expenses that outstrip the institution's capacity *and* could reasonably be viewed as undermining the school's capacity to fulfill its mission based on the speaker's recent expression,[90] then imposing the restriction may be the best approach among imperfect choices.[91] One might even go further and ask whether such dire economic straits should be required or desirable before an institution conducts an analysis along these lines. But that, along with a full assessment of the costs and risks associated with any such restriction, is best left for another day, with thanks in advance to all who will participate in these important, and indeed invaluable, conversations.

Policing, Protesting, and the Insignificance
of Hostile Audiences

Rachel A. Harmon

CITIES LIKE Charlottesville face unclear First Amendment obligations
when confronting major events. In his thoughtful essay, Frederick Schauer
elaborates on the uncertainty that arises from the U.S. Supreme Court's
"hostile audience" cases, which raise, but do not answer, questions about
how vigorously municipalities must protect speakers and at what cost to
other public policy objectives. The hostile audience cases are not only inde-
terminate about what is required of cities; as this commentary argues, they
also misleadingly portray the contemporary project of managing competing
voices in the public square.

First, the cases suggest that prosecutors and permit officials, guided by
First Amendment law, determine who gets to speak. In practice, however, as
the events in Charlottesville in the summer of 2017 illustrate, police departments dictate the scope of speech rights. Although the First Amendment
constrains police decision-making, it allows law enforcement enormous
discretion to manage the streets, subject mostly to political (rather than
legal) review. Second, the hostile audience cases portray disfavored speakers
as being in need of distinctive protection from unruly listeners. But cities and
towns face heterogeneous—and sometimes disorderly—crowds, with more
complicated agendas than competing political messages. Policing speech is
a far more difficult enterprise than the Court's jurisprudence admits.

POLICE, RATHER THAN PROSECUTORS AND PERMITS

The Supreme Court's hostile audience cases have largely arisen through
the same route: a speaker is prosecuted criminally in connection with an

audience's actual or expected response. For instance, Yetta Stromberg was convicted of "display[ing] a red flag and banner in a public place . . . as an invitation and stimulus to anarchistic action."[92] Arthur Terminiello was convicted for a breach of the peace for speech that "stirred people to anger, invited public dispute, or brought about a condition of unrest."[93] Dick Gregory was arrested for failing to disperse when the police ordered him to do so to prevent a crowd from becoming disorderly.[94] In each case, an individual spoke, an audience reacted or threatened to react, a prosecutor charged a crime, and the defendant was convicted. Focused on such prosecutions, these cases collectively reject criminal charges that punish speakers for an audience's response. They bar prosecution for some crimes under some conditions, which in turn prohibits arrests under the same circumstances. In doing so, the cases spotlight prosecutors as key actors in the Court's First Amendment parable.

When prosecutors are not center stage in the "hostile audience" cases, permitting officials are. In *Forsyth County v. Nationalist Movement*, for instance, the Court found facially invalid a city ordinance that granted power to an administrator to set the cost of a permit based on his or her assessment of the likely response to the content of the speaker's message.[95]

But, as is typical for cities preparing for large-scale protests, when the Unite the Right groups came to Charlottesville in 2017, command staff in the police department largely organized the city's response. Prosecutors were mostly marginal, at least until long after the events. True, the city and the Unite the Right rally organizer clashed over whether the city could revoke a permit for the intended location of the rally and move the rally out of town. The city alleged that the park containing the Confederate statue that the rally sought to defend was too small for the protesters and counterprotesters who might attend, and the organizer sued.[96] The First Amendment refereed that fight, suggesting that permitting matters, at least to some degree. But that last-minute litigation was more sideshow than central to the planning process in Charlottesville, both for the city and for the rally's participants.[97]

As flawed as the police department's efforts were in Charlottesville, they led the response. In advance, the department gathered intelligence about who might attend and what they planned to do when they got there. They brought in help from other law enforcement agencies. They developed an operational plan for the day that dictated who would be allowed to go where and when people would be arrested. And they negotiated with the rally's organizer.[98] On the day of the rally, they set up and staffed the physical barriers that channeled participants' movements and controlled the separation between rally participants and counterprotesters. They decided when to break up clashes and when to allow them. They declared an unlawful assembly, effectively ending the rally. And they dispersed the crowd.[99]

The First Amendment guides the police, but only to a limited degree. Certainly, as the cases above suggest, the First Amendment bars cities from choosing two otherwise appealing solutions to the problem of unpopular speakers and their hostile audiences. First, in accordance with *Forsyth County* and similar cases, a city may not preempt the problem of counterprotesters by denying or taxing the speaker's permit. Second, the First Amendment restricts law enforcement's ability to deal with an otherwise peaceful speaker by silencing or arresting him in order to suppress his speech or stem a disorderly response, thus preventing the heckler's veto.[100]

These restrictions are not trivial. But the police tactics they prohibit are hardly the only tools available for the job. Notwithstanding the First Amendment, police have considerable authority to tamp down threats to public order caused by either unruly speakers or hostile crowds using traditional law enforcement means, including orders to move along and arrests to enforce those orders.[101] State law and the Fourth Amendment largely empower rather than constrain the police at such events. Most notably, a significant array of state criminal offenses and local ordinances regulate all kinds of public behavior, from felony assault to jaywalking. Pedestrian laws alone commonly prohibit crossing roads outside of marked crosswalks, walking in roadways when sidewalks are available, and willfully standing, sitting, or lying in a street in a manner that impedes the flow of traffic—all activities that protesters are wont to do. Even when no other law bars participant conduct, state law also often permits police to declare unlawful assemblies, generating additional arrest authority to manage events when violence is imminent. Fourth Amendment law only helps the police in this context, as it allows arrests even for minor offenses,[102] it permits officers to make arrests pretextually,[103] and it permits force as necessary to compel compliance.[104] Although there are First Amendment limits on using state law offenses to silence a speaker for stirring up a crowd, police can usually use arrests for minor crimes to impose peace and order well within these limits.

Despite this broad authority, police often seek to avoid conflict with and arrests of protesters. Best practices in policing protests have largely shifted over time from aggressively responding to threats to order, or what is often called an "escalated force" model, to less coercive means of addressing large-scale crowds, known as "negotiated management," involving fewer arrests and more cooperation.[105] When Schauer notes that police often refrain from aggressively enforcing even laws against violence in the crowd context, he is noticing one consequence of this shift. Whatever policing strategy a department chooses, it is largely the police department rather than the law that determines what constitutes permissible protest and what instead represents a sufficient threat to public order to justify a forceful response.

Those police decisions are not the end of the discussion. When police departments tolerate low-level disorder or aggressively break up crowds, the officers and command staff know they will face a form of appellate review far more intensive than that of the courts. They will hear directly from the press and the public, and when they make similar decisions again, they will read the responses to earlier protests as relevant precedent. In this light, many have speculated that Charlottesville police were reluctant to make arrests at the Unite the Right rally on August 12, 2017, in part because of the community outcry they faced for arrests made on July 8 when the KKK came to town.[106]

The remedies for police mistakes are more often political than legal as well. In Charlottesville, the police chief, the city manager, and the mayor all lost their jobs over their performance around the 2017 summer events.[107] These personnel changes are far more salient to the public than protracted court fights over the same conduct.[108] And justly so. Communities understand that—whether or not they violate the law—poor strategies for handling protests (whether too aggressive or under-protective) can breed distrust in law enforcement and local government, which in turn can undermine a community's other policy and public safety goals. The upshot is that community views about the value of free speech and the costs of police coercion are at least as likely as the law to influence how much unpopular speakers and hostile audiences are permitted to express themselves.

MOVEMENTS, NOT MESSENGERS

Not only do police (regulated by political influence) govern speech more than prosecutors and permit administrators (constrained by the First Amendment), but the "hostile audience" cases also give a misleading impression of the actors on the other side of the free speech equation when they depict distinct speakers opposed by contentious crowds.

First, as Schauer notes, hostile audiences are themselves speakers. Once one accepts the First Amendment principle that would-be speakers cannot lightly be penalized because of actual or expected responses to their message, speakers and audiences start to look simply like competing claimants for the public's eye and ear. From the ground, hostile audiences look very much like rival crowds with something to say, whether what they want to talk about is the KKK, police violence, or Wall Street's greed and corruption.

Second, cities and towns face most of the same challenges even when major events are one-sided. In all likelihood, the possibility of violent clashes is heightened by competing messages and by objectionable speakers, like those who descended on Charlottesville. But many protests become violent even when no competing voices show up. Protests such as those after the death of Michael Brown in Ferguson, Missouri, in 2014 and against the World Trade Organization in Seattle in 1999 managed to generate violence and arrests, strain public services, and interfere with activities of the public, all without an unpopular speaker to target. A motivated crowd with a message is enough to generate a challenge for cities. The fact that the message is hostile to another speaker merely adds complexity to the event.

Third, some of the "speakers" that cities face in protests do not intend to communicate a message in the way that First Amendment doctrine imagines. The only necessary commonality among protesters is the desire to collect en masse in a public space. The First Amendment cases protect speech and other forms of expressive conduct, so they talk mostly about individuals and groups who seek to persuade an audience or highlight a cause. But others attending the same protests may instead pursue social change by disruption, obstruction, or even destruction. Police thus face groups with mixed and sometimes incompatible strategies operating in fluid interaction. In such a case, who is the hostile audience and who is the speaker?

Whatever the First Amendment says about governments remaining content-neutral in their approach to speech, the methods protesters employ have enormous consequences for how they are policed. The shift to "negotiated management" depends on an alignment of interests between those who want the opportunity to convey a message peacefully and a law enforcement agency willing to value speech at the same time that it seeks to promote public safety. According to this model, protest groups assign representatives to meet with the department and cooperate in developing terms for the events, including what conduct will trigger arrests and what lawbreaking will be ignored.[109] But this model can only work with protesters who are willing and able to negotiate. When protests are conceived on social media, or when their leadership is diffuse, there may be no group sufficiently organized to negotiate effectively, even if some elements want to do so. And when protesters reject police as illegitimate and view self-restraint in cooperation with the police as a form of repression, they may be unwilling to work with police to ensure the peace.

Either way, protesters who do not negotiate may face more coercive policing. One modern coercive strategy, sometimes called "strategic incapacitation," involves close surveillance, preemptive arrests, and tight control over the location of protesters. When used on the Occupy Wall Street protests in New York City in 2011, it involved creating free speech zones, where protesters were channeled into public spaces delimited by hard barriers, outside of which policing took aggressive forms.[110] In this way, despite the First Amendment, the tactics law enforcement chooses, though neutral in principle, are necessarily bound to the content and form of the protesters' ideas, which in turn dictate their readiness to cooperate in advance with law enforcement.

In this light, as hateful as the group's message is and as perverse as it may seem, a group like the Pelham, North Carolina, chapter of the KKK that visited Charlottesville on July 8 is an ideal speaker from a police planning perspective. These KKK members were organized, coherent, and identifiable by their black shirts, white robes, and Confederate flags. They coordinated with police regarding their arrival, their rally, and their departure, and they followed police instructions during the event. And the police protected them in precisely the way the cases envisioned. Only counterprotesters clashed with police, leading to disorder and more than twenty arrests.[111] By contrast, the more tragic events of August 12 arose in part because so many disparate groups descended on Charlottesville, some with violent agendas, without much cooperation with law enforcement.

* * *

Whatever the failings of city government and state and local law enforcement on August 12 in Charlottesville—and those failings were many—one has to acknowledge the magnitude of the challenge cities can face. Protesters unwilling to negotiate terms that maximize expression and preserve order in public spaces pose a predicament for communities that prize both free speech and public order, and the First Amendment is only a starting point for understanding the values at stake and the legal tools and constraints applicable to efforts to govern public spaces.

First Amendment values remain central to how communities grapple with public protest. But the complexity of contemporary protest goes far beyond the hostile audience doctrine's image of unpopular speakers and disorderly listeners regulated by permits and prosecutions. As a consequence, doctrine will often be less important than political will and participant preferences in determining what our system of free expression looks like on the streets.

NOTES

1. 505 U.S. 123 (1992).
2. *See, e.g., Christian Knights of Ku Klux Klan Invisible Empire, Inc. v. District of Columbia*, 972 F.2d 365 (D.C. Cir. 1992); *Bible Believers v. Wayne County*, 805 F.3d 228 (6th Cir. 2015).
3. Dan T. Coenen, *Freedom of Speech and the Criminal Law*, 97 B.U. L. Rev. 1533, 1557 (2017).

THE HOSTILE AUDIENCE REVISITED

I am grateful to the Knight Institute and David Pozen for the invitation to contribute this essay, and to my colleagues Risa Goluboff, Rachel Harmon, Leslie Kendrick, and John Harrison for timely comments, valuable information, challenging perspectives, and the patience to endure far too many of my questions.

4. Because many prominent recent events have involved groups protesting against what they perceive to be excess government, rampant liberalism, and too little concern for white people, contemporary discourse describes those challenging these groups as "counterprotesters." I will adhere to this usage, even while recognizing that because some speakers who attract audience hostility are not protesting anything, calling those who protest against them "counterprotesters" is often a misnomer.
5. The label "hostile audience" dates in the case law to Chief Justice Fred Vinson's majority opinion in *Feiner v. New York*, 340 U.S. 315, 320 (1951), but it appeared earlier in academic commentary. *See* Note, *Freedom of Speech and Assembly: The Problem of the Hostile Audience*, 49 Colum. L. Rev. 1118 (1949); *see also* Note, *Constitutional Law—Free Speech and the Hostile Audience*, 26 N.Y.U. L. Rev. 489 (1951).
6. *See, e.g., Gregory v. City of Chicago*, 394 U.S. 111 (1969) (civil rights demonstrators); *Beckerman v. City of Tupelo*, 664 F.2d 502 (5th Cir. 1981) (same); *Wolin v. Port of N.Y. Auth.*, 392 F.2d 83 (2d Cir. 1968) (antiwar protesters); *Dr. Martin Luther King, Jr. Movement, Inc. v. City of Chicago*, 419 F. Supp. 667 (N.D. Ill. 1976) (civil rights parade).

7. *See, e.g., Bible Believers v. Wayne County*, 805 F.3d 228, 248 (6th Cir. 2015); Vincent Blasi, *Learned Hand and the Self-Government Theory of the First Amendment*: Masses Publishing Co. v. Patten, 61 U. Colo. L. Rev. 1, 31–34 (1990); Dan T. Coenen, *Freedom of Speech and the Criminal Law*, 97 B.U. L. Rev. 1533, 1555–57 (2017); Geoffrey R. Stone, *Content Regulation and the First Amendment*, 25 Wm. & Mary L. Rev. 189, 237–39 (1983).

8. Among the more extensive works are Donald Alexander Downs, *Nazis in Skokie: Freedom, Community, and the First Amendment* (1985); David Hamlin, *The Nazi/Skokie Conflict: A Civil Liberties Battle* (1981); Aryeh Neier, *Defending My Enemy: American Nazis, the Skokie Case, and the Risks of Freedom* (2d ed. 2012); Philippa Strum, *When the Nazis Came to Skokie: Freedom for Speech We Hate* (1999); and David Goldberger, *Sources of Judicial Reluctance to Use Psychic Harms as a Basis for Suppressing Racist, Sexist and Ethnically Offensive Speech*, 56 Brook. L. Rev. 1165 (1991).

9. A majority of the town's population in 1977 was Jewish, although prior to World War II Skokie was heavily populated by Christians of German ancestry.

10. In the ensuing litigation, Skokie stressed its official designation as a "village," presumably as a way of suggesting a small and close community, even though, with a population of over 60,000 and adjacent to Chicago, it is more accurately described as a large suburb. *See* Lee C. Bollinger, *The Tolerant Society: Freedom of Speech and Extremist Speech in America* 26 (1986).

11. *Village of Skokie v. Nat'l Socialist Party of Am.*, 373 N.E.2d 21 (Ill. 1978).

12. *Collin v. Smith*, 578 F.2d 1197 (7th Cir. 1978).

13. *Smith v. Collin*, 439 U.S. 916 (1978) (denying certiorari); *Nat'l Socialist Party of Am. v. Village of Skokie*, 432 U.S. 43 (1977) (per curiam) (staying injunction against march).

14. That conclusion follows from some combination of then-entrenched Supreme Court decisions in *Brandenburg v. Ohio*, 395 U.S. 444 (1969) (protecting Ku Klux Klan speaker from prosecution for advocating racial violence); *Cohen v. California*, 403 U.S. 15 (1971) (disallowing offense to unwilling viewers as a justification for restriction); *Hague v. C.I.O.*, 307 U.S. 496 (1939) (recognizing the streets as public forums); and *Police Department of Chicago v. Mosley*, 408 U.S. 92 (1972) (announcing the presumption against content discrimination).

15. *Collin*, 578 F.2d at 1203.

16. Eisenhower famously ordered federal soldiers to Little Rock to enforce U.S. Supreme Court and lower federal court desegregation rulings. *See Cooper v. Aaron*, 358 U.S. 1 (1958); Tony Freyer, *The Little Rock Crisis: A Constitutional Interpretation* (1984). Conceptually, the situations may not be as different as the moral gulf between the Nazis and the fighters for desegregation in Little Rock might initially suggest. The Nazis could have been described as a group seeking to exercise a federal constitutional right that had been explicitly recognized in their case with a federal court injunction against various state officials, just as the basis for Eisenhower's directive was the need to protect a federal judicial order against state officials set on resisting rather than obeying it. We do not know what, if anything, President Jimmy Carter or other federal officials would have done in Skokie had state and local officials either resisted the court's order or, more likely,

obeyed it only grudgingly and with little expenditure of human and financial resources. But the parallels are intriguing.

17. 310 U.S. 296 (1940).
18. *See, e.g., Niemotko v. Maryland*, 340 U.S. 268 (1951) (invalidating standardless requirement to obtain permission before using public park for demonstration); *Marsh v. Alabama*, 326 U.S. 501 (1946) (applying First Amendment to company-owned town); *Schneider v. Irvington*, 308 U.S. 147 (1939) (invalidating blanket prohibition on door-to-door religious and political canvassing).
19. *State v. Cantwell*, 8 A.2d 533 (Conn. 1939).
20. *Cantwell*, 310 U.S. at 309.
21. Although there was no clear precedent at the time *Cantwell* was decided on the impermissibility of allowing angered or offended listeners or viewers to justify restrictions on a speaker, subsequent cases made clear what seems only implicit in *Cantwell*. *See, e.g., Texas v. Johnson*, 491 U.S. 397 (1989) (flag desecration); *Erznoznik v. City of Jacksonville*, 422 U.S. 205 (1975) (non-obscene nudity); *Cohen v. California*, 403 U.S. 15 (1971) (offensive language).
22. 337 U.S. 1 (1949).
23. 283 U.S. 359 (1931).
24. *Terminiello*, 337 U.S. at 6.
25. *Id.* at 13 (Jackson, J., dissenting).
26. 340 U.S. 315 (1951).
27. *Id.* at 320.
28. *Id.* at 317.
29. *Id.* at 321.
30. *See* Harry Kalven, Jr., *A Worthy Tradition: Freedom of Speech in America* 89 (Jamie Kalven, ed., 1988).
31. The law on the power of the police to move or remove people is largely to the effect that the greater includes the lesser, and thus that if the police may lawfully arrest someone then they may lawfully remove them without arrest. *See* Rachel Harmon, *Lawful Orders and Police Use of Force* (Sept. 29, 2017) (unpublished manuscript) (on file with author). But the question, which the doctrine neither answers nor even addresses, is whether the First Amendment might require attempted removal prior to arrest, a requirement that does not exist outside the First Amendment context.
32. 372 U.S. 229 (1963).
33. *Id.* at 236.
34. *Id.* at 237.
35. *Id.* (quoting *Terminiello v. Chicago*, 337 U.S. 1, 4–5 (1949)).
36. 379 U.S. 536 (1965).
37. *Id.* at 550.
38. *Id.* at 551 (quoting *Watson v. City of Memphis*, 373 U.S. 526, 535 (1963)).
39. *Gregory v. City of Chicago*, 394 U.S. 111 (1969).
40. *Id.* at 111.
41. *Cf.* Harry Kalven, Jr., *The Negro and the First Amendment* (1965) (documenting the First Amendment decisions that arose in the context of 1960s civil rights issues).

42. The conclusion in the text is too quick. In fact, there are four possibilities. One is that a subsequent willingness to protect morally undesirable demonstrators even in the face of a hostile audience, as in *Forsyth County v. Nationalist Movement*, 505 U.S. 123 (1992), is indeed evidence that the results in *Edwards, Cox,* and *Gregory* had little or nothing to do with sympathy for the demonstrators and their cause. Second is that a change in the membership of the Court (only Justices William Brennan and Byron White sat for both *Gregory* and *Forsyth County*) makes any generalization across the relevant time period impossible. Third is that stare decisis really does matter for some issues at some times on the Supreme Court, making *Cox, Edwards,* and *Gregory* causally influential of the *Forsyth County* outcome. And fourth is that the identity of the demonstrators genuinely made a difference, given that the ordinance under attack in *Forsyth County* was enacted not in response to the kind of white supremacist parades at issue in the case itself, but against the background of some number of recent black civil rights demonstrations in overwhelmingly white and undeniably hostile Forsyth County.

43. 505 U.S. 123 (1992).

44. In a controversial line of "secondary effects" cases, the Supreme Court has held that secondary effects indirectly caused by the content of speech might be regulated without violating the prohibition on content regulation. Most of those cases have involved zoning and related restrictions on "adult" establishments, where the justification for the regulation was the effect on the neighborhood of such establishments in terms of crime, property values, viability of retail trade, and general quality of life. *See City of Renton v. Playtime Theatres, Inc.,* 475 U.S. 41 (1986). For subsequent applications, discussions, and criticism of the secondary effects idea, see *City of Los Angeles v. Alameda Books, Inc.,* 535 U.S. 425 (2002); *City of Erie v. Pap's A.M.,* 529 U.S. 277 (2000); *Barnes v. Glen Theatre, Inc.,* 501 U.S. 560 (1991); Seana V. Shiffrin, *Speech, Death, and Double Effect,* 78 N.Y.U. L. Rev. 1135 (2003); Philip J. Prygoski, *The Supreme Court's "Secondary Effects" Analysis in Free Speech Cases,* 6 Cooley L. Rev. 1 (1989); and Geoffrey R. Stone, *Content-Neutral Restrictions,* 54 U. Chi. L. Rev. 46 (1987). But if the secondary effects approach is not to be limited to restrictions on places of adult entertainment, the tension between that approach and *Forsyth County,* where an analogous secondary effect was deemed to be content-based, is inescapable.

45. An important open question, however, is whether after *Forsyth County* a municipality may take into account equally content-based predictions of audience size in requiring speakers (in advance) to move to a different location or a different time, or in determining whether a permit application was timely.

46. See especially the extensive and recent analysis in *Bible Believers v. Wayne County,* 805 F.3d 228 (6th Cir. 2015). Also important are *Christian Knights of Ku Klux Klan Invisible Empire, Inc. v. District of Columbia,* 972 F.2d 365 (D.C. Cir. 1992); *Glasson v. City of Louisville,* 518 F.2d 899 (6th Cir. 1975); and *Smith v. Ross,* 482 F.2d 33 (6th Cir. 1973).

47. On the uses of vagueness doctrine to deal with often hostile law enforcement discretion during the era of civil rights protests and demonstrations, see Risa L. Goluboff, *Vagrant Nation: Police Power, Constitutional Change, and the Making of the 1960s* (2016).

48. *See* Alexander M. Bickel, *The Least Dangerous Branch: The Supreme Court at the Bar of Politics* 177–83 (1962); Melvyn R. Durchslag, *The Inevitability (and Desirability?) of Avoidance: A Response to Dean Kloppenberg*, 56 Case W. Res. L. Rev. 1043, 1046 (2006).

49. 395 U.S. 444 (1969).

50. 403 U.S. 15 (1971).

51. Sometimes the violence ensues when counterprotesters provoke—in the "fighting words" sense of provoke, *see Gooding v. Wilson*, 405 U.S. 518 (1972); *see also Lewis v. City of New Orleans*, 415 U.S. 130 (1974); *Rosenfeld v. New Jersey*, 408 U.S. 901 (1972)—violent retaliatory reactions from the protesters.

52. *See supra* note 35 and accompanying text.

53. *See supra* notes 32–40 and accompanying text.

54. Several days before the Unite the Right rally in Charlottesville on August 12, 2017, the Charlottesville police requested the Albemarle County police (whose jurisdiction does not include the city of Charlottesville) and the University of Virginia police (whose jurisdiction does not extend beyond the university) to take all of the Charlottesville police's 9-1-1 calls, because it knew that its security responsibilities for the rally would preclude being able to take or respond to such calls. *See* Brian McKenzie, *Police Prep for Two-Front Response to Rally*, Daily Progress (Aug. 10, 2017), http://www.dailyprogress.com/news/local/police-prep -for-two-front-response-for-rally/article_6966afae-7e38-11e7-aca7-63c574abc7a9. html. The requested departments agreed, although of course they were not required to do so. If they had refused, the costs to general security occasioned by providing security to the Unite the Right demonstrators would have been even more obvious. And with the request having been granted, we might ask whether there was less county and university security because the county and university security forces had taken on additional responsibilities without additional staffing or funding.

55. Among numerous media reports with slightly varying numbers, see Jocelyn Gecker, *The Cost of Free Speech Isn't Cheap at UC Berkeley*, AP News (Sept. 15, 2017), https://apnews.com/f2d6a139cd6b44d7a743932f2b913677; Chris Quintana, *Berkeley's Leader Saw Hints That "Free Speech Week" Was a Stunt. Here's Why She Planned for It Anyway*, Chron. Higher Educ. (Sept. 26, 2017), http://www.chronicle.com/article/Berkeley-s-Leader-Saw-Hints/241299; and Elise Ulwelling, *Ben Shapiro's Visit Cost UC Berkeley an Estimated $600k for Security*, Daily Californian (Sept. 18, 2017), http://www.dailycal.org/2017/09/17 /uc-berkeley-security-costs-ben-shapiros-visit-estimated-600k.

56. *See* Andrew Blake, *"Unite the Right" Rally Costs City $70K in Security: Charlottesville Police Dept.*, Wash. Times (Sept. 26, 2017), http://www.washington times.com/news/2017/sep/26/charlottesville-police-place-70k-price-tag-unite-r. In addition, the University of Virginia itself spent another $63,000 on law enforce-ment for the August 11 white supremacist rally, a rally coordinated with the Unite the Right rally a day later. Ruth Serven, *UVa Spent $63,000 on Response to August Rallies*, Daily Progress (Sept. 27, 2017), http://www.dailyprogress.com /news/uva-spent-on-response-to-august-rallies/article_75a1cf38-a3ea-11e7-b66f -ab5b5925c684.html.

57. The attribution of causation here is tricky. In the language of American tort law, we can say that the August 12 march by the Unite the Right demonstrators was

the "but-for" cause of the violent confrontation in Charlottesville, but the existence of so-called counterprotesters was also a but-for cause, and so may have been the size and nature of the police presence. We know that attributions of causation under circumstances of multiple causation are often morally loaded, such that people may be hesitant to attribute the causation of unpleasant consequences to those whose actions they deem morally desirable, and prone to attribute causation for such consequences to those they are willing to condemn morally. *See* Mark D. Alicke, *Culpable Causation*, 63 J. Personality & Soc. Psych. 368 (1992); *see also* Bertram F. Malle et al., *A Theory of Blame*, 25 Psych. Inquiry 147 (2014). (On the relationship between moral attribution and other factors people use to attribute causation, see Barbara A. Spellman & Elizabeth A. Gilbert, *Blame, Cause, and Counterfactuals: The Inextricable Link*, 25 Psych. Inquiry 245 (2014); and Barbara A. Spellman & Alexandra Kincannon, *The Relation Between Counterfactual ("but for") and Causal Reasoning: Experimental Findings and Implications for Jurors' Decisions*, 64 Law & Contemp. Probs. 241 (2001).) And thus, although both the Charlottesville white supremacist protesters and the politically left counterprotesters were each the but-for causes of the events that ensued, the subsequent discourse tended to assign causal responsibility largely to the white supremacists, the constitutional (and not moral) status of their rally notwithstanding.

58. Again, the labels are tricky here. As mentioned above, *see supra* note 4, it is common to refer nowadays to the initial speakers as "protesters" because they are often protesting what they see as a government excessively sympathetic to the claims of racial and religious minorities, and then to refer to the audience as the "counterprotesters." But there is no reason to think that the scenarios are necessarily so limited, and we can imagine events in which a hostile audience is challenging a speaker or group of speakers who are not protesting anything.

59. Code of Virginia, §§ 18.2-406, 18.2-407 (2014). On the intersection between these statutes and the First Amendment, see *United Steelworkers of America v. Dalton*, 544 F. Supp. 282 (E.D. Va. 1982).

60. Indeed, the previous version of the Virginia unlawful assembly statute had been invalidated for failure to incorporate a "clear and present danger" standard. *Owens v. Commonwealth*, 179 S.E.2d 477 (Va. 1971).

61. On the lack of a constitutional claim against public authorities who do not act against violence, see, albeit in a very different context, *Deshaney v. Winnebago Cnty. Dep't of Soc. Servs.*, 489 U.S. 189 (1989). For the argument that *Deshaney* and police inaction in the face of impending violence are conceptually similar, see David A. Strauss, *Due Process, Government Inaction, and Private Wrongs*, 1989 Sup. Ct. Rev. 53.

62. Which may be less true for major car rental companies and major airlines, and thus as an empirical matter what in antitrust law is called "conscious parallelism" exists less often in the market for higher education.

63. Moreover, such attempts to shift costs might, ironically, produce further demonstrations and counterdemonstrations. We know that Berkeley students are inclined toward public protest in the face of proposed tuition increases, and so an attempt to pass on the costs of demonstrations to them seems likely to do little more than encourage more demonstrations.

64. *See Missouri v. Jenkins*, 495 U.S. 33 (1990).
65. The alternatives discussed here all assume that under existing doctrine it is impermissible simply to deny a permit or shut down an event in advance. But is there some degree of very high likelihood of violence that might justify simply prohibiting the event in advance? If not under current doctrine, is the current doctrine up to the tasks and expenses that recent events have exposed? And if ex ante prohibition is impermissible, can there be content-based advance special security requirements based on prior experiences (or public utterances) with the same or similar protesters and the same or similar counterprotesters?
66. *See generally* Katharine G. Young, *Constituting Economic and Social Rights* (2012).
67. *Government of Republic of South Africa v. Grootboom*, (2001) (1) SA 46 (CC). Perhaps recognizing the difficult allocational problems, the Constitutional Court refused to mandate minimum expenditures, requiring only that the governmental determinations of housing expenditures be reasonable.
68. *Minister of Health v. Treatment Action Campaign*, 2002 (5) SA 721 (CC).
69. The issue of judicial determination of governmental priorities among worthy goals is most obvious with respect to positive social welfare rights, but it exists as well with other rights. The clearest American examples come from those constitutional rights that actually require affirmative government expenditures, as with the right to counsel. *See Gideon v. Wainwright*, 372 U.S. 335 (1963). Such concerns about resource allocation might conceivably have been behind subsequent decisions setting both the nature and the limitations of what the state is required to provide. *Compare Ross v. Moffitt*, 417 U.S. 600 (1974) (no right to appointed counsel for discretionary appeals), *with Mayer v. City of Chicago*, 404 U.S. 189 (1971) (right to state-provided transcript). But even rights that do not seem so obviously to require expenditures—so-called negative rights such as the rights of freedom of speech and the press—are still indirectly costly, in the sense that they impose limits on what the state in its own unconstrained wisdom might decide to do as a matter of policy. *See* Frederick Schauer, *The Annoying Constitution: Implications for the Allocation of Interpretive Authority*, 58 Wm. & Mary L. Rev. 1689 (2017); Frederick Schauer, *Constitutionalism and Coercion*, 54 B.C. L. Rev. 1881 (2013).
70. I have no desire to replay several generations of angst about the so-called counter-majoritarian difficulty, *see, e.g.*, Barry E. Friedman, *The Birth of an Academic Obsession: The History of the Counter-Majoritarian Difficulty, Part Five*, 112 Yale L.J. 153 (2002), but it remains worthwhile to note that every non-majoritarian resource reallocation punctuates and increases the difficulties that trouble those who worry about the counter-majoritarian difficulty in the first place.
71. On obstructing lawful passage as a public nuisance, *see, e.g.*, Cal. Civ. Code §3479 (West 2016); Conn. Gen. Stat. §53a-182a (2016). A useful discussion of the relevant common law can be found in *Watchtower Bible & Tract Society of New York, Inc. v. Sagardia De Jesus*, 634 F.3d 3, 15–16 (1st Cir. 2011).
72. 42 U.S.C. § 1985(3) (2012). I say "ironically" because the statute was originally enacted in 1871 as the Ku Klux Klan Act, designed to provide a cause of action *against* the Klan, even though an action to interfere with the exercise of a constitutional right might, in 2020, be brought *by* the Klan.
73. *See generally* Steven F. Shatz, *The Second Death of 42 U.S.C. Section 1985(3): The Use and Misuse of History in Statutory Interpretation*, 27 B.C. L. Rev. 911 (1986).

74. *See, e.g., United Bhd. of Carpenters & Joiners of Am., Local 610 v. Scott,* 463 U.S. 825 (1983).

75. 336 U.S. 77 (1949).

76. *See* Mark Tushnet, *What the Constitution Says Berkeley Can Do When Controversial Speakers Come Knocking,* Vox (Sept. 23, 2017), https://www.vox.com/the-big-idea/2017/9/22/16346330/free-speech-week-first-amendment-constitution-bannon; *see also* Mark Tushnet, *Free Speech on Campus,* Balkinization (Sept. 24, 2017), https://balkin.blogspot.com/2017/09/free-speech-on-campus.html; Thomas Healy, *Who's Afraid of Free Speech?,* Knight First Amend. Inst. (July 14, 2017), https://knightcolumbia.org/news/whos-afraid-free-speech.

77. As I note in the Conclusion, this claim is soundest if we see a free speech regime as in some sense interactive, as most versions of the arguments based on searching for truth or engaging in democratic decision-making would maintain. But if the arguments for a distinct right to free speech are largely individualistic arguments based on self-expression, it is less clear that assuring an environment in which speakers can be understood is all that important. For those of us who are skeptical of the self-expression arguments, *see* Frederick Schauer, *Free Speech: A Philosophical Enquiry* (1982); Frederick Schauer, *On the Distinction Between Speech and Action,* 65 Emory L. Rev. 427 (2015); Frederick Schauer, *Free Speech on Tuesdays,* 24 Law & Phil. 119 (2015), the notion of a heckler's right to drown out a speaker seems odd, but the self-expression or autonomy theorist might come to a different conclusion.

78. Indeed, many of these issues are implicated by the cases on abortion clinic protests, where the principal argument of the protesters is that they are engaging in controversial public speech in the public forum on question of major policy importance, with the counterargument being that the protests, especially if graphic, create psychological impediments to the exercise of a constitutional right. *See Hill v. Colorado,* 530 U.S. 703 (2000); *Schenck v. Pro-Choice Network of W. N.Y.,* 519 U.S. 357 (1997); *Madsen v. Women's Health Ctr., Inc.,* 512 U.S. 753 (1994).

79. There are also connections between the issues raised in this paragraph and the concerns about silencing that have been raised by the feminist anti-pornography movement. *See* Catharine A. MacKinnon, *Only Words* (1993); *see also* Rae Langton, *Sexual Solipsism: Philosophical Essays on Pornography and Objectification* (2009); *Speech and Harm: Controversies over Free Speech* (Ishani Maitra & Mary Kate McGowan, eds., 2012). If the speech of one (or many) can effectively silence the speech of another by changing the meaning or the force of what another says, as I believe it can, is this to count as interference for legal purposes? And if it is not to count as interference for purposes of legal remedies, is it nevertheless to count as interference for purposes of moral or political evaluation? We think, correctly, that picketers against a speaker whose picketing is outside the venue have First Amendment rights no less valuable than the First Amendment rights of the speaker, but we would be foolish to deny that such picketing may at times simply change the nature of the speaker's speech. Just as Marcel Duchamp's mustachioed Mona Lisa has made it impossible for me ever to see the real Mona Lisa without wondering where the mustache is, and just as *The Lone Ranger* has made it impossible for many people of my generation to appreciate without

distraction Rossini's *"William Tell* Overture," so too can counterprotesters alter the nature of a speaker's speech without ever engaging in physical interference and thus without ever risking legal liability. But when counterprotesters should do so, when we should praise or castigate them for doing it, and whether such actions are inconsistent with the deeper purposes of our free speech regime are questions that go beyond and beneath the law, even as they may be more important than questions about the law. On all of this, albeit without specific application to the problem of the hostile or obstructing audience, see Frederick Schauer, *The Ontology of Censorship,* in *Censorship and Silencing: Practices of Cultural Regulation* 147 (Robert C. Post, ed., 1998).

UNSAFE SPACES

80. The question Schauer raises about the lack of legal distinction between incitement of a sympathetic crowd and provocation of a hostile one is similarly noteworthy. The 1942 Supreme Court decision in *Chaplinsky v. New Hampshire,* 315 U.S. 568 (1942), which established the doctrine of "fighting words"—terms so inflammatory that a rational actor might reasonably be driven to violence—would seem applicable here. The premise of the doctrine is directed specifically at a hostile audience, not an easily incited sympathetic one. The Christian residents of Rochester, New Hampshire, in that case, could be expected to react violently toward Walter Chaplinsky, a Jehovah's Witness, as he denounced their religious beliefs and referred to a local police officer as "a damned Fascist."

COSTING OUT CAMPUS SPEAKER RESTRICTIONS

This commentary explores ideas in my personal capacity only. It does not express views for or on behalf of Columbia University, nor does it address or interpret the university's policies regarding speakers on campus.

81. For discussion of efforts to measure the effects of hostile speech on individuals and communities in the context of the Nazis' 1977 plan to march in Skokie, Illinois, see, for example, Donald A. Downs, *Nazis in Skokie: Freedom, Community, and the First Amendment* (1985) (analyzing interviews of and data regarding Holocaust survivors in Skokie). For discussion of studies showing negative physical effects of verbal abuse and other similar adversity, see Lisa Feldman Barrett, *When Is Speech Violence?,* N.Y. Times (July 14, 2017), https://www.nytimes.com/2017/07/14/opinion/sunday/when-is-speech-violence.html (citing studies showing negative physical effects of verbal abuse and other similar adversity). *But cf.* Philippa Strum, *When the Nazis Came to Skokie: Freedom for the Speech We Hate* 147–48 (1999) (arguing that Skokie residents benefited from challenging the attempted march).

82. Schauer cites the University of California at Berkeley's expenditure of roughly $2 million for three speeches. The University of Florida similarly indicated, in a Q&A published prior to a white nationalist speaking on its campus, that "[m]ore than $500,000 will be spent by UF and other agencies to enhance security on our campus and in the city of Gainesville for this event." Q&A for Richard Spencer 10/19 event, University of Florida, https://freespeech.ufl.edu/qa-for-1019-event (last visited July 18, 2019).

83. I also want to be clear, again, that I offer these thoughts in my personal capacity and not in connection with any aspect of Columbia University's policies.

84. Many have already written thoughtfully and extensively about this challenge, primarily in the context of hate speech. *See, e.g.*, Richard Delgado & Jean Stefancic, *Four Ironies of Campus Climate*, 101 Minn. L. Rev. 1919, 1922 (2017) ("[M]any campus administrators are committed to the goal of educating students for roles in a multicultural and multiracial world, and if the campus is cold or hostile, this goal will be difficult to achieve." (citations omitted)); Charles R. Lawrence III, *If He Hollers Let Him Go: Regulating Racist Speech on Campus*, 1990 Duke L.J. 431, 435–36, 458–61, 472–76 (describing the negative effects of hostile speech on students from marginalized social groups); Mari J. Matsuda, *Public Response to Racist Speech: Considering the Victim's Story*, 87 Mich. L. Rev. 2320, 2321–23, 2336–41, 2370–73, 2375–78 (1989) (same). I offer these ideas with their work in mind and with apologies up front that it is not possible to engage this body of scholarship sufficiently here.

85. Even this approach, though, may not sufficiently take account of a multiplier effect on the risk of violence resulting from the combination of actual previous incidents (for example, the violence in Berkeley or Charlottesville) and the amplification of competing views about the permissibility of that violence.

86. For all three approaches, there is also the basic risk of over-inclusiveness in that speakers cannot be counted on always to deliver the same message. As a result, under each of these approaches, some speakers would potentially be barred even from delivering a nonhostile or unprovocative message.

87. For thoughtful arguments and legislative models that seek to distinguish hate speech from other forms of speech, see generally Jeremy Waldron, *The Harm in Hate Speech* (2012) (arguing that Americans should give greater consideration to the harm caused by hate speech).

88. At the most basic level, evaluators would have to identify the extent to which the speaker's message might elevate individuals' sense of being threatened and the marginal cost of increased services to respond to that sense of threat. Among the difficulties here: measuring the sense of threat, evaluating the causal link between a speaker's message and an individual's sense of vulnerability, and concretizing the degree to which expanded services would provide redress. The assessment of security costs at or near the time of an event, as required by the other options, involves many fewer variables, though it may also be less effective in capturing an event's long-term costs. Indeed, another potential but nearly impossible-to-predict cost of contentious speakers is to an institution's ability to recruit and retain students and employees.

89. Robert Post offers a related observation in a recent commentary. Robert C. Post, *There Is No 1st Amendment Right to Speak on a College Campus*, Vox (Oct. 25, 2017), https://www.vox.com/the-big-idea/2017/10/25/16526442/first-amendment -college-campuses-milo-spencer-protests (arguing that universities "can support student-invited speakers *only* because it serves university purposes to do so" and that "these purposes must involve the purpose of education").

90. Here I would suggest that reasonableness could be gauged by some combination of the institution's administrative and faculty leadership, as these are individuals engaged daily and over the long term in efforts to carry out the mission. For this reason, legislators, trustees, and students are, I would argue, less well positioned to make this assessment in the context at hand.

91. In another essay, I address the interests schools might have and the steps schools might take to address costs to community members' well-being where excluding hostile speakers is not a meaningful option. *See* Suzanne B. Goldberg, *Free Expression on Campus: Mitigating the Costs of Contentious Speakers*, 41 Harv. J.L. & Pub. Pol'y 163 (2018).

POLICING, PROTESTING, AND THE INSIGNIFICANCE OF HOSTILE AUDIENCES

92. *Stromberg v. California*, 283 U.S. 359, 361 (1931).
93. *Terminiello v. Chicago*, 337 U.S. 1, 5 (1949).
94. *Gregory v. City of Chicago*, 394 U.S. 111 (1969).
95. 505 U.S. 123 (1992).
96. *See* Chris Suarez, *City Sued over Rally Permit Decision*, Daily Progress (Aug. 10, 2017), http://www.dailyprogress.com/news/local/city-sued-over-rally -permit-decision/article_5255aa5e-7e1f-11e7-8a16-e37d2241f987.html.
97. *See* Timothy J. Heaphy, *Final Report: Independent Review of the 2017 Protest Events in Charlottesville, Virginia* 69, 81–84 (2018).
98. *See id.* at 69–75, 89–103.
99. *See id.* at 120–42.
100. *See, e.g., Gregory v. City of Chicago*, 394 U.S. 111 (1969); *Cox v. Louisiana*, 379 U.S. 536, 550 (1965).
101. *See Feiner v. New York*, 340 U.S. 315 (1951).
102. *See Atwater v. Lago Vista*, 532 U.S. 318 (2001).
103. *See Whren v. United States*, 517 U.S. 806 (1996).
104. *See Graham v. Connor*, 490 U.S. 390 (1989).
105. *See* Clark McPhail et al., *Policing Protest in the United States: 1960–1995*, in *Policing Protest: The Control of Mass Demonstrations in Western Democracies* 49 (Donatella della Porta & Herbert Reiter, eds., 1998).
106. *See, e.g.*, David A. Graham, *Could Police Have Prevented Bloodshed in Charlottesville?*, Atlantic (Aug. 14, 2017), https://www.theatlantic.com/politics /archive/2017/08/could-the-police-have-prevented-bloodshed-in-charlottesville /536775.
107. *See* Farah Stockman, *Year After White Nationalist Rally, Charlottesville Is in Tug of War over Its Soul*, N.Y. Times (July 21, 2018), https://www.nytimes .com/2018/07/21/us/white-nationalist-rally-charlottesville-mayor.html.
108. *See, e.g.*, Chris Suarez, *City Council Memo Leaked*, Daily Progress (Aug. 25, 2017), http://www.dailyprogress.com/news/local/leaked-memo-shows-councilors -grilled-city-manager-on-rally-response/article_c95a9388-89ac-11e7-ae33 -c7cced6877e7.html.
109. *See* McPhail et al., *supra* note 105, at 52–54.
110. *See* Patrick F. Gillhan et al., *Strategic Incapacitation and the Policing of Occupy Wall Street Protests in New York City, 2011*, 23 Policing and Soc'y 81 (2013).
111. *See* Dean Seal, *KKK Rally in Charlottesville Eclipsed by Protests*, Daily Progress (July 8, 2017), http://www.dailyprogress.com/news/local/kkk-rally-in-charlottesville -eclipsed-by-protests/article_f13cde22-6415-11e7-9756-c3a385058998.html.

3

STRAINING (ANALOGIES) TO MAKE SENSE OF THE FIRST AMENDMENT IN CYBERSPACE

David E. Pozen

IN TRYING to figure out the First Amendment rights and responsibilities of internet search engines and social media platforms, courts and commentators have turned to somewhat anachronistic analogies. Google's search engine compiles and transmits content supplied by third parties—and to this extent, many have pointed out, it looks like a traditional publisher. On the other hand, Google's search engine results do not express critical curatorial judgments by Google or indicate Google's support for their content in the manner we generally expect of publishers. Facebook's Trending News feature ranks and disseminates stories based on algorithms created by humans—and in this sense, it looks like a newspaper editor. On the other hand, Facebook takes pains to minimize the influence of human "biases" on these algorithms and to portray itself as a neutral conduit for information.

For these and other reasons, as Heather Whitney's essay explains, the analogies that get drawn in these contexts are imperfect. There are significant dissimilarities as well as similarities between the things being compared. There are, moreover, other analogies that might be privileged instead: why not compare Google and Facebook to a shopping mall, or to a public trustee, or to a company town? And still more fundamentally, there is an underlying question of whether and why the First Amendment logic of prior cases *should* apply to such technologies. This is a question that analogies in themselves cannot answer.

Whitney's essay deconstructs the use of the "editorial analogy," and of analogical reasoning more generally, in First Amendment litigation and advocacy concerning some of our most powerful tech companies. Whitney does not seek to advance any particular interpretation of Facebook, Google, and the like. Rather, through careful conceptual and empirical analysis, she seeks to expose the pitfalls of relying too heavily on analogies in this area of law and thereby to shift ongoing First Amendment debates onto more solid ground.

Three commentaries engage with Whitney's essay in strikingly different ways. Eric Goldman defends the validity of the editorial analogy for Google and Facebook, while also maintaining that their First Amendment rights do not depend on it to any meaningful degree. Whitney's critique of this analogy, Goldman worries, may create space for overly aggressive or counterproductive forms of regulation.

Genevieve Lakier, in contrast, agrees with Whitney that courts have been clumsy in comparing search engines to newspapers; cable providers, Lakier submits, are closer counterparts to the former in the contemporary public sphere. Yet Lakier disagrees with the notion that courts should therefore move away from analogies altogether. When done well, Lakier argues, analogical reasoning plays an indispensable role in guiding and constraining judicial discretion.

Finally, Frank Pasquale hails Whitney's intervention and asks how it might be pushed further. Underpinning both First Amendment jurisprudence and public policy on large internet intermediaries, Pasquale contends, should be the principle that "free speech protections are primarily for people, and only secondarily (if at all) for software, algorithms, artificial intelligence, and platforms." Whitney's essay concludes by urging us to stop fixating on analogies and start paying more explicit attention to the deep normative issues at stake in our debates over search engine results and social media designs. Pasquale gives a sense of what it looks like to do just that.

Search Engines, Social Media, and the Editorial Analogy

Heather Whitney*

"Its power seems inescapable—but then, so did the divine right of kings."
—URSULA K. LE GUIN[1]

SOCIAL MEDIA companies are in Congress's sights. In May 2016, in the wake of allegations that Facebook workers had suppressed pro-conservative viewpoints and links while injecting liberal stories into the newly introduced Trending Topics section, Senator John Thune sent a letter to Mark Zuckerberg demanding, among other things, a copy of the company's guidelines for choosing Trending Topics, a list of all news stories removed or injected into Trending Topics, and information about what steps the company would take to "hold the responsible individuals accountable."[2] Facebook complied, with Zuckerberg himself meeting with lawmakers.

During the subsequent hearings before the Senate and House intelligence committees on Russian interference in the 2016 presidential campaign, Senator Dianne Feinstein told the general counsels of Facebook, Google, and Twitter, whose CEOs were conspicuously absent: "You bear this responsibility. You've created these platforms. And now they're being misused. And you have to be the ones to do something about it. *Or we will.*"[3] Despite intensive lobbying efforts by these companies, both individually and through their collective trade association,[4] legislation imposing new restrictions on how they operate is, "for the first time in years, . . . being discussed seriously in Washington."[5] As one reporter put it, "In 2008, it was Wall Street bankers. In 2017, tech workers are the world's villain."[6]

That Bay Area tech companies are having something of a PR crisis is clear.[7] And in the rough and tumble of politics, that these companies would meet with and appease legislators is no great surprise. But if Congress does decide to get tough, how credible and wide-ranging is the regulatory threat, under current First Amendment jurisprudence?

Some prominent commentators claim that Facebook is analogous to a newspaper and that its handling of a feature like Trending Topics is analogous to a newspaper's editorial choices.[8] As a result, these commentators find congressional scrutiny of such matters to be constitutionally problematic. Moreover, the editorial analogy has been a remarkably effective shield for these tech companies in litigation. In a series of lower court cases, Google and others have argued that their decisions concerning their platforms — for example, what sites to list (or delist) and in what order, who can buy ads and where to place them, and what users to block or permanently ban — are analogous to the editorial decisions of publishers. And like editorial decisions, they argue, these decisions are protected "speech" under the First Amendment. While mostly wielded against small-fry, often pro se plaintiffs, courts have tended to accept this analogy wholesale.

Large consequences hinge on whether the various choices companies like Facebook and Google make are indeed analogous to editorial "speech." The answer will partly determine whether and how the state can respond to current challenges ranging from the proliferation of fake news to high levels of market concentration to the lack of ad transparency. Furthermore, algorithmic discrimination and the discrimination facilitated by these platforms' structures affect people's lives today and no doubt will continue to do so.[9] But if these algorithms and outputs are analogous to the decisions the *New York Times* makes on what to publish, then attempts to extend antidiscrimination laws to deal with such discrimination will face an onslaught of potentially insuperable constitutional challenges. In short, these companies' deployment of the editorial analogy in the First Amendment context poses a major hurdle to government intervention.

Whether, or to what extent, the editorial analogy *should* work as a shield against looming legislation and litigation for companies like Facebook and Google is something this historical moment demands we carefully consider. My primary aim in this essay is to do just that. I will engage critically with, and ultimately raise questions about, the near-automatic application of the editorial analogy. The core takeaways are these: (1) we should be cognizant of the inherent limitations of analogical reasoning generally and of the editorial analogy specifically; (2) whether these companies' various outputs should receive coverage as First Amendment "speech" is far from clear, both descriptively and normatively;[10] (3) the proposition that regulations compelling these companies to add content (disclaimers, links to competitors, and so on) compel the companies to speak is also far from clear; and, finally and most crucially, (4) given the limits of analogical reasoning, our future debates about First Amendment coverage should focus less on analogy and more on what actually matters—the normative commitments that undergird free speech theory and how our choices either help or hinder their manifestations.

To that end, I start by reviewing some of the cases in which the editorial analogy has been successfully deployed. Next, I lay the groundwork for rethinking the editorial analogy—first, by analyzing its internal weaknesses, and second, by raising other potentially compelling analogical frames. Each new analogy raises far knottier questions than I can address here, so I will briefly mention only a few, ending with the analogy brought to life by the Supreme Court's recent language in *Packingham v. North Carolina*.[11] There, the Court, either strategically or recklessly, "equate[d] the entirety of the internet with public streets and parks"[12] and declared it "clear" that "cyberspace" and "social media in particular" are now "the most important places (in a spatial sense) for the exchange of views."[13] The Court found social media to be "the modern public square"[14] and stated that it is a "fundamental principle of the First Amendment . . . that all persons have access" to such a forum.[15] This language casts doubt on whether the editorial analogy will be successful going forward. Its reliance on highly abstract characterizations also serves as a lesson. We should address First Amendment coverage questions through the lens of normative theory and not through a collection of ill-suited analogies.

THE EDITORIAL ANALOGY IN LITIGATION

Zhang v. Baidu.com, Inc. is the case in which a lower court has most fully explained why, in its view, the editorial analogy applies to a search engine's outputs.[16] The plaintiffs, New York residents and self-described "promoters of democracy in China," alleged that Baidu, the dominant Chinese search engine, intentionally delisted their pro-democracy websites from its search results in the United States at the behest of the Chinese government.[17] And in so doing, they further alleged, Baidu violated their First Amendment rights. Baidu replied that its listing decisions were its protected speech. The Southern District of New York agreed, finding that "First Amendment jurisprudence all but compels the conclusion that Plaintiffs' suit must be dismissed."[18] With no attention paid to the claim that Baidu was acting on behalf of the Chinese government, the court saw the relevant precedent as *Miami Herald Publishing Co. v. Tornillo*.[19] There, the U.S. Supreme Court found unconstitutional a statute that required newspapers to provide political candidates a right of reply to critical editorials.[20] The court in *Baidu* also saw *Hurley v. Irish-American Gay, Lesbian, and Bisexual Group of Boston* as an extension of *Tornillo*, equally applicable to *Baidu*.[21] In *Hurley*, the Court ruled that requiring parade organizers to permit a pro-LGBT group to participate would entail unconstitutionally compelling the parade organizers to speak.[22]

The *Baidu* court's holding followed directly from its analogical reasoning. It saw Baidu as organizing information, which it thought sufficient to make the relevant analogy a "newspaper editor's judgment of which . . . stories to run."[23] The Supreme Court previously found a newspaper's judgment of which stories to run protected "speech" and struck down as compelled speech a requirement that it include content that went against that judgment. Thus, analogizing Baidu to a newspaper, Baidu's judgments about which sites to list were also protected "speech" and requiring Baidu to include sites against its wishes would be unconstitutional compelled speech, too.

The editorial analogy again won out, this time for Google, in *e-ventures Worldwide, LLC v. Google, Inc.*[24] e-ventures is a search engine optimization (SEO) firm. Such firms seek to improve the visibility of client websites in organic (i.e., non-paid) search results. Clients like this because the higher their websites in organic rankings, the heavier the flow of traffic to their sites, which in turn enables them to sell advertising space on their sites at higher rates. Search engine companies are not big fans of SEO firms—they see them as trying to game the system for unpaid rankings.[25] More to the point, when SEO firms are successful, it means that companies spend a portion of their advertising budgets with the SEO firms and not with Google for paid placement in search results. As a result, a perpetual game of cat and mouse ensues.[26] Apparently unable to tweak its search algorithm in a way it liked, Google instead manually delisted 231 websites belonging to e-ventures clients.[27] e-ventures attempted to reach out to Google through several channels with the hopes of getting the sites relisted, but it was unsuccessful. As a result, e-ventures filed suit, at which point Google relisted the sites.

In its suit, e-ventures alleged that the delisting constituted unfair competition under the Lanham Act, tortious interference with business relations, and a violation of Florida's Deceptive and Unfair Trade Practices Act.[28]

e-ventures also alleged that Google's statements about its search results—that "Google search results are a reflection of the content publicly available on the web" and that "it is Google's policy not to censor search results"—were false and deceptive in light of its delisting practices.[29] Google responded by asserting, among other things, that e-ventures' claims were overridden by the First Amendment, as Google's search results were its editorial judgments and opinions.[30] While the court did not grant Google's motion to dismiss, it ultimately agreed with Google at summary judgment that the First Amendment protects its delisting decisions.[31] And the court did so by squarely analogizing Google to a publisher and its judgments about what to list or delist to a publisher's decision about what to publish.[32]

That Google's actions were commercial and arguably anticompetitive did not matter. That Google was alleged to have made deceptive statements did not matter. On the contrary, the court expressly opined that Google's free speech rights protect its listing and delisting decisions "whether they are fair or unfair, or motivated by profit or altruism."[33] The court's conclusion that if Google's results were speech, unfair competition laws could not apply is deeply problematic and difficult to square with the obvious fact that laws addressing unfair and deceptive advertising prohibit certain speech all the time.[34] This conclusion underscores the editorial analogy's powerful influence and what its successful use puts at stake.

That said, while the editorial analogy has proved potent in lower court cases, there is still time to rethink it. First, the Supreme Court has yet to weigh in. As I mentioned before and will discuss below, the Court's most recent comments in this area come in *Packingham*.[35] If we take the majority at its word, that case suggests that it is an analogy to the public square and not to a publisher that ought to guide First Amendment thinking about social media. Second, plaintiffs in these prior cases were much more modestly resourced than the search titans they opposed. Some plaintiffs proceeded pro se. As a practical matter, this means that lower courts have been under little pressure to interrogate the cursory analogical-reasoning rationales that favored the defendants.

But this too might change. In what Yelp's vice president of public policy described as the "most significant enforcement event in consumer tech antitrust" since the action against Microsoft in 2000,[36] Google was fined a record-breaking €2.4 billion by European regulators in June 2017 for abusing its market dominance by giving an illegal advantage to its own products while demoting rivals in its comparison shopping service,

Google Shopping.[37] While EU actions do not ensure any movement domestically, they can bring to light information that further tarnishes Silicon Valley's reputation and thus contributes to the erosion of the basis for its companies' exceptional treatment to date. Within the United States, moreover, Yelp and TripAdvisor have repeatedly argued that Google deliberately diverts users searching for their sites to Google-owned alternatives. Google has said that some of these results are the result of bugs, but its competitors argue otherwise.[38] It is at least possible that a major (and well-funded) lawsuit in the United States—and with it, a vigorous battle over First Amendment coverage, the editorial analogy, and unfair competition laws—may yet materialize.

THE LIMITS OF THE EDITORIAL ANALOGY

The analogical argument works something like this: A does x and merits treatment y. B does x. Therefore, B is analogous to A, and B also merits treatment y. We can challenge arguments of this form in several ways. First, internal to the argument, we can question the relationship between doing x and getting treatment y. We cannot assume that doing x always merits treatment y. Indeed, we cannot assume that doing x has anything to do with why treatment y is merited. An example will help make this more concrete: take the action of eating a sundae without permission. If I work at the ice cream shop from which I took that sundae, a reprimand from my employer might be merited. But say instead that I'm a professor. We likely think that it would be absurd for my employer to reprimand me for eating a sundae without permission. In both cases I did the same thing—ate a sundae without permission—but additional facts change what treatment we think that same action merits.[39] Put simply, even when A and B have some similarities, there can be relevant *dissimilarities* between them that renders treatment y appropriate for one but not the other.

A second challenge, and one I would call external, is to propose a different analogy. Why analogize B to A and not B to C? Consider that newspapers (A) provide people information (x) and that requiring newspapers to provide different information (for example, a right of reply) may be struck down as compelling them to speak (merits treatment y). Search engines (B) also provide people information (x). As a result, search engines are analogous to newspapers (A), and so we might think that requiring a search engine to provide different information should similarly be struck down as compelling it to speak (merits treatment y). Now consider an alternative analogy. Law schools (C) provide information (x) by hosting and organizing recruitment fairs, to which they invite a limited number of employers. Requiring law schools to allow military recruiters into such fairs and to give them equal access to students does not compel the schools to say anything (they remain free to protest the military's policies), so this requirement is constitutional (merits treatment z).[40] Search engines (B) provide information (x) via their rankings, in which a limited number of sites are included. Therefore, requiring search engines to allow sites into those rankings and to give them equal access to the search engine's users similarly does not compel the search engine to speak (it remains free to protest the competitor's speech). Thus, that requirement is constitutional as well (merits treatment z). Treatments y and z are incompatible. Yet, we can construct analogies that call for search engines to get both. That's a problem.

Like all analogies, the editorial analogy is vulnerable on both the internal and external front.

INTERNAL WEAKNESSES OF THE ANALOGY

In a white paper paid for by Google at the same time that the Federal Trade Commission was investigating whether the company had abused its market dominance,[41] Eugene Volokh and Donald Falk argue that Google's organic search results are fully protected speech and, as a result, are insulated from antitrust scrutiny.[42] Relatedly, they argue that requiring Google to change its search results (for example, by placing Yelp higher) would unconstitutionally compel Google to speak in much the same way that a right-of-reply law would unconstitutionally compel a newspaper editor to speak.[43] In making their argument, the authors rely heavily on the editorial analogy. As they put it, companies like Google are "analogous to newspapers and book publishers" in that they both "convey a wide range of information."[44] They claim that search results are also analogous to editorial publications, as both involve choices about "how to rank and organize content,"[45] "what should be presented to users,"[46] and "what constitutes useful information."[47] This description of (some of) what Google does is accurate. But, crucially, these analogies do not substantiate the authors' two claims—namely, that (1) search engines and search results merit the same treatment as publishers and editorial judgments for First Amendment purposes, and (2) requiring Google to modify its search results would compel Google to speak.

Let's start with the first claim—that Google is analogous to a publisher because it, too, conveys a wide range of information. Now consider the application of that argument to a familiar saying: "Actions speak louder than words." We say this because actions convey a wide range of information, often more truthful information than is conveyed through speech alone. Yet we certainly do not think that whenever people act, they are analogous to newspaper editors under the First Amendment and that their actions are therefore covered as speech. Thus, we can conclude that conveying a wide range of information is not sufficient for being treated like a publisher under the First Amendment.[48] And given this, it straightforwardly follows that pointing out that Google conveys a wide range of information does not yet tell us whether Google should be treated like a publisher under the First Amendment.

Now consider the layout of a grocery store. There are good reasons that pharmacies are in the back,[49] that certain brands are at eye level,[50] and that candy is near the checkout.[51] All those choices convey a wide range of information to consumers. Do we think that for purposes of First Amendment analysis, grocery stores are therefore analogous to publishers, because grocery stores convey a wide range of information through their organizing of products? Is the layout of the grocery store analogous to an editorial for purposes of speech coverage? My guess is most people think the answer is an obvious no.

If any individual or organization who satisfies this "conveys a wide range of information" criterion is deemed analogous to newspaper and book publishers for First Amendment purposes, then we have misunderstood how liberal political theory and free speech theory work. At the heart of liberal political theory is the idea that everyone is free to live according to their own ideals, so long as doing so does not unduly interfere with other people's ability to do likewise. As a result, the government can only legitimately restrict people's freedom when it is necessary to prevent harm or secure the demands of justice. The idea at the heart of liberal free speech theory is that when it comes to certain communicative acts, a commitment to individual freedom isn't enough and must be bolstered by extra protections that make what counts as "speech" less liable to regulation than similarly harmful or unjust non-speech. This doesn't mean that the government can willy-nilly regulate whatever it wants except for speech. It must always show the harm or injustice that results from the object of regulation. Instead, liberal free speech theory says that regulating a subset of those harms or injustices—those that come directly from "speech"—should be more difficult, even acknowledging that they are harmful or unjust.[52] But this whole scheme presupposes that what gets covered as "speech" for this purpose is limited, a special domain of extra protection. We should remember that this special domain comes at a cost. "Free" speech isn't truly free.[53] When we grant "speech" coverage, we require those who are harmed or treated unjustly by that speech to absorb more of its costs. Once any entity that conveys a wide range of information is suddenly analogous to a newspaper, we have begun making what was supposed to be exceptional treatment the new rule. While some might welcome this libertarian, deregulatory move in the short run, it is not only anathema to liberal theory but also, I suspect, unlikely to yield attractive outcomes in the long run.

Volokh and Falk next say that search results are analogous to editorial publications because both involve choices about "how to rank and organize content,"[54] "what should be presented to users,"[55] and "what constitutes useful information."[56] These similarities to publishers fare no better. As I said before, every store organizes and ranks content through its layout.[57] Are all store layouts now akin to editorial publications under the First Amendment? Are all stores First Amendment publishers? Again, I think the answer is no. But as an ex-Google product philosopher (and who doesn't want that title?) points out, companies like Facebook, Google, and Twitter seek to influence users by means of various organizational and content choices in much the same way that grocery stores do by their layout and product placement.[58]

One might respond here by saying that ranking and organizing only counts as analogous to editorial functions if what is ranked and organized is itself speech. But this is implausible. Surely Volokh and Falk think that a restaurant ranking qualifies as speech even though the underlying things ranked and organized—restaurants—are not. Thus, that the thing being ranked and organized is itself speech is not necessary for coverage. Is it sufficient?

Here is an argument for that position: a bookstore selects which books to sell. Wouldn't we say that its selection of those books is itself speech? And if so, doesn't that show that curating other people's speech is necessarily speech itself? Once again, I think the answer is no. First, I hesitate to grant the premise—that we would call a bookseller's book selections an independent instance of protected speech. I say this because in cases where the state has banned the sale of protected speech, the Court has invoked either the First Amendment rights of speech creators or would-be speech buyers. When sellers challenge these bans, they point to the First Amendment rights of those *other* parties. Take *Brown v. Entertainment Merchants Association*, where the Court struck down a law banning the sale of violent video games.[59] Although its opinion was admittedly not a paragon of clarity, the Court in *Brown* considered the First Amendment rights of game creators and child buyers. Nowhere did the Court consider whether the ban might violate the speech rights of video game sellers. Second, and more fundamentally, even if a bookseller's choice of which books to sell counts as speech, that still does not show that (1) every time an entity curates third-party speech that curation is itself speech, nor does it show what might ultimately be more crucial—namely, that (2) like the newspaper in *Tornillo*, requiring a modification of that curation constitutes compelled speech. I have already gone over the reason for (1). To see (2), consider the military recruitment case *Rumsfeld v. Forum for Academic and Institutional Rights* (FAIR).[60]

In *FAIR*, a federal statute required law schools to provide military recruiters the same access to students as that given to other recruiters or lose funding.[61] A group of law schools argued that requiring them to include the military in their fairs would send students the message that the schools endorsed the military's "don't ask, don't tell" policy, which they did not. As a result, the schools argued that the requirement constituted unconstitutional compelled speech.[62] The Court disagreed, holding that requiring law schools to give military recruiters equal access and even sending out scheduling emails to students on behalf of the military recruiters did not compel the law schools to speak at all. As the Court saw it, "schools are not speaking when they host interviews and recruiting receptions."[63] Even more, the Court thought some of the schools' compelled-speech claims "trivialize[d] the freedom protected" in its prior compelled-speech cases.[64] Given the Court's ruling in *FAIR*, and even granting that the curation of third-party speech is itself speech, it is not the case that requiring an entity to include speech it dislikes within its curation necessarily entails compelling that entity to speak.

A final move someone might suggest to rehabilitate the Volokh and Falk position entails looking at the restaurant ranking differently—it doesn't rank and organize restaurants but instead information about those restaurants. And so, any entity that makes such rankings is in the business of ranking and organizing information and is relevantly analogous to a publisher making editorial selections.[65] Two points here. First, I find it difficult to characterize a restaurant ranking as the organization of information about restaurants. It seems more natural to say that it is a ranking of restaurants that also generates information (which restaurants are best and which are worst). Second, as already noted, virtually any activity that involves the creation of information entails some curatorial decisions. Unless we are willing to say that every such activity warrants constitutional protection, we must concede that the fact that newspaper editors and search engines both engage in the curation of information is not sufficient for finding the latter analogous, for First Amendment purposes, to the former.

POTENTIALLY RELEVANT DISSIMILARITIES

While often unnoticed, the extent to which we find analogical reasoning convincing is based not only on relevant similarities but also on the absence of relevant dissimilarities. And as many have already pointed out, there are significant and arguably relevant dissimilarities between the outputs of tech companies like Facebook, Google, and Twitter, on the one hand, and newspapers, on the other.

To make this point about the importance of dissimilarity more concrete, consider the development of oil and gas rights in the United States. Courts were faced with the question of whether land owners had property rights to oil and gas reservoirs that lay underneath their land. Reasoning by analogy, early American courts were "captured" by an analogy to the law of capture. If you capture a wild animal while you're on your own property, it's yours.[66] Therefore, analogously, so long as you take out the gas and oil while you're on your own property, it's also yours. But of course, while in the grip of this analogy, courts failed to see the relevant dissimilarities between hunting wild animals and extracting oil and gas that made the analogy, and thus the application of the law of capture to oil and gas, problematic. For starters, such a rule incentivized landowners to over-drill so as to extract as much oil and gas as possible before their neighbors could do the same. Eventually we figured out that sometimes the dissimilarities are more important than the similarities and changed the rule.[67]

Returning to editorial publications and tech company outputs, some scholars have argued that the use of algorithms creates a relevant dissimilarity. As Oren Bracha and Frank Pasquale have put it, we should distinguish between dialogical and functional expression and only give First Amendment coverage to the former.[68] The rough idea is that dialogical expression is perceived by the audience as something with which it can agree or disagree, criticize or support, argue for or against. In contrast, functional expression, while not clearly defined, is expression that the audience does not perceive as speech to which it can respond in these ways. Bracha and Pasquale argue that algorithmically generated search outputs are functional because users do not perceive rankings as expression with which they can dialogically engage.

Volokh and Falk object to claims that algorithms and their outputs are not speech, pointing in part to the fact that algorithms are written by humans and result from engineers' judgments.[69] However, if we instead put them in conversation with Bracha and Pasquale, they might argue that audiences do perceive these outputs as judgments with which they can critically engage — just consider the public outcry over certain rankings and what does or does not trend. Even if we accept the dialogical/functional methodology,[70] it seems that both sides are only partially right. Bracha and Pasquale are wrong to suggest that algorithmically encoded curation is necessarily functional. As others have suggested, we can conjure up some cases of algorithmic operations that look dialogical.[71] This undermines the claim that the algorithm is what makes Facebook's and Google's curation non-speech.

Yet all of this is consistent with the plausible view, contra Volokh and Falk, that in light of how these companies portray themselves and their outputs to the public, outputs like search results, lists of what is trending, and newsfeed fodder are not understood by most members of the public as dialogical expression on the order of the content a newspaper publishes. While newspapers generally stand behind their content, Google,[72] Facebook,[73] and Twitter[74] have all explicitly disavowed the substance of their results. Newspapers also (and unsurprisingly) hold themselves out as editors, whereas these tech companies do everything they can to run from that categorization. It strikes me that selling themselves to the public in this way does lessen users' perception that their outputs are dialogical. I doubt many people enter a search query into Google and think, "I now know Google's views on my query." And part of the reason for this may well be that these companies expressly tell users not to think the results are their speech (even as they claim the opposite in litigation). Self-presentation as not-a-speaker has another important consequence: users may not perceive requirements that these companies alter their results as tantamount to compelling the companies to speak.[75]

To see why the public might not perceive these algorithmic outputs as the speech of these companies, let's turn to a few specific examples.

GOOGLE'S POSITION: NOT A SPEAKER   We can start with the controversy over Google's autocomplete function. As most reading this will be aware, when you start typing a search query into Google's search box, Google automatically makes suggestions for how the query should be completed. These suggestions, which are generated algorithmically, depend on several variables, including what you are typing, what you have previously searched for, what others have searched for, and what is currently trending. In 2016, users noticed that when they typed "are Jews" or "are women," Google suggested "evil" to complete the query. Similarly, when users typed "are Muslims," Google suggested "bad."[76] In 2011, when a certain Italian citizen's name was typed into Google's search box, autocomplete suggestions included the Italian words for "con man" and "fraud." The individual then sued Google for defamation and won.[77]

If we really think the outputs of Google's algorithms are its speech, this defamation suit makes sense. But Google argued the opposite. In its statement after losing the suit in Italian court, Google said, "We believe that Google should not be held liable for terms that appear in autocomplete as these are predicted by computer algorithms based on searches from previous users, not by Google itself."[78] If you go to Google's support pages today and look under "Search using autocomplete," you will see the following: "Note: Search predictions aren't the answer to your search. They're also not statements by other people or Google about your search terms."[79] We should pause to reflect on this. Google is not simply saying that the views of those it ranks are not its speech. More than that, it expressly disavows as its own speech the very rankings and algorithmic outputs it claims in litigation to be its editorial speech.[80]

There are, in fact, numerous situations in which Google disavows as its speech the very rankings that commentators like Volokh and Falk argue are both its speech and analogous to the speech of editorial publications. Stuart Benjamin describes a case in which Google's top result for the term "Jew" was an anti-Semitic site called "Jew Watch." When civil rights groups pressured Google to delist the site, Google instead posted a note stating that its results rely on "algorithms using thousands of factors to calculate a page's relevance to a given query" and that they don't reflect "the beliefs and preferences of those who work at Google."[81] Google thus presented itself as a conduit for the speech of others—not so different from how Google saw internet service providers (ISPs) as conduits, at least when I worked there.[82] Now consider *Tornillo*, where the newspaper was so intimately tied to the content it published that a mere right of reply was thought to compel the newspaper to speak. The difference between *Tornillo* and Google's situation is clear. Google's point is that its search-related outputs aren't its speech at all.

Google most recently and explicitly eschewed the editorial analogy in its testimony before the Senate Judiciary Subcommittee on Crime and Terrorism in October of 2017. It is worth reproducing in full the relevant dialogue between Louisiana Senator John Kennedy and Richard Salgado, Google's law enforcement and information security director:

> **KENNEDY:** Are you a media—let me ask Google this, to be fair. Are you a media company, or a neutral technology platform?
>
> **SALGADO:** We're the technology platform, primarily.
>
> **KENNEDY:** That's what I thought you'd say. You don't think you're one of the largest, the largest newspapers in 92 countries?
>
> **SALGADO:** We're not a newspaper. We're a platform for sharing of information that can include news from sources such as newspapers.
>
> **KENNEDY:** Isn't that what newspapers do?
>
> **SALGADO:** This is a platform from which news can be read from news sources.[83]

If we are stuck making First Amendment coverage determinations by analogy, we might want to look beyond the analogy Google explicitly rejected in its congressional testimony.

FACEBOOK'S POSITION: NOT A SPEAKER The history of Facebook's Trending News and the recent controversy surrounding how its architecture facilitates—indeed, encourages—the proliferation of inflammatory and weaponized misinformation and propaganda provide further examples of a company that deliberately disclaims its curatorial products as its speech and itself as editor.

Facebook launched Trending News in January 2014. By this time, Twitter had established itself as the go-to social media site for breaking news and minute-by-minute coverage of live events. As a result, Twitter could "gobble up enormous amounts of engagement during TV premieres, award shows, sport matches, and world news events."[84] Twitter also successfully commercialized its Trending Topics feature, selling lucrative advertising space in the form of "promoted trends."[85] Facebook's Trending News was viewed as the company's attempt to emulate and compete with Twitter in this commercial space.[86]

By the summer of 2014, Facebook was already facing criticism for its lack of serious news, both in Trending News and its main news feeds. The civil unrest in Ferguson was considered the year's "most important domestic news story," and while Twitter was hailed for its second-by-second coverage of Ferguson, there was scant evidence of the conflict on Facebook, which instead seemed dominated by the ALS ice bucket challenge.[87] Some observers conjectured that Facebook's feed algorithms were to blame.[88] At one point, a senior Facebook employee said that the company was "actually working on it," but uncertainty about the nature of the problem and Facebook's response remained.[89] Should we understand the lack of Ferguson coverage in people's feeds as the editorial decision of Facebook? Did Facebook see the lack of Ferguson coverage as its own speech? After all, according to Volokh and Falk, that absence was clearly the result of algorithmic construction choices, which in turn reflected the judgments of the company's engineers. And Facebook was criticized for its algorithm's design, which basically hid controversial content and showed users more universally agreeable content, because the latter is what "keeps people coming back."[90] But once again, and unsurprisingly, this is not how Facebook saw it. Facebook did not see the resulting absence of Ferguson coverage as its own speech, let alone the product of a deliberate decision akin to the choices made by a newspaper to write about or neglect that same topic. Nor does Facebook's recognition that it needed to respond to the controversy by tweaking its algorithm, which it did,[91] necessarily suggest that the lack of Ferguson coverage in Facebook feeds was an editorial judgment.

As this episode underscored, Facebook straightforwardly does not see itself as an editor or its curation as its speech. Instead, in a Q&A session, Zuckerberg, much like Google, characterized Facebook as more analogous to a neutral conduit or tool that enables the speech of others:

> What we're trying to do is make it so that every single person in the world has a voice and a channel and can share their opinions, or research, or facts that they've come across, and can broadcast that out to their friends and family and people who follow them and want to hear what they have to say. . . . We view it as our job to . . . giv[e] everyone the richest tools to communicate and share what's important to them.[92]

This innocent-conduit-for-the-speech-of-others framing is not inconsistent with the facts that, by 2014, Facebook was the primary driver of traffic to most of the top news websites[93] and that, by 2017, 45 percent of U.S. adults were getting at least some of their news from Facebook.[94] Facebook has become "to the news business what Amazon is to book publishing—a behemoth that provides access to hundreds of millions of consumers and wields enormous power."[95] Nevertheless, Greg Marra, the engineer who oversees Facebook's News Feed algorithm, said in an interview that he and his team "explicitly view ourselves as not editors. . . . We don't want to have editorial judgment over the content," because users are in the best position to decide what they want to see.[96]

Facebook's response to the 2016 controversy surrounding the curation of Trending Topics further drives home the editorial disanalogy. Back in 2014, Facebook said that its Trending Topics articles were ranked by an algorithm based on metrics like popularity and timeliness.[97] Until the publication of a story by Recode in August 2015, there appears to have been no awareness that this was not the whole truth.[98] That story suggested that Facebook's workers had some hand in shaping Trending Topics content—not by selecting which articles appeared ("that's done automatically by the algorithm") but by writing headlines.[99] But in two explosive pieces on the tech news site Gizmodo in May 2016, Michael Nunez reported that the involvement of workers went much further: material appearing in Trending News was curated by Facebook contractors who, in addition to writing headlines, selected which topics trended and which sites they linked to.[100] These contractors reported that they were told to link to stories from preferred outlets like the *New York Times*; that they had a prerogative, which they regularly exercised, to blacklist topics that weren't covered by multiple traditional news sources or that concerned Facebook itself; and that they were told not to publicize that they were working for Facebook, presumably because the company "wanted to keep the magic about how trending topics work a secret."[101] Contractors subsequently reported that they had also injected stories about topics like Black Lives Matter into Trending News at the behest of management, who thought certain topics should be trending regardless of algorithmic metrics.[102] Most controversially, the contractors reported that pro-conservative stories were regularly excluded from Trending News, not at management's instruction, but on account of left-leaning colleagues using their prerogative to blacklist topics.[103] Based on these reports, Nunez argued that Facebook wanted to "foster the illusion of a bias-free news ranking process" and that Facebook was obscuring its workers' involvement because it "risk[ed] losing its image as a non-partisan player in the media industry" rather than "an inherently flawed curator."[104] In Nunez's view, Facebook worked like a newsroom, expressing the views of its staff in its reporting, in "stark contrast" to the company's depiction of Trending News as merely "topics that have recently become popular on Facebook"[105] or "a neutral pipeline for distributing content."[106]

This did not sit well with Republicans. Within hours of Nunez's second report, Republican National Committee Chairman Reince Priebus demanded that Facebook "answer for conservative censorship."[107] A post on the GOP's official blog argued (presciently) that "Facebook has the power to greatly influence the presidential election" and objected to its platform "being used to silence viewpoints and stories that don't fit someone else's agenda."[108] Shortly thereafter, Senate Commerce Committee chairman John Thune—a leading critic of the Federal Communications Commission's fairness doctrine until it was officially repealed (after years of non-enforcement) in 2011[109]—notified Facebook that his committee was exploring a consumer protection investigation. In his words:

> If Facebook presents its Trending Topics section as the result of a neutral, objective algorithm, but it is in fact subjective and filtered to support or suppress particular political viewpoints, Facebook's assertion that it maintains a platform for people and perspectives from across the political spectrum misleads the public.[110]

Thune gave Facebook fourteen days to provide details of its guidelines for preventing the suppression of political views, the training it provided workers in relation to those guidelines, and its methods for monitoring compliance.[111] Despite the view of lawyers who thought that Facebook could (and perhaps should) invoke the editorial analogy and reject Thune's demands on First Amendment grounds,[112] the company responded to Thune,[113] explained its practices, and shared its internal Trending Topics review guidelines.[114] Facebook's senior leaders also met with a number of top Republican leaders to reassure them that it was an impartial platform.[115] In its letter to Senator Thune, Facebook said that it found "no evidence of systematic political bias" but couldn't rule out occasional biased judgment by its curators.[116] It also identified, and pledged to reform, two parts of its process for generating Trending News. First, it would end its practice of boosting topics being covered by preferred major media players like BBC News, CNN, Fox News, and the *New York Times* (a change, looking back, that we might wish Facebook had not made). Second, the company stated that it would "take prompt remedial actions" should it find evidence of "improper actions taken on the basis of political bias."[117]

Facebook's response to this issue, in the following months and amid a contentious U.S. election cycle, was to replace the Trending News curatorial team with engineers who had a more mechanical role in approving stories generated by the Trending News algorithm. These engineers, as one writer poetically put it, would be "the algorithm's janitors."[118] Per its revised guidelines, Facebook removed its own headlines and summaries, and all featured news stories, including their accompanying excerpt, became algorithmically generated, based on "spikes in conversation."[119] The only non-algorithmic effect on content was when reviewers found clear mistakes—such as duplicate topics,[120] posts about non-news,[121] and posts about fictional events—and when they separated topics that had been automatically clustered under a single heading by the algorithm.[122] Before approving a topic, reviewers also confirmed that each topic contained at least three recently posted articles or five recently published posts, reviewed the keywords associated with the topic, nominated related topics, and set the topic location and category (for example, business, sports, or politics). From this point on, the source of posted articles no longer had a bearing on whether a topic would appear in Trending News.

Facebook thus changed its practices to become more "neutral," however amorphous the concept. The company wanted to make clear that its rankings were not its speech. Recall that in the *FAIR* case, the Court thought that requiring law schools to include military recruiters was not compelled speech, as even "high school students can appreciate the difference between speech a school sponsors and speech the school permits because legally required to do so, pursuant to an equal access policy."[123] Facebook is asking users to do this very same thing—to appreciate that what is trending is not Facebook's speech, even though it is on its platform.

Unfortunately, the more Facebook went out of its way to not be an editor, the more its Trending News algorithm was, as various news outlets characterized it, a "disaster,"[124] an algorithm "go[ne] crazy."[125] A few days after the change, Megyn Kelly was trending with a false headline: "Fox News Exposes Traitor Megyn Kelly, Kicks Her Out for Backing Hillary."[126] At the same time, four *Washington Post* journalists ran an experiment on their personal

Facebook accounts to look at the sorts of stories in Trending News and uncovered that, from August 31 to September 22, there were "five trending stories that were indisputably fake and three that were profoundly inaccurate."[127] Throughout all of this, Zuckerberg did not reconsider his prior insistence that Facebook is "a tech company, not a media company."[128] For better or worse, it is hard to imagine Facebook trying harder to distance itself from both the editorial analogy and any claim that what showed up in Trending News was its speech. Even in the wake of Trump's win, when "everyone from President Obama to the Pope . . . raised concerns about fake news and the potential impact on both political life and innocent individuals,"[129] Zuckerberg reiterated that he and his company "do not want to be arbiters of truth ourselves, but instead [want to] rely on our community and trusted third parties."[130]

When we diagnose what went wrong with regard to fake news, we need not conclude that Facebook made the mistake of trying to be too neutral. Instead, we can realize that our (and their) previous conception of what "neutrality" entailed—not privileging certain news sources and treating all sources of "news" the same—was wrong. Facebook, and the rest of us, learned that treating fake news sites on a par with the *Wall Street Journal* and the *New York Times* is saying something very not "neutral" about how we should treat information from those sites. Just recently, Facebook announced that it will once again rank news sources, but this time it plans to do so based on user evaluations of those sources.[131] We can debate this method as well, but it represents yet another attempt by Facebook to figure out what "neutral" means and then do it.

Finally, like Google, Facebook and Twitter were asked during recent congressional hearings how they "respond to . . . the growing concerns that [they] and other Silicon Valley companies are putting a thumb on the scale of political debate and shifting it in ways consistent with the political views of [their] employees?"[132] Facebook general counsel Colin Stretch replied, "Senator, again, we think of ourselves as a platform of all ideas—for all ideas and we aspire to that."[133] Stretch then discussed training given to prevent bias in its employees, saying, "We want to make sure that people's own biases are not brought to bear in how we manage the platform."[134] Responding to the same question, Sean Edgett of Twitter insisted that "our goal and . . . one of our fundamental principles at the company is to remain impartial."[135]

Whatever the analogical similarities they share with publishers, these companies see the analogical dissimilarities as more salient. Given this, it is hard to see why we should extend First Amendment coverage to the choices they make about how to run their platforms. And perhaps more significantly, these companies' self-conception dramatically weakens the claim that requirements to change their outputs would unconstitutionally compel them to speak.

COMPETING ANALOGIES

In addition to delving into some internal weaknesses of the editorial analogy, we can cast further doubt on its near-automatic acceptance by raising rival analogical frameworks that either (1) suggest that these companies' judgments should not receive free speech coverage or (2) assume some coverage but suggest ways that government regulation would not count as compelling these companies to speak. The ISP-like conduit analogy has already been discussed extensively by others (and briefly by me above),[136] so here I will mention three other sets: shopping malls or law schools, fiduciaries or public trustees, and company towns or public forums. My goal here is not to convince you of one analogy above the rest but instead to show the limitations and (often unstated) normative judgments inherent in making First Amendment coverage determinations via analogy at all.

SHOPPING MALL OR LAW SCHOOL

In *Pruneyard Shopping Center v. Robins*,[137] the appellees, a group of high school students, set up a stand to gather signatures for a petition in a privately owned shopping center. Security guards forced the students to leave; the students sued, claiming a right to solicit signatures on the premises under the California Constitution. The California Supreme Court ruled in their favor, but the Pruneyard Shopping Center appealed, claiming a violation of its speech rights under the federal Constitution. Most interestingly for our purposes, in its briefs Pruneyard cited *Tornillo* to argue analogically. That is, Pruneyard argued that requiring it to allow the students to petition was analogous to compelling newspapers to publish replies by political candidates they criticize.[138] Now, we can see that there are some similarities between a shopping center and a newspaper — for example, both decide what to present to consumers, and both convey information to those consumers by means of their curatorial decisions (i.e., they share the same similarities Volokh and Falk identified between newspapers and Google). But crucially, the U.S. Supreme Court did not think those similarities were salient. Instead, the Court took a different, and better, methodological approach. It looked at the reasoning underlying *Tornillo* to see whether that same reasoning was applicable to a shopping mall.[139] As the *Pruneyard* Court saw it, the state cannot force newspapers to publish right-of-reply articles because doing so would deter editors "from publishing controversial political statements" and thus limit the "vigor" and "variety" of public debate.[140] But such concerns did not apply in the case of a shopping center, and so the analogy did not hold sway. The Court ruled that Pruneyard's First Amendment rights were not infringed by the students' state-given rights of expression and petition on its property. Indeed, the Court did not think allowing the students to petition compelled Pruneyard to speak at all.[141]

The Court again discussed and rejected the *Tornillo* analogy in *FAIR*.[142] While the law schools argued that requiring them to treat military and nonmilitary recruiters alike unconstitutionally compels them to speak— to send a message about their views on a military policy with which they disagreed—the Court thought otherwise. Unlike a newspaper engaging in First Amendment–protected activity in choosing which editorials to run, the Court held that "schools are not speaking when they host interviews and recruiting receptions."[143]

We can analogize both the Pruneyard Shopping Center and the law schools to Facebook Trending and Google Search in a way that has prima facie appeal. Like Pruneyard and the schools, neither Facebook nor Google is literally a newspaper. Both companies' platforms, like the shopping center, are generally accessible to all. Like the shopping center's selecting which retailers to lease space to and the law schools' selecting which employers to participate in their recruitment fairs, Facebook and Google make curatorial decisions. As I have discussed at length above, Facebook and Google can and do publicly dissociate themselves from the views expressed by people who speak through their platforms and from the products of their own curatorial efforts (such as a particular ranking). The Supreme Court thought it important that Pruneyard and the law schools were capable of doing the same. Thus, if we reason by this analogy, Facebook and Google are also not compelled to speak when required to let others speak on their platform.

Analogous to *Pruneyard*, it is also not obvious that regulations preventing Facebook, Google, and Twitter from making certain curatorial and architectural choices—for example, from delisting competitors' sites or refusing their ads, deactivating user live streams at the behest of police with no judicial oversight,[144] striking deals with record labels to preemptively block the upload of certain user videos,[145] or relying on monetization models that encourage addictive behaviors[146] and the development of polarized epistemic bubbles that in turn facilitate the viral spread of fake news and propaganda[147]—would limit the vigor or variety of public debate. Indeed, it's important to remember that even if, like in *Pruneyard*, the state can force these private actors to permit third-party speech in ways that do not require the companies themselves to speak, the First Amendment rights of users remain. The government could not have silenced the high school petitioners in *Pruneyard*, and the same can be said for political dissent on Facebook.

In short, we can plausibly analogize Facebook, Google, and Twitter to the shopping center in *Pruneyard* or the law schools in *FAIR*, instead of to the newspaper in *Tornillo*. And when we do, certain regulations don't look constitutionally problematic after all.

FIDUCIARY OR PUBLIC TRUSTEE

An alternative analogical approach conceives of major tech companies as information fiduciaries.[148] In chapter 1 of this volume, Tim Wu raises a similar idea when he asks whether new laws and regulations should "requir[e] that major speech platforms behave as public trustees, with general duties to police fake users, remove propaganda robots, and promote a robust speech environment surrounding matters of public concern."[149] As Wu points out, such a move would require a reorientation of the First Amendment so as to renew the concern the Court evinced for the speech rights of listeners (or users) in cases like *Red Lion Broadcasting Co. v. FCC*.[150]

While this analogy may seem unlikely to be adopted in practice, such a move accords with the Court's recognition in *Packingham* of cyberspace as "the most important place" for the exchange of views.[151] In the recent congressional hearings with social media companies, it was also clear that all the participants were operating on a background assumption that while dealing with problems like those generated by Russian interference in the election, these companies had to be mindful of First Amendment principles. At one point, Senator Dick Durbin remarked, "Now take the word Russian out of it. A Facebook account that promotes anti-immigrant, anti-refugee sentiment in the United States. I don't know if you would characterize that as vile. I sure would."[152] Pursuing this concern, Senator Durbin asked, "How are you going to sort this out, consistent with the basic values of this country when it comes to freedom of expression?"[153]

If we thought of these companies as the same as any other private company, the idea that their solutions need to be consistent with the First Amendment would seem confused. Under existing doctrine, the tech companies don't need to comply with the First Amendment, nor concern themselves with the First Amendment rights of users, because they aren't engaged in state action. But even putting aside a finding of state action, members of the government, ordinary citizens, and the companies themselves do seem to see the companies as having a fiduciary-type role, given the importance of their platforms as spaces of public debate.[154]

Further movement toward a public trustee role was also essentially called for by a shareholder proposal filed with Facebook and Twitter by Arjuna Capital (an activist investment firm) and the New York State Common Retirement Fund (the nation's third-largest public pension fund).[155] And Zuckerberg embraced a public trustee model in his 2018 annual self-challenge[156] and Yom Kippur atonement.[157] Zuckerberg did not commit to turning Facebook into a better newspaper editor; he suggested that the company would "assume the responsibilities implied by [its] power," much like a public trustee would.[158] And while these latter two are Zuckerberg's personal commitments, as Facebook's CEO and a controlling shareholder, he has fiduciary duties of his own to think about.

Like the editorial analogy, analogizing these companies to fiduciaries or public trustees is prima facie plausible. Indeed, even more so than in the case of the editorial analogy, pretty much all of the relevant parties act (at least outside of litigation) as if something like this were the case today. If these companies were analogized to fiduciaries for purposes of First Amendment law, then as with lawyers and doctors, case law supports the regulation of their fiduciary-related choices, even assuming those choices are speech.

COMPANY TOWN OR PUBLIC FORUM

When considering the company town or limited public forum analogy, we should distinguish two distinct positions: (1) the social media sites themselves are like company towns or create limited public forums such that when the company bans or delists someone, there are First Amendment implications; and (2) government officials who communicate to the public through their pages on these privately owned platforms can violate users' First Amendment rights by banning the users or deleting their comments.

Up until recently, courts have rejected the first and been uncertain about the second.[159] As all lawyers know, for the First Amendment to apply, there must be state action. And rarely does a private actor's power rise to that level. But historical moments—and the nature of emerging threats—matter. As Eric Goldman observes, "We can't ignore that there is such skepticism towards internet companies' consolidation of power."[160] Goldman was focused on antitrust, but the point generalizes. If we combine this skepticism with the Court's broad language in *Packingham*, the once off-the-wall theory that these companies should count as state actors for First Amendment purposes is starting to look a bit more on the table. And indeed, both the language of *Packingham* and its public square analogy have made appearances in recent suits by users alleging that social media companies violated their First Amendment rights.[161] More than that, they have already appeared in court opinions concerning the same.[162] It seems possible that the Court has signaled a willingness to return to an earlier and more capacious reading of the state action doctrine.

The second question concerns whether government officials' pages on private social platforms can amount to limited public forums under the First Amendment. And while certain cases suggesting an affirmative answer predate *Packingham*,[163] *Packingham* has already been used to bolster that conclusion. Most obviously, the Knight First Amendment Institute itself has argued, citing *Packingham*, that Trump's @realDonaldTrump Twitter account is a designated public forum and that his banishment of seven Twitter users violates their First Amendment rights.[164]

As for the company town or limited public forum analogy, there are two strands of state action doctrine worth mentioning here. The first concerns public function and the second entanglement. And we can make out analogies to cases in both.

The classic public function case is *Marsh v. Alabama*,[165] which involved a company town. As happened not infrequently in the early 1900s, companies would build "towns" and then have their workers live and buy within them. Often, companies would use a claim of private property to prohibit certain individuals, particularly union organizers, from entering the town, bringing out the police in the event of any trespass.[166] In *Marsh*, it was not a union organizer but a Jehovah's Witness who was arrested for trespass while distributing religious literature on the company-owned sidewalk. The Court held that the company's actions constituted state action, because the entire company town had "all the characteristics of any other American town," save for the fact that it was privately owned.[167] The company executed a public function, and that meant it could be treated as a state actor for constitutional purposes.

So when it comes to Facebook, Google, and Twitter, what counts as a "public function"? As the history of the state action doctrine attests, the Court has changed its mind on this very issue. In *Amalgamated Food Employees Union Local 590 v. Logan Valley Plaza*, for instance, the Court held that so long as union picketers used a private shopping center in a manner and purpose "generally consonant" with the use the owners had intended, they could not be banned from it consistent with the First Amendment.[168] In the Court's view, the shopping center was "clearly the functionally equivalent of the business district . . . involved in *Marsh*."[169] And "because the shopping center serve[d] as the community business block and [was] freely accessible and open to the people in the area and those passing through, the State [could] not delegate the power, through the use of its trespass laws, wholly to exclude those members of the public wishing to exercise their First Amendment rights on the premises."[170] If *Logan Valley Plaza* were still good law, it would seem that the platforms run by Facebook, Google, and Twitter could easily be analogized to the plaza, and users and advertisers would have First Amendment claims against these private companies.

But *Logan Valley Plaza* was overruled in *Hudgens v. NLRB*.[171] There, the Court thought itself bound by its earlier decision in *Lloyd Corporation v. Tanner*,[172] which held that a shopping center did enough to make clear that it was not dedicated to public use, so that members of the public had no First Amendment right to distribute handbills protesting the Vietnam War. In *Hudgens*, the Court said it was its "institutional duty . . . to follow until changed the law as it now is" and thought the rationale in *Logan Valley Plaza* could not survive *Lloyd*.[173] *Hudgens* reread *Marsh* as standing for something narrower: namely, that private entities that are the functional equivalent of a municipality cannot, consistent with the First Amendment, wholly restrict the speech of others on their property.[174]

From these precedents, two questions naturally arise. First, and reasoning analogically, we can ask whether platforms such as those run by Facebook, Google, and Twitter are more like municipalities or more like shopping centers. Because I see these platforms as sufficiently different from both (and because I am skeptical of analogical reasoning in this space generally), this framing of the issue strikes me as unattractive. Alternatively, we might instead ask whether a majority of the current Court is open to finding a public forum well before a company has created the equivalent of an entire town. The language in *Packingham* supports an affirmative answer.

Again, in *Packingham* the Court "equate[d] the entirety of the internet with public streets and parks"[175] and declared it "clear [that] cyberspace . . . and social media in particular" are "the most important places (in a spatial sense) for the exchange of views."[176] It found social media "the modern public square"[177] and suggested it is "a fundamental principle of the First Amendment . . . that all persons have access" to it.[178] This might be read as analogizing social media to the company towns of the past. If these spaces are the "modern public square," they are clearly taking on important government functions.

One might reply—as these companies always do—that users are just a click away from going somewhere else. Two thoughts about this. First, this reply only highlights how open to the public these platforms are. And since *Hudgens*, when courts have tried to make sense of when private property becomes a public forum, they find relevant whether the site has been dedicated to public use.[179] If people can seamlessly move between social media sites, it may be easier to find these sites dedicated to public use. Like walking into a park or entering a shopping mall, it is true that you agree to follow some basic rules upon entry, but overall such barriers are low. The emphasis that leading social media companies placed on openness and non-bias in their recent congressional testimony[180] buttresses this point. Second, we know that such freedom of online movement would only exist if the costs of switching platforms were zero or close to it. But we (and they) know that this is not true, given network effects, switching costs, and first-mover advantages, among other things. Moreover, and as the more analogically inclined have put it, even if you do switch, it tends to be a move from one online feudal lord (such as Google) to another (such as Facebook).[181] Like moving from company town to company town, moving from one online feudal lord to another does not obviously diminish the sense in which either engages in the functional equivalent of state action.

A separate strand of cases within the "murky waters of the state action doctrine"[182] concerns government entanglement. This is considered the "category of exceptions that has produced—and continues to produce—the most confusion."[183] Given this, how the Court will evolve the doctrine going forward is anybody's guess. With that said, and putting aside cases concerning state action via judicial enforcement of private contractual agreements (*Shelley v. Kraemer* being the apex of this[184]), the Court has previously found state action when "the State so far insinuated itself into a position of interdependence with" a private non-state actor "that it must be recognized as a joint participant in the challenged activity."[185] Relatedly, in *Evans v. Newton* the Court said that "conduct that is formally 'private' may become so entwined with governmental policies or so impregnated with a governmental character as to become subject to the constitutional limitations placed upon state action."[186]

The government-like character of the leading tech companies has been acknowledged by the companies themselves. A decade ago, Zuckerberg opined, "In a lot of ways Facebook is more like a government than a traditional company. We have this large community of people, and more than other technology companies we're really setting policies."[187] But governments also hold substantial power over these companies, often in ways invisible to the public. Take government "requests" for data, without judicial oversight. It isn't hard to see what is technically a private decision by companies like Facebook (to hand over user data to the government) as so entwined with the government that finding state action would be reasonable. Or take the pervasive—and, in most of academia, deeply underappreciated—informal pressures that governments put on these platforms to regulate certain content: a technique sometimes called "jawboning."[188] The recent congressional hearings and various letters from congressional committees to these companies underscore how responsive the companies are to the concerns and recommendations of U.S. government officials, even where the government's legal authority to demand such responsiveness is unclear. If members of the public were more aware of all the ways that the U.S. government works with and makes "requests" of these companies, I suspect findings of state action would be more forthcoming.[189]

THE TAKEAWAY

As with the editorial analogy, other proposed analogies highlight certain facts while obscuring others. Yet all these analogies have prima facie purchase. When it comes to programs that organize, rank, and transmit third-party communication to users, some of what they do is similar, in some respects, to some of what publishers or editors do; some of what they do is similar, in some respects, to what fiduciaries do; and some of their functions are similar, in some respects, to what shopping malls and law schools do; and some of what they do makes them look analogous to public squares or to state actors. The question that everything hinges on is this: which similarities and dissimilarities are the ones that matter from the point of view of free speech principles?

In the First Amendment context, to invoke the compelled speech doctrine and cite *Tornillo* as the relevant precedent, based on the mere fact that both search engines and newspapers rank and organize content, is to beg this question instead of properly addressing it. In asking which similarities and dissimilarities matter from the perspective of free speech principles, we are posing a question the answer to which cannot but reside in normative considerations. Analogical methods that respond to questions of free speech coverage by noting similarities between different types of communication, without examining these underlying normative concerns, are at best limited and at worst misleading. The limits of analogical reasoning help explain why some find the concept of "similarity" nearly useless.[190] Indeed, the very use of analogical reasoning in law remains contested, with some finding it to be the "cornerstone of common law reasoning" while others see it as "mere window-dressing, without normative force."[191] As I have suggested elsewhere, if analogical reasoning is to be useful at all, we may need to distinguish between types of analogy and recognize the limited value of each.[192]

The above point is focused on the threshold question of First Amendment coverage. There also remains an enormous amount of uncertainty concerning how these different framings, if adopted, would play out in practice. Take the fiduciary analogy. Determining to whom these companies would owe fiduciary obligations is far less clear than some acknowledge. Even among domestic users, interests will conflict, as we see in debates about these companies' policies concerning hate speech and on university campuses when the need for open debate runs up against the need for safe spaces. Similarly, while finding these companies to be analogous to public squares or company towns might be straightforward in some respects, it is worth noting that neither government officials nor a majority of users seem to *want* these companies to be confined by the First Amendment.[193] Returning to hate speech, it remains protected under the First Amendment, yet there has been a steady stream of controversies surrounding the failure of these platforms to remove hate speech and the users who engage in it. Users expect a level of content moderation that would likely be unachievable by a platform constrained by the First Amendment.[194] Even more than this, applying the First Amendment would likely mean that each of these companies' community standard guidelines are unconstitutional. If the state can't eject you from the public square for saying something, these companies wouldn't be able to do so either.

If the First Amendment rights of users were deployed to overturn content moderation as we know it, I suspect these platforms would witness a mass exodus. If I may analogize a bit myself, there is something to be said for the Nintendo way, where systems are more closed and curated. Such systems often end up creating more value for users (and persisting longer) than alternatives like Sega or MySpace, which try to be too many things to too many people at once, with minimal quality control.[195] If the First Amendment really did apply to today's tech giants, it's not clear to me that they could avoid the latter's fate.

NORMATIVE BEGINNINGS

Instead of focusing on plausible analogies, we need to think through the normative theories undergirding the free speech principle and which of them, singular or plural, we want to privilege when making First Amendment coverage determinations.[196] Here I will only mention two major contenders—democratic participation theory and thinker-based theory—and leave it to readers to decide whether these theories or others are what ought to be privileged at this historical moment.

Democratic ideals are invoked by many influential First Amendment scholars to explain and defend U.S. free speech doctrine.[197] Building on this tradition, the democratic participation theory of free speech says that speech must be protected in order to ensure "the opportunity for individuals to participate in the speech by which we govern ourselves."[198] How do we decide what counts as "speech" using democratic participation as our normative reference point? We cannot construe the ideal too broadly, such that all parts of social life are part of the project of self-government, for in encompassing everything, the ideal would prioritize nothing. Instead, the ideal of democratic participation requires us to conceptually divide society into two domains: public life, where we act as citizens cooperating in collective self-governance, and private life, where we act independently in the service of our own projects. For free speech principles grounded in democratic participation, "speech" denotes whatever forms of communication are integral to collective self-governance. Of course, there will be complications at the margins, but the basic implications of the democratic participation theory are discernible all the same. Free speech principles are not meant to immunize all communication against legitimate regulatory aims. They are meant to support the project of collective self-government by safeguarding the communicative conduct that is essential to that project's realization.

With those clarifications in place, the pertinent question for our purposes is which sorts of ostensible "speech"—be it algorithmic outputs in the form of rankings, listing decisions, trending topics, and so on—help the project of democratic self-government and which do not? At this moment, we can certainly appreciate how troll armies, fake accounts, and bots can be anathema to these projects. The economic decisions that companies like Google make in determining which ads to run or whether to privilege their own products against rivals like Yelp and TripAdvisor are, as I said, commercial and need not be seen as worth protecting as "speech" for the sake of democratic self-governance, at least across the board.[199] That's not to say that these decisions should necessarily be regulated but instead to show why, under democratic participation theory, they could be, without running afoul of the First Amendment.

The "thinker-based" theory, recently developed by Seana Shiffrin, identifies "the individual agent's interest in the protection of the free development and operation of her mind" as the normative keystone of free speech.[200] Whereas other theories situate the value of the thinker in relation to extrinsic ideals or desiderata, this theory identifies a direct and noncontingent link between the value of mental autonomy and the justification for the protected status of communicative conduct. Again, however, not all communication is privileged under such a theory. If we prioritize the "fundamental function of allowing an agent to transmit . . . the contents of her mind to others and to externalize her mental content,"[201] then we will need to have special protections for people sharing all of this "content" with others. This is part of what makes Shiffrin's theory distinctive: the expression of thoughts about politics and government does not occupy an exalted position relative to the expression of thoughts about everyday life. But crucially, what is especially protected in this theory is not communication as such but the communication of the thought of individuals. And this will tend to assign a less privileged status to much commercial communication. So when we revisit our key questions—whether programs that synthesize, organize, rank, and transmit third-party communication to users are implicated in "the fundamental function of allowing an agent to transmit the contents of her mind to others"—the diagnosis is mixed, as in the previous case.

One interesting consequence of the thinker-based theory is that, unlike the democratic participation theory, it suggests that facilitation of everyday online chatter by search engines and social networks may be as much a part of the case for protecting (some of) their operations as their role in facilitating political discourse. But as with the democratic participation theory, much of what these programs do—including running ads and allowing for the creation of bot armies and the spread of fake and inflammatory news—will likely fall outside the scope of free speech coverage by the lights of this normative approach.

CONCLUDING THOUGHTS

In debates over tech companies and free speech coverage, neither the gravity of the policy stakes nor the complexity of the things being compared has dampened the willingness of courts and scholars to use tenuous analogies in charting the way forward. Most everybody seems to agree that search engines and social media platforms should be covered by principles of a free press, if and to the extent that the reasons underlying our protection of the press apply to them. But the point of this essay is that casual analogical methods—observing that both types of things "convey a wide range of information" or "rank and organize content"—do not tell us whether or to what extent they do. There are multiple plausible analogies that might be used, each with different First Amendment implications, and none tells us whether the normative considerations underlying free speech coverage for the one apply to the other. But if those normative considerations are inapplicable, the reason to extend coverage disappears.

Of Course the First Amendment Protects Google and Facebook (and It's Not a Close Question)

Eric Goldman

INTERNET GIANTS like Google and Facebook have accumulated unprecedented scale and power, and this has spurred many academic papers strategizing ways to regulatorily "fix" them. Heather Whitney's essay in this volume fits in that genre. The essay questions whether Google and Facebook are best analogized to traditional publishers like newspapers. If the analogy does not fit, the essay suggests, Google and Facebook may not qualify for full, or perhaps any, First Amendment protection. After undermining the "editorial analogy," the essay suggests several potential alternative analogies that might let regulators "fix" Google and Facebook.

I offer two responses to Whitney's essay. First, the essay's parsing of analogies doesn't resolve the constitutional questions, because it is so clear that Google's and Facebook's activities qualify for First Amendment protection that no analogies are required. Second, the essay seeks to enable regulation that would be a net loss for all of us.

GOOGLE AND FACEBOOK ENGAGE IN SPEECH AND PRESS ACTIVITIES (NO ANALOGY REQUIRED)

Whitney's essay never precisely defines the "editorial analogy" that it deconstructs. This passage from the essay provides one of several examples of the analogy: "Facebook is analogous to a newspaper and . . . its handling of a feature like Trending Topics is analogous to a newspaper's editorial choices." This analogy, if apt, should mean that Facebook (and Google) qualify for First Amendment protection just like newspapers do. Whitney's essay questions this argument in several ways, including by distinguishing Google's and Facebook's practices from those of newspapers.

However, Google and Facebook qualify for First Amendment protection without needing to rely on the editorial analogy or any other analogy. The First Amendment expressly protects "freedom of speech [and] of the press," and Google and Facebook clearly engage in both speech and press activities when they republish third-party content.

The First Amendment's references to "speech" and "press" have many definitions, but the essay focuses on editorial activities, so that deserves a closer look. *Zeran v. America Online, Inc.*[202] provides an exemplary definition. The *Zeran* court said that "a publisher's traditional editorial functions" include "deciding whether to publish, withdraw, postpone or alter content."[203] That's exactly what Google's search engine and Facebook's newsfeed do.

First, both Google's search engine and Facebook's newsfeed decide what third-party content to publish. They implement their publication decisions using automated screens to filter out third-party content that their human editors have deemed unsuitable. Google and Facebook sort and prioritize the remaining third-party content using complex algorithms reflecting human-established editorial decisions, and then they publish the content to their readers.

Second, Google's search engine and Facebook's newsfeed frequently withdraw previously published third-party content using a combination of automated removal tools and human decisions.

Even though some of these operations are automated, both Google and Facebook rely on humans to make all publication and withdrawal editorial decisions. For example, Google refines its search results using the feedback of "search quality evaluators" who apply 160 pages of editorial guidelines.[204] Furthermore, Google employees withdraw content from its search database through manual bans or downgrades (such as what happened in the e-ventures case discussed in Whitney's essay). Facebook relies on over 10,000 "safety and security" human editors to apply extensive and very detailed editorial guidelines to decide whether to keep publishing or withdraw third-party content.[205] And as Whitney's essay documents, Facebook has a robust editorial procedure for its Trending Topics feature.

Thus, we don't need to compare Google and Facebook to newspapers, grocery stores, malls, parade organizers, law school career fairs, doctors, or anything else to conclude that the publication and withdrawal of third-party content constitute traditional editorial functions. We can resolve the constitutional question via the plain meaning of the Constitution's words.

That makes it irrelevant how many times Google and Facebook have publicly disclaimed editorial control over their databases of third-party content. Google and Facebook also routinely say the opposite (which the essay doesn't recount), and their inconsistent statements reflect the disparate audiences for their messages.

IF WHITNEY IS RIGHT, WHERE'S THE WIN?

Let's assume that the essay's analysis is right and that, having rejected the editorial analogy, courts decide that Google and Facebook should receive only limited or no First Amendment protection. The essay does not really explore the regulatory implications of this possibility. One of two alternative scenarios would likely occur.

One scenario is that Google and Facebook would be classified as "neutral conduits." In that case, they would lack discretion to moderate content, so they would have to carry all content, including content from spammers, fraudsters, bots, foreign election manipulators, and so on.

To avoid this unfavorable legal characterization, Google and Facebook might revamp their services to qualify for First Amendment treatment. However, if revamping requires human pre-review of all content and the acceptance of full liability for all published content, many of their existing services would not be tenable. (Imagine Facebook where human editors must review and approve all user status updates before publication, or Google where human editors must review and approve every search listing before incorporating it into the search database.) Otherwise, if they try to function as neutral conduits, Google and Facebook quickly would be overwhelmed by harmful and useless content, and that surely would spur the "mass exodus" of users mentioned by the essay.

An alternative scenario is that regulators would have virtually unlimited discretion to tell Google and Facebook how to run their services. Remember, if the First Amendment does not apply, regulators can impose obligations on Google and Facebook that are motivated by anti-speech, anti-technology, or even authoritarian objectives. The cumulative effect of these newly imposed regulations would likely make Google and Facebook functionally unusable, which would also lead to a "mass exodus" of users.

Thus, without First Amendment protection, it seems to me that the two most likely scenarios both result in the functional destruction of Google and Facebook. I know some might cheer that outcome, but I would not. Google, Facebook, and other user-generated-content services have created enormous social value that enriches our lives many times an hour. Allowing regulators to destroy that value is something we should aggressively resist.

CONCLUSION

I understand the widespread suspicion and fear of the power held by internet giants like Google and Facebook. I too am skeptical of any institution that has so much power. Plus, Google and Facebook have made many unforced gaffes and errors that erode our trust.

However, these are not good reasons to clip the First Amendment's wings. The rights to free speech and press are cherished civil liberties, and they have been essential components of our republic's centuries-long successes. Whatever issues we have with Google and Facebook, the robust application of the First Amendment is almost certainly part of the solution. Whether it is based on the editorial analogy, the plain language of the Constitution, or some other ground, the courts have recognized that fundamental point, and I hope legislators will too.

The Problem Isn't the Use of Analogies but the Analogies Courts Use

Genevieve Lakier

THE SEARCH ENGINE is one of the most important technologies of the twenty-first century. Just as was true of the television, the motion picture, and the radio before it, the widespread dissemination of this new technology is reshaping the speech environment in which we operate in profound and often unexpected ways. Search engines raise, as a result, a whole host of novel constitutional as well as regulatory questions.[206] Yet, as Heather Whitney's interesting and incisive essay demonstrates, courts confronted with free speech challenges to laws that regulate search engines tend to analyze them by means of an often-unpersuasive analogy to older technologies, chief among them the newspaper. This is a problem because it makes complex issues seem unduly simple.

Take, for example, one of the more influential of the cases Whitney discusses in her essay, *Zhang v. Baidu.com, Inc.*[207] As Whitney notes, the plaintiffs in that case sued the Chinese internet company Baidu after it prevented their pro-democracy websites, and other websites that provided information about the democracy movement in China, from appearing in the results of the very popular search engine it operated.[208] The plaintiffs claimed that Baidu censored the search results at the behest of the Chinese government, which did not want its citizens exposed to democratic ideas, and that Baidu's actions violated their federal and state civil rights.[209] The district court dismissed the complaint because it found Baidu's decision not to include the plaintiffs' websites in its search engine results to involve the same kind of editorial discretion as the decision by a newspaper editor not to publish an article in the newspaper.[210] Because the First Amendment clearly immunizes the latter decision against the kind of civil rights claims the plaintiffs asserted, the court concluded that it immunizes Baidu's decision as well.

The *Baidu* court strongly suggested that the conclusion it reached was inevitable—and obvious—given existing precedents. It noted, for example, that "to allow [the] suit to proceed would plainly violate the fundamental rule of protection under the First Amendment, that a speaker has the autonomy to choose the content of his own message."[211] And the court suggested that although the constitutional analysis might be different in a case in which the search engine was not alleged to have exercised "editorial control over its search results," the First Amendment "plainly shields Baidu from Plaintiffs' claims."[212] Two "plainlies" in one paragraph! How much more straightforward can you get?

In fact, there is reason to doubt that the First Amendment issues raised by the case were as plain and simple as the district court suggested. For one thing, if Baidu truly was acting at the behest of the Chinese government—as the plaintiffs alleged in their complaint—was it actually exercising its *own* expressive autonomy when it removed their websites from its search engine results? Or was it instead acting as an agent of the censorial Chinese state?[213] The answer to this question surely matters—or should matter—to the First Amendment analysis.

Even if one assumes that Baidu acted on its own volition when it removed the plaintiffs' websites from its search results, it is far from clear that requiring it to list the plaintiffs' websites in its search results would create the same kinds of expressive harms as would requiring a newspaper to print articles it did not choose. This is because of the important differences in the relationship between search engines and the websites they find, on the one hand, and newspapers and the articles or advertisements they print, on the other. Newspapers are legally responsible for the defamatory or otherwise unlawful content of the articles and advertisements they publish, but search engines are not.[214] Newspapers also tend to be associated in readers' minds with the ideological and aesthetic viewpoint of the articles or advertisements that fill their pages. This is not true of search engines and the websites they link to. How could it be? The list of websites produced by a single search will often express a cacophony of competing views; it would be very difficult, as a result, to glean from the actions of the search engine a discernible perspective. From both a legal and a cultural standpoint, then, the websites that populate search engine results are not understood to express the viewpoint of the search engine that finds them. And this, in turn, suggests that preventing search engines from removing websites from search results would not undermine the search engines' ability to "control the content of [their] message."[215] It would not create, in other words, the kinds of harms the Court was worried about when it struck down the right-of-reply statute in *Miami Herald Publishing Co. v. Tornillo*.[216]

Whitney is entirely correct, therefore, that even if there are important similarities between newspapers and search engines, there are important dissimilarities that complicate the straightforward analogy the district court relied on in *Baidu*. These dissimilarities call into question whether precedents like *Tornillo* compel the conclusion that the court reached in *Baidu* and that other courts have reached as well: namely, that, because of its concern with the expressive autonomy of editorial speakers, "the First Amendment fully immunizes search-engine results from most, if not all, kinds of civil liability and government regulation."[217]

I am less convinced by the conclusion that Whitney reaches from the problematic analogical reasoning employed in cases like *Baidu*: namely, that courts should whenever possible "address First Amendment coverage questions through the lens of normative theory and not through a cacophony of ill-suited analogies." Analogical reasoning plays an incredibly important role in our law, including in the law of the First Amendment.[218] Given the centrality of analogical argument to legal practice, it is hard to believe that judges *would* take up Whitney's suggestion to chuck the analogies and restrict themselves instead to a more straightforward normative analysis of the constitutional and other interests at stake in these cases. Nor, I think, *should* they. The interests that the First Amendment is said to advance — Whitney identifies two (democracy and thinker autonomy), but there are others one could name (the search for truth, for example) — tend to be articulated at an extremely high level of generality. Their application in concrete situations will, as a result, almost always be up for debate. Analogical reasoning helps constrain judicial discretion on these matters and thereby brings some degree of consistency and predictability to the law.[219] It also allows judges who cannot agree on what interests the First Amendment advances to reach agreement in particular cases.[220] And, by concretizing the abstract, it helps illuminate complexities that a court more focused on abstractions might miss.[221] Perhaps most importantly, analogies encourage the creation of generalizable rules: rules that extend beyond a particular fact pattern or kind of speech act. They therefore make it more difficult for courts to treat speakers differently based on a political or cultural or idiosyncratic judgment of the value of their speech. Certainly this is the role that analogies have historically played in free speech law.[222]

There are thus both First Amendment–specific and more general legal process reasons to believe analogies play a useful, and not just a familiar, role in judicial decision-making. This is not to say that analogies cannot go wrong. Nor is it to contest the fact that, as Whitney points out, analogical reasoning is fundamentally incomplete. It is absolutely true that, to know whether two things are similar or dissimilar, one must have a view of the relevant criteria against which similarity is to be measured. But what the incompleteness of analogical reasoning means is *not* that analogies cannot provide a useful aid to judicial analysis; what it means, instead, is that analogies will prove useful only to the extent they are used thoughtfully, to illuminate the similarities and dissimilarities that matter for the purposes of the law.

The problem with the decision in *Baidu* need not be seen, therefore, as a consequence of the court's reliance on analogical reasoning per se. It is better understood as a consequence of the court's reliance on an overly formal analogy between newspapers and search engines, one that fails to take into account the very different functions that newspapers and search engines play in the contemporary public sphere. It may be true that both newspapers and search engines rank and order information that they then provide to the public—that they perform in this sense an editorial function. But they do so for very different purposes. Newspapers articulate views, and provide information, that contribute to the "uninhibited, robust, and wide-open . . . debate on public issues" that the First Amendment protects against government control.[223] Search engines, in contrast, allow users to navigate among different sources of information and perspective.

This suggests that the most illuminating analogy for purposes of constitutional analysis is not to the newspaper but instead to the cable provider or, less directly perhaps, the telephone company—to other technologies that provide users access to views and information that those technologies neither author nor control. It is somewhat surprising that Whitney does not mention the cable-provider analogy as a possible alternative to the newspaper analogy she criticizes, since Oren Bracha and Frank Pasquale first suggested it over ten years ago in an article that the district court discussed in *Baidu*.[224] And it is a very good analogy in many respects: like cable companies, search engines provide access to the speech of others; like cable companies, search engines exercise some degree of editorial discretion over whom they provide access to.[225] They both speak and act as a conduit of speech, in other words.

The analogy is, like all analogies, not a perfect one. Because cable providers have to create at least part of the physical infrastructure of their cable system before they can operate, barriers to entry in the cable market may be significant.[226] The same is not true of search engines. For these companies, the only significant barrier to entry is the development of a search algorithm (and perhaps also access to sufficient marketing dollars to attract consumers away from competitor search engines). The consequence is that cable companies may possess a kind of monopoly power that search engines do not.[227]

The power of the analogy nevertheless arises from the fact that it takes into account not only the formal features of search engines' speech but also the functional role they play in the public sphere. In so doing, it makes clearer why it is we might worry about an interpretation of the First Amendment that immunizes search engines from most kinds of regulation—and why we might worry, in particular, about a constitutional rule that prevents the government from being able to prohibit the kind of content-based discrimination at issue in *Baidu*. Such a rule is problematic because, just like cable operators, search engines have tremendous influence over "a critical pathway of communication"—influence that they can use to "to restrict . . . the free flow of information and ideas" when it suits their interests to do so.[228] Rather than a vindication of free speech values, in other words, what the analogy to the cable operator suggests is that the outcome in *Baidu* and similar cases poses a threat to freedom of speech. What it also suggests, as a result, is an alternative approach to the constitutional review of search engine expression: one that vests the government with significant, albeit by no means unlimited, power to regulate when doing so serves important (in this case, speech-promoting) ends.[229] This is all to the good, I think, given the power that search engines possess in our contemporary media landscape.

Ultimately, therefore, I disagree with Whitney's primary normative conclusion. I remain convinced that analogies play a vital role in free speech law because they force courts to toggle back and forth between the concrete and the abstract and thereby make possible a better understanding of both new legal questions and the normative principles we use to resolve them. I also think the most powerful response to the shortcomings of cases like *Baidu* is not to chuck the analogies but instead to suggest why another analogy works better.

Whitney's essay nevertheless performs a valuable function by suggesting how difficult the process of analogical reasoning can be. It also makes clear—in a way I find heartening—that there remains considerable opportunity for courts to think more deeply about what analogies best make sense of the multiple interests at stake when the government regulates the power of search, and about the constitutional rules that consequently apply.

Preventing a Posthuman Law of Freedom of Expression

Frank Pasquale

LARGE INTERNET PLATFORMS' pleas for First Amendment protection have vexed policy-makers and scholars for over a decade. I am presently trying to reconcile the type of intermediary responsibility I call for in recent work with my earlier characterization of platforms as common carriers.[230] These platforms assume a variety of distinctive roles and responsibilities that arise situationally. Sometimes a platform takes on real editorial responsibility.[231] In other scenarios, it is unable or unwilling to exercise control over users, and regulators are unwilling or unable to formulate rules requiring it to act.

Heather Whitney's essay challenges these distinctions by highlighting how media organizations and intermediaries that were the subjects of leading First Amendment precedents are unlike contemporary platforms. Whitney's subtle intervention carefully parses the role and purpose of media outlets, fiduciaries, and other entities with a longer history of regulation than platforms. It should be a vital corrective to the anachronistic metaphors that bog down First Amendment discourse to this day.

The question now is how to craft free expression doctrine capable of addressing platforms that are far more centralized, pervasive, and powerful than the vast majority of entities that pressed free expression claims before 2000.[232] That is a project worthy of a treatment as expansive as Thomas Emerson's classic *The System of Freedom of Expression*.[233] In this brief commentary, I merely hope to advance a perspective congruent with Whitney's turn to Seana Shiffrin's "thinker-based" theory of free expression. I believe that free speech protections are primarily for people, and only secondarily (if at all) for software, algorithms, artificial intelligence, and platforms.[234]

"Free speech for people" is a particularly pressing goal given ongoing investigations into manipulation of public spheres around the world. American voters still do not know to what extent foreign governments, non-state actors, and bots manipulated social media during the presidential election of 2016. The Federal Election Commission failed to require disclosure of the source of much political advertising on Facebook and Twitter. Explosive reports now suggest that the goal of the Russian buyers of many ads "was to amplify political discord in the U.S. and fuel an atmosphere of divisiveness and chaos."[235] Social media firms are cooperating with investigators now. But they will likely fight proactive regulation by arguing that their algorithmic feeds are speech. They have already deleted critical information.[236]

Courts are divided on whether algorithmic generation of search results and newsfeeds merits full First Amendment protection.[237] As Tim Wu has observed, "Computers make trillions of invisible decisions each day; the possibility that each decision could be protected speech should give us pause."[238] He and other scholars have argued forcefully for limiting constitutional protection of "machine speech." By contrast, Stuart Benjamin has predicted that courts will expand the coverage of First Amendment protection to artificial intelligence (AI), including algorithmic data processing.[239]

Given the growing concern about the extraordinary power of secret algorithmic manipulation to target influential messaging to persons with little to no appreciation of its ultimate source, courts should not privilege algorithmic data processing in these scenarios as speech. As James Grimmelmann has warned with respect to "robotic copyright," First Amendment protection for the products of AI could systematically favor machine over human speech.[240] This is particularly dangerous as bots begin mimicking actual human actors. Henry Farrell paints a vivid picture:

> The world that the Internet and social media have created is less a system than an ecology, a proliferation of unexpected niches, and entities created and adapted to exploit them in deceptive ways. Vast commercial architectures are being colonized by quasi-autonomous parasites. . . . Such fractured worlds are more vulnerable to invasion by the non-human. . . . Twitterbots vary in sophistication from automated accounts that do no more than retweet what other bots have said, to sophisticated algorithms deploying so-called "Sybil attacks," creating fake identities in peer-to-peer networks to invade specific organizations or degrade particular kinds of conversation.[241]

There is also a growing body of empirical research on the troubling effects of an automated public sphere.[242] In too many scenarios, bot interventions are less speech than anti-speech, calculated efforts to disrupt democratic will formation and fool the unwary.

To restore public confidence in democratic deliberation, Congress should require rapid disclosure of the data used to generate algorithmic speech, the algorithms employed, and the targeting of that speech. American legislation akin to the "right to explanation" in the European Union's General Data Protection Regulation would not infringe on, but would rather support, First Amendment values. Affected firms may assert that their algorithms are too complex to disclose.[243] If so, Congress should have the power to ban the targeting and arrangement of information at issue, because the speech protected by the Constitution must bear some recognizable relation to human cognition.

Authorities should also consider banning certain types of manipulation. The UK Code of Broadcast Advertising states that "audiovisual commercial communications shall not use subliminal techniques."[244] In a less esoteric mode, there is a long line of U.S. Federal Trade Commission (FTC) guidance forbidding misleading advertisements and false or missing indication of sponsorship. Given the FTC's manifold limitations, U.S. states will also need to develop more specific laws to govern an increasingly automated public sphere. California Senator Robert Hertzberg recently introduced the so-called Blade Runner Bill, which "would require digital bots, often credited with spreading misinformation, to be identified on social media sites."[245] Another proposed bill would "would prohibit an operator of a social media Internet Web site from engaging in the sale of advertising with a computer software account or user that performs an automated task, and that is not verified by the operator as being controlled by a natural person."[246] I applaud such interventions as concrete efforts to assure that critical forums for human communication and interaction are not overwhelmed by a post-human swarm of spam, propaganda, and distraction.[247]

As theorists develop a philosophy of free expression for the twenty-first century, they might take the principles underlying interventions like the Blade Runner Bill as fixed points of considered convictions to guide a reflective equilibrium on the proper balance between the rights of speakers and listeners, individuals and community, technology users, and those subject to technology's effects.[248] Even if free expression protections extend to algorithmic targeting and bot expression, disclosure rules are both essential and constitutionally sound.[249] Courts should avoid intervening to protect "speech" premised on elaborate and secretive human-subject research on internet users. The future of human expression depends on strict rules limiting the power and scope of technological substitutes for real thinkers and real thoughts.

NOTES

SEARCH ENGINES, SOCIAL MEDIA, AND THE EDITORIAL ANALOGY

For helpful feedback, my sincerest thanks to Adam Shmarya Lovett, Chris Franco, Daniel Viehoff, David Pozen, Eric Goldman, Jameel Jaffer, Jane Friedman, Katie Fallow, Neil Martin, Robert Hopkins, and Robert Mark Simpson. Additional thanks to David Pozen, who also served as editor for this essay, and to Knight Institute interns Joseph Catalanotto and Sam Matthews for editorial assistance.

1. Ursula K. Le Guin, speech in acceptance of the National Book Foundation Medal for Distinguished Contribution to American Letters (Nov. 19, 2014), available at http://www.theguardian.com/books/2014/nov/20/ursula-k-le-guin -national-book-awards-speech.

2. Letter from Sen. John Thune to Mark Zuckerberg 2–3 (May 10, 2016), http:// www.commerce.senate.gov/public/_cache/files/fe5b7b75-8d53-44c3-8a20 -6b2c12b0970d/C5CF587E2778E073A80A79E2A6F73705.fb-letter.pdf [hereinafter Thune Letter].

3. Craig Timberg et al., *Fiery Exchanges on Capitol Hill as Lawmakers Scold Facebook, Google and Twitter*, Wash. Post (Nov. 1, 2017), http://www.washingtonpost .com/news/the-switch/wp/2017/11/01/fiery-exchanges-on-capitol-hill-as-lawmakers -scold-facebook-google-and-twitter (emphasis added).

4. *See* Mark Bergen et al., *Google, Facebook, Twitter Scramble to Hold Washington at Bay*, Bloomberg (Oct. 10, 2017), http://www.bloomberg.com/news/articles /2017-10-10/google-facebook-and-twitter-scramble-to-hold-washington-at-bay; Ben Brody & Bill Allison, *Lobbying Group for Facebook and Google to Pitch Self-Regulation of Ads*, Bloomberg (Oct. 23, 2017), http://www.bloomberg.com/news /articles/2017-10-24/lobby-group-for-facebook-google-to-pitch-self-regulation-of -ads; Sarah Frier & Bill Allison, *Facebook Fought Rules That Could Have Exposed Fake Russian Ads*, Bloomberg (Oct. 4, 2017), http://www.bloomberg.com/news /articles/2017-10-04/facebook-fought-for-years-to-avoid-political-ad-disclosure-rules.

5. Timberg et al., *supra* note 3. In addition, "[i]n a rare act of unanimity, all current FEC commissioners voted [in October 2017] to reopen public comments" on the Federal Election Commission's rule exempting Facebook from its political advertising disclosure regulations. Frier & Allison, *supra* note 4. Since 2011, Facebook has asked for exemptions, arguing that "political ad disclosures could hinder free speech" and that the FEC "should not stand in the way of innovation." *Id.*

6. Erin Griffith, *The Other Tech Bubble*, Wired (Dec. 16, 2017), http://www.wired .com/story/the-other-tech-bubble.

7. Growing disenchantment with Bay Area tech companies is certainly not limited to concerns about fake news and foreign propaganda. From their association with massive economic inequality and neighborhood gentrification, to purported attempts at union-busting at Tesla, to sexual harassment and other forms of discrimination both within these companies and facilitated through their platforms, to the recent uproar over Apple's iPhone-slowdown "misunderstanding," the last few years have done much to erode the utopian view some once held of Silicon Valley. *See, e.g.,* Brady Dale, *The Economic Justice Fight Inside Silicon Valley's Commuter Buses,* Observer (Apr. 6, 2017), http://observer.com/2017/04/teamsters-facebook-google-linkedin; Megan Rose Dickey, *In Light of Discrimination Concerns, Uber and Lyft Defend Their Policies to Show Rider Names and Photos,* TechCrunch (Dec. 29, 2016), http://techcrunch.com/2016/12/29/uber-lyft-respond-al-franken-about-discrimination; Zac Estrada, *Tesla Hit with Labor Complaint on Behalf of Fired Factory Workers,* Verge (Oct. 26, 2017), http://www.theverge.com/2017/10/26/16553554/tesla-labor-complaint-fired-factory-workers-elon-musk; Jordan McMahon, *Apple Had Way Better Options than Slowing Down Your iPhone,* Wired (Dec. 21, 2017), http://www.wired.com/story/apple-iphone-battery-slow-down; Alexandra Simon-Lewis, *What Is Silicon Valley's Problem with Women?,* Wired (June 12, 2017), http://www.wired.co.uk/article/tesla-sexism-lawsuit-harassment-uber.

8. *See* Hope King, *Is Facebook Protected Under the First Amendment?,* CNN (May 12, 2016), http://money.cnn.com/2016/05/12/media/facebook-first-amendment; Hope King & Brian Stelter, *Senate Demands Answers from Facebook,* CNN (May 10, 2016), http://money.cnn.com/2016/05/10/technology/facebook-news-senate; Jeff John Roberts, *Like It or Not, Facebook Has the Right to Choose Your News,* Fortune (May 10, 2016), http://fortune.com/2016/05/10/facebook-first-amendment.

9. *See, e.g.,* Julia Angwin, *Making Algorithms Accountable,* ProPublica (Aug. 1, 2016), http://www.propublica.org/article/making-algorithms-accountable (reviewing mounting concerns over algorithmic secrecy and "bias"); Katharine T. Bartlett & Mitu Gulati, *Discrimination by Customers,* 102 Iowa L. Rev. 223 (2016) (discussing regulation of online discrimination of customers); Nancy Leong & Aaron Belzer, *The New Public Accommodations: Race Discrimination in the Platform Economy,* 105 Geo. L.J. 1271 (2017) (arguing that existing public accommodation laws should evolve to regulate businesses in the online platform economy); *cf.* Heather M. Whitney, *The Regulation of Discrimination by Individuals in the Market,* 2017 U. Chi. Legal F. 537 (2017) (laying the groundwork for thinking through whether, descriptively and normatively, consumers have a right to discriminate online and online companies a right to help them); Heather M. Whitney, *Markets, Rights, and Discrimination by Customers,* 102 Iowa L. Rev. Online 346 (2017) (responding to Bartlett & Gulati).

10. *See generally* Frederick Schauer, *Free Speech: A Philosophical Enquiry* (1982) (describing the question of which classes of communicative acts warrant free speech protection as the question of coverage).

11. 137 S. Ct. 1730 (2017).

12. *Id.* at 1738 (Alito, J., concurring in judgment).

13. *Id.* at 1735.

14. *Id.* at 1737.
15. *Id.* at 1735.
16. 10 F. Supp. 3d 433 (S.D.N.Y. 2014).
17. *Id.* at 435.
18. *Id.* at 436.
19. *Id.* at 436–43 (citing *Tornillo*, 418 U.S. 241 (1974)).
20. *Tornillo*, 418 U.S. at 258.
21. *Baidu*, 10 F. Supp. 3d at 437–442 (citing *Hurley*, 515 U.S. 557 (1995)).
22. For an interesting criticism of the *Hurley* Court's analysis, see John Gardner, Case Note, Hurley and South Boston Allied War Veterans Council v. Irish American Gay, Lesbian, and Bi-Sexual Group of Boston, *115 S. Ct. 2338*, 1 Int'l J. Discrimination & L. 283 (1996).
23. *Baidu*, 10 F. Supp. 3d at 438.
24. No. 2:14-cv-646-FtM-PAM-CM, 2017 WL 2210029 (M.D. Fla. Feb. 8, 2017).
25. Note the oddity here. Search engine companies don't like SEO firms because they don't like how those firms boost their clients' sites in the search engine's own rankings. This fact—that search engine companies cannot fully control their own results—makes it harder to then call those rankings the company's speech.
26. *See* Alexia Tsotsis, *Google's Algorithmic Cat and Mouse Game [Infographic]*, TechCrunch (Mar. 23, 2011), http://techcrunch.com/2011/03/23/googles-algorithmic-cat-and-mouse-game-infographic (illustrating this game).
27. *e-ventures Worldwide, LLC v. Google, Inc.*, 188 F. Supp. 3d 1265, 1271 (M.D. Fla. 2016).
28. *Id.*
29. *Id.* at 1270–71. You might notice that this latter argument is similar in spirit to the one made by Senate Commerce Committee Chairman John Thune when writing Zuckerberg about Facebook's allegedly liberal-biased Trending Topics. *See* Thune Letter, *supra* note 2, at 1–2 ("If Facebook presents its Trending Topics section as the result of a neutral, objective algorithm, but it is in fact subjective and filtered to support or suppress particular political viewpoints, Facebook's assertion that it maintains a 'platform for people and perspectives from across the political spectrum' misleads the public." (quoting Josh Constine & Sarah Buhr, *Facebook Now Directly Denies Report of Biased Trends, Says There's No Evidence*, TechCrunch (May 9, 2016), http://techcrunch.com/2016/05/09/facebook-workers)). A similar move has been made against Yelp. Companies have alleged that Yelp deleted their positive reviews, leaving only the negatives, and then blackmailed them into paying for ads. Given that Yelp portrays itself as a neutral platform that accurately reflects the reviews of users (indeed, that's why people use it), this would also seem like a clear case of false advertising if the allegations are true. But sometimes courts, misapplying Section 230 of the Communications Decency Act, have failed to see this. *See, e.g., Levitt v. Yelp! Inc.*, 2011 WL 5079526 (N.D. Cal. Oct. 26, 2011). Thankfully, however, not all courts have made this mistake. *See Demetriades v. Yelp, Inc.*, 175 Cal. Rptr. 3d 131 (Cal. Ct. App. 2014). For more on this problem, compare Rebecca Tushnet, *A Cry for Yelp*, Rebecca Tushnet's 43(B)log (Nov. 1, 2011), http://tushnet.blogspot.com/2011/11/cry-for-yelp.html (agreeing with me), with Eric Goldman, *Yelp Gets Complete Win in Advertiser "Extortion" Case—Levitt v. Yelp*, Tech. &

Marketing L. Blog (Oct. 26, 2011), http://blog.ericgoldman.org/archives/2011/10/yelp_gets_compl.htm (disagreeing).

30. *e-ventures Worldwide*, 188 F. Supp. 3d at 1273–74.

31. *e-ventures Worldwide, LLC v. Google, Inc.*, 2:14-cv-00646-PAM-CM (M.D. Fla. Feb. 8, 2017), 2017 WL 2210029, at *4.

32. *Id.* ("A search engine is akin to a publisher, whose judgments about what to publish and what not to publish are absolutely protected by the First Amendment." (citing *Miami Herald Publ'g Co. v. Tornillo*, 418 U.S. 241, 258 (1974))).

33. *Id.*

34. The California Attorney General's Office has also set out arguments for why Google search results can both be covered by the First Amendment and still be open to antitrust scrutiny. *See* Paula Lauren Gibson, *Does the First Amendment Immunize Google's Search Engine Search Results from Government Antitrust Scrutiny?*, 23 Competition: J. Antirust & Unfair Comp. L. Sec. St. B. Cal. 125, 136 (2014); *see also supra* note 29.

35. *Packingham v. North Carolina*, 137 S. Ct. 1730 (2017).

36. Klint Finley, *Google's Big EU Fine Isn't Just About the Money*, Wired (June 27, 2017), http://www.wired.com/story/google-big-eu-fine.

37. Josie Cox, *Google Hit with Record EU Fine over "Unfair" Shopping Searches*, Independent (June 27, 2017), http://www.independent.co.uk/news/business/news/google-eu-fine-latest-competition-shopping-searches-prepare-online-european-commission-results-a7809886.html.

38. Mark Bergen, *Google Says Local Search Results That Buried Rivals Yelp, TripAdvisor Is Just a Bug*, Recode (Nov. 24, 2015), http://www.recode.net/2015/11/24/11620920/google-says-local-search-result-that-buried-rivals-yelp-tripadvisor.

39. Thanks to Jane Friedman for help with this example.

40. *Rumsfeld v. Forum for Acad. & Institutional Rights, Inc.*, 547 U.S. 47, 58 (2006).

41. *See* Debra Cassens Weiss, *Law Prof Volokh Argues Google Has a Free Speech Right to Determine Search Results*, ABA J. (May 14, 2012), http://www.abajournal.com/news/article/law_prof_volokh_argues_google_has_a_free_speech_right_to_determine_search_r; Thomas Catan & Amir Efrati, *Feds to Launch Probe of Google*, Wall St. J. (June 24, 2011), http://www.wsj.com/articles/SB10001424052702303339904576403603764717680.

42. Eugene Volokh & Donald M. Falk, *First Amendment Protection for Search Engine Search Results* (2012), https://ssrn.com/abstract=2055364.

43. *Id.* at 21.

44. *Id.* at 27.

45. *Id.* at 11.

46. *Id.* at 14.

47. *Id.* at 27.

48. *See* J.L. Austin, *How to Do Things with Words* 4–11 (J.O. Urmson & Marina Sbisà, eds., 2d ed. 1975) (preliminarily developing the notion of "performatives"—utterances that are the performance of an action, such as promising).

49. *See* Paco Underhill, *Why We Buy: The Science of Shopping* 85–86 (2009).

50. *See id.* at 80.

51. *See id.* at 205, 209.
52. A further complication is that, as any law student can tell you, not even all of what we would colloquially call "speech" is necessarily covered under the First Amendment—for instance, lying under oath, yelling "fire" in a theater, or threatening or defrauding someone.
53. *Cf.* Stanley Fish, *There's No Such Thing as Free Speech* (1994).
54. Volokh & Falk, *supra* note 42, at 11.
55. *Id.* at 14.
56. *Id.* at 27.
57. *See* Underhill, *supra* note 49, at 77–88.
58. Tristan Harris, *How Technology Is Hijacking Your Mind—from a Magician and Google Design Ethicist,* Thrive Global (May 18, 2016), http://journal .thriveglobal.com/how-technology-hijacks-peoples-minds-from-a-magician -and-google-s-design-ethicist-56d62ef5edf3; *see also* Paul Lewis, *"Our Minds Can Be Hijacked": The Tech Insiders Who Fear a Smartphone Dystopia,* Guardian (Oct. 6, 2017), http://www.theguardian.com/technology/2017/oct/05 /smartphone-addiction-silicon-valley-dystopia.
59. 564 U.S. 786 (2011).
60. 547 U.S. 47 (2006).
61. *Id.* at 51.
62. *Id.*
63. *Id.* at 64.
64. *Id.* at 62.
65. I thank Eric Goldman for making this argument to me.
66. *See, e.g., Pierson v. Post,* 3 Cai. 175 (N.Y. 1805).
67. For further discussion, see Richard Posner, *How Judges Think* 186–87 (2008); and Grant Lamond, *Analogical Reasoning in the Common Law,* 34 Oxford J. Legal Stud. 567, 582–84 (2014).
68. Oren Bracha & Frank Pasquale, *Federal Search Commission? Access, Fairness and Accountability in the Law of Search,* 93 Cornell L. Rev. 1149, 1197–1200 (2008).
69. *See* Volokh & Falk, *supra* note 42, at 11. While I will not rehash it here, we can contest Volokh and Falk's argument that the presence of judgments in constructing algorithms provides a reason why those algorithms' outputs are analogous to editorial speech. Judgments are ubiquitous; First Amendment coverage is not.
70. And I am reluctant to do so. The method seems to distinguish communicative acts from acts that communicate information, and I worry that such a divide is as unstable and illusory as philosophers of language have shown the communication-conduct distinction to be. *See* Austin, *supra* note 48, at 4–11. Thanks to Rob Hopkins for raising this issue.
71. *See, e.g.,* Stuart Minor Benjamin, *Transmitting, Editing, and Communicating: Determining What "the Freedom of Speech" Encompasses,* 60 Duke L.J. 1673, 1704–05 (2011) (exploring, but ultimately rejecting, the possibility that network-design choices that the network operator makes to optimize certain types of communications might be understood as substantive speech protected by the First Amendment).

72. *See, e.g.*, Tom Warren, *Google's Top Search Results Promote Offensive Content, Again*, Verge (Nov. 22, 2017), http://www.theverge.com/2017/11/22/16689534 /google-search-results-offensive-material (describing Google's decision to remove offensive web pages and images that ranked highly in their search results for certain terms).

73. *See, e.g.*, Jordan Crook, *Fake Times*, TechCrunch (Mar. 19, 2017), http:// techcrunch.com/2017/03/19/facebook-will-never-take-responsibility-for-fake-news ("As part of a nationwide tour, Zuck[erberg] expressed that Facebook doesn't *want* fake news on the platform.").

74. *See, e.g.*, Marty Swant, *Twitter Is Cracking Down on Trolls and Offensive Tweets with These New Tools*, Adweek (Feb. 7, 2017), http://www.adweek.com/digital /twitter-is-cracking-down-on-trolls-and-offensive-tweets-with-these-new-tools (describing steps Twitter has taken to identify and minimize content on the platform that is "potentially abusive and low-quality").

75. *Cf. Rumsfeld v. Forum for Acad. & Institutional Rights, Inc.*, 547 U.S. 47, 65 (2006) ("Nothing about recruiting suggests that law schools agree with any speech by recruiters, and nothing in the [statute] restricts what the law schools may say about the military's policies. We have held that high school students can appreciate the difference between speech a school sponsors and speech the school permits because legally required to do so, pursuant to an equal access policy.").

76. *See* Samuel Gibbs, *Google Alters Search Autocomplete to Remove "Are Jews Evil" Suggestion*, Guardian (Dec. 5, 2016), http://www.theguardian.com/technology /2016/dec/05/google-alters-search-autocomplete-remove-are-jews-evil-suggestion.

77. David Meyer, *Google Loses Autocomplete Defamation Case in Italy*, ZDNet (Apr. 5, 2011), http://www.zdnet.com/article/google-loses-autocomplete -defamation-case-in-italy.

78. *Id.*

79. Google, *Search Using Autocomplete*, Google Search Help, http://support.google .com/websearch/answer/106230 (last visited July 18, 2019).

80. Thanks to Daniel Viehoff for encouraging me to emphasize this point.

81. Stuart Minor Benjamin, *Algorithms and Speech*, 161 U. Pa. L. Rev. 1445, 1470 (2013) (quoting *An Explanation of Our Search Results*, Google, http://www .google.com/explanation.html (as visited Apr. 10, 2013)).

82. Joe Pinsker, *Where Were Netflix and Google in the Net-Neutrality Fight?*, Atlantic (Dec. 20, 2017), http://www.theatlantic.com/business/archive/2017/12 /netflix-google-net-neutrality/548768. As Evgeny Morozov has pointed out, Google has also relied on a mirror metaphor that paints Google as simply and neutrally reflecting back the state of the world, where it is not a speaker and its outputs are not its speech. *See* Evgeny Morozov, *To Save Everything, Click Here* 144–46 (2013).

83. Thanks to Evelyn Douek for most helpfully sharing her summary and transcript excerpts from those hearings. *See* Evelyn Douek, *Summary of Congressional Tech Hearings* 16 (2017), http://lawfare.s3-us-west-2.amazonaws.com/staging/2018 /DOUEK%20Summary%20of%20Congressional%20Tech%20Hearings.pdf.

84. Josh Constine, *Facebook Launches Trending Topics on Web with Descriptions of Why Each Is Popular*, TechCrunch (Jan. 16, 2014), http://techcrunch.com /2014/01/16/facebook-trending.

85. *See How Much Does It Cost to Advertise on Twitter?*, ThriveHive (Feb. 21, 2017), http://thrivehive.com/how-much-does-it-cost-to-advertise-on-twitter.

86. Garett Sloane, *Facebook Lends Trending Hand to Brands*, Adweek (Jan. 17, 2014), http://www.adweek.com/digital/facebook-lends-trending-hand-brands-155060. Accordingly, Facebook contacted advertising agencies to explain how brands could feature in Trending Topics and to explain the incentives for advertising on Facebook's platform more generally. *See id.* This raises an important question: how ought the commerciality of these sites and the profit-driven decisions of which content to put before users alter our First Amendment analysis? Volokh and Falk recognized the potential relevance of the commercial divide and limited their analysis to Google's organic results. *See* Volokh & Falk, *supra* note 42, at 5–6 ("We focus in this submission on Google search results for which no payment has been made to Google. . . ."). Given the economic motivations behind organic rankings, it is not obvious to me that they should be considered noncommercial. Then again, given how the current Supreme Court has chipped away at the commercial-noncommercial distinction, it is hard to say how much commerciality will even matter moving forward.

87. Charlie Warzel, *How Ferguson Exposed Facebook's Breaking News Problem*, BuzzFeed (Aug. 19, 2014), http://www.buzzfeed.com/charliewarzel/in-ferguson -facebook-cant-deliver-on-its-promise-to-deliver; *see also* Ravi Somaiya, *Facebook Takes Steps Against "Click Bait" Articles*, N.Y. Times (Aug. 25, 2014), http://www .nytimes.com/2014/08/26/business/media/facebook-takes-steps-against-click-bait -articles.html (describing updates to Facebook's algorithm designed to increase the quality of articles that users see).

88. *See* Warzel, *supra* note 87.

89. *Id.*

90. Gail Sullivan, *How Facebook and Twitter Control What You See About Ferguson*, Wash. Post (Aug. 19, 2014), http://www.washingtonpost.com/news/morning-mix /wp/2014/08/19/how-facebook-and-twitter-control-what-you-see-about-ferguson. Again we see the tight connection between these companies' "organic" algorithmic decisions and commercial objectives. *Cf. supra* note 86.

91. Martin Beck, *Timely Change? Facebook Adjusts News Feed Algorithm to Surface More Trending Stories*, Marketing Land (Sept. 18, 2014), http://marketingland. com/facebook-adjusts-news-feed-algorithm-surface-timely-stories-100630. By August, Facebook had already announced tweaks to its algorithm meant to reduce clickbait articles, by considering how long users spent reading an article and whether they shared it (though, as we eventually learned, these metrics did not weed out fake news). *See* Somaiya, *supra* note 87.

92. David Cohen, *Mark Zuckerberg Q&A: Dislike Button, Ferguson, Graph Search, News Feed Study Controversy*, Adweek (Dec. 12, 2014), http://www.adweek.com /digital/mark-zuckerberg-qa-121114.

93. Amy Mitchell et al., Pew Research Ctr., *Social, Search & Direct: Pathways to Digital News* 23–24 (2014), http://assets.pewresearch.org/wp-content/uploads /sites/13/2014/03/SocialSearchandDirect_PathwaystoDigitalNews.pdf.

94. Elisa Shearer & Jeffrey Gottfried, Pew Research Ctr., *News Use Across Social Media Platforms 2017* (2017), http://www.journalism.org/2017/09/07 /news-use-across-social-media-platforms-2017.

95. Somaiya, *supra* note 87.
96. *Id.* A common reply is that conduits can be neutral, but platforms and their algorithms cannot. *See, e.g.*, Eric Goldman, *Search Engine Bias and the Demise of Search Engine Utopianism*, 8 Yale J.L. & Tech. 188 (2006) (making an argument along these lines). I take this to be a false dichotomy. There aren't neutral conduits on one side and non-neutral platforms on the other. Something being "neutral" just means neutral against some baseline. But the threshold choice of that baseline is itself a non-neutral judgment. Many say, for example, that ISPs should be neutral with respect to content; this is a cornerstone of the net neutrality movement. But what is "neutral" here? Making all content creators pay the same amount? Treating similar kinds of content similarly? Our definition of "neutral" does not emerge from the sea fully grown—we decide it.
97. *Updates to Trending*, Facebook Newsroom (Dec. 10, 2014), http://newsroom.fb.com/news/2014/12/updates-to-trending.
98. Kurt Wagner, *How Facebook Decides What's Trending*, Recode (Aug. 21, 2015), http://www.recode.net/2015/8/21/11617880/how-facebook-decides-whats-trending.
99. *Id.*
100. Michael Nunez, *Want to Know What Facebook Really Thinks of Journalists? Here's What Happened When It Hired Some*, Gizmodo (May 3, 2016), http://gizmodo.com/want-to-know-what-facebook-really-thinks-of-journalists-1773916117.
101. Nunez, *supra* note 100.
102. Michael Nunez, *Former Facebook Workers: We Routinely Suppressed Conservative News*, Gizmodo (May 9, 2016), http://gizmodo.com/former-facebook-workers-we-routinely-suppressed-conser-1775461006.
103. *Id.* Nunez reported that the contractors, in addition to having a liberal political bent, had all previously worked in the news industry and mostly came from Ivy League and elite East Coast colleges. *See* Nunez, *supra* note 100.
104. Nunez, *supra* note 100.
105. Nunez, *supra* note 102.
106. Nunez, *supra* note 100.
107. Tony Romm & Hadas Gold, *Inside Facebook's GOP Charm Offensive*, Politico (May 16, 2016), http://www.politico.com/story/2016/05/facebook-conservatives-zuckerberg-bias-223244.
108. Team GOP, *#MakeThisTrend: Facebook Must Answer for Conservative Censorship*, GOP.com: Blog (May 9, 2016), http://gop.com/makethistrend-facebook-must-answer-for-liberal-bias.
109. Robinson Meyer, *Facebook Doesn't Have to Be Fair*, Atlantic (May 13, 2016), http://www.theatlantic.com/technology/archive/2016/05/facebook-isnt-fair/482610.
110. Thune Letter, *supra* note 2, at 1–2 (internal quotation marks omitted).
111. *Id.* at 2–3.
112. *See, e.g.*, Nick Corasaniti & Mike Isaac, *Senator Demands Answers from Facebook on Claims of "Trending" List Bias*, N.Y. Times (May 10, 2016), http://www.nytimes.com/2016/05/11/technology/facebook-thune-conservative.html; Thomas C. Rubin, *Facebook's Trending Topics Are None of the Senate's Business*, Slate (May 23, 2016), http://www.slate.com/articles/news_and_politics/jurisprudence/2016/05/facebook_s_trending_topics_are_none_of_the_senate_s_business.html.

113. Colin Stretch, *Response to Chairman John Thune's Letter on Trending Topics*, Facebook Newsroom (May 23, 2016), http://newsroom.fb.com/news/2016/05/response-to-chairman-john-thunes-letter-on-trending-topics.

114. Justin Osofsky, *Information About Trending Topics*, Facebook Newsroom (May 12, 2016), http://newsroom.fb.com/news/2016/05/information-about-trending-topics. A link to the guidelines can be found in this article.

115. Romm & Gold, *supra* note 107.

116. Letter from Colin Stretch, Facebook Gen. Counsel, to Sen. Thune 1–2 (May 23, 2016), http://www.commerce.senate.gov/public/_cache/files/93a14e98-2443-4d27-bf04-1fc59b8cf2b4/22796A1389F52BE16D225F9A03FB53F8.facebook-letter.pdf.

117. *Id.* at 11.

118. Abby Ohlheiser, *Three Days After Removing Human Editors, Facebook Is Already Trending Fake News*, Wash. Post (Aug. 29, 2016), http://www.washingtonpost.com/news/the-intersect/wp/2016/08/29/a-fake-headline-about-megyn-kelly-was-trending-on-facebook. For further explanation of these changes, see *Search FYI: An Update on Trending*, Facebook Newsroom (Aug. 26, 2016), http://newsroom.fb.com/news/2016/08/search-fyi-an-update-to-trending; and Sam Thielman, *Facebook Fires Trending Team, and Algorithm Without Humans Goes Crazy*, Guardian (Aug. 29, 2016), http://www.theguardian.com/technology/2016/aug/29/facebook-fires-trending-topics-team-algorithm.

119. *Trending Review Guidelines*, Facebook Newsroom (Aug. 26, 2016), http://fbnewsroomus.files.wordpress.com/2016/08/trending-review-guidelines.pdf.

120. For example, if "NBA Finals" is a live Trending Topic, the team would not accept "#NBAFinals" as a new topic. *See id.*

121. For example, while "#lunch" peaks in usage across the site during lunchtime every day and around the world, curators would not allow #lunch to be a trending topic because it is not tied to a news event. *See id.*

122. For instance, when Congressman John Lewis said that he didn't believe Trump was a legitimate president and Trump tweeted against Lewis in response, the Trending Topics algorithm might pick up a spike in references to Trump and Lewis together, and the two might be clustered together as if they were all part of one conversation. The reviewer's job would be to ensure that the algorithmically suggested clustering is correct. *See id.*

123. *Rumsfeld v. Forum for Acad. & Institutional Rights, Inc.*, 547 U.S. 47, 65 (2006).

124. Will Oremus, *Trending Bad: How Facebook's Foray into Automated News Went from Messy to Disastrous*, Slate (Aug. 30, 2016), http://www.slate.com/articles/technology/future_tense/2016/08/how_facebook_s_trending_news_feature_went_from_messy_to_disastrous.html.

125. Thielman, *supra* note 118.

126. *See* Ohlheiser, *supra* note 118.

127. Caitlin Dewey, *Facebook Has Repeatedly Trended Fake News Since Firing Its Human Editors*, Wash. Post (Oct. 12, 2016), http://www.washingtonpost.com/news/the-intersect/wp/2016/10/12/facebook-has-repeatedly-trended-fake-news-since-firing-its-human-editors.

128. Giulia Segreti, *Facebook CEO Says Group Will Not Become a Media Company*, Reuters (Aug. 29, 2016), http://www.reuters.com/article/us-facebook-zuckerberg/facebook-ceo-says-group-will-not-become-a-media-company-idUSKCN1141WN.

129. Michael Barthel et al., *Many Americans Believe Fake News Is Sowing Confusion*, Pew Research Ctr. (Dec. 15, 2016), http://www.journalism.org/2016/12/15 /many-americans-believe-fake-news-is-sowing-confusion.

130. Mark Zuckerberg, Facebook (Nov. 19, 2016), http://www.facebook.com/zuck /posts/10103269806149061.

131. *See* Deepa Seetharaman, *Facebook to Rank News Sources by Quality to Battle Misinformation*, Wall St. J. (Jan. 19, 2018), http://www.wsj.com/articles /facebook-to-rank-news-sources-by-quality-to-battle-misinformation-1516394184.

132. Douek, *supra* note 83, at 18.

133. *Id.*

134. *Id.* at 19.

135. *Id.*

136. The *New York Times* recently used similar language when describing these tech platforms. *See* Farhad Manjoo, *How 2017 Became a Turning Point for Tech Giants*, N.Y. Times (Dec. 13, 2017), http://www.nytimes.com/2017/12/13 /technology/tech-companies-social-responsibility.html ("Think of these platforms as the roads, railroads and waterways of the information economy—an essentially inescapable part of life for any business or regular person who doesn't live in a secluded cabin in the woods.").

137. 447 U.S. 74 (1980).

138. *See* Brief of Appellants, *Pruneyard Shopping Ctr. v. Robins*, 447 U.S. 74 (1980) (No. 79–289), 1979 WL 199940, at *13.

139. This same move was made by the ACLU in its amicus brief. *See* Brief of the American Civil Liberties Union of Northern California et al. as Amici Curiae, *Pruneyard Shopping Ctr. v. Robins*, 447 U.S. 74 (1980) (No. 79–289), 1980 WL 339574, at *39–*41.

140. 447 U.S. at 88.

141. *See id.*

142. *Rumsfeld v. Forum for Acad. & Institutional Rights, Inc.*, 547 U.S. 47 (2006).

143. *Id.* at 64.

144. As was the case when Korryn Gaines, a black woman, was shot and killed, and her five-year-old son shot twice, during a standoff at her home with police officers. *See* Hanna Kozlowska, *Facebook Is Giving the US Government More and More Data*, Quartz (Dec. 19, 2017), http://qz.com/1160719/facebooks-transparency -report-the-company-is-giving-the-us-government-more-and-more-data; Baynard Woods, *Facebook Deactivated Korryn Gaines' Account During Standoff, Police Say*, Guardian (Aug. 3, 2016), http://www.theguardian.com/us-news/2016 /aug/03/korryn-gaines-facebook-account-baltimore-police; *see also* Mike Isaac & Sydney Ember, *Live Footage of Shootings Forces Facebook to Confront New Role*, N.Y. Times (July 8, 2016), http://www.nytimes.com/2016/07/09/technology /facebook-dallas-live-video-breaking-news.html (discussing the Facebook live stream of the killing of Philando Castile by police and how "it was taken down by Facebook for a few hours without explanation. Facebook blamed a technical glitch for the video's removal, but declined to speak further of the incident").

145. *See Videos Removed or Blocked Due to YouTube's Contractual Obligations*, YouTube Help, http://support.google.com/youtube/answer/3045545 (last visited July 18, 2019); Mike Masnick, *YouTube Won't Put Your Video Back Up, Even If*

It's Fair Use, If It Contains Music from Universal Music, TechDirt (Apr. 5, 2013), http://www.techdirt.com/articles/20130405/01191322589/youtube-wont-put-your -video-back-up-even-if-its-fair-use-if-it-contains-content-universal-music.shtml.

146. *See generally* Adam Alter, *Irresistible: The Rise of Addictive Technology and the Business of Keeping Us Hooked* (2017); Julian Morgans, *Your Addiction to Social Media Is No Accident*, Vice (May 19, 2017), http://www.vice.com/en_us/article /vv5jkb/the-secret-ways-social-media-is-built-for-addiction.

147. *See* Renee Diresta & Tristan Harris, *Why Facebook and Twitter Can't Be Trusted to Police Themselves*, Politico Mag. (Nov. 1, 2017), http://www.politico .com/magazine/story/2017/11/01/why-facebook-and-twitter-cant-be-trusted -to-police-themselves-215775; Kurt Wagner, *Facebook Is Making a Major Change to the News Feed That Will Show You More Content from Friends and Family and Less from Publishers*, Recode (Jan. 11, 2018), http://www.recode .net/2018/1/11/16881160/facebook-mark-zuckerberg-news-feed-algorithm-content -video-friends-family-media-publishers.

148. Many have suggested something along these lines. *See, e.g.*, Jack Balkin, *Information Fiduciaries and the First Amendment*, 49 U.C. Davis L. Rev. 1183 (2016); James Grimmelmann, *Speech Engines*, 98 Minn. L. Rev. 868 (2014).

149. Wu, this volume.

150. 395 U.S. 367 (1969).

151. *Packingham v. North Carolina*, 137 S. Ct. 1730, 1735 (2017).

152. Douek, *supra* note 83, at 14.

153. *Id.*

154. *See also* Franklin Foer, *Facebook Finally Blinks*, Atlantic (Jan. 11, 2018), http:// www.theatlantic.com/technology/archive/2018/01/facebook/550376 ("The company finally acted as if it might assume the responsibilities implied by its power. . . .").

155. *See* Nitaska Tiku, *Investors Join Calls for Facebook, Twitter to Take More Responsibility*, Wired (Jan. 11, 2018), http://www.wired.com/story/investors-join -calls-for-facebook-twitter-to-take-more-responsibility.

156. Mark Zuckerberg, Facebook (Jan. 4, 2018), http://www.facebook.com/zuck/posts /10104380170714571 ("The world feels anxious and divided, and Facebook has a lot of work to do—whether it's protecting our community from abuse and hate, defending against interference by nation states, or making sure that time spent on Facebook is time well spent.").

157. *See* Ian Sherr, *Zuckerberg Says He's Committed to Fixing Facebook This Year*, CNET (Jan. 4, 2018), http://www.cnet.com/news/zuckerberg-says-hes-committed -to-fixing-facebook-hate-harassment-russia (describing Zuckerberg's apology "for the ways my work was used to divide people rather than bring us together").

158. Foer, *supra* note 154.

159. *See, e.g.*, *Zhang v. Baidu.com, Inc.*, 10 F. Supp. 3d 433 (S.D.N.Y. 2014). First Amendment arguments leveled against online platforms go back at least to *Cyber Promotions, Inc. v. American Online, Inc.*, 948 F. Supp. 436 (E.D. Pa. 1996). As for the latter position, while courts have found several government-run websites not to be open public forums, those same courts have also suggested that the outcomes would be different if the sites were more dynamic and open to the public. *See, e.g.*, *Sutliffe v. Epping Sch. Dist.*, 584 F.3d 314, 334–35 (1st Cir. 2009);

Page v. Lexington Cty. Sch. Dist. One, 531 F.3d 275, 284 (4th Cir. 2008); *Putnam Pit, Inc. v. City of Cookeville, Tennessee*, 221 F.3d 834, 842 (6th Cir. 2000). Prior to *Packingham*, the district court in *Davison v. Loudoun County Board of Supervisors*, 1:16-cv-932 (JCC/IDD), 2017 WL 1929406 (E.D. Va. May 10, 2017), a case involving comments on a county chair's Facebook page, found that the question could not be answered at summary judgment.

160. Joseph Bernstein & Charlie Warzel, *Far-Right Activist Charles Johnson Has Sued Twitter over His Suspension*, BuzzFeed (Jan. 8, 2018), http://www.buzzfeed.com /josephbernstein/far-right-activist-charles-johnson-has-sued-twitter-over.

161. *See, e.g., id.* (complaint embedded in article); Caitlin Dewey, *Charles Johnson, One of the Internet's Most Infamous Trolls, Has Finally Been Banned from Twitter*, Wash. Post (May 26, 2015), http://www.washingtonpost.com/news /the-intersect/wp/2015/05/26/charles-johnson-one-of-the-internets-most-infamous -trolls-has-finally-been-banned-from-twitter; Elizabeth Dwoskin & Craig Timberg, *Google, Twitter Face New Lawsuits Alleging Discrimination Against Conservative Voices*, Wash. Post (Jan. 8, 2018), http://www.washingtonpost. com/news/the-switch/wp/2018/01/08/google-faces-a-lawsuit-over-discriminating -against-white-men-and-conservatives; Ian Lovett & Jack Nicas, *PragerU Sues YouTube in Free-Speech Case*, Wall St. J. (Oct. 23, 2017), http://www.wsj.com /articles/prageru-sues-youtube-in-free-speech-case-1508811856; Heather Whitney, *Does the Packingham Ruling Presage Greater Government Control over Search Results? Or Less?*, Tech. & Marketing L. Blog (June 22, 2017), http://blog.eric goldman.org/archives/2017/06/does-the-packingham-ruling-presage-greater -government-control-over-search-results-or-less-guest-blog-post.htm. Litigants have also used *Packingham* to bolster arguments that private commercial websites, and not only physical structures, can be "public accommodations" for purposes of Title III of the Americans with Disabilities Act. *See, e.g., Andrews v. Blick Art Materials, LLC*, 268 F. Supp. 3d 381, 393 (E.D.N.Y. 2017); *Del-Orden v. Bonobos, Inc.*, No. 17 CIV. 2744 (PAE) (S.D.N.Y. Dec. 20, 2017), 2017 WL 6547902, at *10.

162. *See, e.g., hiQ Labs, Inc. v. LinkedIn Corp.*, No. 17-CV-03301-EMC (N.D. Cal. Aug. 14, 2017), 2017 WL 3473663, at *7 ("The Court's analogy of the Internet in general, and social networking sites in particular, to the 'modern public square,' embraces the social norm that assumes the openness and accessibility of that forum to all comers." (quoting *Packingham v. North Carolina*, 137 S. Ct. 1730, 1737 (2017))); *see also* Venkat Balasubramani, *LinkedIn Enjoined from Blocking Scraper—hiQ v. LinkedIn*, Techn. & Marketing L. Blog (Aug. 15, 2017), http://blog.ericgoldman.org/archives/2017/08/linkedin-enjoined-from -blocking-scraper-hiq-v-linkedin.htm (response from Eric Goldman noting that "[c]ollectively, it looks like some courts are reading *Packingham* to enshrine a general purpose right of users to get content without restriction on the Internet—which would be an interesting and potentially far-reaching implica- tion of the ruling").

163. *See, e.g., Davison v. Plowman*, 247 F. Supp. 3d 767, 776 (E.D. Va. 2017) ("The Court has already ruled that the Loudoun County Social Media Comments Policy—both as originally written and as amended—serves to create a limited

public forum as applied to the Loudoun County Commonwealth's Attorney Facebook page."); *see also supra* note 159 (citing additional cases).

164. Complaint for Declaratory & Injunctive Relief at 16, Knight First Amendment Inst. at Columbia Univ. v. Trump, No. 1:17-cv-05205 (S.D.N.Y. July 11, 2017); *see also Davison v. Loudoun Cty. Bd. of Supervisors*, 267 F. Supp. 3d 703, 715–19 (E.D. Va. 2017) (citing *Packingham* and holding, without deciding on the nature of the forum, that the banning of a resident from a local politician's Facebook page for twelve hours violated the First Amendment).

165. 326 U.S. 501 (1945).

166. For an example of this tactic, see Mary Harris Jones, *Autobiography of Mother Jones* 156 (1996) (Mary Field Parton, ed., 1925) (describing how the author had to drive through a creek bed to reach miners "as that was the only public road and I could be arrested for trespassing if I took any other").

167. 326 U.S. at 502.

168. 391 U.S. 308, 319–20 (1968).

169. *Id.* at 318.

170. *Id.* at 319.

171. 424 U.S. 507 (1976).

172. 407 U.S. 551 (1972).

173. 424 U.S. at 518.

174. *Id.* at 520.

175. *Packingham v. North Carolina*, 137 S. Ct. 1730, 1738 (2017) (Alito, J., concurring).

176. *Id.* at 1735.

177. *Id.* at 1737.

178. *Id.* at 1732.

179. *See, e.g., Venetian Casino Resort LLC v. Local Joint Exec. Bd.*, 257 F.3d 937, 943 (9th Cir. 2001); *Freedom from Religion Found., Inc. v. City of Marshfield*, 203 F.3d 487, 494 (7th Cir. 2000).

180. *See* Douek, *supra* note 83, at 16–19.

181. *See* Tai Liu et al., *The Barriers to Overthrowing Internet Feudalism*, in *Sixteenth ACM Workshop on Hot Topics in Networks* (2017), http://cs.nyu.edu/~jchen/ publications/hotnets17-liu.pdf. The feudalism analogy has been made for many years. *See, e.g.*, Ben Johnson, *How Tech Giants Are Like Feudal Lords and Users Are Like Serfs*, Marketplace (Nov. 27, 2012), http://www.marketplace. org/2012/11/27/tech/how-tech-giants-are-feudal-lords-and-users-are-serfs; Bruce Schneier, *The Battle for Power on the Internet*, Atlantic (Oct. 24, 2013), http://www.theatlantic.com/technology/archive/2013/10/the-battle-for -power-on-the-internet/280824; Bruce Schneier, *When It Comes to Security, We're Back to Feudalism*, Wired (Nov. 26, 2012), http://www.wired.com/2012/11 /feudal-security.

182. *Fitzgerald v. Mountain Laurel Racing, Inc.*, 607 F.2d 589, 591 (3d Cir. 1979).

183. Christopher W. Schmidt, *On Doctrinal Confusion: The Case of the State Action Doctrine*, 2016 BYU L. Rev. 575, 589.

184. 334 U.S. 1 (1948).

185. *Burton v. Wilmington Parking Auth.*, 365 U.S. 715, 725 (1961).

186. 382 U.S. 296, 299 (1966) (holding segregation not permitted in a private park maintained by city and granted tax exemption); *see also Lugar v. Edmondson Oil Co.*, 457 U.S. 922 (1982) (finding state action where prohibited act could fairly be attributed to the state); *Jackson v. Metro. Edison*, 419 U.S. 345, 351 (1974) (finding state action when "there is a sufficiently close nexus between the State and the challenged actions of the [private] entity" that the state can be deemed responsible for the actions).

187. David Kirkpatrick, *The Facebook Effect* 254 (2010).

188. Derek E. Bambauer, *Against Jawboning*, 100 Minn. L. Rev. 51 (2015). The term *jawboning* "became fashionable in the 1960s" and signifies "an effort by the government, usually the president, to persuade companies—through intimidation, bullying or shaming—to do what the president asked in the 'national interest' even if it wasn't in the firms' immediate self-interest." Robert J. Samuelson, *Trump's Job "Jawboning" May Be Good Politics—But It's Not Good Economics*, Wash. Post (Jan. 8, 2017), http://www.washingtonpost.com /opinions/trumps-job-jawboning-may-be-good-politics—but-its-not-good-economics /2017/01/08/a1496dc2-d44b-11e6-a783-cd3fa950f2fd_story.html.

189. I do not mean to suggest that these companies always comply with government requests. Apple's refusal to unlock the iPhone of Syed Rizwan Farook, an American-born terrorist and one of the two people responsible for the San Bernardino attack, even in the face of a court order, is just one example of company resistance. *See* Mark Berman & Ellen Nakashima, *FBI Director: Victory in the Fight with Apple Could Set a Precedent, Lead to More Requests*, Wash. Post (Mar. 1, 2016), http://www.washingtonpost.com/news/post-nation/wp/2016/03/01 /fbi-apple-bringing-fight-over-encryption-to-capitol-hill. These companies have reasons both to comply and not to comply in such situations, and users have few ways of knowing what happened one way or the other. *See* Bruce Schneier, *Data and Goliath: The Hidden Battles to Collect Your Data and Control Your World* 85 (2015). To the extent that we worry about this, an expansive approach to state action might provide companies an attractive shield against informal government requests.

190. Nelson Goodman, *Seven Strictures on Similarity*, in *Problems and Projects* 437, 437–46 (1972).

191. Lamond, *supra* note 67, at 567–68; *see also* Larry Alexander & Emily Sherwin, *Demystifying Legal Reasoning* (2008); Posner, *supra* note 67, at 180–92; Larry Alexander, *Bad Beginnings*, 145 U. Pa. L. Rev. 57 (1996); Emily Sherwin, *A Defense of Analogical Reasoning in Law*, 66 U. Chi. L. Rev. 1179 (1999); Cass Sunstein, *On Analogical Reasoning*, 106 Harv. L. Rev. 741 (1993).

192. *See generally* Heather M. Whitney & Robert Mark Simpson, *Search Engines and Free Speech Coverage*, in *Free Speech in the Digital Age* 33 (Susan J. Brison & Katharine Gelber, eds., 2019).

193. *See, e.g.*, Thomas Wheatley, *Why Social Media Is Not a Public Forum*, Wash. Post (Aug. 4, 2017), http://www.washingtonpost.com/blogs/all-opinions-are-local /wp/2017/08/04/why-social-media-is-not-a-public-forum.

194. Users' expectations on this score, it bears mention, are compatible both with objections to specific moderation decisions and with calls for these companies' content moderation policies to be less opaque.

195. For more on this and confirmation that the Cylons were right (this has all happened before and all of this will happen again), see Blake J. Harris, *Console Wars: Sega, Nintendo, and the Battle That Defined a Generation* (2014); and Adam Gabbatt, *Myspace Tom to Google+: Don't Become a Cesspool Like My Site*, Guardian (Dec. 30, 2011), http://www.theguardian.com/technology/2011/dec/30/myspace-tom-google-censorship.

196. In this way, I agree with Robert Simpson that we should move from a confused and tacit subtractive approach to speech coverage to an additive one. *See* Robert Mark Simpson, *Defining "Speech": Subtraction, Addition, and Division*, 29 Canadian J.L. & Jurisprudence 457 (2016); *see also* Robert C. Post, *The Constitutional Status of Commercial Speech*, 48 UCLA L. Rev. 1 (2000) (using an additive methodology to discuss the protection of commercial speech).

197. *See, e.g.*, Alexander Meiklejohn, *Free Speech and Its Relation to Self-Government* 22–27 (1948); Robert Post, *The Constitutional Conception of Public Discourse: Outrageous Opinion, Democratic Deliberation, and* Hustler Magazine v. Falwell, 103 Harv. L. Rev. 601 (1990).

198. James Weinstein, *Participatory Democracy as the Central Value of American Free Speech Doctrine*, 97 Va. L. Rev. 491, 491 (2011).

199. *See supra* notes 37–38 and accompanying text.

200. Seana Valentine Shiffrin, A *Thinker-Based Approach to Freedom of Speech*, 27 Const. Comment. 283, 287 (2011). *See generally* Seana Valentine Shiffrin, *Speech Matters: On Lying, Morality, and the Law* (2014).

201. Shiffrin, A *Thinker-Based Approach, supra* note 200, at 295.

OF COURSE THE FIRST AMENDMENT PROTECTS GOOGLE AND FACEBOOK (AND IT'S NOT A CLOSE QUESTION)

202. 129 F.3d 327 (4th Cir. 1997).

203. *Id.* at 330.

204. *See generally* Google, *Search Quality Evaluator Guidelines* (July 27, 2017), http://static.googleusercontent.com/media/www.google.com/en//insidesearch/howsearchworks/assets/searchqualityevaluatorguidelines.pdf.

205. *See* Anita Balakrishnan, *Facebook Pledges to Double Its 10,000-Person Safety and Security Staff by End of 2018*, CNBC (Oct. 31, 2017), http://www.cnbc.com/2017/10/31/facebook-senate-testimony-doubling-security-group-to-20000-in-2018.html.

THE PROBLEM ISN'T THE USE OF ANALOGIES BUT THE ANALOGIES COURTS USE

206. It is worth noting that the First Amendment problems raised by search engines are only the tip of the iceberg. For more discussion of the regulatory questions that search engines raise, see James Grimmelmann, *The Structure of Search Engine Law*, 93 Iowa L. Rev. 1 (2007).

207. 10 F. Supp. 3d 433 (S.D.N.Y. 2014).

208. *Id.* at 434–35.
209. *Id.* at 439.
210. *Id.*
211. *Id.*
212. *Id.* at 439–40.
213. There is considerable evidence to support the allegation in the plaintiffs' complaint that internet companies like Baidu face pressure from the Chinese government to help enforce its repressive and censorial policies. *See, e.g.,* U.S.–China Econ. & Sec. Review Comm'n, *2010 Report to Congress* 231–32 (2010), http://www.uscc.gov/sites/default/files/annual_reports/2010-Report-to-Congress. pdf (noting that "the Chinese government outsources Internet censorship to the private sector" and that "Baidu is now very much a part of China's comprehensive oppression on the Internet").
214. *See* 47 U.S.C. § 230(c)(1) (2012) (absolving search engines and other "interactive computer services" of liability as the "publisher or speaker of any information provided by another information content provider").
215. *Baidu,* 10 F. Supp. 3d at 437.
216. 418 U.S. 241, 258 (1974) (striking down a Florida right-of-reply law on the ground that it undermined a newspaper's ability to decide, among other things, how it would "treat[] . . . public issues and public officials").
217. *Baidu,* 10 F. Supp. 3d at 436–37; *see also La'Tiejira v. Facebook, Inc.,* 272 F. Supp. 3d 981, 995 (S.D. Tex. 2017); *e-ventures Worldwide, LLC v. Google, Inc.,* 188 F. Supp. 3d 1265, 1274 (M.D. Fla. 2016); *Langdon v. Google, Inc.,* 474 F. Supp. 2d 622, 629–30 (D. Del. 2007).
218. This is true when it comes to cases dealing with First Amendment coverage questions, as it is true of cases that deal with other areas of First Amendment law. Whitney mentions the recent decision in *Packingham v. North Carolina,* 137 S. Ct. 1730 (2017), but this is by no means the only First Amendment opinion that relies upon analogical reasoning to determine how broadly the First Amendment applies. *See, e.g., Brown v. Entm't Merchs. Ass'n,* 564 U.S. 786, 790 (2011); *Winters v. New York,* 333 U.S. 507, 510 (1948).
219. *See* Cass R. Sunstein, *On Analogical Reasoning,* 106 Harv. L. Rev. 741, 783 (1993) ("[B]y constraining the areas of reasonable disagreement . . . analogical reasoning introduces a degree of stability and predictability. These are important virtues for law, and they sharply reduce the costs of reaching particular decisions.").
220. *See id.* at 782 ("[R]easoning by analogy may have the significant advantage of allowing people unable to reach anything like an accord on general principles to agree on particular outcomes. Sometimes it is exceedingly difficult to get people to agree on the general principles that account for their judgments. But it may be possible for them to agree on particular solutions or on low-level principles.").
221. *See id.* at 779 ("[A]nalogies . . . are not simply unanalyzed fact patterns; they are used to help people think through contested cases and to generate low-level principles. In this way they have a constitutive dimension, for the patterns we see are a product not simply of preexisting reality, but of our cognitive structures and our principles as well.").
222. Consider here the 1948 decision in *Winters v. New York,* 333 U.S. 507 (1948). A bookdealer was convicted of violating a New York law that prohibited the

distribution of what were colloquially known as "true crime" magazines—magazines that provided, often in salacious detail, stories and pictures of criminals and the crimes they committed. *Id.* 508. Both lower courts upheld the conviction against the bookdealer's First Amendment challenge because they found that the magazines in question contained so little "social value" that their unimpeded distribution did not contribute to the First Amendment's democratic or social purposes. *People v. Winters*, 63 N.E.2d 98, 101 (N.Y. 1945), *aff'g* 48 N.Y.S.2d 230, 234 (App. Div. 1944). The Supreme Court reversed because it found that these magazines were, in relevant respects, like other kinds of literature the First Amendment protected and that their democratic or social value could not therefore be so easily dismissed. *Winters*, 333 U.S. at 510.

223. *New York Times Co. v. Sullivan*, 376 U.S. 254, 270 (1964).

224. Oren Bracha & Frank Pasquale, *Federal Search Commission? Access, Fairness, and Accountability in the Law of Search*, 93 Cornell L. Rev. 1149 (2008).

225. As the Supreme Court noted in *Turner Broadcasting System, Inc. v. FCC*, "[t]hrough 'original programming, or by exercising editorial discretion over which stations or programs to include in [their] repertoire,' cable programmers and operators 'see[k] to communicate messages on a wide variety of topics and in a wide variety of formats.'" 512 U.S. 622, 636 (1994) (third alteration in original) (quoting *Los Angeles v. Preferred Commc'ns, Inc.*, 476 U.S. 488, 494 (1986)).

226. A recent report found that capital investment by providers of cable television and internet equaled $87.2 billion in 2015. Free Press, *It's Working: How the Internet Access and Online Video Markets Are Thriving in the Title II Era* 5 (2017), http://www.freepress.net/sites/default/files/resources/internet-access-and-online-video-markets-are-thriving-in-title-II-era.pdf.

227. *See Turner*, 512 U.S. at 656 ("[S]imply by virtue of its ownership of the essential pathway for cable speech, a cable operator can prevent its subscribers from obtaining access to programming it chooses to exclude. A cable operator, unlike speakers in other media, can thus silence the voice of competing speakers with a mere flick of the switch.").

228. *Id.* at 657. For an influential, relatively early discussion of the power that search engines possess to "shape the web," see Lucas D. Introna & Helen Nissenbaum, *Shaping the Web: Why the Politics of Search Engines Matters*, 16 Info. Soc'y 169 (2000).

229. *Turner*, 512 U.S. at 653 (rejecting the proposition that a law requiring cable operators to transmit local broadcast stations "trigger[s] strict scrutiny because [it] compel[s] cable operators to transmit speech not of their choosing" and instead upholding the law under an intermediate standard of review).

PREVENTING A POSTHUMAN LAW OF FREEDOM OF EXPRESSION

230. *See generally* Frank Pasquale, *The Automated Public Sphere*, in *The Politics and Policies of Big Data: Big Data, Big Brother?* (Ann Rudinow Sætnan et al., eds., 2018) (translated into German and Portuguese); Frank Pasquale, *Internet Nondiscrimination Principles: Commercial Ethics for Carriers and Search Engines*, 2008 U. Chi. Legal F. 263; Frank Pasquale, *Platform Neutrality: Enhancing Freedom of Expression in Spheres of Private Power*, 17 Theoretical Inquiries L. 487 (2016)

(translated into Hungarian); Frank Pasquale, *Reforming the Law of Reputation*, 47 Loyola L. Rev. 515 (2016). As the translations suggest, I intend my work for a global audience and do not limit my consideration of free expression policy to First Amendment–dominated U.S. perspectives.

231. In this sentence, and for the rest of this commentary, the term "platform" refers to large internet platforms with over 10 million users. As the regulation of platforms evolves, legislators, regulators, and courts should hold large platforms to higher standards than smaller platforms.

232. On the evolution of the structure of the internet, see Chelsea Barabas, Neha Narul & Ethan Zuckerman, Ctr. for Civic Media & Digital Currency Initiative, *Defending Internet Freedom Through Decentralization: Back to the Future?* 1 (2017), https://static1.squarespace.com/static/59aae5e9a803bb10bedeb03e/t /59ae908a46c3c480db42326f/1504612494894/decentralized_web.pdf ("[S]ince its development, the Web has steadily evolved into an ecosystem of large, corporate-controlled mega-platforms which intermediate speech online.").

233. Thomas I. Emerson, *The System of Freedom of Expression* (1970).

234. My position here echoes the name of the anti–*Citizens United* group Free Speech for People, as I believe the doctrine of "computer speech" could evolve in the same troubling ways that corporate speech doctrine has.

235. Dylan Byers, *Facebook Gives Russian-linked Ads to Congress*, CNN (Oct. 2, 2017), http://money.cnn.com/2017/10/01/media/facebook-russia-ads-congress.

236. Kieren McCarthy, *Facebook, Twitter Slammed for Deleting Evidence of Russia's US Election Mischief*, Register (Oct. 13, 2017), http://www.theregister.co .uk/2017/10/13/facebook_and_twitter_slammed_for_deleting_evidence_of_russian _election_interference.

237. Scholars compiling cases limiting such coverage include Ashutosh Bhagwat, *When Speech Is Not "Speech,"* 78 Ohio St. L.J. 839 (2017); Oren Bracha, *The Folklore of Informationalism: The Case of Search Engine Speech*, 82 Fordham L. Rev. 1629 (2014); and Tim Wu, *Machine Speech*, 161 U. Pa. L. Rev. 1495 (2013).

238. Tim Wu, *Free Speech for Computers?*, N.Y. Times (June 19, 2012), http://www .nytimes.com/2012/06/20/opinion/free-speech-for-computers.html; *see also* Morgan Weiland, *Expanding the Periphery and Threatening the Core: The Ascendant Libertarian Speech Tradition*, 69 Stan. L. Rev. 1389 (2017).

239. Stuart Minor Benjamin, *Algorithms and Speech*, 161 U. Pa. L. Rev. 1445 (2013); *see also Zhang v. Baidu.com, Inc.*, 932 F. Supp. 2d 561 (S.D.N.Y. 2013).

240. James Grimmelmann, *Copyright for Literate Robots*, 101 Iowa L. Rev. 657 (2016).

241. Henry Farrell, *Philip K. Dick and the Fake Humans*, Boston Rev. (Jan. 16, 2018), http://bostonreview.net/literature-culture/henry-farrell-philip-k-dick -and-fake-humans.

242. *See* Robyn Caplan et al., Data & Soc'y, *Dead Reckoning: Navigating Content Moderation After "Fake News"* (2018), http://datasociety.net /pubs/oh/DataAndSociety_Dead_Reckoning_2018.pdf; Alice Marwick & Rebecca Lewis, Data & Soc'y, *Media Manipulation and Disinformation Online* (2017), http://datasociety.net/pubs/oh/DataAndSociety_Media ManipulationAndDisinformationOnline.pdf.

243. On the need to limit the scope and power of such "inexplicable" artificial intelligence, see Frank Pasquale, *Toward a Fourth Law of Robotics: Preserving Attribution, Responsibility, and Explainability in an Algorithmic Society*, 78 Ohio St. L.J. 1243 (2017).

244. The BCAP Code: The UK Code of Broadcast Advertising, App'x 2 (Sept. 1, 2010), http://www.asa.org.uk/uploads/assets/uploaded/e6e8b10a-20e6-4674 -a7aa6dc15aa4f814.pdf. The U.S. Federal Communications Commission has twice considered the issue but done nothing.

245. Sen. Robert Hertzberg, *Press Release: Hertzberg Announces Legislation to Encourage Social Media Transparency* (Feb. 1, 2018), http://sd18.senate .ca.gov/news/212018-hertzberg-announces-legislation-encourage-social-media -transparency.

246. An act to add Article 10 (commencing with Section 17610) to Chapter 1 of Part 3 of Division 7 of the Business and Professions Code, relating to advertising, A.B. 1950, 2017–2018 Reg. Sess. (Jan. 29, 2018), available at http://leginfo.legislature .ca.gov/faces/billNavClient.xhtml?bill_id=201720180AB1950.

247. Frank Pasquale, *Campaign 2020: Bots United*, Balkinization (Feb. 14, 2012), https://balkin.blogspot.com/2012/02/campaign-2020-bots-united.html. Like much in my Cassandran oeuvre, this post was too cautious—its title suggested that dynamics that emerged only a few years after publication would take at least eight years to occur.

248. I draw here on terms developed in Rawlsian theoretical methodology. John Rawls, *Political Liberalism* 8 (1993).

249. *See, e.g.*, *McConnell v. FEC*, 540 U.S. 93, 194–202 (2003) (upholding disclosure provisions of the Bipartisan Campaign Reform Act of 2002); Frank Pasquale, *Reclaiming Egalitarianism in the Political Theory of Campaign Finance Reform*, 2008 Ill. L. Rev. 599 (2008) (cited in *Citizens United v. FEC*, 130 S. Ct. 876, 963 (Stevens, J., dissenting)).

4

INTERMEDIARY IMMUNITY AND DISCRIMINATORY DESIGNS

David E. Pozen

SECTION 230 of the Communications Decency Act of 1996 is widely credited with helping free expression flourish online. With limited exceptions, internet service providers, social networking sites, and other online intermediaries are protected under Section 230 against state civil and criminal claims for the third-party content they host. This immunity has allowed intermediaries to publish enormous volumes of speech.

Yet in so doing, Section 230 has arguably shaped the development of the public sphere in worrisome ways—subsidizing digital platforms over analog ones, rewarding reliance on user-generated rather than employee-generated content, and allowing website operators to avoid internalizing many of the social costs of the materials they disseminate. Without the expansive immunity granted by Section 230, the internet might not have become the remarkably rich discursive domain that it is today. It also might not be quite so saturated with racist, misogynistic, defamatory, fraudulent, and otherwise harmful speech.

That, at least, is the premise of Olivier Sylvain's essay. Sylvain worries that Section 230 doctrine has drifted away from the goal of encouraging intermediaries to clean up the tortious and discriminatory content on their sites, and that the human costs of this immunity regime have been borne disproportionately by women and by racial and ethnic minorities who are subject to myriad forms of online mistreatment and abuse. Sylvain calls attention, in particular, to the ways in which intermediaries' interface design features may enable or elicit such behaviors. Airbnb's requirement that users share racially suggestive profile information, for example, resulted in widespread racial discrimination by its hosts. Civil rights groups have alleged that Facebook's marketing categories allow advertisers to exclude protected groups in contravention of fair housing statutes.

Although he does not go into detail, Sylvain suggests that intermediaries that knowingly or negligently facilitate the distribution of unlawful content should not benefit from Section 230 immunity, at least when violations of civil rights laws are at issue. Critics of this proposal will worry about chilling effects on lawful speech. But Sylvain maintains that the status quo *already* chills lawful speech—the speech of members of vulnerable groups—and that a more nuanced approach to intermediary liability could bring internet law into greater harmony with antidiscrimination norms while increasing the vitality and diversity of online expression. One way to read Sylvain's essay, then, is as a brief against the fatalistic claim that intermediary immunity simply cannot be reined in without destroying the dynamism of the internet.

Sylvain's argument will evoke, for many readers, the pioneering work of Danielle Citron highlighting law's complicity in the proliferation of hateful and illicit internet speech, from cyberbullying to revenge pornography. Responding to Sylvain's essay, Citron embraces his critique of current doctrine and his contention that "platforms should not enjoy immunity from liability for their architectural choices that violate antidiscrimination laws." Although she agrees with Sylvain that Section 230 can be read in this way, Citron proposes a statutory revision that would condition intermediaries' immunity on their compliance with a reasonable standard of care to prevent or address unlawful behaviors.

James Grimmelmann points out that any intermediary liability rule is likely to be over- or under-inclusive (or both). Without robust immunity, intermediaries can be expected to suppress some "good" speech by third parties; with immunity, they will fail to suppress some "bad" speech. How to weigh these different sorts of mistakes, Grimmelmann explains, depends not only on one's view of their relative incidence and importance but also on how crisply the categories can be defined and how accurately and cheaply platforms can distinguish between the two. The normative question of whether Section 230 ought to be reformed cannot be divorced from these practical and empirical questions about how any reform would play out.

Daphne Keller sounds an additional note of caution. While sympathizing with Sylvain's distress about the prevalence of online discrimination,

Keller questions whether Section 230 is really an important contributing factor to many of its manifestations. Moreover, in situations where Section 230 does seem to license invidious discrimination, Keller draws on adjacent bodies of law to question the wisdom of tying intermediary liability to the absence of "neutrality" or to a knowledge-based standard.

Keller concludes with an appeal for morally motivated yet legally and institutionally grounded deliberation about the troubling developments that Sylvain describes. The pieces in this chapter model such deliberation and, one hopes, will prompt more of it.

Discriminatory Designs on User Data

Olivier Sylvain

THE STATED AIM of online intermediaries like Facebook, Twitter, and Airbnb is to provide the platforms through which users freely meet people, purchase products, and discover information.[1] As "conduits" for speech and commerce,[2] intermediaries such as these are helping to create a more vibrant and democratic marketplace for goods and ideas than any the world has seen before.[3]

That, at least, is the theory on which Congress enacted Section 230 of the Communications Decency Act (CDA) in 1996.[4] One of the central objectives of Section 230's drafters was to ensure that intermediaries are "unfettered" by the obligation to police third-party user content.[5] They believed that conventional tort principles and regulatory rules were simply not workable in an environment in which so much user content flows,[6] and they doubted that intermediaries would be able to create new value for users if they constantly had to monitor, block, or remove illicit content. In the words of free speech doctrine, members of Congress worried the intermediaries would be "chilled" by the fear that they could be held legally responsible for content posted by users.[7]

Section 230 of the CDA therefore protects intermediaries from liability for distributing third-party user content. Courts have read Section 230 broadly, creating an immunity for intermediaries who do all but "materially contribute" to the user content they distribute.[8] That is, courts have read the statute's protections to cover services that "augment[]" user content, but not services that demonstrably "help" to develop the alleged illegal expressive conduct.[9] Many believe that the internet would not be as dynamic and beguiling today were it not for the protection that Section 230 has been construed to provide for online intermediaries.[10]

This may be true. But Section 230 doctrine has also had a perverse effect. By providing intermediaries with such broad legal protection, the courts' construction of Section 230 effectively underwrites content that foreseeably targets the most vulnerable among us. In their ambition to encourage an "unfettered" market for online speech, the developers of Section 230 immunity have set up a regime that makes online engagement more difficult for children, women, racial minorities, and other predictable targets of harassment and discriminatory expressive conduct. Examples abound: the gossip site that enabled users to anonymously post salacious images of unsuspecting young women;[11] the social media site through which an adult male lured a young teenage girl into a sexual assault;[12] the classifieds site that has allegedly facilitated the sex trafficking of minors;[13] the online advertising platform that allows companies to exclude Latinos from apartment rentals and older people from job postings;[14] the unrelenting social media abuse of feminist media critics[15] and a prominent black female comedian;[16] the live video stream of a gang rape of a teenage girl.[17]

The standard answer to the charge that current immunity doctrine enables these acts is that the originators of the illicit content are to blame, not the "neutral" services that facilitate online interactions.[18] Intermediaries, this position holds, merely pass along user speech. They do not encourage its production or dissemination, and, in any case, Section 230 immunity exists to protect against a different problem: the "collateral censorship" of lawful content.[19]

This answer, however, is either glib or too wedded to an obsolete conception of how online intermediaries operate. Intermediaries today do much more than passively distribute user content or facilitate user interactions. Many of them elicit and then algorithmically sort and repurpose the user content and data they collect. The most powerful services also leverage their market position to trade this information in ancillary or secondary markets.[20]

Intermediaries, moreover, design their platforms in ways that shape the form and substance of users' content. Intermediaries and their defenders characterize these designs as substantively neutral technical necessities, but as I explain below, recent developments involving two of the most prominent beneficiaries of Section 230 immunity, Airbnb and Facebook, suggest otherwise. Airbnb and Facebook have enabled a range of harmful expressive acts, including violations of housing and employment laws, through the ways in which they structure their users' interactions.

At a minimum, companies should not get a free pass for enabling unlawful discriminatory conduct, regardless of the social value their services may otherwise provide. But more than this, I argue here,[21] Section 230 doctrine requires a substantial reworking if the internet is to be the great engine of democratic engagement and creativity that it should be. Section 230 is no longer serving all the purposes it was meant to serve. The statute was intended at least in part to ensure the vitality and diversity, as well as the volume, of speech on new communications platforms. By allowing intermediaries to design their platforms without internalizing the costs of the illegal speech and conduct they facilitate, however, the statute is having the opposite effect.

This essay has four parts. The first discusses the basic contours of the prevailing doctrine, including the legislative purposes behind Section 230 and the logic courts have relied on to support broad immunity for intermediaries. The second part identifies ways in which the doctrine, in assuming that intermediaries are passive disseminators of information, may accelerate the mass distribution of content that harms vulnerable people and members of historically subordinated groups. I focus in particular on the distribution of nonconsensual pornography as a species of content that not only exacts a discrete reputational or privacy toll on victims but also fuels the circulation of misogynist views that harm young women in particular.

The third part of the essay turns to the designs that intermediaries employ to structure and enhance their users' experience, and how these designs themselves can further discrimination. While the implications of this analysis reach beyond injuries to historically marginalized groups, my goal is to explain how the designs employed by two of the most prominent intermediaries today, Airbnb and Facebook, have enabled unlawful discrimination. The fourth and final part of the essay proposes a reform to the doctrine: I argue that courts should account for the specific ways in which intermediaries' designs do or do not enable or cause harm to the predictable targets of discrimination and harassment. As recent developments underscore, Section 230 immunity doctrine must be brought closer in line with long-standing equality and universality norms in communications law.[22]

SECTION 230 IMMUNITY: A BRIEF OVERVIEW

The immunity that intermediaries enjoy under Section 230 of the CDA[23] has helped to bring about the teeming abundance of content in today's online environment. The prevailing interpretation of Section 230 bars courts from imposing liability on intermediaries that are the "mere conduits" through which user-generated content passes.[24] This doctrine protects services that host all kinds of content—everything from customer product reviews to fake news to dating profiles.

Congress invoked a very old concept when it drafted this law. The central provision of Section 230, titled "Protection for 'Good Samaritan' blocking and screening of offensive material,"[25] resembles laws in all the states that in one way or another shield defendants from liability arising from their good-faith efforts to help those in distress.[26] Good Samaritan laws are inspired by the Biblical parable that praises the do-gooder who risks ridicule and censure to help a stranger left for dead.[27]

Section 230's drafters applied this concept to online activity. They created an exception under tort law, which traditionally holds publishers liable for distributing material they know to be unlawful, but does not hold them liable if they lack notice about the illegality of the communicative act at issue.[28] Proponents of Section 230 worried that, without this legislation, claims for secondary liability would either stifle expressive conduct in the then-nascent medium or discourage intermediaries from policing content altogether.[29] They further insisted that government regulators such as the Federal Communications Commission should play no role in deciding what sorts of content prevailed online; viewers (and their parents) should make those decisions for themselves.[30]

While an interest in both free speech and the Good Samaritan concept drove Congress to enact Section 230, courts interpreting the statute have been far more influenced by the free speech concerns. In contrast to the nuanced requirements of the Digital Millennium Copyright Act's notice-and-takedown regime,[31] online intermediaries have not been required under Section 230 to block or screen offensive material in any particular way. Today, Section 230 doctrine provides a near-blanket immunity to intermediaries for hosting tortious third-party content. Long-established internet companies like AOL and Craigslist that host massive amounts of user content have been clear beneficiaries. Relying on Section 230, courts have immunized them from liability for everything from defamatory posts on electronic bulletin boards to racially discriminatory solicitations in online housing advertisements.[32] Leading opinions have reasoned that the scale at which third-party content passes through online services makes that content infeasible to moderate; requiring services to try would not only chill online speech but also stunt the internet's development as a transformative medium of communication.[33] This immunity now applies to a wide range of online services that host and distribute user content, including

Twitter's microblogging service, Facebook's flagship social media platform, and Amazon's online marketplace. Thanks to Section 230, these companies have no legal obligation to block or remove mendacious tweets, fraudulent advertisements, or anticompetitive customer reviews by rivals.[34]

As a result, most targets of illicit online user content in the United States have little to no effective recourse under law to have that content blocked or removed. They can sue the original posters of the content. But such litigation often presents serious challenges, including the cost of bringing a lawsuit, the difficulty of discovering the identities of anonymous posters, and, even if the suit is successful on the merits, the difficulty of obtaining remedies that are commensurate with the harm.[35] Targets can also enlist services like search engine optimizers that make it harder to find the offending material. They can complain to the intermediaries about offending posts. And they can press intermediaries to improve their policies generally. If none of these strategies succeeds, users can boycott the service, as many people did recently—for one day—to protest the failure of Twitter to protect women from "verbal harassment, death threats, and doxing."[36] Even if effective, however, this last option sometimes feels far from optimal, given that the promise of the internet is understood to lie in its unrivaled opportunities for commercial engagement and social integration. Exit would only exacerbate extant disparities.[37]

The threat of losing consumers, it must be said, is potent enough to have moved many intermediaries to develop content-governance protocols and automated systems for content detection. Even though Section 230 doctrine has removed any legal duty to moderate third-party content, certain companies routinely block or remove content when its publication detracts from the character of the service they mean to provide. And so, for instance, Google demotes or delists search engine optimizers and sites that host "fake news" and offensive content.[38] Facebook removes clickbait articles and has now partnered with fact-checking organizations like Snopes and PolitiFact to implement a notification process for removing "fake news."[39]

The reform that the news aggregation and discussion site Reddit undertook in 2015 is especially striking in this regard. Reddit, which had been evangelical about its laissez-faire approach to user-generated content, implemented rules that ban "illegal" content, "involuntary pornography," material that "encourages or incites violence," and content that "threatens, harasses, or bullies or encourages others to do so."[40] Many "redditors" rebelled, voting up user comments that addressed Reddit's Asian American female CEO in racist and misogynist ways.[41] These posts were popular enough among redditors to make it to the site's front page, the prime position on the site that touts itself as "the first page of the Internet." Reddit subsequently buttressed its restrictions on violent and harassing content.[42] Moreover, it recently banned a "subreddit" of self-identified misogynists.[43] Reddit's reforms have been met with fierce resistance from self-styled free speech enthusiasts.[44] But the company does not appear to be backpedaling at this time.

As this example indicates, and as new scholarship illuminates,[45] attention to consumer demand and a sense of corporate responsibility have motivated certain intermediaries to moderate certain user content. It may be tempting to conclude that reforms to Section 230 law are therefore unnecessary. Unregulated intermediaries might be the best gauges of authentic user sentiment about what is or is not objectionable. Section 230 doctrine, on this view, allows users to express and learn from each other in a dynamic fashion, without the distortions that may be caused by tort liability or government mandates. This is part of why free speech enthusiasts ascribe so much significance to the statute: Section 230 doctrine, for them, is premised on a noble faith in the moral and democratic power of unregulated information markets.[46]

THE LIVED HUMAN COSTS OF "UNFETTERED" ONLINE SPEECH: THE EXAMPLE OF NONCONSENSUAL PORNOGRAPHY

These arguments for near-blanket immunity only go so far, though. As much as some intermediaries may try, the fact is that many others do not make any effort to block or remove harmful expressive conduct. According to their critics, sites like Backpage (a classifieds site through which users are known to engage in the sex trafficking of minors) or TheDirty (a gossip site known for soliciting derogatory content about unsuspecting young women) are unabashed solicitors and distributors of a species of content that attacks members of historically subordinated groups. Under current doctrine, they are immune for acting in this way. They are just as immune under Section 230 as are intermediaries like Facebook and Twitter that purport to remove or block various categories of illicit user content but nevertheless sometimes distribute it.[47] The prevailing justification for this approach is to protect against the "collateral censorship" of lawful content.[48] This view holds that slippage in the direction of occasionally hosting hurtful material is the price of ensuring free speech online.

It may be correct that tolerating harmful content every now and again is the cost of promoting the statutory objective of an "unfettered" online speech environment. But just as a wide range of offline expressive acts like fraud, sexual harassment, and racially discriminatory advertisements for housing are not entitled to legal protection, we might wonder whether online services should be entirely immune for similar behaviors by their users.[49] To be sure, there is a significant qualitative and quantitative difference between the reach of offline and online expressive acts: the latter travel further and faster than the former by a long shot. But this fact hardly removes the need to regulate harmful online behaviors. Quite the contrary. The human costs of "unfettered" online speech may be aggravated by the internet's reach, and the costs themselves are disproportionately shouldered by those who are most likely to be the targets of attacks and abuse both online and off. That is to say, the victims of online abuse tend to be the same sorts of people who have always been subject to attack and harassment offline in the United States and elsewhere—in particular, young women, racial minorities, and sexual "deviants."[50]

The harm that these users experience is made worse by the way in which illicit or inflammatory content, once distributed, can spread across the internet at a speed and scale that is hard, if not impossible, to control. This unforgiving ecology raises the stakes of occasional slippage for the predictable targets and systemic victims of harmful content. The internet thus reinforces some of the classic arguments for the regulation of assaultive speech acts that target members of historically subordinated groups.[51] The vitriolic content that flows through online intermediaries affects members of these groups distinctively, discouraging them from participating fully in public life online and making their social and commercial integration even more difficult than it might otherwise be.[52]

Consider nonconsensual pornography, the distribution of nude images of a person who never authorized their distribution. On the internet, such images are generally shared in order to humiliate or harass the depicted person. In some instances, third parties then exploit the images to extort the victim, as in the case of sites that require a fee to take the images down.[53] Other parties discover and distribute such images for free, without necessarily knowing anything about the depicted individual.

The injuries caused by nonconsensual pornography are clear and are felt most immediately and painfully by its victims. Section 230 jurisprudence is riddled with cases that illustrate these harms. In one of the more cited ones, *Barnes v. Yahoo!, Inc.*,[54] a young woman sued Yahoo! for failing to remove a false dating site profile of her created by her ex-boyfriend. The profile contained her work phone number and address, as well as nude and suggestive photographs accompanied by promises of sex. Would-be suitors and predators soon came looking for her at work. The harm caused by this cruel hoax was plain.

Victims of nonconsensual pornography may experience many other indignities. Once posted, the offending image takes on a life of its own, exacting something that resembles an endlessly repeating privacy invasion. Danielle Citron and Mary Anne Franks, who have been thinking and writing compellingly about the issue for almost a decade now, explain the phenomenon:

> Today, intimate photos are increasingly being distributed online, potentially reaching thousands, even millions of people, with a click of a mouse. A person's nude photo can be uploaded to a website where thousands of people can view and repost it. In short order, the image can appear prominently in a search of the victim's name. It can be e-mailed or otherwise exhibited to the victim's family, employers, coworkers, and friends. The Internet provides a staggering means of amplification, extending the reach of content in unimaginable ways.[55]

The scale of distribution magnifies the harm to depicted individuals far beyond what is possible through other communications technologies. In this environment, taking down nonconsensual pornography, once it has been posted on an online intermediary, often becomes a futile and agonizing game of whack-a-mole.

In addition to the direct harms to those whose images are being exploited, the distribution of nonconsensual pornography also exacts a more general harm that mirrors and reinforces the routine subjugation of young women.[56] It is different in this regard from defamatory user posts, the prototypical subject of Section 230 jurisprudence, in which the injury caused by the defamatory posts are reputational in nature.[57] Nonconsensual pornography sweeps its victims into a network of blogs, pornography sites, social media groups, Tumblrs, and Reddit discussion threads that enthusiastically traffic in the collective humiliation of young women.[58]

And yet, Section 230 doctrine relieves online intermediaries of any legal obligation to block or remove nonconsensual pornography. When sued for distributing such images and videos, the intermediaries cite Section 230 to justify their passive role. Courts have generally sided with them, explaining that the immunity is not contingent on sites' policing of illicit user content.[59] The result is not only grief for the predictable victims of online abuse and harassment but also a regulatory regime that helps to reinforce systemic subordination.

MORE THAN A CONDUIT: ONLINE INTERMEDIARIES' DESIGNS ON USER DATA

As pernicious as it is, cyberharassment does not reflect the full scope of the threat that such broad legal protection for online intermediaries poses to vulnerable persons. This is because, today, most if not all intermediaries affirmatively shape the form and substance of user content. Adding to the arguments that scholars like Citron and Franks have ably made, I want to call attention here to this crucial way in which Section 230 immunity entrenches extant barriers to social and commercial integration for historically subordinated groups. I want to suggest, furthermore, that more than two decades into the development of the networked information economy, online intermediaries should not be able to claim blissful indifference when their designs predictably elicit or even encourage expressive conduct that perpetuates discrimination and subjugation.

I make these arguments in this part in several sections. First, I illustrate the ways in which intermediaries pervasively influence users' online experiences. Next, I explain how such designs can enable and exacerbate certain categories of harmful expressive acts. Finally, I look at the courts' responses.

INTERMEDIARY DESIGNS AND USER EXPERIENCES

Popular services like Facebook, Twitter, and Airbnb offer good examples of how intermediary designs interact with user experiences. Twitter immediately distributes its users' posts (tweets) after the users type them. But its user interface affects the nature and content of those tweets. Twitter's 280-character limitation, for example, has generated its own abbreviated syntax and conventions (for example, hashtags and subtweets).[60] The company also allows pseudonyms, effectively allowing users to be anonymous. This liberal approach to attribution invites creativity and useful provocation but also the harassment and targeted attacks mentioned above. Twitter knows this, and in many cases it will take down such attacks after the fact and remove users who routinely violate the company's no-harassment policy.

These superficial interface design features are distinct from the designs on content that occur behind (so to speak) the user interface. Some companies are intentionally deceptive about how they acquire or employ content. Take, for example, the online marketing company that placed deceptive information about its clients' products on affiliated "fake news" sites.[61] Or consider the online sleuthing company that, in response to solicited user requests for information about people, routinely contracted with third-party researchers to retrieve information in ways it allegedly knew violated privacy law.[62]

Without necessarily resorting to outright deception, many more intermediaries administer their platforms in obscure or undisclosed ways that are meant to influence how users behave on the site.[63] Many intermediaries, for example, employ user interfaces designed to hold user attention by inducing something like addictive reliance.[64] Facebook employs techniques to ensure that each user sees stories and updates in her News Feed that she may not have seen on her last visit to the site.[65] And its engineers constantly tweak the algorithms that manage the user experience.[66] In addition, many intermediaries analyze, sort, and repurpose the user content they elicit. Facebook and Twitter, for example, employ software to make meaning out of their users' "reactions," search terms, and browsing activity in order to curate the content of each user's individual feed, personalized advertisements, and recommendations about "who to follow." (A *Wired* magazine headline from 2015 comes to mind: "How Facebook Knows You Better than Your Friends Do."[67]) Intermediaries ostensibly do all of these things to improve user experiences, but their practices are often problematic and opaque to the outside world.[68] As recent revelations involving Cambridge Analytica underscore, Facebook for years shared its unrivaled trove of user data with third-party researchers, application developers, and data brokers in the interest of deepening user engagement.[69] Facebook reportedly took 30 percent of developer profits in the process.[70]

This is all to say that intermediaries now have near-total control of users' online experience. They design and predict nearly everything that happens on their site, from the moment a user signs in to the moment she logs out. The lure of "big" consumer data pushes them to be ever more aggressive in their efforts to attract new users, retain existing users, and generate information about users that they can mine and market to others. It is neither surprising nor troubling that companies make handsome profits in this way. But these developments undermine any notion that online intermediaries deserve immunity because they are mere conduits for or passive publishers of their users' expression. Online intermediaries pervasively shape, study, and exploit communicative acts on their services.

All of this, moreover, belies the old faith that such services operate at too massive a scale to be asked to police user content. Online intermediaries are already carefully curating and commoditizing this content through automated "black box" processes that would seem unworkable were they not working so well. The standard justifications for broad immunity under Section 230—grounded in fears of imposing excessive burdens on intermediaries and chilling their distribution of lawful material—have become increasingly divorced from technological and economic realities. As intermediaries have figured out how to manage and distribute user data with ever greater precision, the traditional case for Section 230 immunity has become ever less compelling, if not altogether inapt.

DISCRIMINATORY DESIGNS ON USER CONTENT AND DATA: THE EXAMPLE OF ONLINE HOUSING MARKETPLACES

These developments in intermediary design have been underway for over a decade now and have become far-reaching and consequential enough in themselves to warrant rethinking of Section 230 doctrine. The problems with the doctrine, however, are made worse when intermediaries' designs facilitate expressive conduct that harms vulnerable people and members of historically subordinated groups.[71] We often hear about the dangerous content that intermediaries automatically distribute by algorithm, as in the notorious ways in which Facebook and Twitter facilitated the targeted dissemination of "fake news" in the months leading up to the 2016 presidential election,[72] or the advertisement that Instagram made of a user's personal photo of a violently misogynist threat she had received through her account.[73] My point here, however, is that the stakes of automated intermediary designs are especially high for certain predictable communities.

Unpoliced, putatively neutral online application and service designs can entrench long-standing racial and gender disparities.

Consider Airbnb's popular home-sharing service. Quite unlike Twitter's liberal approach to personal attribution, Airbnb's main service requires each guest to create an online profile with certain information, including a genuine name and phone number. It also encourages inclusion of a real photograph.[74] For Airbnb, the authenticity of this profile information is vital to the operation of the service, as it engenders a sense of trust and connection between hosts and guests. Guests' physical characteristics may contain social cues that instill familiarity and comfort on the one hand, or suspicion and distrust on the other. The sense of authentic connection that Airbnb is adamant about cultivating, however, has dangerous consequences in a market long plagued by discrimination against racial and ethnic minorities. In its more insidious manifestations, access to a guest's name and profile picture affords hosts the ability to assess the trustworthiness of a guest based on illicit biases—against, say, Latinos or blacks—that do not accurately predict a prospective guest's reliability as a tenant. In this way, Airbnb's service directly reinforces discrimination when it requires users to share information that suggests their own race.

That race would matter so much to Airbnb hosts should not be a surprise. Race, after all, has long played an enormous—and pernicious—role in U.S. housing markets, online as well as offline. SketchFactor, the crowd-sourced neighborhood safety rating application, for example, became little more than a platform for users to share racist stereotypes about "shady" parts of town.[75] Match.com, the ostensibly race-neutral online dating application, facilitates users' discrimination against blacks.[76] Similarly, Airbnb hosts use the home-sharing service to discriminate against racial minorities whose identities as such are suggested in their profiles. Guests have complained publicly about this phenomenon, giving rise to the hashtag #AirbnbWhileBlack.[77] One guest reported that a host abruptly canceled her reservation after sending an unambiguously bigoted explanation: "I wouldn't rent to u if u were the last person on earth. One word says it all. Asian."[78] Researchers at the Harvard Business School have substantiated individual claims like these, finding that Airbnb guests "with distinctively African-American names are 16 percent less likely to be accepted relative to identical guests with distinctively White names."[79] Airbnb felt compelled to commission a well-regarded civil rights attorney to conduct a study on the topic. Her review, too, found a distinct pattern of host discrimination against users whose profiles suggest they are a member of a racial minority group.[80]

The difference between these racially discriminatory patterns as they appear on Airbnb versus dating or neighborhood rating apps is that the former are illegal because they violate fair housing laws. The 1968 Fair Housing Act (FHA), for example, specifically forbids home sellers or renters, as well as brokers, property managers, and agents, from distributing advertisements "that indicate[] any preference, limitation, or discrimination based on race, color, religion, sex, handicap, familial status, or national origin."[81] States have similar laws. In light of the mounting evidence that hosts use its service to discriminate unlawfully, Airbnb has augmented its efforts to police discriminatory behavior by hosts. In addition to requiring users to forswear that practice, the company now also requires new users to agree "to treat everyone in the Airbnb community—regardless of their race, religion, national origin, ethnicity, skin color, disability, sex, gender identity, sexual orientation or age—with respect, and without judgment or bias."[82] Airbnb has also promoted its "instant bookings" service as an alternative to its main service.[83] "Instant bookings" does not require elaborate profiles (including racially suggestive names or pictures) to complete transactions.

However, Airbnb still facilitates discrimination through its main service to the extent that it continues to rely on names and pictures. The "instant bookings" feature, paired with the main service, creates a "two-tiered reservations system": in one system (instant bookings), guests lose a sense of conviviality with hosts but obtain some peace of mind in knowing that they will not be discriminated against on the basis of race, while in the other system (the main service), discrimination is inevitable but also exploited to promote "authentic" connections.[84]

Section 230 doctrine arguably insulates Airbnb's design choices from antidiscrimination law's scrutiny. The company and its defenders have routinely cited Section 230 as a protection against liability for a wide range of illicit host activities, including discrimination that violates fair housing laws.[85] In their view, the statutory immunity is robust enough to protect Airbnb from liability for these expressive acts by third-party hosts because the company only facilitates transactions between users.[86] It does not contribute anything material to the transactions themselves.[87]

Airbnb is far from alone in deploying designs that routinely generate serious forms of discrimination. Late in 2016, ProPublica published the first in a series of illuminating reports on Facebook Ads, the social media company's powerful microtargeted advertising platform. This service enables advertisers to customize campaigns to social media users based on the information that Facebook gathers about those users. Facebook Ads is a bargain (at a clip of $30 for each advertisement) compared to the going rate of top social media marketing and advertising firms. It can be a great help to entrepreneurs of all sizes because it identifies salient market segments in real time.

Facebook Ads is also distinctive because the company employs software, first, to analyze the unrivaled troves of user data that it collects and, second, to create dozens of categories from which advertisers may choose. These include targeted classifications within geographic locations, demographics, friendship networks, and online user behaviors.[88] Among the more notorious categories in the recent past were ones that "enabled advertisers to direct their pitches to the news feeds of almost 2,300 people who expressed interest in the topics of 'Jew hater,' 'How to burn jews,' or 'History of "why jews ruin the world."'"[89] No human at Facebook created these specific anti-Semitic classifications. Facebook's algorithms determined that they were salient based on user interest at the time.[90]

Facebook's algorithms likewise seem to have created various controversial demographic classifications for "ethnic" or "multicultural" affinities, a category that does not connote race as such so much as users' cultural associations and inclinations.[91] These classifications are predictive proxies, however, for race and ethnicity. Recent news reports have shown that, through these classifications, Facebook Ads has enabled building managers and employers to exclude racial minorities from advertisements about apartment rentals and to exclude older people from advertisements about jobs.[92] When faced with stories of discrimination on the advertising platform in late 2016, Facebook immediately announced a plan to stamp out the practice.[93] Among other things, Facebook now requires advertisers to certify that they do not discriminate in contravention of civil rights laws.[94] But, as with Airbnb, reports of illicit use of the site continue to surface.[95]

Critics and victims of these practices would greatly prefer to seek relief and reform from the intermediary itself—from Facebook—rather than from thousands of individual users. Aggrieved parties have thus filed federal class action lawsuits against Facebook alleging fair housing and employment discrimination violations.[96] Predictably, Facebook has cited Section 230 to defend its advertising platform. It argues that the company does not control the reach or content of targeted ads; third-party advertisers do. According to

Facebook, its platform is nothing more than a "neutral tool" to help these advertisers "target their ads to groups of users most likely to be interested in the goods or services being offered."[97] This activity, it asserts, falls squarely in the category of "publishing" for which companies like Facebook are granted immunity under the CDA.

DOCTRINAL RESPONSES AND RESOURCES

Section 230 doctrine could very well lead courts to side with Facebook on this matter. But it is hardly obvious that it should, given that the alleged discrimination would not be possible but for the way in which Facebook leverages its unrivaled access to social media user data to generate the illicit categories. In Facebook's favor, courts have read Section 230 to immunize intermediaries that host racially discriminatory advertisements or solicitations. In 2008, the U.S. Court of Appeals for the Seventh Circuit explained that the popular classifieds site Craigslist could not be held liable for hosting third-party housing advertisements that overtly expressed preferences for people on the basis of race, sex, religion, sexual orientation, and family status.[98] The panel explained that Congress enacted the statute to protect services exactly like Craigslist. The company neither had a hand in the authorship of the discriminatory advertisements nor caused or induced advertisers to post such content.[99] Craigslist, the panel reasoned, acts as nothing more than a publisher of (sometimes racist) user content and, as such, could not be liable under federal fair housing law.[100] Had Congress meant to include an exception under Section 230 for such laws, it would have said so.[101]

But the Section 230 case law also contains some resources and opportunities for plaintiffs like those in the current Facebook Ads case. In the same year that the Seventh Circuit ruled in favor of Craigslist, the Ninth Circuit sitting en banc held that an important design element of Roommates. com, a website that also brokers connections between people in the housing market, was not immune under Section 230.[102] As a condition of participation on the site, Roommates.com required subscribers to express preferences that are strictly forbidden under fair housing law.[103] Among other things, the site's developers designed a dropdown menu that listed gender, sexual orientation, and family status as potential options. (Notably, the menu did not include race among the listed items.) A participant had to share such a preference to find a match. The Ninth Circuit held that this design feature "materially contributed" to a fair housing law violation every time a user expressed a preference for one of those prohibited classifications.[104] This conclusion flowed from language in Section 230 that does not extend protection to intermediaries that help to "create or develop" illicit third-party content.[105]

As important as the *Roommates.com* opinion has become in limiting the scope of immunity under Section 230, it is worth noting that the Ninth Circuit was very careful in how it discussed its holding. The court made a point of limiting its no-immunity conclusion to the dropdown menu. The plaintiffs had argued that a separate, blank dialogue box that Roommates. com makes available to subscribers also permits them to express bigoted preferences and share information in violation of fair housing law.[106] For example, subscribers had posted comments that they "prefer white Male roommates," that "the person applying for the room MUST be a BLACK GAY MALE," or that they are "NOT looking for black muslims."[107] The court held that Section 230 immunizes Roommates.com from liability for statements like these. It is not enough, the court reasoned, that the site encourages subscribers to share preferences and information, as this is "precisely the kind of situation for which section 230 was designed to provide immunity."[108] Roommates.com only "passively displayed" the statements and had "no way to distinguish unlawful discriminatory preferences from perfectly legitimate statements."[109] This conclusion jibes with the Seventh Circuit's approach to Craigslist.[110] Indeed, these two opinions neatly mapped out the basic contours of Section 230 doctrine when they were decided in 2008. The *Roommates.com* opinion, in particular, is now routinely cited as authority for the "material contribution" standard.[111]

The Ninth Circuit's other notable conclusion in that case, decided a couple of years after a post-remand trial court finding for Roommates. com, was that the plaintiff civil rights organization, the Fair Housing Council of the San Fernando Valley (FHC), had standing to seek relief even if it was not itself the victim of a discrete discriminatory act.[112] FHC had alleged that Roommates.com was strictly liable for designing its site in a way that discriminated against prospective renters. It claimed standing to sue, however, because its research into the company's discriminatory designs was a drain on its resources and frustrated its mission.[113] The Ninth Circuit agreed, holding that FHC had suffered an actual injury sufficient to have standing.

In essence, the court determined that the organization could stand in for a hypothetical Roommates.com subscriber who would be harmed by users' discriminatory preferences and postings.[114] This holding makes good sense, as discriminatory targeted advertisements and solicitations subjugate racial minorities even when their victims do not witness or otherwise experience the discriminatory act directly. Civil rights laws often reach beyond discrete acts of exclusion in order to redress systemic patterns of subordination and exclusion. Roommates.com's design choices, FHC had argued, facilitated communicative acts of discrimination in a market long plagued by that very problem. And if not for FHC's intervention, the court reasoned, these patterns of bias would continue.

TOWARD A MORE NUANCED IMMUNITY DOCTRINE

The *Roommates.com* opinion, issued a decade ago, helps to show the way forward. The Ninth Circuit's careful treatment of the two contested features of the website design of Roommates.com demonstrated an appreciation for the diversity of ways in which the company elicits content from users, and its standing ruling demonstrated an appreciation for the realities of civil rights harms.

However, the Ninth Circuit's opinion did not go far enough; it did not address the increasingly subtle and tentacular kinds of control that online intermediaries exert over users' experiences today. The system through which Facebook algorithmically sorts and repurposes user data to support microtargeted advertising is a far cry from the clumsy dropdown menu in the *Roommates.com* case. Two decades after the CDA's enactment, it has become increasingly implausible to equate this powerful manipulation of users' data and content with traditional publishing under Section 230.

Section 230 doctrine must be adapted to the political economy of contemporary online information flows. Judges and litigants already have a rich set of tools from antidiscrimination and consumer protection law for determining liability and providing remedies for harmful expressive conduct. But the current Section 230 doctrine cuts cyberspace off from these other bodies of law, foreclosing liability analysis for companies whose service designs routinely facilitate or even encourage illicit content.

It is important to emphasize, moreover, that holding intermediaries to account for such designs does not require anything like strict liability for the harms caused by nonconsensual pornography or any other user-generated content. Consistent with the neglected Good Samaritan goal of the statute, Section 230 can quite comfortably be interpreted to provide a safe harbor for intermediaries that try in good faith to block or take such content down.[115] That is, after all, precisely what the text of Section 230(c)(2)(A) says, at least with regard to "objectionable" speech.[116] At the same time, courts could allow plaintiffs to seek redress from intermediaries that knowingly or negligently facilitate the distribution of harmful content. As the Ninth Circuit's ruling against Roommates.com shows, we do not need new statutory language to assess intermediary liability when the user interface at issue enables illegal online conduct.

But the experience of two decades of Section 230 litigation does suggest that new statutory language could help, particularly since the prevailing view prevents the plain meaning of the Good Samaritan title and Section 230(c)(2)(A) from doing any meaningful work. The statute itself, moreover, fails to give clear direction on the kinds of torts it covers. Nor, for that matter, does the statute address the extent to which a defendant must "create[] or develop[]" the offending material.[117] This has been left to the courts to sort out. Distressed by the wide scope of the doctrine and some of these textual gaps, legislators and activists have been promoting amendments to Section 230 that would create exceptions for prostitution, nonconsensual pornography, and the sex trafficking of minors.[118] There is no reason why Congress couldn't also write in an explicit exception to Section 230 immunity for violations of civil rights laws.

Such proposals will face substantial pushback from intermediaries and others.[119] A company like Facebook has a lot to lose from any change that would require it to be more careful about how it distributes user content or generates personal or targeted advertisements.[120] Even a shift to what some are now calling "contextual advertising," where an advertiser buys the context in which social media users engage with each other rather than individual users' profiles, could cost a company like Facebook billions of dollars.[121] And to be sure, apart from the commercial interests at stake, there are important free speech arguments for keeping Section 230 broad: the content and data flowing through the online speech environment may not be as abundant in a world in which intermediaries are held to account for their users' content and their own designs on user data. But then again, it is difficult to weigh this "chilling" concern against the chilling of members of historically subordinated groups that is already happening under existing law.[122]

CONCLUSION

Whether legal reform in this area takes place in the legislature or the judiciary or both, reform is necessary. Judges, lawyers, and legislators should stop shielding intermediaries from liability on the basis of implausible assumptions about their neutrality or passivity—and should instead start looking carefully at how intermediaries' designs on user content do or do not result in actionable injuries. This attention to design will further sensitize intermediaries to the ways in which their services perpetuate systemic harms. Equipped with a more nuanced approach to intermediary immunity, we might come to expect an online environment that is hospitable to all comers.

Section 230's Challenge to Civil Rights and Civil Liberties

Danielle Keats Citron

IN SECTION 230 of the Communications Decency Act, lawmakers thought they were devising a safe harbor for online providers engaged in self-regulation. The goal was to encourage platforms to "clean up" offensive material online. Yet Section 230's immunity has been stretched far beyond that purpose to immunize platforms that solicit or deliberately host illegality. As Olivier Sylvain's thoughtful essay shows, it has been invoked to shield from liability platforms whose architectural choices lead ineluctably to illegal discrimination.

Section 230's immunity provision has secured important breathing space for innovative new ways to work, speak, and engage with the world. But the law's overbroad interpretation has been costly to expression and equality, especially for members of traditionally subordinated groups.

This commentary highlights Sylvain's important normative contributions to the debate over Section 230. It provides some practical reinforcements for his reading of Section 230. Our central disagreement centers on the way forward. Congress should revise Section 230's safe harbor to apply only to platforms that take reasonable steps to address unlawful activity. I end with thoughts about why it is time for platforms to pair their power with responsibility.

THE "DECENCY" ACT AND ITS COSTS TO FREE SPEECH AND EQUALITY

In the technology world, Section 230 of the Communications Decency Act (CDA) is a kind of sacred cow—an untouchable protection of near-constitutional status.[123] It is, in some circles anyway, credited with enabling the development of the modern internet.[124] As Emma Llansó recently put it, "Section 230 is as important as the First Amendment to protecting free speech online."[125]

Before we tackle the current debate, it is important to step back to the statute's history and purpose. The CDA, which was part of the Telecommunications Act of 1996, was not a libertarian enactment.[126] At the time, online pornography was considered *the* scourge of the age. Senators James Exon and Slade Gorton introduced the CDA to make the internet safe for kids.[127] Besides proposing criminal penalties for the distribution of sexually explicit material online, the Senators underscored the need for private sector help in reducing the volume of noxious material online.[128] In that vein, Representatives Christopher Cox and Ron Wyden offered an amendment to the CDA titled "Protection for Private Blocking and Screening of Offensive Material."[129] The Cox-Wyden amendment, codified in Section 230, provided immunity from liability for "Good Samaritan" online service providers that either over- or under-filtered objectionable content.[130]

Twenty years ago, federal lawmakers could not have imagined how essential to modern life the internet would become. The internet was still largely a tool for hobbyists. Nonetheless, Section 230's authors believed that "if this amazing new thing—the Internet—[was] going to blossom," companies should not be "punished for *trying* to keep things clean."[131] Cox recently noted that "the original purpose of [Section 230] was to help clean up the Internet, not to facilitate people doing bad things on the Internet."[132] The key to Section 230, explained Wyden, was "making sure that companies in return for that protection—that they wouldn't be sued indiscriminately—were being responsible in terms of policing their platforms."[133]

Courts, however, have stretched Section 230's safe harbor far beyond what its words, context, and purpose support.[134] Attributing the broad interpretation of Section 230 to "First Amendment values [that] drove the CDA,"[135] courts have extended immunity from liability to platforms that republished content knowing it violated the law;[136] solicited illegal content while ensuring that those responsible could not be identified;[137] altered their user interface to ensure that criminals could not be caught;[138] and sold dangerous products.[139]

Granting immunity to platforms that deliberately host, encourage, or facilitate illegal activity would have seemed absurd to the CDA's drafters.[140]

The law's overbroad interpretation means that platforms have no reason to take down illicit material and that victims have no leverage to insist that they do so.[141] Rebecca Tushnet put it well a decade ago: Section 230 ensures that platforms enjoy "power without responsibility."[142]

Although Section 230 has been valuable to innovation and expression,[143] it has not been the net boon for free speech that its celebrants imagine.[144] The free expression calculus, devised by the law's supporters, fails to consider the loss of voices in the wake of destructive harassment that platforms have encouraged or deliberately tolerated. As ten years of research has shown, cyber mobs and individual harassers shove people offline with sexually threatening and sexually humiliating abuse;[145] targeted individuals are more often women, women of color, lesbian and trans women, and sexual minorities.[146] The benefits that Section 230's immunity has enabled likely could have been secured at a lesser price.

DISCRIMINATORY DESIGN AND WHAT TO DO ABOUT IT

Sylvain wisely urges us to think more broadly about the costs to historically disadvantaged groups wrought by Section 230's overbroad interpretation. Platforms disadvantage the vulnerable not just through their encouragement of cyber mobs and individual abusers but also through their design choices. As Sylvain argues, conversations about Section 230's costs to equality should include the ways that a platform's design can "predictably elicit or even encourage expressive conduct that perpetuates discrimination."

Sylvain's focus on discriminatory design deserves the attention of courts and lawmakers. More than twenty years ago, Joel Reidenberg and Lawrence Lessig highlighted code's role in channeling legal regulation and governance.[147] A platform's architecture can prevent illegal discrimination, just as it can be designed to protect privacy,[148] expression,[149] property,[150] and due process rights.[151]

As Sylvain has shown, platforms have instead chosen architectures that undermine legal mandates. Airbnb's site, for instance, asks guests to include real names in their online profiles even though the company knows illegal discrimination is sure to result. As studies have shown, Airbnb guests with distinctively African American names are 16 percent less likely to be accepted relative to identical guests with distinctively white names.[152] Facebook's algorithms mine users' data to create categories from which advertisers choose, including ones that facilitate illegal discrimination in hiring and housing.

Sylvain's normative argument is compelling. Platforms are by no means neutral, no matter how often or loudly tech companies say so. They are not *merely* publishing others' content when their carefully devised user interfaces and algorithms damage minorities' and women's opportunities. When code enables invidious discrimination, law should be allowed to intervene.[153] Facebook has built an advertising system that inevitably results in fair housing violations. Airbnb's user interface still requires guests to include their names, which predictably results in housing discrimination. Sylvain is right—platforms should not enjoy immunity from liability for their architectural choices that violate antidiscrimination laws.

The question, of course, is strategy. Do we need to change Section 230 to achieve Sylvain's normative ends? Section 230 should not be read to immunize platforms from liability related to user interface or design. Platforms are being sued for their code's illegality, not for their users' illegality or the platforms' subsequent over- or under-removal of content. What is legally significant is the platform's adoption of a design (such as Facebook's algorithmic manipulation of user data to facilitate ads) that enables illegal discrimination.

Sylvain's argument finds support in recent state and federal enforcement efforts.[154] For instance, in a suit against revenge porn operator Craig Brittain, the Federal Trade Commission (FTC) argued that it was unfair—and a violation of Section 5 of the FTC Act—for Brittain to exploit individuals' personal information shared in confidence for financial gain.[155] The FTC's theory of wrongdoing had roots in prior decisions related to companies that unfairly induced individuals to betray another's trust.[156] Theories of inducement focus on acts, not the publication of another's speech. Section 230 would not bar such actions because they are not premised on platforms' publication of another's speech but rather on platforms' inducing others to breach a trust. So, too, with claims asserting that a platform's wrongful activity is its design that induces or enables illegal discrimination.

What if courts are not convinced by this argument? Sylvain urges Congress to maintain the immunity but to create an explicit exception from the safe harbor for civil rights violations. He notes that other exceptions could be added, such as those related to combating nonconsensual pornography, sex trafficking, or child sexual exploitation.[157] A recent example of that approach is the Allow States and Victims to Fight Online Sex Trafficking Act, enacted in 2018.[158] The Act amends Section 230 by rendering websites liable for hosting sex trafficking content.[159]

Congress, however, should avoid a piecemeal approach going forward.[160] Carving out exceptions risks leaving out other areas of the law that should not be immunized. The statutory scheme would require updating as new problems arise that would seem to demand it. Legislation requiring piece-by-piece exemptions would most likely not get updated.

Benjamin Wittes and I have offered a broader though balanced legislative fix. In our view, platforms should enjoy immunity from liability if they can show that their response to unlawful uses of their services is reasonable. Accordingly, Wittes and I have proposed a revision to Section 230(c)(1) as follows (revised language is italicized):

> No provider or user of an interactive computer service that *takes reasonable steps to prevent or address unlawful uses of its services* shall be treated as the publisher or speaker of any information provided by another information content provider *in any action arising out of the publication of content provided by that information content provider.*[161]

The determination of what constitutes a reasonable standard of care would take into account differences among online entities. Internet service providers (ISPs) and social networks with millions of postings a day cannot plausibly respond to complaints of abuse immediately, or even within a day or two. On the other hand, they may be able to deploy technologies to detect content previously deemed unlawful.[162] The duty of care will evolve as technology improves.[163]

A reasonable standard of care will reduce opportunities for abuses without interfering with the further development of a vibrant internet or unintentionally turning innocent platforms into involuntary insurers for those injured through their sites. Approaching the problem as one of setting an appropriate standard of case more readily allows for differentiating among different kinds of online actors, setting a different rule for websites designed to facilitate mob attacks or to enable illegal discrimination from the one that would apply to large ISPs linking millions to the internet.

PARTING THOUGHTS

We have come to an important inflection point. The public is beginning to understand the extraordinary power that platforms wield over our lives. Consider the strong, negative public reaction to journalistic reports of Cambridge Analytica's mining of Facebook data to manipulate voters, or Facebook's algorithms allowing advertisers to reach users who "hate Jews," or YouTube's video streams that push us to ever more extreme content.[164] Social media companies can no longer hide behind the notion that they are neutral platforms simply publishing people's musings. Their terms-of-service agreements and content moderation systems determine if content is seen or heard or if it is muted or blocked.[165] Their algorithms dictate the advertisements that are visible to job applicants and home seekers.[166] Their systems act with laser-like precision to target, score, and manipulate each and every one of us.[167]

To return to Rebecca Tushnet's framing, with power comes responsibility. Law should change to ensure that such power is wielded responsibly. Content intermediaries have moral obligations to their users and others affected by their sites, and companies are beginning to recognize this. As Mark Zuckerberg told CNN, "I'm not sure we shouldn't be regulated."[168]

While the internet is special, it is not so fundamentally special that all normal legal rules should not apply to it. Online platforms facilitate expression, along with other key life opportunities, but no more so than do workplaces, schools, and various other civic institutions, which are zones of conversation and are not categorically exempted from legal responsibility for operating safely. The law has not destroyed expression in workplaces, homes, and other social venues.

When courts began recognizing claims under Title VII for sexually hostile work environments, employers argued that the cost of liability would force them to shutter and, if not, would ruin the camaraderie of workspaces.[169] That grim prediction has not come to pass. Rather, those spaces are now available to all on equal terms, and brick-and-mortar businesses have more than survived in the face of Title VII liability. The same should be true for networked spaces. We must make policy for the internet and society that we actually have, not the internet and society that we believed we would get twenty years ago.

To Err Is Platform

James Grimmelmann*

SECTION 230 is law for a world of mistakes. Its fundamental premise is that everyone makes mistakes. Platforms make mistakes about which user-generated content is legal; courts make mistakes about how hard platforms are trying to remove illegal content; platforms and victims make mistakes about what courts will decide. Section 230's rule of blanket immunity absolves platforms for their filtering mistakes, and keeps everyone away from inquiries where they are likely to make legal mistakes.

Because mistakes are central to Section 230, to understand Section 230 policy one must worry about mistakes, who makes them, and when. It is not enough to point to the bad speech that stays online because of Section 230, or to the good speech that platforms also host.[170] One must also ask when these two types of speech might be mistaken for each other. More than anything else, it is this question that should inform discussions about how broad Section 230 should be. In its current form, Section 230 reflects a judgment that *in general* mistakes about good and bad content are so pervasive that immunity for platforms is justified. Any proposal to create exceptions to Section 230 should be based on a judgment that *in a specific setting* these mistakes can be reduced to an acceptable level.

To be more precise, Felix Wu persuasively argues that the best theory of Section 230 is *collateral censorship*: without immunity "a (private) intermediary suppresses the speech of others in order to avoid liability that otherwise might be imposed on it as a result of that speech."[171] A platform facing liability will predictably protect itself by removing too much content: it throws the baby out with the bathwater. Section 230 takes away the risk of liability. As a result, platforms will fail to remove some content that is legally actionable: the baby stays, and so does some dirty bathwater.

Section 230 reflects a policy judgment that babies are more important than bathwater.

This is an error costs argument.[172] Its premise is that the mistakes caused by liability are worse than the mistakes caused by immunity. Given the immense scale of the internet and the immense value of the good content on it, there are good reasons to think that the argument is often correct. But the argument can fail in one of two ways. First, where *good filtering is possible*, liability will not lead to much collateral censorship because platforms will rarely mistake good content for bad. Second, where *bad content dominates good* (in terms of its volume and in terms of the harms it causes), then collateral censorship is still better than the alternative.

Courts and plaintiffs also make mistakes. If the standard for platforms' liability is anything other than blanket immunity, courts must decide whether platforms have met that standard, and plaintiffs must predict what courts will decide. Any mistakes will be costly for platforms: paying judgments in cases you lose and paying lawyers in cases you win both get expensive quickly. If those costs get too high, we are back to collateral censorship, because platforms will overfilter rather than take their chances in court. So for any exception to immunity, *the standard of liability must be clear* so platforms on the right side of the line can win their cases cheaply and reliably.

It should be clear by now that I approach the question of whether and how to restrict Section 230 rather differently than Professor Olivier Sylvain does. Something like his analysis is necessary to the case for a narrower immunity, but it is not sufficient. He argues clearly and powerfully that what I have bloodlessly referred to as "bad" or "illegal" content is both widely present on major platforms and often quite harmful. Nonconsensual pornography is awful for its victims; some Airbnb hosts discriminate illegally; Facebook enables advertisers to target ads by race.

But Sylvain never quite engages with what I see as the crucial question: *how crisply is it possible to define these categories?* Instead of talking about filtering, he talks about platforms. He argues that even if platforms were once passive intermediaries relaying user content, today they actively "sort and repurpose the user content and data they collect." This distinction between active and passive intermediaries is intuitively appealing. But the best normative case for intermediary immunity—collateral censorship—has never really rested on intermediary passivity. Even a passive intermediary has still acted by providing a platform that is a but-for cause of the harm.

Courts and commentators sometimes talk about platform passivity as a justification for immunity. But this is best understood as a shorthand for the argument that a truly passive intermediary typically lacks the *knowledge* about specific harmful content that it would need to make reliable filtering decisions. For example: a user posts a defamatory screed to YouTube about an ex-spouse's neglectful parenting. The user knows the allegations are false, but this is not something YouTube can know without detailed investigation. It lacks such knowledge not because it was passive rather than active, but because it is missing a crucial piece of information.

Not all activity is created equal. Sorting, for example, may be automated but not in a way that yields specific knowledge about the meaning of content, let alone whether it is illegal. Sorting on the basis of video length, a user's likes of previous ads, or a guest's past bookings does not tell a platform anything about whether a new video is pornographic, a new ad is hateful, or a new host is rejecting minority guests. Take nonconsensual pornography. The "pornography" half of the definition is probably something that many platforms can detect at scale—certainly this is true for the sort of platforms that let users tag videos by the race of participants and the sexual acts they perform. But the "nonconsensual" half will almost always depend on facts not in evidence, no matter how intensively the platform categorizes videos and analyzes user engagement with them. The active pornography platform and the passive one are equally able (or equally unable) to identify nonconsensual pornography. That the platform filters content along one dimension is only circumstantial evidence that it is capable of filtering along another.

Facebook's ad platform may be different because some of the categories it exposed to advertisers were so transparent. A "Demographic" category for an "affinity" of "African American (US)," for example, is fairly obviously a strong proxy for racial identity, even if the "affinity" is supposedly based only on what links a user has liked. But even here, things are not always clear-cut. Being able to target an ad to a person who has expressed interest in "how to burn jews" sounds damning, but the list of categories this was drawn from was generated algorithmically based on "what users explicitly share with Facebook and what they implicitly convey through their online activity."[173] The difference is subtle but significant. It is likely that no one at Facebook even realized it was offering a "how to burn jews" category until ProPublica reported on it, whereas it seems more likely that Facebook employees knew about a category as large and prominent as "African American (US)" but failed to appreciate its legal and ethical dangers. So now the question becomes, what would Facebook need to do to detect and exclude not just "how to burn jews" but everything else of equal odiousness, and what would the rate of false positives be?

Experience with Facebook's voluntary attempts to restrict hate speech by users does not provide reason for optimism. According to its internal guidelines, "Poor black people should still sit at the back of the bus" is acceptable (it targets only a subset of a protected group), but "White men are assholes" is not (cursing is considered an attack).[174] Speech-hosting platforms have proven repeatedly incompetent at understanding speech in context, unable to distinguish criticism, parody, and reporting from endorsement. This is a double cause for despair. First, even well-intentioned platforms run by supposedly smart and hard-working people blunder again and again in ways that are shameful or worse. And second, any threat of liability that might clean up some of the worst abuses would likely also curtail a good deal of speech trying to counter those abuses.

There is a close and often neglected connection between the proper scope of Section 230 and the underlying substantive law. Section 230 carve-outs are easier to justify when the underlying law is clearer. It is no accident that the heartland of Section 230 is defamation:[175] it is a doctrinal swamp where cases often turn on subtle nuances of meaning. And it is no accident that copyright law is exempted from Section 230:[176] fair use may be messy in the extreme, but the prima facie question of whether a particular piece of content is or is not a nearly identical copy of a particular copyrighted work is something a platform can delegate to a hashing algorithm. Similarly, federal child pornography laws—not subject to Section 230[177]—are in practice enforced against platforms by asking them to take action only when a hashing algorithm detects an already-known item, or when they acquire specific knowledge about a specific piece of content.[178]

It is reasonable to ask proponents of a narrower Section 230 to explain not just *why* it should be narrower but *how*. I look forward to future work from Sylvain and others that delves into the substantive law of nonconsensual pornography, civil rights violations, harassment, and the other mountains of garbage washing up on the internet's polluted shores,[179] and that explains in more detail how to distinguish the good from the bad quickly, cheaply, reliably, and at scale.

Toward a Clearer Conversation About Platform Liability

Daphne Keller*

IN HIS CONTRIBUTION to this volume, Fordham Law School's Olivier Sylvain critiques a core U.S. internet law, Section 230 of the Communications Decency Act (CDA 230).[180] CDA 230 immunizes platforms like YouTube and Craigslist from most liability for speech posted by their users. By doing so, it protects lawful and important speech that risk-averse platforms might otherwise silence. But it also lets platforms tolerate unlawful and harmful speech.

Sylvain argues that the net result is to perpetuate inequities in our society. For women, ethnic minorities, and many others, he suggests, CDA 230 facilitates harassment and abuse — and thus "helps to reinforce systemic subordination."[181] We need not tolerate all this harm, Sylvain further suggests, given the current state of technology. Large platforms' ever-improving ability to algorithmically curate users' speech "belies the old faith that such services operate at too massive a scale to be asked to police user content."

CDA 230 has long been a pillar of U.S. internet law. Lately, though, it has come under sustained attack. In the spring of 2018, Congress passed the first legislative change to CDA 230 in two decades: the Allow States and Victims to Fight Online Sex Trafficking Act, commonly known as FOSTA.[182] FOSTA has an important goal — protecting victims of sex trafficking. But it is so badly drafted, no one can agree on exactly what it means. It passed despite opposition from advocates for trafficking victims[183] and the ACLU,[184] and despite the Justice Department's concern that aspects of it could make prosecutors' jobs harder.[185] More challenges to CDA 230 are in the works. That makes close attention to the law, including both its strengths and its weaknesses, extremely timely.

Supporters of CDA 230 generally focus on three broad benefits. The first is promoting innovation and competition. When Congress passed the law in 1996, it was largely looking to future businesses and technologies. In today's age of powerful mega-platforms, the concern about competition is perhaps even more justified. When platform liability risks expand, wealthy incumbents can hire lawyers and armies of moderators to adapt to new standards. Startups and smaller companies can't. That's why advocates for startups opposed FOSTA,[186] while Facebook[187] and the incumbent-backed Internet Association supported it.[188]

The second benefit of CDA 230 is its protection for internet users' speech rights. When platforms face liability for user content, they have strong incentives to err on the side of caution and take it down, particularly for controversial or unpopular material. Empirical evidence from notice-and-takedown regimes tells us that wrongful legal accusations are common, and that platforms often simply comply with them.[189] The Ecuadorian government, for example, has used spurious copyright claims to suppress criticism and videos of police brutality.[190] Platform removal errors can harm any speaker, but a growing body of evidence suggests that they disproportionately harm vulnerable or disfavored groups.[191] So while Sylvain is surely right to say that vulnerable groups suffer disproportionately when platforms take down too little content, they may also suffer disproportionately when platforms take down too much.

The third benefit is that CDA 230 encourages community-oriented platforms like Facebook or YouTube to weed out offensive content. This was Congress's goal in enacting the CDA's "Good Samaritan" clause, which immunizes platforms for voluntarily taking down anything they consider "objectionable."[192] Prior to CDA 230, platforms faced the so-called moderator's dilemma—any effort to weed out illegal content could expose them to liability for the things they missed, so they were safer not moderating at all.[193]

Against these upsides, Sylvain marshals a compelling list of downsides. Permissive speech rules and hands-off attitudes by platforms, especially when combined with what Sylvain calls "discriminatory designs on user content and data," enable appalling abuses, particularly against members of minority groups. Nonconsensual pornography, verbal attacks, and credible threats of violence are all too common.

Does that mean it is time to scrap CDA 230? Some people think so. Sylvain's argument is more nuanced. He identifies specific harms, and specific advances in platform technology and operations, that he argues justify legal changes. While I disagree with some of his analysis and conclusions, the overall project is timely and useful. It arrives at a moment of chaotic, often rudderless public dialogue about platform responsibility. Pundits depict a maelstrom of online threats, often conflating issues as diverse as data breaches, "fake news," and competition. The result is a moment of real risk, not just for platforms but for internet users. Poorly thought-through policy responses to misunderstood problems can far too easily become laws.

In contrast to this panicked approach, Sylvain says we should be "looking carefully at how intermediaries' designs on user content do or do not result in actionable injuries." This is a worthy project. It is one that, in today's environment, requires us to pool our intellectual resources. Sylvain brings, among other things, a deep understanding of the history of communications regulation. I bring practical experience from years in-house at Google and familiarity with intermediary liability laws around the world.

To put my own cards on the table—and surely surprising no one— I am very wary of tinkering with intermediary liability law, including CDA 230. That's mostly because I think the field is very poorly understood. It was hardly a field at all just a few years ago. A rising generation of experts, including Sylvain, will fix that before long. In the meantime, though, we need careful and calm analysis if we are to avoid shoot-from-the-hip legislative changes.

Whatever we do with the current slew of questions about platform responsibility, the starting point should be a close look at the facts and the law. The facts include the real and serious harms Sylvain identifies. He rightly asks why our system of laws tolerates them and what we can do better.

CDA 230, though, is not the driver of many of the problems he identifies. In the first section of my commentary, I will walk through the reasons why. Hateful or harassing speech, for example, often doesn't violate any law at all, for reasons grounded in the First Amendment. If platforms tolerate content of this sort, it is not because of CDA 230. Quite the contrary: a major function of the law is to *encourage* platforms to take down lawful but offensive speech.

Other problems Sylvain describes are more akin to the practices that put Facebook user data in the hands of Cambridge Analytica.[194] They involve breaches of trust (or of privacy or consumer protection law) between a platform and the user who shared data or content in the first place. Legal claims for breaching this trust are generally not immunized by CDA 230. If we want to change laws that apply in these situations, CDA 230 is the wrong place to start.

In the second section of my commentary, I will focus on the issues Sylvain surfaces that really do implicate CDA 230. In particular, I will discuss his argument that platforms' immunities should be reduced when they actively curate content and target it to particular users. Under existing intermediary liability frameworks outside of CDA 230, arguments for disqualifying platforms from immunity based on curation typically fall into one of two categories. I will address both.

The first argument is that platforms should not be immunized when they are insufficiently neutral. This framing, I argue, is rarely helpful. It leads to confusing standards and in practice deters platforms from policing for harmful material.

The second argument is that immunity should depend on whether a platform knows about unlawful content. Knowledge is a slippery concept in the relevant law, but it is a relatively well-developed one. Knowledge-based liability has problems—it poses the very threats to speech, competition, and good-faith moderation efforts that CDA 230 avoids. But by talking about platform knowledge, we can reason from precedent and experience with other legal frameworks in the United States and around the world. That allows us to more clearly define the factual, legal, and policy questions in front of us. We can have an intelligent conversation, even if we don't all agree. That's something the world of internet law and policy badly needs right now.

ISOLATING NON-CDA 230 ISSUES

In this section I will walk through issues and potential legal claims mentioned by Sylvain that are not, I think, controlled by CDA 230. Eliminating them from the discussion will help us focus on his remaining important questions about intermediary liability.

TARGETING CONTENT OR ADS BASED ON DISCRIMINATORY CLASSIFICATIONS

Sylvain's legal arguments are grounded in a deep moral concern with the harms of online discrimination. He provides numerous moving examples of bias and mistreatment. But many of the internet user and platform behaviors he describes are not actually illegal, or are governed by laws other than CDA 230.

As one particularly disturbing example, Sylvain describes how Facebook allowed advertisers to target users based on algorithmically identified "interests" that included phrases like "how to burn jews" and "Jew hater." When ProPublica's Julia Angwin broke this story, Facebook scrambled to suspend these interest categories. Sylvain recounts this episode to illustrate the kinds of antisocial outcomes that algorithmic decision-making can generate. However repugnant these phrases are, though, they are not illegal. Nor is using them to target ads. So CDA 230 does not increase platforms' willingness to tolerate this content—although it does increase their legal flexibility to take it down.

To outlaw this kind of thing, we would need different substantive laws about things like hate speech and harassment. Do we want those? Does the internet context change First Amendment analysis? Like other critics of CDA 230 doctrine, Sylvain emphasizes the "significant qualitative and quantitative difference between the reach of [harmful] offline and online expressive acts." But it's not clear how reducing CDA 230 immunity would curb many of these harms if the speech at issue is legal.

CDA 230 also has little or no influence on Facebook ads that target users based on their likely race, age, or gender. Critics raise well-justified concerns about this targeting. But, as Sylvain notes, it generally is not illegal under current law. Antidiscrimination laws, and hence potential CDA 230 defenses, only come into play for ads regarding housing, employment, and possibly credit.[195] Even for that narrower class of ads, it's not clear that Facebook is doing anything illegal under the Fair Housing Act (FHA) and similar laws by offering a targeting tool that has both lawful and unlawful uses.[196] Finally, if Facebook *did* violate the FHA, one of the leading cases suggests that CDA 230 might offer no defense.[197] In 2019, Facebook settled cases that might have answered these questions and told us whether CDA 230 is relevant to the problems Sylvain describes.[198]

Sylvain's more complicated claim is that CDA 230 allows Airbnb to facilitate discrimination by requiring renters to post pictures of themselves. Given Airbnb's importance to travelers, discrimination by hosts is a big deal. But CDA 230's relevance is dubious. First, it's not clear if anyone involved—even a host—violates the FHA by enforcing discriminatory preferences for shared dwellings.[199] Even if the hosts are liable, it seems unlikely that Airbnb violates the FHA by requiring photos, which serve legitimate as well as illegitimate purposes. Prohibiting the photos might even be unconstitutional. A court recently struck down under the First Amendment a California statute that, following reasoning similar to Sylvain's, barred the Internet Movie Database from showing actors' ages because employers might use the information to discriminate.[200] Finally, if Airbnb's photo requirement did violate the FHA, it seems unlikely that CDA 230 would provide immunity.[201] The upshot is that CDA 230 is probably irrelevant to the problem Sylvain is trying to solve in this case.

None of this legal analysis refutes Sylvain's moral and technological point: the internet enables new forms of discrimination, and the law should respond. The law may very well warrant changing. But for these examples, CDA 230 isn't the problem.

TARGETING CONTENT BASED ON DATA MINING

Sylvain also describes a set of problems that seem to arise from platforms' directly harming or breaching the trust of their users. Some of these commercial behaviors, like "administer[ing] their platforms in obscure or undisclosed ways that are meant to influence how users behave on the site," don't appear to implicate CDA 230 even superficially.[202] Others, like using user-generated content in ways the user did not expect, look more like CDA 230 issues because they involve publication. But I don't think they really fall under CDA 230 either.

In one particularly disturbing example, Sylvain describes an Instagram user who posted a picture of a rape threat she received—only to have Instagram reuse the picture as an ad. An analogous fact pattern was litigated under CDA 230 in *Fraley v. Facebook, Inc.*[203] In that case, users sued Facebook for using their profile pictures in ads, claiming a right-of-publicity violation. A court upheld their claim and rejected Facebook's CDA 230 defense.[204] If that ruling is correct, there should no CDA 230 issue for the case Sylvain describes.

But there is a deeper question about what substantive law governs in cases like this. The harm comes from a breach of trust between the platform and individual users, the kind of thing usually addressed by consumer protection, privacy, or data protection laws. U.S. law is famously weak in these areas. Compared to other countries, we give internet users few legal tools to control platforms' use of their data or content.[205] U.S. courts enforce privacy policies and terms of service that would be void in other jurisdictions,[206] and they are stingy with standing or damages for people claiming privacy harms.[207] That's why smart plaintiffs' lawyers bring claims like the right-of-publicity tort in *Fraley*. But the crux of those claims is not a publishing harm of the sort usually addressed by CDA 230. The crux is the user's lack of control over her *own* speech or data—what Jack Balkin or Jonathan Zittrain might call an "information fiduciary" issue.[208] Framing cases like these as CDA 230 issues risks losing sight of these other values and legal principles.

ADDRESSING CDA 230 ISSUES

Sylvain suggests that platforms should lose CDA 230 immunity when they "employ software to make meaning out of their users' 'reactions,' search terms, and browsing activity in order to curate the content" and thereby "enable[] illegal online conduct." For issues that really do involve illegal content and potential liability for intermediaries—like nonconsensual pornography—this argument is important. At least one case has reviewed a nearly identical argument and rejected it.[209] But Sylvain's point isn't to clarify the current law. It's to work toward what he calls "a more nuanced immunity doctrine." For that project, the curation argument matters.

I see two potential reasons for stripping platforms of immunity when they "elicit and then algorithmically sort and repurpose" user content.[210] First, a platform might lose immunity because it is not neutral enough, given the ways it selects and prioritizes particular material. Second, it could lose immunity because curation efforts give it knowledge of unlawful material. Both theories have important analogues in other areas of law—including the Digital Millennium Copyright Act (DMCA), pre-CDA U.S. law, and law from outside the United States—to help us think them through.

NEUTRALITY

All intermediary liability laws have some limit on the platform operations that are immunized—a point at which a platform becomes too engaged in user-generated content and starts being held legally responsible for it.

Courts and lawmakers often use words like "neutral" or "passive" to describe immunized platforms. Those words don't, in my experience, have stable enough meanings to be useful.

For example, the Court of Justice of the European Union has said that only "passive" hosts are immune under EU law. Applying that standard in the leading case, it found Google immune for content in ads, which the company not only organizes and ranks but also ranks based in part on payment.[211] And in a U.S. case, a court said a platform was neutral when it engaged in the very kinds of curation that, under Sylvain's analysis, makes platforms *not* neutral.[212]

In the internet service provider (ISP) context, neutrality—as in net neutrality—means something very different. Holding ISPs to a "passive conduit" standard makes sense as a technological matter. But that standard doesn't transfer well to other intermediaries. It would eliminate immunity for topic-specific forums (Disney's Club Penguin or a subreddit about knitting, for example) or for platforms like Facebook that bar lawful but offensive speech. That seems like the wrong outcome given that most users, seemingly including Sylvain, *want* platforms to remove this content.

Policy-makers could in theory draw a line by saying that, definitionally, a platform that algorithmically curates content is not neutral or immunized. But then what do we do with search engines, which offer algorithmic ranking as their entire value proposition? And how exactly does a no-algorithmic-curation standard apply to social media? As Eric Goldman has pointed out, there is no such thing as neutrality for a platform, like Facebook or Twitter, that hosts user-facing content.[213] Whether it sorts content chronologically, alphabetically, by size, or some other metric, it unavoidably imposes a hierarchy of some sort.

All of this makes neutrality something of a Rorschach test. It takes on different meanings depending on the values we prioritize. For someone focused on speech rights, neutrality might mean not excluding any legal content, no matter how offensive. For a competition specialist, it might mean honesty and fair competition in ranking search results.[214] Still other concepts of neutrality might emerge if we prioritize copyright, transparency, or, as Sylvain does in this piece, protecting vulnerable groups in society.

One way out of this bind is for the law to get very, very granular—like the DMCA. It has multiple overlapping statutory tests that effectively assess a defendant's neutrality before awarding immunity.[215] By focusing on just a few values, narrowly defining eligible technologies, and spelling out rules in detail, it's easier to define the line between immunized behavior and non-immunized behavior.

DMCA litigators on both sides hate these granular tests. Maybe that means the law is working as intended. But highly particular tests for immunity present serious tradeoffs. If every intermediary liability question looked like the DMCA, then only companies with armies of lawyers and reserves of cash for litigation and settlement could run platforms. And even they would block user speech or decide not to launch innovative features in the face of legal uncertainty. Detailed rules like the DMCA's get us back to the problems that motivated Congress to pass the CDA: harm to lawful speech, harm to competition and innovation, and uncertainty about whether platforms could moderate content without incurring liability.

Congress's goal in CDA 230 was to get away from neutrality tests as a basis for immunity and instead to encourage platforms to curate content. I think Congress was right on this score, and not only for the competition, speech, and Good Samaritan reasons identified at the time. Abstract concepts of neutrality do not provide workable answers to real-world platform liability questions.

KNOWLEDGE

The other interpretation I see for Sylvain's argument about curation is that platforms shouldn't be able to claim immunity if they know about illegal content—and that the tools used for curation bring them ever closer to such knowledge. This factual claim is debatable. Do curation, ranking, and targeting algorithms really provide platforms with meaningful information about legal violations?[216] Whatever the answer, focusing on questions like this can clarify intermediary liability discussions.

Like the neutrality framing, this one is familiar from non–CDA 230 intermediary liability. Many laws around the world, including parts of the DMCA, say that if a platform knows about unlawful content but doesn't take it down, it loses immunity. These laws lead to litigation about what counts as "knowledge," and to academic, NGO, and judicial attention to the effects on the internet ecosystem. If a mere allegation or notice to a platform creates culpable knowledge, platforms will err on the side of removing lawful speech. If "knowledge" is an effectively unobtainable legal ideal, on the other hand, platforms won't have to take down anything.

Some courts and legislatures around the world have addressed this problem by reference to due process. Platforms in Brazil,[217] Chile,[218] Spain,[219] India,[220] and Argentina[221] are, for some or all claims, not considered to know whether a user's speech is illegal until a court has made that determination. Laws like these often make exceptions for "manifestly" unlawful content that can, in principle, be identified by platforms. This is functionally somewhat similar to CDA 230's exception for child pornography and other content barred by federal criminal law.[222]

Other models, like the DMCA, use procedural rules to cabin culpable knowledge. Sylvain rightly invokes these as important protections against abuse of notice-and-takedown systems. Claimants must follow a statutorily defined notice process and provide a penalty-of-perjury statement. A DMCA notice that does not comply with the statute's requirements cannot be used to prove that a platform knows about infringing material.[223] Claimants also accept procedures for accused speakers to formally challenge a removal or to seek penalties for bad-faith removal demands.[224]

A rapidly expanding body of material from the United Nations and regional human rights systems,[225] as well as a widely endorsed civil society standard known as the Manila Principles,[226] spell out additional procedures designed to limit over-removal of lawful speech. Importantly, these include public transparency to allow NGOs and internet users to crowdsource the job of identifying errors by platforms and patterns of abuse by claimants. Several courts around the world have also cited constitutional free expression rights of internet users in rejecting—as Sylvain does—strict liability for platforms.[227]

As Sylvain notes, liability based on knowledge is common in pre-CDA tort law. Platforms differ from print publishers and distributors in important respects. But case law about "analog intermediaries" can provide important guidance, some of it mandatory under the First Amendment. The "actual malice" standard established in New York Times Co. v. Sullivan is an example.[228] Importantly, the Times in that case acted as a platform, not as a publisher of its own reporting. The speech at issue came from paying advertisers, who bought space in the paper to document violence against civil rights protesters. As the court noted in rejecting the Alabama Supreme Court's defamation judgment, high liability risk "would discourage newspapers from carrying 'editorial advertisements' of this type, and so might shut off an important outlet for the promulgation of information and ideas by persons who do not themselves have access to publishing facilities."[229] Similar considerations apply online.

Knowledge-based standards for platform liability are no panacea.[230] Any concept of culpable knowledge for speech platforms involves tradeoffs of competing values, and not ones I necessarily believe we should make. What the knowledge framing and precedent provide, though, is a set of tools for deliberating more clearly about those tradeoffs.

CONCLUSION

Talk of platform regulation is in the air. Lawyers can make sense of this chaotic public dialogue by being lawyerly. We can crisply identify harms and parse existing laws. If those laws aren't adequately protecting important values, including the equality values Sylvain discusses, we can propose specific changes and consider their likely consequences.

At the end of the day, not everyone will agree about policy tradeoffs in intermediary liability—how to balance speech values against dignity and equality values, for example. And not everyone will have the same empirical predictions about what consequences laws are likely to have. But we can get a whole lot closer to agreement than we are now. We can build better shared language and analytic tools, and identify the right questions to ask. Sylvain's observations and arguments, coupled with tools from existing intermediary liability law, can help us do that.

NOTES

DISCRIMINATORY DESIGNS ON USER DATA

1. *See, e.g.,* Mark Zuckerberg, *Bringing the World Closer Together,* Facebook (June 22, 2017), http://www.facebook.com/zuck/posts/10154944663901634; *About Us,* Airbnb, https://press.airbnb.com/about-us (last visited July 18, 2019); Ricardo Castro, *A Better Way to Connect with People,* Twitter Blog (May 3, 2016), http://blog.twitter.com /official/en_us/a/2016/a-better-way-to-connect-with-people.html.
2. *Zeran v. America Online, Inc.,* 129 F.3d 327, 332 (4th Cir. 1997).
3. *See* Orly Lobel, *The Law of the Platform,* 101 Minn. L. Rev. 87, 89 (2016) (discussing "the digital platform revolution").
4. 47 U.S.C. § 230 (2012).
5. *Id.* § 230(b)(2).
6. *See, e.g.,* 104 Cong. Rec. H8469 (statements of Rep. Cox and Rep. Wyden); H.R. Rep. No. 104–58, at 194 (1996); *see also* Eugene Volokh, *Freedom of Speech in Cyberspace from the Listener's Perspective: Private Speech Restrictions, Libel, State Action, Harassment, and Sex,* 1996 U. Chi. Legal F. 377, 405–06;

Alan H. Bomser, *A Lawyer's Ramble down the Information Superhighway*, 64 Fordham L. Rev. 697, 799–800 (1996).

7. *See* Anthony Ciolli, *Chilling Effects: The Communications Decency Act and the Online Marketplace of Ideas*, 63 U. Miami L. Rev. 137, 148 (2008); Seth F. Kreimer, *Censorship by Proxy: The First Amendment, Internet Intermediaries, and the Problem of the Weakest Link*, 155 U. Pa. L. Rev. 11, 28–29 (2006); Rebecca Tushnet, *Power Without Responsibility: Intermediaries and the First Amendment*, 76 Geo. Wash. L. Rev. 986, 991, 998–99, 1006–09, 1015–16 (2008); Felix T. Wu, *Collateral Censorship and the Limits of Intermediary Immunity*, 87 Notre Dame L. Rev. 293, 300, 315–18 (2011).

8. *See, e.g., Jones v. Dirty World Entm't Recordings*, 755 F.3d 398, 413 (6th Cir. 2014); *Fair Hous. Council of San Fernando Valley v. Roommates.com, LLC*, 521 F.3d 1157, 1167–71 (9th Cir. 2008) (en banc).

9. *Roommates.com*, 521 F.3d at 1167–68.

10. *See, e.g., id.* at 1180 (McKeown, J., concurring in part and dissenting in part) ("We have underscored that this broad grant of webhost immunity gives effect to Congress's stated goals 'to promote the continued development of the Internet and other interactive computer services' and 'to preserve the vibrant and competitive free market that presently exists for the Internet and other interactive computer services.'" (quoting *Carafano v. Metrosplash.com*, 339 F.3d 1119, 1123 (9th Cir. 2003))).

11. *Jones v. Dirty World Entm't Recordings, LLC*, 755 F.3d 398 (6th Cir. 2014).

12. *Doe v. MySpace*, F. Supp. 2d 843 (W.D. Tex. 2007).

13. *Doe v. Backpage.com, LLC*, 817 F.3d 12 (1st Cir. 2016), *cert. denied*, 137 S. Ct. 622 (2017).

14. Julia Angwin & Terry Parris Jr., *Facebook Lets Advertisers Exclude Users by Race*, ProPublica (Oct. 28, 2016), http://www.propublica.org/article/facebook-lets-advertisers-exclude-users-by-race.

15. Nick Wingfield, *Feminist Critics of Video Games Facing Threats in "GamerGate" Campaign*, N.Y. Times (Oct. 15, 2014), http://www.nytimes.com/2014/10/16/technology/gamergate-women-video-game-threats-anita-sarkeesian.html.

16. Anna Silman, *A Timeline of Leslie Jones's Horrific Online Abuse*, Cut (Aug. 24, 2016), http://www.thecut.com/2016/08/a-timeline-of-leslie-joness-horrific-online-abuse.html.

17. Emanuella Grinberg, *Police: At Least 40 People Watched Teen's Sexual Assault on Facebook Live*, CNN (Mar. 22, 2017), http://www.cnn.com/2017/03/21/us/facebook-live-gang-rape-chicago.

18. *See* Rob Goldman, *This Time, ProPublica, We Disagree*, Facebook Newsroom (Dec. 20, 2017), http://newsroom.fb.com/news/h/addressing-targeting-in-recruitment-ads.

19. *See* Wu, *supra* note 7, at 315–18.

20. *See generally* Kenneth Bamberger & Orly Lobel, *Platform Market Power*, 32 Berkeley Tech. L.J. 1, 37–39 (2018) (discussing ways in which intermediaries leverage their market position to exploit user data in different markets); Lina M. Khan, Note, *Amazon's Antitrust Paradox*, 126 Yale L.J. 710 (2017) (discussing ways in which intermediaries may raise antitrust concerns to the extent they cultivate their position as "essential infrastructure" for commerce across industries).

21. This argument builds on my recent writing. *See* Olivier Sylvain, *Intermediary Design Duties*, 50 Conn. L. Rev. 202 (2018) [hereinafter Sylvain, *Design Duties*]; Olivier Sylvain, AOL v. Zeran: *The Cyberlibertarian Hack of Section 230 Has Run Its Course*, Law.com (Nov. 10, 2017), http://www.law.com /therecorder/sites/therecorder/2017/11/10/aol-v-zeran-the-cyberlibertarian -hack-of-%C2%A7230-has-run-its-course.

22. On these norms, see generally Olivier Sylvain, *Network Equality*, 67 Hastings L.J. 443 (2016).

23. The pertinent language provides as follows:

> (1) Treatment of publisher or speaker
> No provider or user of an interactive computer service shall be treated as the publisher or speaker of any information provided by another information content provider.
> (2) Civil liability. No provider or user of an interactive computer service shall be held liable on account of—
> (A) any action voluntarily taken in good faith to restrict access to or avail-ability of material that the provider or user considers to be obscene, lewd, lascivious, filthy, excessively violent, harassing, or otherwise objectionable, whether or not such material is constitutionally pro-tected; or
> (B) any action taken to enable or make available to information content providers or others the technical means to restrict access to material described in paragraph (1).

   47 U.S.C. § 230(c) (2012). The statute excludes from immunity intermediar-ies that are "responsible, in whole or in part, for the creation or development" of illicit user content. *Id.* § 230(f)(3). Applying this language, courts have sub-jected defendant intermediaries to liability when they "materially contribute" to the offending content. *See, e.g., Fair Hous. Council of San Fernando Valley v. Roommates.com, LLC*, 521 F.3d 1157, 1167–71 (9th Cir. 2008) (en banc). In principle, the "material contribution" standard limits the scope of the protection to services that are only conduits of content. In practice, however, it is a very high bar for plaintiffs to clear.

24. *Zeran v. Am. Online, Inc.*, 129 F.3d 327, 332 (4th Cir. 1997).

25. 47 U.S.C. § 230(c).

26. *See* Benjamin C. Zipursky, *Online Defamation, Legal Concepts, and the Good Samaritan*, 51 Val. U. L. Rev. 1, 31 (2016); Benjamin C. Zipursky, *Thinking in the Box in Legal Scholarship: The Good Samaritan and Internet Libel*, 50 J. Legal Educ. 55, 60 (2016).

27. *Luke* 10:23–37 ("[A] Samaritan, as he traveled, came where the man was; and when he saw him, he took pity on him. He went to him and bandaged his wounds, pouring on oil and wine. Then he put the man on his own donkey, brought him to an inn and took care of him.").

28. *Zeran*, 129 F.3d at 330–32.

29. 104 Cong. Rec. H8469 (statement of Rep. Wyden).

30. *Id.* (statement of Rep. Cox).

31. *See* 17 U.S.C. § 512(c) (2012); *see also Viacom v. YouTube*, 676 F.3d 19 (2d. Cir. 2012).

32. *See, e.g., Fair Hous. Council of San Fernando Valley v. Roommates.com, LLC*, 521 F.3d 1157 (9th Cir. 2008) (en banc); *Zeran*, 129 F.3d 327.
33. *See, e.g., Zeran*, 129 F.3d at 333.
34. *See, e.g., Klayman v. Zuckerberg*, 753 F.3d 1354 (D.C. Cir. 2014); *Joseph v. Amazon.com*, 46 F. Supp. 3d 1095 (W.D. Wash. 2014); *Goddard v. Google*, 640 F. Supp. 2d 1193 (N.D. Cal. 2009).
35. *See* Danielle Keats Citron, *Hate Crimes in Cyberspace* 122 (2014).
36. *See* Debbie Chachra, *Twitter's Harassment Problem Is Baked into Its Design*, Atlantic (Oct. 16, 2017), http://www.theatlantic.com/technology/archive/2017/10 /twitters-harassment-problem-is-baked-into-its-design/542952.
37. *See* Sylvain, *supra* note 22, at 462–64.
38. *See Search King v. Google*, 2003 WL 21464568 (W.D. Okla. 2003). *See generally* Deepa Seetharaman, *Google Retools Search Engine to Demote Hoaxes, Fake News*, Wall St. J. (Apr. 25, 2017), http://www.wsj.com/articles /google-retools-search-engine-to-downplay-hoaxes-fake-news-1493144451.
39. Erin Griffith, *Facebook Can Absolutely Control Its Algorithm*, Wired (Sept. 26, 2017), http://www.wired.com/story/facebook-can-absolutely-control-its-algorithm; Amber Jamieson & Olivia Solon, *Facebook to Begin Flagging Fake News in Response to Mounting Criticism*, Guardian (Dec. 15, 2016), http://www.theguardian .com/technology/2016/dec/15/facebook-flag-fake-news-fact-check.
40. *Reddit Content Policy*, Reddit, http://www.reddit.com/help/contentpolicy (last visited July 18, 2019); *see also Removing Harassing Subreddits*, Reddit (June 10, 2015), http://np.reddit.com/r/announcements/comments/39bpam /removing_harassing_subreddits.
41. Charlie Warzel, *Reddit Is a Shrine to the Internet We Wanted and That's a Problem*, BuzzFeed (June 19, 2015), http://www.buzzfeed.com/charliewarzel /reddit-is-a-shrine-to-the-internet-we-wanted-and-thats-a-pro.
42. ModNews, *Update on Site-Wide Rules Regarding Violent Content*, Reddit (Oct. 25, 2017), http://www.reddit.com/r/modnews/comments/78p7bz /update_on_sitewide_rules_regarding_violent_content.
43. *See* Aja Romano, *Reddit Just Banned One of Its Most Toxic Forums. But It Won't Touch the Donald*, Vox (Nov. 13, 2017), http://www.vox.com/culture /2017/11/13/16624688/reddit-bans-incels-the-donald-controversy.
44. *Id.*
45. *See generally* Kate Klonick, *The New Governors: The People, Rules, and Processes Governing Online Speech*, 131 Harv. L. Rev. 1598 (2018); Karen Levy & Solon Barocas, *Designing Against Discrimination in Online Markets*, 32 Berkeley Tech. L.J. 1183 (2017).
46. *See* Derek Khanna, *The Law That Gave Us the Modern Internet—and the Campaign to Kill It*, Atlantic (Sept. 12, 2017), http://www.theatlantic.com /business/archive/2013/09/the-law-that-gave-us-the-modern-internet-and-the -campaign-to-kill-it/279588.
47. *See, e.g.,* Ariana Tobin et al., *Facebook's Uneven Enforcement of Hate Speech Rules Allows Vile Posts to Stay Up*, ProPublica (Dec. 27, 2017), http://www .propublica.org/article/facebook-enforcement-hate-speech-rules-mistakes; Julia Angwin et al., *Facebook (Still) Letting Housing Advertisers Exclude Users by Race*, ProPublica (Nov. 21, 2017), http://www.propublica.org/article /facebook-advertising-discrimination-housing-race-sex-national-origin.

48. *See* sources cited *supra* note 7.
49. There also is a toll on the human moderators responsible for censoring illicit content. Recent reporting suggests that these workers are traumatized by the material they censor. *See* Lauren Weber & Deepa Seetharaman, *The Worst Job in Technology: Staring at Human Depravity to Keep It off Facebook*, Wall St. J. (Dec. 27, 2017), http://www.wsj.com/articles/the-worst-job-in-technology-staring -at-human-depravity-to-keep-it-off-facebook-1514398398.
50. *See* Citron, *supra* note 35, at 13–16.
51. *See, e.g.*, Mari J. Matsuda et al., *Words that Wound: Critical Race Theory, Assaultive Speech, and the First Amendment* (1993); Charles R. Lawrence, III, *Crossburning and the Sound of Silence: Antisubordination Theory and the First Amendment*, 37 Vill. L. Rev. 787 (1992).
52. *Cf.* Richard Delgado & Jean Stefancic, *Understanding Words that Wound* 217–18 (2004) (advocating a "new approach" that "points out how speech and equality stand in reciprocal relation; neither can thrive without the other. Speech without equality is a lecture, a sermon, a rant. Speech, in other words, presumes equality, or something like it, among participants in a dialogue").
53. *See* Margaret Talbot, *The Attorney Fighting Revenge Porn*, New Yorker (Dec. 5, 2016), http://www.newyorker.com/magazine/2016/12/05/the-attorney-fighting -revenge-porn.
54. 570 F.3d 1096 (9th Cir. 2009).
55. Danielle Keats Citron & Mary Anne Franks, *Criminalizing Revenge Porn*, 49 Wake Forest L. Rev. 345, 350 (2014).
56. *See* Danielle Keats Citron, *Law's Expressive Value in Combating Cyber Gender Harassment*, 108 Mich. L. Rev. 373 (2009); *see also* Clare McGlynn et al., *Beyond "Revenge Porn": The Continuum of Image-Based Sexual Abuse*, 25 Feminist Legal Stud. 25 (2017); Catherine Buni & Soraya Chemaly, *The Unsafety Net: How Social Media Turned Against Women*, Atlantic (Oct. 9, 2014), http://www.theatlantic.com/technology/archive/2014/10/the -unsafety-net-how-social-media-turned-against-women/381261.
57. *See, e.g.*, *Barrett v. Rosenthal*, 146 P.3d 510 (Cal. 2006); *Batzel v. Smith*, 333 F.3d 1018 (9th Cir. 2003); *Zeran*, 129 F.3d 327. *See generally* Joel R. Reidenberg et al., Ctr. on Law & Info. Pol'y at Fordham Law Sch., *Section 230 of the Communications Decency Act: A Survey of the Legal Literature and Reform Proposals* (Apr. 25, 2012), http://ssrn.com/abstract=2046230 (surveying sixteen years of Section 230 cases).
58. *See* Citron, *supra* note 35, at 127 ("Cyber harassment reinforces gender stereotypes by casting women as sex objects that are unfit for life's important opportunities.").
59. *See, e.g.*, *Barnes v. Yahoo!, Inc.*, 570 F.3d 1096 (9th Cir. 2009); *Jones v. Dirty World Entm't Recordings, LLC*, 755 F.3d 398 (6th Cir. 2014).
60. Twitter recognizes the significance of its character limitation; it increased the limitation from 140 in November 2017 to improve the user experience. *See* Aatif Sulleyman, *Twitter Introduces 280 Characters to All Users*, Independent (Nov. 7, 2017), http://www.independent.co.uk/life-style/gadgets-and-tech/news/twitter -280-characters-tweets-start-when-get-latest-a8042716.html.
61. *See FTC v. LeadClick Media*, 838 F.3d 158 (2d Cir. 2016).
62. *See FTC v. Accusearch*, 570 F.3d 1187 (10th Cir. 2009).

63. *See* Frank Pasquale, *The Black Box Society* 3, 28–31 (2015).

64. *See* Adam Alter, *Irresistible: The Rise of Addictive Technology and the Business of Keeping Us Hooked* (2017); Paul Lewis, *"Our Minds Can Be Hijacked": The Tech Insiders Who Fear a Smartphone Dystopia*, Guardian (Oct. 6, 2017), http://www .theguardian.com/technology/2017/oct/05/smartphone-addiction-silicon -valley-dystopia. *See generally* Tim Wu, *The Attention Merchants: The Epic Scramble to Get Inside Our Heads* (2016); Nir Eyal, *Hooked: How to Build Habit-Forming Products* (2014).

65. Noam Cohen, *Silicon Valley Is Not Your Friend*, N.Y. Times (Oct. 13, 2017), http://www.nytimes.com/interactive/2017/10/13/opinion/sunday/Silicon-Valley-Is -Not-Your-Friend.html.

66. Julia Carrie Wong, *Facebook Overhauls News Feed in Favor of "Meaningful Social Interactions,"* Guardian (Jan. 11, 2018), http://www.theguardian.com /technology/2018/jan/11/facebook-news-feed-algorithm-overhaul-mark-zuckerberg.

67. Issie Lapowsky, *How Facebook Knows You Better Than Your Friends Do*, Wired (Jan. 13, 2015), http://www.wired.com/2015/01/facebook-personality-test.

68. *See* Christina Passariello, *Facebook: Media Company or Technology Platform?*, Wall St. J. (Oct. 30, 2016), http://www.wsj.com/articles/facebook-media-company -or-technology-platform-1477880520.

69. *See* Matthew Rosenberg et al., *How Trump Consultants Exploited the Facebook Data of Millions*, N.Y. Times (Mar. 17, 2018), http://www.nytimes. com/2018/03/17/us/politics/cambridge-analytica-trump-campaign.html; *see also* Paul Lewis, *"Utterly Horrifying": Ex-Facebook Insider Says Covert Data Harvesting Was Routine*, Guardian (Mar. 20, 2018), http://www.theguardian.com/news/2018 /mar/20/facebook-data-cambridge-analytica-sandy-parakilas.

70. Lewis, *supra* note 69.

71. *Cf.* Solon Barocas & Andrew D. Selbst, *Big Data's Disparate Impact*, 104 Calif. L. Rev. 671 (2016) (discussing ways in which algorithmic analysis and machine learning may produce discriminatory impacts); Levy & Barocas, *supra* note 45 (discussing ways in which intermediary designs may have discriminatory impacts).

72. *See, e.g.,* Nancy Scola & Josh Meyer, *Twitter Takes Its Turns in the Russian Probe Spotlight*, Politico (Sept. 28, 2017), http://www.politico.com/story/2017/09/28 /twitter-russia-probe-spotlight-243239.

73. Sam Levin, *Instagram Uses "I Will Rape You" Post as Facebook Ad in Latest Algorithm Mishap*, Guardian (Sept. 21, 2017), http://www.theguardian.com /technology/2017/sep/21/instagram-death-threat-facebook-olivia-solon.

74. Airbnb also gives users the option of importing information from users' Facebook accounts.

75. Andrew Marantz, *When an App Is Called Racist*, New Yorker (July 29, 2015), http://www.newyorker.com/business/currency/what-to-do-when-your-app-is-racist. *See generally* Anthony G. Greenwald & Linda Hamilton Krieger, *Implicit Bias: Scientific Foundations*, 94 Calif. L. Rev. 945 (2006); Jerry Kang & Kristin Lane, *Seeing through Colorblindness: Implicit Bias and the Law*, 58 UCLA L. Rev. 465 (2010).

76. *See* Emanuella Grinberg, *When It Comes to Dating Sites, Race Matters*, CNN (Jan. 13, 2016), http://www.cnn.com/2016/01/13/living/where-white-people -meet-feat. This is to say nothing of sites like WhereWhitePeopleMeet that openly exploit this phenomenon. *Id.*

77. *See, e.g.*, Kristen Clarke, *Does Airbnb Enable Racism?*, N.Y. Times (Aug. 23, 2016), http://www.nytimes.com/2016/08/23/opinion/how-airbnb-can-fight -racial-discrimination.html; Carla Javier, *A Trump-Loving Airbnb Host Canceled This Woman's Reservation Because She's Asian*, Splinter News (Apr. 6, 2017), http://splinternews.com/a-trump-loving-airbnb-host-canceled-this-womans -reserva-1794086239; Carla Herreria, *Amsterdam Airbnb Host Accused of Pushing South African Down Stairs Is Arrested*, Huffington Post (July 13, 2017), http:// www.huffingtonpost.com/entry/amsterdam-airbnb-host-pushes-guest-stairs-racist _us_59680a7de4b03389bb164286.

78. Javier, *supra* note 78.

79. Benjamin Edelman et al., *Racial Discrimination in the Sharing Economy: Evidence from a Field Experiment*, 9 Am. Econ. J.: Applied Econ. 1, 2 (2017).

80. Laura Murphy, Laura Murphy & Assocs., *Airbnb's Work to Fight Discrimination and Build Inclusion: A Report Submitted to Airbnb* 16–17 (2016), http://blog .atairbnb.com/wp-content/uploads/2016/09/REPORT_Airbnbs-Work-to-Fight -Discrimination-and-Build-Inclusion.pdf.

81. 42 U.S.C. § 3604(c) (2012).

82. Airbnb, *General Questions About the Airbnb Community Commitment*, http:// www.airbnb.com/help/article/1523/general-questions-about-the-airbnb-community -commitment (last visited July 18, 2019).

83. Airbnb, *Business Is Better with Instant Book*, http://www.airbnb.com/host/instant (last visited July 18, 2019).

84. Katie Benner, *Airbnb Adopts Rules to Fight Discrimination by Its Hosts*, N.Y. Times (Sept. 8, 2016), http://www.nytimes.com/2016/09/09/technology/airbnb -anti-discrimination-rules.html. As Nancy Leong and Aaron Belzer have recently shown, moreover, the guest-rating systems on online platforms like Airbnb and Uber further entrench discrimination by aggregating illicit biases over time. *See* Nancy Leong & Aaron Belzer, *The New Public Accommodations: Race Discrimination in the Platform Economy*, 105 Geo. L.J. 1271, 1293–95 (2017).

85. Tracey Lien, *Airbnb's Legal Argument: Don't Hold Us Accountable for the Actions of Our Hosts*, L.A. Times (June 29, 2016), http://www.latimes.com/business /technology/la-fi-tn-airbnb-free-speech-20160629-snap-story.html.

86. *Id.*; *see also* Julia Carrie Wong, *How a Failed Attempt to Get Porn off the Internet Protects Airbnb from the Law*, Guardian (June 29, 2016), http://www.theguardian .com/technology/2016/jun/29/airbnb-lawsuit-san-francisco-regulation-internet -porn.

87. On the other hand, Airbnb's decision to settle in some of these cases may suggest that the company worries about its role in perpetuating discrimination, irrespective of whether Section 230 supplies immunity. *Cf.* Sam Levin, *Airbnb Gives in to Regulator's Demand to Test for Racial Discrimination by Hosts*, Guardian (Apr. 27, 2017), http://www.theguardian.com/technology/2017/apr/27 /airbnb-government-housing-test-black-discrimination.

88. *See* Facebook Business, *Facebook Ads*, http://www.facebook.com/business /products/ads (last visited July 18, 2019).

89. Julia Angwin et al., *Facebook Enabled Advertisers to Reach "Jew Haters,"* ProPublica (Sept. 14, 2017), http://www.propublica.org/article/facebook-enabled -advertisers-to-reach-jew-haters.

90. Jaclyn Peiser, *Anti-Semitism's Rise Gives the Forward New Resolve*, N.Y. Times (Oct. 8, 2017), http://www.nytimes.com/2017/10/08/business/media/the-forward -antisemitism.html.

91. ProPublica, which first broke the story about this practice, *see* Angwin & Parris, *supra* note 14, has not reported on whether Facebook generates these categories manually or by algorithm. I do not take up the question here, but the roles of automation and machine learning raise difficult questions about proof of intention under current nondiscrimination law.

92. *See* Julia Angwin et al., *Facebook Job Ads Raise Concerns About Age Discrimination*, N.Y. Times (Dec. 20, 2017), http://www.nytimes.com /2017/12/20/business/facebook-job-ads.html; Angwin & Parris, *supra* note 14.

93. Sapna Maheshwari & Mike Isaac, *Facebook Will Stop Some Ads from Targeting Users by Race*, N.Y. Times (Nov. 11, 2016), http://www.nytimes.com/2016/11/12 /business/media/facebook-will-stop-some-ads-from-targeting-users-by-race.html.

94. Rachel Goodman, *Facebook's Ad Targeting Problems Prove How Easy It Is to Discriminate Online*, NBC News (Nov. 30, 2017), http://www.nbcnews.com /think/opinion/facebook-s-ad-targeting-problems-prove-how-easy-it-discriminate -ncna825196.

95. *Id.*

96. *See, e.g.*, Complaint, *Mobley v. Facebook, Inc.*, No. 5:16-cv-06440-EJD (N.D. Cal. Nov. 3, 2016), 2016 WL 6599689.

97. Defendant's Notice of Motion and Motion to Dismiss First Amendment Complaint; Memorandum of Points and Authorities in Support Thereof at 10, *Mobley v. Facebook, Inc.* (N.D. Cal.) (June 1, 2017) (No. 5:16-cv-06440-EJD), available at http://assets.documentcloud.org/documents/4333515/Outten-FB -FB-Motion-to-Dismiss-4-3–17.pdf. Facebook also asserts that the plaintiffs lack standing and that, in any event, it is not discriminating within the meaning of the pertinent civil rights laws. *Id.* at 14–25.

98. *Chicago Lawyers' Comm. for Civil Rights v. Craigslist, Inc.*, 519 F.3d 666 (7th Cir. 2008).

99. *Id.* at 671.

100. *Id.*

101. *Id.*

102. *Fair Hous. Council of San Fernando Valley v. Roommates.com, LLC*, 521 F.3d 1157 (9th Cir. 2008) (en banc).

103. *Id.* at 1165–72.

104. *Id.*

105. 47 U.S.C. § 230(f)(3) (2012). After remand, a three-judge panel did nothing to alter this conclusion in its ruling four years later. *Fair Hous. Council of San Fernando Valley v. Roommate.com, LLC*, 666 F.3d 1216 (9th Cir. 2012). In this later opinion, the panel held that, while the immunity under Section 230 did not bar the suit against Roommates.com for its drop-down menu, Roommates.com's specific conduct at issue did not violate the FHA because "the FHA doesn't apply to the sharing of living units" as opposed to "the sale or rental of a dwelling." *Id.* at 1222 (discussing the scope of 42 U.S.C. § 3604(c)).

106. *Roommates.com*, 521 F.3d at 1173.

107. *Id.*

108. *Id.* at 1174.

109. *Id.*

110. *See id.* at 1173 n.33 (explaining that the court's holding is consistent with the Seventh Circuit's *Craigslist* opinion).

111. *See, e.g., Jones v. Dirty World Entm't Recordings*, 755 F.3d 398, 410–12 (6th Cir. 2014); *FTC v. Accusearch*, 570 F.3d 1187, 1200 (10th Cir. 2009).

112. *Fair Hous. Council of San Fernando Valley v. Roommate.com, LLC*, 666 F.3d 1216, 1219 (9th Cir. 2012).

113. *Id.*

114. *Id.*

115. *See* Facebook Business, *Take the Work out of Hiring* (Feb. 15, 2017), http://www .facebook.com/business/news/take-the-work-out-of-hiring.

116. *See* 47 U.S.C. § 230(c)(2)(A) (2012) ("No provider or user of an interactive computer service shall be held liable on account of . . . any action voluntarily taken in good faith to restrict access to or availability of material that the provider or user considers to be obscene, lewd, lascivious, filthy, excessively violent, harassing, or otherwise objectionable, whether or not such material is constitutionally protected.").

117. *Id.* § 230(f)(3). *See generally* Sylvain, *Design Duties, supra* note 21, at 239–42.

118. *See* Stop Enabling Sex Traffickers Act of 2017, S. 1693, 115th Cong. (2017); Allow States and Victims to Fight Online Sex Trafficking Act of 2017, H.R. 1865, 115th Cong (2017).

119. *See, e.g., Intermediary Liability*, Internet Ass'n, http://internetassociation. org/positions/intermediary-liability (last visited July 18, 2019); *see also Stop SESTA: Congress Doesn't Understand How Section 230 Works*, Electronic Frontier Found. (Sept. 7, 2017), http://www.eff.org/deeplinks/2017/09/stop-sesta -congress-doesnt-understand-how-section-230-works.

120. John Battelle, *Facebook Can't Be Fixed*, NewCo Shift (Jan. 5, 2018), https://shift .newco.co/2018/01/05/Facebook-Cant-Be-Fixed.

121. *Id.*

122. It is also difficult to disentangle this free speech argument from the intermediaries' commercial interests. European regulators, for instance, fined Google almost two and a half billion Euros last summer for abusing its market dominance in search to give "an illegal advantage to another Google product." European Commission, Press Release, *Antitrust: Commission Fines Google €2.42 Billion for Abusing Dominance as Search Engine by Giving Illegal Advantage to Own Comparison Shopping Service* (June 27, 2017), http://europa.eu/rapid /press-release_IP-17-1784_en.htm.

SECTION 230's CHALLENGE TO CIVIL RIGHTS AND CIVIL LIBERTIES

123. *See CDA 230: The Most Important Law Protecting Internet Speech*, Electronic Frontier Found., http://www.eff.org/issues/cda230/legal (last visited July 18, 2019).

124. *See* Christopher Zara, *The Most Important Law in Tech Has a Problem*, Wired (Jan. 3, 2017), http://www.wired.com/2017/01/the-most-important-law-in-tech-has -a-problem.

125. Alina Selyukh, *Section 230: A Key Legal Shield for Facebook, Google Is About to Change*, NPR (Mar. 21, 2018), http://www.wbur.org/npr/591622450/section-230 -a-key-legal-shield-for-facebook-google-is-about-to-change (quoting Llansó).

126. *See* Danielle Keats Citron & Benjamin Wittes, *The Internet Will Not Break: Denying Bad Samaritans Section 230 Immunity*, 86 Fordham L. Rev. 401 (2017).

127. S. Rep. No. 104–23, at 59 (1995). Key provisions criminalized the transmission of indecent material to minors.

128. *Id.*

129. H.R. Rep. No. 104–223, Amendment No. 2–3 (1995) (proposed to be codified at 47 U.S.C. § 230).

130. 47 U.S.C. § 230(c) (2012); *see* H. Conf. Rep. No. 104–458 (1996).

131. Selyukh, *supra* note 125.

132. *Id.* (quoting Cox).

133. *Id.* (quoting Wyden).

134. *See* Danielle Keats Citron, *Cyber Civil Rights*, 89 B.U. L. Rev. 61, 118 (2009). In the landmark *Reno v. ACLU* decision, the Supreme Court struck down the CDA's blanket restrictions on internet indecency under the First Amendment. 521 U.S. 844, 853 (1997). Online expression was too important to be limited to what government officials think is fit for children. *Id.* at 875. Section 230's immunity provision, however, was left intact.

135. *Jane Doe No. 1 v. Backpage.com LLC*, 817 F.3d 12, 25 (1st Cir. 2016). The judiciary's insistence that the CDA reflected "Congress' desire to promote unfettered speech on the Internet" so ignores its text and history as to bring to mind Justice Scalia's admonition against selectively determining legislative intent in the manner of someone at a party who "look[s] over the heads of the crowd and pick[s] out [their] friends." Antonin Scalia, *A Matter of Interpretation: Federal Courts and the Law* 36 (1997).

136. *Shiamili v. Real Estate Group of New York*, 2011 WL 2313818 (N.Y. App Ct. June 14, 2011); *Phan v. Pham*, 2010 WL 658244 (Cal. App. Ct. Feb. 25, 2010).

137. *Jones v. Dirty World Entertainment Holding*, 2014 WL 2694184 (6th Cir. June 16, 2014); *S.C. v. The Dirty LLC*, No. 11-CV-00392-DW (W.D. Mo. Mar. 12, 2012).

138. 817 F.3d 12 (1st Cir. 2016).

139. *See, e.g., Hinton v. Amazon*, 72 F. Supp. 3d 685, 687 (S.D. Miss. 2014).

140. Cox recently said as much: "I'm afraid . . . the judge-made law has drifted away from the original purpose of the statute." Selyukh, *supra* note 125. In his view, sites that solicit unlawful materials or have a connection to unlawful activity should not enjoy Section 230 immunity. *Id.*

141. *See* Citron, *supra* note 134, at 118; Mark A. Lemley, *Rationalizing Internet Safe Harbors*, 6 J. Telecomm. & High Tech. L. 101 (2007); Doug Lichtman & Eric Posner, *Holding Internet Service Providers Accountable*, 14 Sup. Ct. Econ. Rev. 221 (2006).

142. Rebecca Tushnet, *Power Without Responsibility: Intermediaries and the First Amendment*, 76 Geo. Wash. L. Rev. 986 (2008).

143. *See* Jack M. Balkin, *The Future of Free Expression in a Digital Age*, 36 Pepp. L. Rev. 427, 434 (2009).

144. *See* Citron & Wittes, *supra* note 126, at 410; Danielle Keats Citron & Neil M. Richards, *Four Principles for Digital Expression (You Won't Believe #3!)*, 95 Wash. U. L. Rev. 1353 (2018).

145. *See, e.g.*, Maeve Duggan, Pew Research Ctr., *Online Harassment 2017*, at 31 (2017), http://assets.pewresearch.org/wp-content/uploads/sites/14/2017 /07/10151519/PI_2017.07.11_Online-Harassment_FINAL.pdf (finding that people "whose most recent incident involved severe forms of harassment are more likely to say they changed their username or deleted their profile, stopped attending offline venues[,] or reported the incident to law enforcement"). The individual and societal costs are considerable when victims go offline, lose their jobs and cannot find new ones, or suffer extreme emotional harm in the face of online abuse. *See generally* Danielle Keats Citron, *Civil Rights in Our Information Age*, in *The Offensive Internet* 31 (Saul Levmore & Martha C. Nussbaum, eds., 2010).

146. *See* Danielle Keats Citron, *Hate Crimes in Cyberspace* (2014); Citron, *supra* note 134; Danielle Keats Citron, *Law's Expressive Value in Combating Cyber Gender Harassment*, 108 Mich. L. Rev. 373 (2009); Danielle Keats Citron, *Online Engagement on Equal Terms*, B.U. L. Rev. Online (2015); Danielle Keats Citron & Mary Anne Franks, *Criminalizing Revenge Porn*, 49 Wake Forest L. Rev. 345 (2014); Mary Anne Franks, *Unwilling Avatars: Idealism and Discrimination in Cyberspace*, 20 Colum. Gender J.L. 220 (2011); Mary Anne Franks, *Sexual Harassment 2.0*, 71 Md. L. Rev. 655 (2012); Danielle Keats Citron, *Yale ISP— Reputation Economies in Cyberspace Part 3*, YouTube (Dec. 8, 2007), http://www .youtube.com/watch?v=XVEL4RfN3uQ.

147. Lawrence Lessig, *Code and Other Laws of Cyberspace* 60 (1999) ("How the code regulates . . . [is a] question[] that any practice of justice must focus in the age of cyberspace."); Joel R. Reidenberg, *Lex Informatica: The Formulation of Information Policy Rules Through Technology*, 76 Tex. L. Rev. 553, 554 (1998) (exploring how system design choices provide sources of rulemaking and make a "useful extra-legal instrument that may be used to achieve objectives that otherwise challenge conventional laws").

148. Woodrow Hartzog's recent book *Privacy's Blueprint: The Battle to Control the Design of New Technologies* (2018) demonstrates how the design of digital technologies determines our privacy rights.

149. Jonathan Zittrain, *The Future of the Internet—And How to Stop It* 101–26 (2008).

150. *See generally* Eduardo Moisés Peñalver & Sonia K. Katyal, *Property Outlaws: How Squatters, Pirates, and Protesters Improve the Law of Ownership* (2010).

151. Danielle Keats Citron, *Technological Due Process*, 85 Wash. U. L. Rev. 1249 (2008); Danielle Keats Citron, *Open Code Governance*, 2008 U. Chi. Legal F. 355.

152. Benjamin Edelman et al., *Racial Discrimination in the Sharing Economy: Evidence from a Field Experiment*, Am. Econ. J.: Applied Econ., Apr. 2017, at 1.

153. *Cf.* Danielle Keats Citron, *Mainstreaming Privacy Torts*, 98 Calif. L. Rev. 1805, 1836–40 (2010) (considering potential claims against platforms for tortious enablement of criminal conduct).

154. Danielle Citron & Woodrow Hartzog, *The Decision That Could Finally Kill the Revenge Porn Business*, Atlantic (Feb. 3, 2015), http://www.theatlantic.com /technology/archive/2015/02/the-decision-that-could-finally-kill-the-revenge -porn-business/385113 (discussing the FTC's consent decree with revenge porn operator); *see also* Complaint for Permanent Injunction and Other Equitable

Relief, *FTC v. EMP Media, Inc.*, No. 2:18-cv-00035 (D. Nev. Jan. 9, 2018), http://www.ftc.gov/system/files/documents/cases/1623052_myex_complaint_1-9-18.pdf; Stipulated Order for Permanent Injunction and Monetary Judgment as to Defendant Aniello Infante, *FTC v. EMP Media, Inc.*, 2:18-cv-00035-APG-NJK (D. Nev. Jan. 10, 2018), http://www.ftc.gov/system/files/documents/cases/1623052myexinfanteorder.pdf.

155. Then–California attorney general Kamala Harris prosecuted revenge-porn site operators for exploiting confidential nude images for commercial ends. Revenge porn operator Kevin Bollaert, for instance, unsuccessfully raised Section 230 as a defense to state criminal prosecution. Danielle Citron, *Can Revenge Porn Operators Go to Prison?*, Forbes (Jan. 17, 2015), http://www.forbes.com/sites/daniellecitron/2015/01/17/can-revenge-porn-operators-go-to-jail.

156. Citron & Hartzog, *supra* note 154.

157. I contemplated this possibility in my book *Hate Crimes in Cyberspace*, *supra* note 146. Benjamin Wittes and I offered this possibility as an intermediate, though not ideal, step in recent work. Citron & Wittes, *supra* note 126, at 419.

158. Pub. L. No. 115–164, 132 Stat. 1253 (2018).

159. Quinta Jurecic and I discuss this reform in Danielle Citron & Quinta Jurecic, Hoover Inst., *Platform Justice: Content Moderation at an Inflection Point* (2018), https://www.hoover.org/sites/default/files/research/docs/citron-jurecic_webreadypdf.pdf.

160. Citron & Wittes, *supra* note 126, at 419.

161. *Id.*

162. What comes to mind is Facebook's effort to use hashing technology to detect and remove nonconsensual pornography that has been banned as terms-of-service violations. I serve on a small task force advising Facebook about the use of screening tools to address the problem of nonconsensually posted intimate images.

163. Current screening technology is far more effective against some kinds of abusive material than others; progress may produce cost-effective means of defeating other attacks. With current technologies, it is difficult, if not impossible, to automate the detection of certain illegal activity. That is certainly true of threats, which requires an understanding of the context to determine its objectionable nature.

164. Citron & Richards, *supra* note 144. Julia Angwin, writing for the *Wall Street Journal* and later ProPublica, has been a pioneer in this effort, educating the public on the various and sundry ways that tech companies control crucial aspects of our lives and our personal data.

165. *See* Danielle Keats Citron, *Extremist Speech, Compelled Conformity, and Censorship Creep*, 93 Notre Dame L. Rev. 1035 (2018).

166. *See* Olivier Sylvain, *Intermediary Design Duties*, 50 Conn. L. Rev. 1 (2018).

167. *See generally* Ryan M. Calo, *Digital Market Manipulation*, Geo. Wash. L. Rev. (2014).

168. *Mark Zuckerberg in his Own Words*, CNN (Mar. 21, 2018), http://money.cnn.com/2018/03/21/technology/mark-zuckerberg-cnn-interview-transcript.

169. *See* Jeffrey Rosen, *The Unwanted Gaze: The Destruction of Privacy in America* 107 (2001).

TO ERR IS PLATFORM

My thanks to Aislinn Black, Eric Goldman, Kate Klonick, David Pozen, and Vitaly Shmatikov for their comments on earlier drafts of this commentary.

170. I will use "bad" as shorthand to describe content that would subject the poster to civil or criminal liability under some non–Section 230 body of law, and "good" as shorthand to describe content that would not. Of course, these categories reflect contestable political judgments and can change over time. But for purposes of discussing Section 230, they provide a useful baseline because they embody collective judgments about what content society considers acceptable and what content it does not; they challenge us to explain why those judgments do or do not carry over from users to platforms.

171. Felix T. Wu, *Collateral Censorship and the Limits of Intermediary Immunity*, 87 Notre Dame L. Rev. 293, 295–96 (2011).

172. For an earlier and more detailed economic analysis of Section 230 including error costs, see Matthew Schruers, *The History and Economics of ISP Liability for Third Party Content*, 88 Va. L. Rev. 205 (2002).

173. Julia Angwin et al., *Facebook Enabled Advertisers to Reach "Jew Haters,"* ProPublica (Sept. 14, 2017), https://www.propublica.org/article/facebook -enabled-advertisers-to-reach-jew-haters.

174. Audrey Carlsen & Fahima Haque, *What Does Facebook Consider Hate Speech? Take Our Quiz*, N.Y. Times (Oct. 13, 2017), https://www.nytimes.com/interactive /2017/10/13/technology/facebook-hate-speech-quiz.html.

175. *See, e.g., Zeran v. America Online, Inc.*, 129 F.3d 327 (4th Cir. 1997).

176. 47 U.S.C. § 230(e)(2) (2012).

177. *Id.* § 230(e)(1).

178. *United States v. Ackerman*, 831 F.3d 1292, 1294–95 (10th Cir. 2016).

179. *See generally* Sarah Jeong, *The Internet of Garbage* (2015).

TOWARD A CLEARER CONVERSATION ABOUT PLATFORM LIABILITY

In the interest of full disclosure, I was formerly associate general counsel to Google. The Center for Internet and Society (CIS), where I currently work, is a public interest technology law and policy program at Stanford Law School. A list of CIS donors and funding policies is available at https://cyberlaw.stanford.edu /about-us.

180. 47 U.S.C. § 230 (2012). Under long-standing exceptions, platforms have no CDA 230 immunity for intellectual property law claims, federal criminal claims, and Electronic Communications Privacy Act claims. *Id.* § 230(e).

181. These arguments build on work developed by a number of scholars, prominently including Danielle Citron. *See, e.g.,* Danielle Keats Citron, *Law's Expressive Value in Combating Cyber Gender Harassment*, 108 Mich. L. Rev. 373 (2009).

182. H.R. 1865, 115th Cong. (2018).

183. *See, e.g.,* Shannon Roddel, *Online Sex Trafficking Bill Will Make Things Worse for Victims, Expert Says*, Notre Dame News (Mar. 28, 2018), http://news.nd.edu /news/online-sex-trafficking-bill-will-make-things-worse-for-victims-expert-says.

184. ACLU, *ACLU Vote Recommendation on FOSTA* (2018), http://www.aclu.org /letter/aclu-vote-recommendation-fosta.

185. *See* Letter from Stephen E. Boyd, Ass't Att'y Gen., to Rep. Robert W. Goodlatte 2 (Feb. 27 2018), http://docs.techfreedom.org/DOJ_FOSTA_Letter.pdf.

186. *See* Engine, *Startup Advocates Address Implications of Sex Trafficking Legislation on Tech* (Feb. 26, 2018), http://static1.squarespace.com/static/571681753c44d835 a440c8b5/t/5a9608df419202d2af99166f/1519782111557/FOSTA _SESTA+Media+Advisory.pdf.

187. *See* Ali Breland, *Facebook's Sandberg Backs Controversial Online Sex Trafficking Bill*, Hill (Feb. 26, 2018), http://thehill.com/policy/technology/375680-facebooks -sheryl-sandberg-backs-legislation-to-curb-online-sex-trafficking.

188. *See* Internet Association, *Statement in Support of Allow States and Victims to Fight Online Sex Trafficking Act of 2017 (FOSTA)* (Dec. 11, 2017), http:// internetassociation.org/statement-support-allow-states-victims-fight-online-sex -trafficking-act-2017-fosta.

189. *See* Daphne Keller, *Empirical Evidence of "Over-Removal" by Internet Companies Under Intermediary Liability Laws*, Stanford Law School Center for Internet & Society (Oct. 12, 2015), http://cyberlaw.stanford.edu/blog/2015/10/empirical -evidence-over-removal-internet-companies-under-intermediary-liability-laws; Jennifer M. Urban et al., *Notice and Takedown in Everyday Practice* 10–13, 116–17 (unpublished manuscript) (Mar. 2017), http://ssrn.com/abstract=2755628.

190. *See* José Miguel Vivanco, *Censorship in Ecuador Has Made It to the Internet*, Human Rights Watch (Dec. 15, 2014), http://www.hrw.org/news/2014/12/15 /censorship-ecuador-has-made-it-internet.

191. *See* Daphne Keller, *Inception Impact Assessment: Measures to Further Improve the Effectiveness of the Fight Against Illegal Content Online* 6–7 (2018), http:// cyberlaw.stanford.edu/files/publication/files/Commission-Filing-Stanford -CIS-26-3_0.pdf (describing discriminatory impact of platform efforts to remove "terrorist" content); Tracy Jan & Elizabeth Dwoskin, *A White Man Called Her Kids the N-Word. Facebook Stopped Her from Sharing It.*, Wash. Post (July 31, 2017), http://www.washingtonpost.com/business/economy/for-facebook -erasing-hate-speech-proves-a-daunting-challenge/2017/07/31/922d9bc6 -6e3b-11e7-9c15-177740635e83_story.html; Sam Levin, *Civil Rights Groups Urge Facebook to Fix "Racially Biased" Moderation System*, Guardian (Jan. 18 2017), http://www.theguardian.com/technology/2017/jan/18/facebook-moderation -racial-bias-black-lives-matter.

192. 47 U.S.C. § 230(c)(2)(A) (2012).

193. Congress specifically set out to correct this perverse incentive, as embodied in two 1990s internet defamation cases. *See* H.R. Rep. No. 104–458, at 194 (1996). In one case, a platform that enforced content policies was held liable for a user's defamatory post. *Stratton Oakmont, Inc. v. Prodigy Servs. Co.*, No. 31063/94, 1995 WL 323710 (N.Y. Sup. Ct. May 24, 1995). In another, a platform with no such guidelines was held immune. *Cubby, Inc. v. CompuServe, Inc.*, 776 F. Supp. 135 (S.D.N.Y. 1991).

194. *See* Daphne Keller with Sharon Driscoll, *Data Analytics, App Developers, and Facebook's Role in Data Misuse*, SLS Blogs: Legal Aggregate (Mar. 20, 2018), http://law.stanford.edu/2018/03/20/data-analytic-companies-app-developers -facebooks-role-data-misuse.

195. *See generally* Fair Housing Act, 42 U.S.C. §§ 3601–19; Title VII of the Civil Rights Act of 1964, 42 U.S.C. § 2000e et seq.; Age Discrimination in Employment Act, 29 U.S.C. §§ 621–34; Equal Credit Opportunity Act, 15 U.S.C. §§ 1691 et seq.

196. *Cf. Sony Corp. of America v. Universal City Studios, Inc.*, 464 U.S. 417 (1984) (VCR manufacturer not liable for user copyright infringement because of device's substantial noninfringing uses). *See also Mitchell v. Shane*, 350 F.3d 39 (2d Cir. 2003) (no FHA violation where defendant was unaware of discrimination). The FHA does recognize *respondeat superior* liability: a principal cannot avoid liability under the FHA by delegating duties to an agent. *See Green v. Century 21*, 740 F.2d 460 (6th Cir. 1984). But if a *respondeat* relationship exists for online advertising platforms, presumably the platforms are the agents, not the principals.

197. *Fair Hous. Council of San Fernando Valley v. Roommates.com, LLC*, 521 F.3d 1157 (9th Cir. 2008) (en banc).

198. Jessica Guynn, *Facebook Vows to Stop Ad Discrimination Against African-Americans, Women and Older Workers*, USA Today (Mar. 19, 2019), http://www .usatoday.com/story/news/2019/03/19/facebook-pledges-block-ad-discrimination -targeting-older-workers-blacks/3208282002.

199. *See Fair Hous. Council of San Fernando Valley v. Roommate.com, LLC*, 666 F.3d 1216, 1221 (9th Cir. 2012) (FHA and California equivalent do not apply to listings for roommates, based on statutory language and constitutional privacy concerns activated by "a roommate's unfettered access to the home").

200. *IMDb.com, Inc. v. Becerra*, 16-CV-06535-VC, 2017 WL 772346 (N.D. Cal. Feb. 22, 2017).

201. If Airbnb's liability derives from the hosts' actions, it's hard to see a publication element that CDA 230 would immunize. If the theory is that Airbnb violates the FHA by de facto requiring users to disclose their race, that's almost exactly the thing that falls *outside* CDA 230 immunity under controlling precedent in the Ninth Circuit. *See Fair Hous. Council of San Fernando Valley v. Roommates.com, LLC*, 521 F.3d 1157 (9th Cir. 2008) (en banc) (no CDA 230 immunity where platform required users to provide FHA-violating information as a condition of using the service).

202. This behavior and the claimed product design to "hold user attention by inducing something like addictive reliance," if actionable, sound like some form of fraud or consumer protection violation by the platform itself. Sylvain also says that some platforms "are intentionally deceptive about how they acquire or employ content," but CDA 230 does not provide immunity for that. In both cases he cites, courts held platforms liable for their actions—and rejected CDA 230 defenses. *FTC v. LeadClick Media, LLC*, 838 F.3d 158 (2d Cir. 2016); *FTC v. Accusearch, Inc.*, 570 F.3d 1187 (10th Cir. 2009).

203. 830 F. Supp. 2d 785 (N.D. Cal. 2011).

204. *Id.* at 801–03.

205. For a very rough overview, see Mark Scott & Natasha Singer, *How Europe Protects Your Online Data Differently than the U.S.*, N.Y. Times (Jan. 31, 2016), http://www.nytimes.com/interactive/2016/01/29/technology/data-privacy-policy -us-europe.html.

206. *See, e.g.*, European Commission, Press Release, *Facebook, Google and Twitter Accept to Change Their Terms of Services to Make Them Customer-Friendly and Compliant with EU Rules* (Feb. 15, 2018), http://ec.europa.eu/newsroom/just /item-detail.cfm?item_id=614254.

207. *See, e.g., Spokeo, Inc. v. Robins,* 136 S. Ct. 1540 (2016).

208. *See* Jack M. Balkin & Jonathan Zittrain, *A Grand Bargain to Make Tech Companies Trustworthy,* Atlantic (Oct. 3 2016), http://www.theatlantic.com /technology/archive/2016/10/information-fiduciary/502346.

209. *Dyroff v. Ultimate Software Group, Inc.,* 2017 WL 5665670, at *8–*10 (N.D. Cal. 2017) (assessing allegations that a platform used data mining and machine learning to understand "the meaning and intent behind posts" and target illegal material to individual users).

210. Platforms could also lose immunity when they effectively create the unlawful communication themselves, by specifically eliciting or changing user content. As discussed above, though, CDA 230 already limits immunity in this situation.

211. Joined Cases C-236/08C-238/08, *Google France SARL v. Louis Vuitton Malletier SA,* 2010 E.C.R. I-2417.

212. *Dyroff,* 2017 WL 5665670, at *8–*10.

213. Eric Goldman, *Social Networking Site Isn't Liable for User's Overdose of Drugs He Bought via the Site–Dyroff v. Ultimate Software,* Tech. & Marketing L. Blog (Dec. 5, 2017), http://blog.ericgoldman.org/archives/2017/12/social-networking -site-isnt-liable-for-users-overdose-of-drugs-he-bought-via-the-site-dyroff-v-ultimate -software.htm.

214. *See* James Grimmelmann, *Some Skepticism About Search Neutrality,* in *The Next Digital Decade: Essays on the Future of the Internet* 435 (Berin Szoka & Adam Marcus, eds., 2010).

215. Defendant hosts must offer one of four defined technical services. 17 U.S.C. § 512(a)–(d) (2012). They additionally must not have both the right and the ability to control and direct financial benefits. *Id.* § 512(c)(1)(B).

216. *See* Center for Democracy & Tech., *Mixed Messages? The Limits of Automated Social Media Content Analysis* 18 (2017), http://cdt.org/files/2017/11/Mixed -Messages-Paper.pdf (reporting accuracy rates in the 70 to 80 percent range for commercially available natural language processing filters). *See generally* Evan Engstrom & Nick Feamster, Engine, *The Limits of Filtering: A Look at the Functioning & Shortcomings of Content Detection Tools* (2017), http://static1 .squarespace.com/static/571681753c44d835a440c8b5/t/58d058712994ca536bbfa 47a/1490049138881/FilteringPaperWebsite.pdf. My personal doubts about plat-form omniscience are reinforced by the ads I see, which routinely feature men's clothing and software engineering jobs. People with higher expectations about the capabilities of curation and targeting technology must, I assume, be seeing better ads.

217. Lei No. 12.965, de 23 de Abril de 2014, Diário Oficial da União [D.O.U.] de 24.4.2014 (Braz.).

218. Law No. 20435 art. 71N, Abril 23, 2010, Diario Oficial [D.O.] (Chile).

219. *See Royo v. Google* (Barcelona appellate court judgment 76/2013), 13 February 2013.

220. *See Singhal v. India,* A.I.R. 2015 S.C. 1523.

221. *See* Corte Suprema de Justicia de la Nación [CSJN] [National Supreme Court of Justice], 29/10/2014, "Rodriguez María Belen c/Google y Otro s/ daños y perjuicios" (Arg.).

222. In intermediary liability regimes like this, one can move the needle by calling more or fewer things "manifestly unlawful" and thus subject to de facto adjudication by a platform. Such choices involve substantive tradeoffs; they force us to ask what harms are worth risking platform error. One can also move the needle by allowing accelerated proceedings, such as temporary restraining orders or administrative review. This involves tradeoffs between access to justice for victims of speech harms, on the one hand, and due process and expression rights for speakers, on the other. Within those parameters—and subject to the recognition that all these systems attract abuse— I see ample room for intelligent advocacy on all sides.

223. 17 U.S.C. §§ 512(c)(3)(B)(i), (c)(3)(A) (2012).

224. *Id.* §§ 512(f), (g)(2)(B).

225. *See, e.g., Report of the Special Rapporteur on the Promotion and Protection of the Right to Freedom of Opinion and Expression*, U.N. Doc. A/HRC/32/38 (May 11, 2016); U.N. Special Rapporteur on Freedom of Opinion & Expression et al., *Joint Declaration on Freedom of Expression on the Internet* (June 1, 2011), http://www .osce.org/fom/78309.

226. Manila Principles on Intermediary Liability, http://www.manilaprinciples.org (last visited July 18, 2019).

227. *See, e.g., Singhal v. India*, A.I.R. 2015 S.C. 1523; Corte Suprema de Justicia de la Nación [CSJN] [National Supreme Court of Justice], 29/10/2014, "Rodriguez María Belen c/Google y Otro s/ daños y perjuicios" (Arg.); *Scarlet v. SABAM*, Case C-70/10, 2011 E.C.R. I-11959 (rejecting ISP monitoring remedy in a copyright case); *MTE v. Hungary*, App. No. 22947/13 (Eur. Ct. H.R. 2016) (rejecting platform monitoring obligation for defamation because of harm to internet user speech rights). *But see Delfi AS v. Estonia*, 64569/09 Eur. Ct. H.R. (2015) (permitting monitoring obligation for hate speech).

228. 376 U.S. 254 (1964).

229. *Id.* at 266; *see also Smith v. California*, 361 U.S. 147, 153 (1959) (rejecting strict obscenity liability for bookstores and noting that a bookseller subject to such liability "will tend to restrict the books he sells to those he has inspected; and thus the State will have imposed a restriction upon the distribution of constitutionally protected, as well as obscene literature"); *Bantam Books, Inc. v. Sullivan*, 372 U.S. 58 (1963) (rejecting administrative notice obscenity liability for bookstores).

230. The DMCA, for example, applies a knowledge standard buttressed with procedural protections for accused speakers but still leads to widespread removal of lawful speech. *See generally* Urban et al., *supra* note 189.

5

THE DE-AMERICANIZATION OF INTERNET FREEDOM

David E. Pozen

"THE INTERNET," Ira Magaziner opined in a 1998 speech, is "a force for the promotion of democracy" as well as "individual freedom and individual empowerment."[1] At the time he gave this speech, Magaziner was the Clinton administration's internet guru. He began his remarks in a tentative register, observing that "humility is an important quality for anyone working to develop policies for the Internet," given the "uncharted" nature of the terrain. A minute or so later, Magaziner informed his audience that the internet would "be the primary driver of the broader economy for the next couple of decades," make dictatorships and other non-democratic forms of government "impossible in the long run," and "bring all the peoples of the world closer together."

At least, the internet would deliver these revolutionary benefits if policymakers regulated it appropriately. And that, Magaziner explained, meant regulating it as little as possible: pursuing a "market-driven model" in which "the government role is not in regulating, but rather in setting the terms for a predictable legal environment for contracts to form." A "regulated model" would stifle the growth of the medium and cause "distortion." Nation-states, accordingly, should abandon most efforts to tax the internet, to subject it to traditional telecommunications and competition laws, or to censor or control content. (Intellectual property in electronic commerce, on the other hand, would require "strong protection.") "If I could wave a magic wand," Magaziner summed up his message, "I would say we should go through a complete deregulation here, and let the market go."

Thus was launched the United States' "internet freedom" agenda. Its precise elements have shifted some over time, but as Jack Goldsmith explains in his riveting essay, it has consistently been anchored in the principles of (as Goldsmith puts it) "commercial nonregulation" and "anti-censorship." This agenda has been a boon for the commercial development of the internet, particularly for the large U.S. firms that dominate life online.

Yet in virtually every other respect, Goldsmith argues, the agenda has been an abject failure. Authoritarian regimes—most notably China, but also states in the Caucasus, the Arabian Peninsula, and beyond—"have become adept at clamping down on unwelcome speech and at hindering the free flow of data across and within their borders." European regulators have become increasingly aggressive in going after U.S. technology companies and in repudiating U.S. notions of privacy and free expression. Edward Snowden's leaks exposed the hypocrisy of the U.S. government's "hands-off" approach to digital networks. And years of lax regulation have contributed to a domestic online environment saturated with falsehoods, conspiracy theories, troll armies, cyberthefts, cyberattacks, and related ills— an environment that Russian president Vladimir Putin "was able to exploit," in Goldsmith's telling, "to cause unprecedented disruption in [American] democratic processes, possibly denying [Hillary Clinton] the presidency." As with other aspects of U.S. economic and social policy, President Trump inherits, and is himself the political product of,[2] a baneful legacy of neoliberalism with regard to managing the internet.

* * *

Why did the internet freedom agenda fail? Goldsmith's essay tees up—but does not fully explore—a range of explanatory hypotheses.

The most straightforward have to do with unrealistic expectations and unintended consequences. The idea that a minimally regulated internet would usher in an era of global peace, prosperity, and mutual understanding, Goldsmith tells us, was always a fantasy. As a project of democracy and human rights promotion, the internet freedom agenda was premised on a wildly overoptimistic view about the capacity of information flows, on their own, to empower oppressed groups and effect social change. Embracing this market-utopian view led the United States to underinvest in cybersecurity, social media oversight, and any number of other regulatory tools. In suggesting this interpretation of where U.S. policy-makers and their civil society partners went wrong, Goldsmith's essay complements recent critiques of the neoliberal strains in the broader human rights[3] and transparency[4] movements.

Perhaps, however, the internet freedom agenda has faltered not because it was so naïve and unrealistic but because it was so *effective* at achieving its realist goals. The seeds of this alternative account can be found in Goldsmith's concession that the commercial nonregulation principle helped companies like Apple, Google, Facebook, and Amazon grab "huge market share globally." The internet became an increasingly valuable cash cow for U.S. firms and an increasingly potent instrument of U.S. soft power over the past two decades; foreign governments, in due course, felt compelled to fight back. If the internet freedom agenda is understood as fundamentally a national economic project, rather than an international political or moral crusade, then we might say that its remarkable early success created the conditions for its eventual failure.

Goldsmith's essay also points to a third set of possible explanations for the collapse of the internet freedom agenda, involving its internal contradictions. Magaziner's notion of a completely deregulated marketplace, if taken seriously, is incoherent.[5] As Goldsmith and Tim Wu have discussed elsewhere,[6] it takes quite a bit of regulation for any market, including markets related to the internet, to exist and to work. And indeed, even as Magaziner proposed "complete deregulation" of the internet, he simultaneously called for new legal protections against computer fraud and copyright infringement, which were soon followed by extensive U.S. efforts to penetrate foreign networks and to militarize cyberspace. Such internal dissonance was bound to invite charges of opportunism and to render the American agenda unstable.

Developments outside of government only heightened the contradictions. As private platforms increasingly came to function as the "new governors" of online speech,[7] the noncommercial regulation principle and the anti-censorship principle came into increasing tension with each other. Magaziner envisioned the state as the source of all undesirable restrictions on and distortions of online speech. Yet many of the ways in which digital content is controlled today are the product of corporate decisions, not government policies. And in some instances, public regulation may be the most effective means to *combat* the speech-restrictive or speech-distortive effects of those decisions. As Nani Jansen Reventlow and Jonathan McCully observe in their commentary, by "seeking to take a 'hands-off' approach when it comes to regulating these platforms, the internet freedom agenda . . . jeopardizes the anti-censorship principle."

* * *

Whatever the causes—and there are likely multiple, overlapping contrib-uting factors—it is hard to gainsay Goldsmith's descriptive claim that the U.S. internet freedom agenda now finds itself derailed and discredited around the globe. The fact that the U.S. internet freedom agenda is fail-ing, however, does not necessarily mean that the larger project of internet freedom is failing. On the contrary, the growing detachment of this project from American commercial and ideological interests may suggest a new path forward.

This is the glass-half-full perspective offered by Jansen Reventlow and McCully and by David Kaye in their responses to Goldsmith. While endorsing Goldsmith's basic critique of U.S. policy, these noted interna-tional lawyers push back against the parochialism inherent in evaluating internet freedom in U.S.-centric terms. "If we reorient the internet freedom analysis away from U.S. supply or geopolitical struggle," Kaye submits, we will find a wide variety of actors—from the United Nations Human Rights Council (UNHRC) to regional courts to grassroots activists—who are mobilizing to meet the global demand for online access, privacy, and security and thereby "laying the groundwork for resistance to authoritarian policies and laws." Jansen Reventlow and McCully likewise praise such developments, identifying the UNHRC's "comprehensive, human rights–based approach" as an especially promising and legitimate alternative to the hegemonic projection of U.S. power.

As compared to the Clinton, Bush, and Obama administrations' vision of internet governance, the vision that seems to be emerging from this global movement is less deferential to market logic and more concerned with peo-ple's capacity to control their own data—more concerned, that is, with the positive liberty to use the internet constructively and autonomously than with the negative liberty to be spared state interference. Participants in this movement see themselves as the true defenders of internet freedom and the United States as its false or fickle friend. And so, twenty years in the future, we may find that reforms taken in the name of internet freedom bear little resemblance to the ideas Magaziner set forth in 1998. Humility counsels that we be open to the possibility.

The Failure of Internet Freedom

Jack Goldsmith*

FROM THE SECOND TERM of the Clinton administration to the end of the Obama administration, the U.S. government pursued an internet freedom agenda abroad. The phrase "internet freedom" signaled something grand and important, but its meaning has always been hard to pin down. For purposes of this essay, I will use the phrase to mean two related principles initially articulated by the Clinton administration during its stewardship of the global internet in the late 1990s.

The first principle is that "governments must adopt a non-regulatory, market-oriented approach to electronic commerce," as President Clinton and Vice President Gore put it in 1997.[8] Their administration opposed government taxes, customs duties and other trade barriers, telecommunications constraints, advertisement limitations, and most other forms of regulation for internet firms, communications, or transactions. The premise of this *commercial nonregulation principle*, as I'll call it, was that "the Internet is a medium that has tremendous potential for promoting individual freedom and individual empowerment" and "therefore, where possible, the individual should be left in control of the way in which he or she uses this medium."[9] In other words, markets, individual choice, and competition should presumptively guide the development of the internet. When formal governance is needed, it should be supplied by "private, nonprofit, stakeholder-based" institutions not tied to nations or geography.[10] The Clinton administration acknowledged the need for traditional government regulation in narrow circumstances — most notably, and self-servingly, to protect intellectual property — but otherwise strongly disfavored it.[11]

The second principle of internet freedom, which I'll call the *anti-censorship principle*, argued for American-style freedom of speech and expression on the global internet. This principle originated as a component of the effort to promote electronic commerce. Over time, however, it developed into an independent consideration that sought to influence foreign political structures. The Clinton administration devoted less policy attention to the anti-censorship principle than to the commercial nonregulation principle because it believed that "censorship and content control are not only undesirable, but effectively impossible," as the administration's internet czar Ira Magaziner put it.[12] China's effort "to crack down on the Internet," Bill Clinton famously quipped in 2000, was "like trying to nail Jell-O to the wall."[13]

The George W. Bush administration embraced both internet freedom principles, and it took novel institutional steps to push the anti-censorship principle. In 2006, the State Department established the Global Internet Freedom Task Force (GIFT). The main aims of GIFT were to "maximize freedom of expression and the free flow of information and ideas," to "minimize the success of repressive regimes in censoring and silencing legitimate debate," and to "promote access to information and ideas over the Internet."[14] GIFT provided support for "unfiltered information to people living under conditions of censorship," and it established "a $500,000 grant program for innovative proposals and cutting-edge approaches to combat Internet censorship in countries seeking to restrict basic human rights, including freedom of expression."[15] In this way, the Bush administration got the U.S. government openly in the business of paying for and promoting "freedom technologies" to help break authoritarian censorship and loosen authoritarian rule across the globe.

The Obama administration continued to advocate for the commercial nonregulation principle and further expanded the United States' commitment to the anti-censorship principle.[16] The landmark statement of its approach, and the most elaborate and mature expression of the American conception of internet freedom, came in Secretary of State Hillary Clinton's much-lauded January 2010 speech on the topic.[17] Invoking American traditions from the First Amendment to the Four Freedoms, Clinton pledged American support for liberty of speech, thought, and religion on the internet and for the right to privacy and connectivity to ensure these liberties for all. Clinton's successor to GIFT, the State Department's

NetFreedom Task Force, oversaw "U.S. efforts in more than 40 countries to help individuals circumvent politically motivated censorship by developing new tools and providing the training needed to safely access the Internet."[18] Other federally funded bodies served similar goals.[19] The Obama administration spent at least $105 million on these programs, which included investment in encryption and filter-circumvention products and support to fight network censorship abroad.[20]

Across administrations, the U.S. internet freedom project has pursued numerous overlapping aims. It has sought to build a stable and robust global commercial internet. It has sought to enhance global wealth—especially the wealth of the U.S. firms that have dominated the computer and internet technology industries. It has sought to export to other countries U.S. notions of free expression and free trade. And it has sought to impact politics abroad by spreading democracy with the ambitious hope of ending authoritarianism. "The Internet," Magaziner proclaimed, is "a force for the promotion of democracy, because dictatorship depends upon the control of the flow of information. The Internet makes this control much more difficult in the short run and impossible in the long run."[21] The Bush administration and especially the Obama administration engaged in high-profile and expensive diplomatic initiatives to use and shape the internet to spread democracy and human rights.

The U.S. internet freedom project deserves significant credit for the remarkable growth of the global internet, and especially global commerce, in the last two decades. But on every other dimension, the project is failing, and many of its elements lie in tatters. In response to perceived American provocations, other nations have rejected the attempted export of American values and are increasingly effective at imposing their own values on the internet. These nations have become adept at clamping down on unwelcome speech and at hindering the free flow of data across and within their borders. Authoritarian countries, in particular, are defeating unwanted internet activities within their borders and are using the internet to their advantage to deepen political control. The optimistic hope that the internet might spread democracy overseas has been further belied by the damage it has done to democracy at home. Digital technologies "are not an unmitigated blessing," Secretary Clinton acknowledged in her 2010 speech.[22] She understated the point. The relatively unregulated internet in the United States is being used for ill to a point that threatens basic American institutions.

HYPOCRISY

Hillary Clinton's 2010 speech took place against the background of fifteen years of growing global digital conflict.[23] On the surface, this conflict was mostly about control over internet content. The internet was an American invention that, in its very code, seemed to embody the American values of free speech and resistance to regulation. But global connectivity and access initially challenged local political control and sparked resentment and fear among governments in authoritarian and nonauthoritarian states alike. These sentiments were exacerbated by the fact that the American technology giants—Amazon, Google, Facebook, Apple, and Microsoft— dominated online life, raking in hundreds of billions of dollars in profits through the relentless growth of their increasingly indispensable digital products. They were also stoked by the United States' control of the naming and numbering system for the internet.[24]

More than any other nation, China fought back against these trends. It developed powerful systems of censorship and control over the internet in order to protect the Communist Party and the nation from what the party viewed as subversive online forces. And it forced American firms seeking to do business in China to play by its rules or be denied access. Other authoritarian nations took steps in this direction, although none matched China's vigor or commitment.[25]

But it wasn't only authoritarian governments that the U.S. internet freedom project threatened. Europe's prevailing conception of government's relationship to the individual, and the individual's relationship to personal data, differs sharply from the prevailing American conception. Since the 1990s, European regulators have held American technology firms to higher standards of privacy and competition than American regulators have required of them. European regulators have also sought to eliminate from their networks hate speech that is tolerated by the First Amendment but is illegal in Europe.[26]

Below the surface of disputes about content was a different but no less fierce battle about theft of private and proprietary data. Computer systems are inevitably filled with vulnerabilities that can be exploited to gain entry. When a computer is connected to the internet, actors from around the globe have potential access. And the internet's architecture makes anonymity and spoofing (fake emails or web pages disguised to appear genuine) easy, which further facilitates unauthorized entry. The combination of these factors sparked a growing wave of cybertheft in the first decade of the twenty-first century.

The U.S. government participated in this bonanza of digital extraction, although it focused on acquiring military and intelligence secrets rather than commercial theft to benefit U.S. firms.[27] But the United States was also among the most digitally dependent of nations, and a good deal of its military and economic and cultural power was embedded in digital networks. By the time of Hillary Clinton's 2010 speech, the United States worried that it was losing more from cybertheft than it was gaining. American government networks suffered embarrassing intrusions that resulted in the exfiltration of cherished intelligence and military secrets.[28] Just as alarming was the digital theft from abroad of the commercial secrets of American firms. U.S. companies reportedly lost hundreds of billions of dollars of commercial value each year in what National Security Agency (NSA) director Keith Alexander described as "the greatest transfer of wealth in history."[29] China was public enemy number one for this great digital heist. But other nation-state adversaries and sophisticated organized crime networks also figured out how to steal information from American computer systems.

One important innovation in Clinton's 2010 speech was to tie the imperative of internet security to the ideal of internet freedom. She did so by drawing on the fourth of President Franklin Roosevelt's Four Freedoms, the freedom from fear. The United States must "work against those who use communication networks as tools of disruption and fear," Clinton said.[30] Nations and individuals that "engage in cyberattacks should face consequences and international condemnation."[31] To further resist the rise of cyberattacks, the United States should "create norms of behavior among states and encourage respect for the global networked commons."[32]

The hypocrisy in the linkage between internet freedom and internet security was apparent even before Clinton finished her speech. Eight paragraphs after complaining about cyberattacks, she boasted that the State Department was "supporting the development of new tools" to fight authoritarian censorship online.[33] These tools—which, as noted above, were supported by tens of millions of dollars in U.S. grants—were designed to help activists advocate for freedom in foreign networks in ways that foreign governments viewed as disrupting those networks and violating their sovereignty.

Authoritarian states had worried since the 1990s about ties between the U.S. government and U.S. technology firms; they feared that the United

States would use its internet dominance to foster regime openness and regime change.[34] Their fears grew as U.S. internet technology firms rose to global dominance in the 2000s and as American social media companies like Facebook and Twitter seemed to provide the organizational tools for the protests that shook the Arab world during the Obama administration. In the midst of the demonstrations in Iran following its 2009 presidential election, a State Department official asked Twitter to delay a scheduled maintenance of its network that might "cut off service while Iranians were using Twitter to swap information and inform the outside world about the mushrooming protests around Tehran," as the *New York Times* put it in a story titled "Washington Taps Into a Potent New Force in Diplomacy."[35] The event confirmed for Iranian officials that "the Internet is an instrument of Western power and that its ultimate end is to foster regime change in Iran," as Evgeny Morozov noted.[36] Iran and other authoritarian governments saw U.S. social media firms in particular as "a 'made in America' digital missile that could undermine authoritarian stability."[37]

That perception intensified after Secretary Clinton delivered a second speech on internet freedom in January 2011, during the early days of the Arab Spring. Clinton emphasized how much Facebook and Twitter had aided the Arab Spring and touted U.S. financial and technical support "to help people in oppressive Internet environments get around filters [and] stay one step ahead of the censors."[38] That same month, the State Department intervened with U.S. tech companies to help protect protesters in Tunisia who would soon force President Zine El Abidine Ben Ali to step down.[39] As former NSA and Central Intelligence Agency (CIA) director Michael Hayden described these efforts, "The Secretary of State is laundering money through NGOs to populate software throughout the Arab world to prevent the people in the Arab street from being tracked by their government."[40] Authoritarian nations got the message.

The United States also seemed to be militarizing cyberspace in ways that were hard to square with its rhetorical commitment to digital security. Seven months before Clinton's 2010 speech, the Obama administration established U.S. Cyber Command to integrate American cyber operations, including offensive military cyber operations abroad.[41] It was no accident that the administration placed the director of the NSA in charge of Cyber Command. NSA is responsible for breaking into and extracting intelligence from communications and computer systems abroad—activities that are typically prerequisites to the computer network attacks contemplated for

Cyber Command. "We have U.S. warriors in cyberspace [who] are deployed overseas and are in direct contact with adversaries overseas," bragged Bob Gourley, a former chief technology officer for the Defense Intelligence Agency, to a reporter a few months after Cyber Command was created.[42] These experts "live in adversary networks," he added.[43]

The astounding degree to which the U.S. government lived in adversary networks would became apparent to the world over the next few years. In November 2010, diplomatic cables pilfered by Chelsea Manning and published by WikiLeaks showed that Clinton herself had sent diplomatic directives about ways to break into the communications channels of diplomats from several nations as well as of the secretary general of the United Nations.[44] This is a standard secret intelligence practice, but it was nonetheless embarrassing for Clinton, who had insisted a few months earlier that "in an internet-connected world, an attack on one nation's networks can be an attack on all."[45]

Then, in June 2012, the New York Times reported that President Obama had authorized an elaborate cyberattack to disrupt the centrifuges in Iran's nuclear enrichment facilities.[46] "Olympic Games," as the operation was called, marked a new era in the militarization of cyberspace, according to Hayden, because it was "the first attack of a major nature in which a cyberattack was used to effect physical destruction" rather than simply to steal data or disrupt a computer's normal operation.[47] "Somebody crossed the Rubicon," he stated, comparing the attack on Iran to August 1945, when the world first witnessed the destructive power of nuclear weapons.[48] Olympic Games, on top of Cyber Command, accelerated the global arms race for cyber weapons and cyber forces, with ominous implications for internet freedom.

And finally, in the spring of 2013, Edward Snowden stole many thousands of documents from the NSA and gave them to a group of journalists to publish. The documents revealed that the NSA had penetrated every conceivable form of computer and communications system around the globe, sweeping up unfathomable masses of electronic intelligence about foreign governments and foreign citizens.[49] They also showed that it had set up a system to collect huge quantities of intelligence information, not just by breaking into foreign networks but also by (among other means) demanding information from Google, Yahoo!, Facebook, and other American firms that themselves collected data from abroad, especially communications of individuals.[50] In these and other ways, the NSA seemed to be succeeding in its stated aim of (as one of the leaked documents put it) achieving "global network dominance."[51]

"It would be hard to overstate the extent to which Edward Snowden's disclosures about US mass surveillance techniques in the post-9/11 period have shaken up geopolitical dynamics on Internet freedom, security and governance," wrote Eileen Donahoe of Human Rights Watch two years after the leaks.[52] The Snowden disclosures, on top of everything else, gravely damaged the internet freedom project.

They made it seem like the "hands-off" approach to the internet was, as many nations had feared, a mask for U.S. government manipulation and control. They thus exacerbated the resentment that had been building against the United States due to U.S. firms' dominance of the internet economy and the U.S. government's control over the internet's naming and numbering system. The disclosures also showed that the NSA was heavily involved, on a global scale, in the very forms of surreptitious network surveillance that the U.S. government decried when done by authoritarian nations, albeit for different ends. They indicated that the NSA was secretly trying to undermine the very encryption tools that the State Department and other U.S. agencies were promoting to fight oppression abroad.[53] And the disclosures revealed that the United States was acting directly contrary to the cybersecurity imperative that Clinton had linked to the internet freedom agenda in 2010.

The harm to internet freedom from the Snowden and related disclosures went beyond mere revelations of U.S. hypocrisy. The disclosures chilled certain forms of online communications for fear of government snooping.[54] Most significantly, they gave nations a powerful incentive and a powerful excuse to exert more control over their domestic networks in response to perceived U.S. cyber incursions, along with a roadmap for doing so.[55]

FAILURE ABROAD

By the time that Secretary Clinton began to speak about internet freedom, a decade after Bill Clinton's presidency had ended, China was doing a pretty good job of nailing the Jell-O of undesirable speech to the wall of Communist Party control. Some in 2010 still had doubts that China would succeed. Today, a half-dozen years after Snowden's revelations, China is approaching mastery over the internet communications that it cares most about, which are mainly forms of organizational speech and collective expression that it believes threaten the party and public order generally.[56]

China has established digital filters at the border that allow in only the types and quantities of information the party wants. CNN, ESPN, and the *Washington Post* can currently be accessed in China, but Facebook, Google, YouTube, Twitter, and Instagram are blocked and replaced by homegrown and government-friendly substitutes that flourish behind the Great Firewall.[57] China has also been tightening its grip on the "virtual private networks" that allow sophisticated users to defeat these filters.[58]

Inside the country, an intricate regime of surveillance, counterspeech, censorship, and targeted disruption enables additional party control, often in real time.[59] These tools are supported by a deterrence strategy of prominent arrests, fines, extralegal detentions, and forced confession for writers, journalists, and dissidents who violate China's speech rules. China has also been developing a real-name identity registration system to prevent anonymity and to enhance surveillance, as well as a related "social credit system" that (among many other things) seeks to tie online access to online behavior.[60] And China requires foreign and domestic firms to keep the "critical information infrastructure" they collect inside China and to give the government access for security purposes.[61] Apple is typical among U.S. firms in complying with China's law enforcement and security demands, even as it has resisted in court several U.S. government efforts at cooperation on law enforcement.[62]

A core assumption of the U.S. internet freedom agenda is that online censorship and control retard innovation and modernization. "Countries that restrict free access to information or violate the basic rights of internet users risk walling themselves off from the progress of the next century," Clinton warned China and other authoritarian states in her 2010 speech.[63] China is in the process of proving this assumption false. It is creating an internet that reflects the party's values and protects its interests. At the same time, China permits its nearly 800 million internet users to communicate with each other and the rest of the world on a vast array of topics. It also fosters a sophisticated and robust e-commerce space, led by Chinese companies that include four of the world's largest internet firms: Alibaba (online shopping), Baidu (search), Tencent (social media and messaging), and Xiaomi (smartphones and related products). China has a vibrant technology start-up scene that is starting to rival Silicon Valley's.[64] It is probably ahead of the United States in digital payment systems, mobile commerce, and next-generation wireless technology, and it appears to be holding its own in the important fields of artificial intelligence and quantum computing.[65] Its technology firms, meanwhile, are making the turn from copycats to innovators and are starting to compete abroad, especially in Asia.[66]

The U.S. government has been unable to stymie China's singular approach to mixing political control and commercial freedom on the internet. Since Snowden destroyed its remaining moral leverage and Donald Trump became president, it has practically stopped trying. Access to China's gargantuan market is so cherished by American firms that they acquiesce in policies of government intrusion and surveillance they would not tolerate in the United States. The U.S. government has, in turn, tolerated this acquiescence, perhaps because it realizes that too much pressure on Beijing over censorship would result in retaliation that would harm American companies and the American economy on balance. American efforts to introduce digital tools to defeat China's control over the political aspects of its internet have also failed. Proposals to invoke international trade law to fight back against what the United States sees as the digital protectionism of the Great Firewall have gone nowhere and are unlikely to succeed even if pursued with more vigor.

China is an extreme case. At the dawn of the Arab Spring, it seemed that the internet, especially social media platforms such as Twitter, YouTube, and Facebook, had a better chance of fostering freedom in Arab nations. Many of the leaders of the 2010–2011 uprisings in Tunisia, Libya, Egypt, Yemen, Syria, and Bahrain were trained to use digital technologies by organizations sponsored by the U.S. government and U.S. internet firms. But whatever advantages these technologies initially brought—a debated point—they now appear to have been reversed. The communications tools that seemed to mark a decisive advantage against Arab governments reflected only a temporary advantage due to government incompetence and inattention. In the last five years, authoritarian Arab regimes have reasserted control. They have done so by using tanks, to be sure. But they have also begun to master digital technologies and to deploy them to censor, surveil, and disrupt protesters and to actively cultivate alternative nationalist movements using "bots" and armies of fake users. "The very technologies that many heralded as 'tools of liberation' . . . are now being used to stifle dissent and squeeze civil society," Ron Deibert has observed.[67] These governments have also grown adept at employing internet shutdowns and slowdowns, at blocking encrypted communication tools, and at cracking down on circumvention efforts.

The trend of increasing internet control by governments extends beyond China and the Arab states. In 2009, Freedom House initiated an annual global survey of internet freedom that measured national limits on internet content, internet access, and violations of user rights, including undue surveillance, privacy violations, and penalties for online speech. Its 2017 report found that internet freedom, so measured, was becoming increasingly precarious. "Disinformation tactics contributed to a seventh consecutive year of overall decline in internet freedom, as did a rise in disruptions to mobile internet service and increases in physical and technical attacks on human rights defenders and independent media," Freedom House concluded.[68] "A record number of governments have restricted mobile internet service for political or security reasons, often in areas populated by ethnic or religious minorities," and "governments around the world have dramatically increased their efforts to manipulate information on social media over the past year."[69]

It is not just authoritarian nations that have defied American-style internet freedom. In recent years, the nations of the European Union have come to see the hegemony of U.S. internet firms as nothing less than a danger to the European way of life. In part, this is due to the revelation that the NSA had been sucking up massive amounts of data about European citizens initially collected by U.S. firms. And in part, it is because U.S. internet firms wield their enormous power to shape morals, politics, news, consumer choice, and much more in ways that many European officials abhor. "We are afraid of Google" because it threatens "our values, our understanding of the nature of humanity, our worldwide social order and, from our own perspective, the future of Europe," wrote Mathias Döpfner, the CEO of Axel Springer SE, Germany's largest media group, in a much-noted open letter to Google CEO Eric Schmidt in 2014.[70] In recent years, European regulators have embraced this philosophy and significantly ramped up their legal pressure of American technology firms. Many believe that this pressure is motivated in part by economic protectionism.[71] Perhaps so. The point for now is that Europe's internet regulators are becoming more active within European borders and sometimes beyond.

European regulators have, for example, fined Google $2.7 billion for abusing its economic power in the arena of internet search and Apple $15.3 billion for unpaid taxes.[72] Several other antitrust investigations against Google and other U.S. tech firms are in the works, and European regulators are searching for ways to impose billions more in taxes. They have also threatened these firms with severe sanctions if they do not clamp down on hate speech, incitement, and terrorist violence. They have recognized a "right to be forgotten," which allows individuals to remove detrimental personal information from search results on the web—not just in Europe but possibly everywhere in the world. European courts, alarmed by the Snowden revelations, have raised the privacy bar for sending data collected in Europe to the United States, for fear of NSA snooping. And most significantly, the new General Data Protection Regulation (GDPR) in Europe imposes burdensome new data disclosure and privacy rules for firms handling the information of EU citizens.[73] These rules are in the process of being adopted by firms globally, including in the United States.[74]

The GDPR is one of scores of recent national and regional regulations related to privacy, security, surveillance, and law enforcement that limit the flow of information across national borders and pressure firms to store data about users in a given country on servers located within that country.[75] Other non-tariff barriers to digital free trade that have grown sharply in recent years include local infrastructure or computing requirements, local partnership requirements, intellectual property infringement, cross-border cybertheft, and the various means of filtering and blocking information from abroad noted above.[76] The United States has gotten in the game, mostly through an interagency committee to review foreign investments known as the Committee on Foreign Investment in the United States (CFIUS). CFIUS now regularly flouts the commercial nonregulation principle with its aggressive crackdown on attempts by foreign firms, notably from China, to own or control U.S. information technology firms.[77] The ostensible justification for CFIUS's growing vetoes of foreign takeovers of these firms is cybersecurity. But the trend also reflects retaliation against Chinese protectionism and worries about strategic control over crucial technology sectors.[78]

While the commercial nonregulation principle is everywhere under assault, it would be wrong to ignore its successes. The principle largely prevailed for almost two decades during which the internet boomed and large U.S. firms grabbed huge market share globally, in some instances approaching monopoly power. The United States has a big trade surplus in digital industries.[79] Both U.S. firms and U.S. consumers continue to reap the benefits of the continuing growth in the digital economy, even though U.S. firms and digital free trade are suffering pushback abroad and even though other countries and firms in other countries are catching up. It is an open question how far nations will go down the road of digital protectionism, how burdensome foreign regulations will prove to be for U.S. firms, and what impact these trends will have, especially in the burgeoning tech battle with China.

The anti-censorship principle, by contrast, is much further down the road to collapse and indeed was always a delusional goal. Nations have different values and priorities, and the American conception of freedom, especially our conception of free speech, is a global outlier. As the very different examples of China and Europe show, when the internet threatens those values and priorities, nations can preserve them by exercising sovereign muscle — brute coercive power — over local firms and communication intermediaries within their borders.[80] The internet freedom agenda never really had a plan to fight this logic. The United States lacks the economic or diplomatic power to bend China or the European Union to its will on internet matters. If anything, the dependency of American firms on access to these giant markets gives China and Europe the upper hand. Nor has the United States been able to deliver to activists abroad the digital tools to defeat control in weaker nations, which have largely succeeded in reversing the impact of these tools for their own ends.

FAILURE AT HOME

The United States' internet freedom project is not just failing abroad. It is also failing at home. I explained above that the United States is increasingly engaged in forms of digital protectionism that it once decried. But both the commercial nonregulation principle and the anti-censorship principle are allowing real harms within the country's borders as well. "Modern information networks and the technologies they support can be harnessed for good or for ill," Clinton acknowledged in her 2010 speech.[81] The premise of the U.S. internet freedom agenda is that an open, unregulated internet is great at home on balance and thus should be exported abroad. This premise — built on an optimism about the impact of digital technologies on American public life — is now being called into question.

The first problem concerns cybersecurity. Not a week goes by without reports of major cybersecurity breaches, data thefts, information compromises, or cyberattacks in which major U.S. firms and their consumers are the victims. The U.S. government is not doing much better. A May 2018 report by the Office of Management and Budget and the Department of

Homeland Security concluded that an overwhelming majority of U.S. federal agencies are ill equipped to defend their networks and cannot even "detect when large amounts of information leave their networks, which is particularly alarming in the wake of some of the high-profile incidents across government and industry in recent years."[82] The U.S. government and U.S. firms have seen this problem coming for over a decade, but they have been unable to check it. "We're the frog in the pot that's getting boiled," said Rob Joyce, then the Trump administration's cybersecurity coordinator, at a conference in 2017.[83] "I watch these breaches every day," he added. "It's getting to a point where we're getting numb."[84]

Among the many reasons the United States is failing at cybersecurity is its commitment at home to the commercial nonregulation principle. Inadequate regulation is a primary cause of poor cybersecurity hygiene in the United States. Individuals have inadequate incentives to use security software and take other precautions, and firms lack proper incentives to harden their defenses and share information with each other and the government. The vast majority of software companies, internet technology firms, and individuals will not internalize the many negative cybersecurity costs they impose due to weak security standards or poor security investments unless the government provides some prodding through liability, regulation, tax incentives, standard-setting, or some other means.[85] But the United States' nonregulation commitment and concerns about the impact on innovation have significantly hampered progress on this front.

Another unfortunate side effect of internet freedom at home, and one caused more by the anti-censorship principle, is susceptibility to information operations from abroad. Explaining the difficulty of preventing Russia from stealing emails from Democratic National Committee (DNC) accounts, President Obama explained shortly before leaving office that "our economy is more digitalized and it is more vulnerable, partly because . . . we have a more opened society and we are engaged in less control or censorships [sic] over what happens on the internet."[86] The United States has a wider and more readily accessible digital attack space than any nation in the world, and much of this attack space lies in the private sector, including private channels of communication. The U.S. commitment to free speech, relative anonymity, and sharp limitations on domestic government surveillance — all virtues from a civil liberties perspective, of course — makes it hard for our government to identify, prevent, and respond to malicious cyber operations, especially ones that seek to manipulate information for nefarious ends.

This is the very problem of social disruption and instability from online foreign meddling that Russia and China have been harping about, and taking steps to check, for years.

Another way in which internet freedom threatens American institutions is in the pathological forms of speech that it fosters. There are many reasons for the political and social fracturing of American society, but arguably near the top of the list is the balkanization of information consumption, and the attendant coarsening of public discourse, that digital technologies foster. The internet, and especially social media platforms such as Facebook and Twitter, promote the sort of fine-grained, self-serving, and exclusionary information consumption that Cass Sunstein has called "self-insulation."[87] As Sunstein and others have argued, self-insulation makes it harder to empathize with citizens whose concerns and opinions differ; enhances mutual alienation, misunderstanding, and polarization; and subsidizes the spread of falsehoods, conspiracies, and counterfeit news. The internet has also enabled a proliferation of specialty news and information sites that tend to be more extreme and partisan than traditional "meat-space" media and that intensify self-insulation, especially in a heterogeneous society like the United States. All these tendencies have a devastating impact on our deliberative democracy, which depends for its success on mutual understanding, compromise, and learning.

A final problem comes in the form of the weaponization of speech.[88] The internet has made speech cheap to produce and to aggregate. This has allowed private actors to engage in vicious group attacks by "troll armies" that aim to discredit or to destroy the reputation of disfavored speakers and to discourage them from speaking again. A related practice is to distort or overcome disfavored speech by using fake news, fake commentators, and other forms of misinformation or propaganda to muffle the disfavored speech or confuse the audience. Both practices take advantage of the pathologies of self-insulation. And the impact of both can be magnified by bots that automatically send and resend the weaponized speech on a large scale. The aim of weaponized speech is often to create a fog that prevents all news sources, and all informed critical commentary, from being trusted.

These maladies of internet freedom at home converged in the historic event that may one day be seen as its death knell: the Russian information operation in the presidential election of 2016. In 2010, Hillary Clinton spoke of internet freedom as a means to end censorship and control in authoritarian nations like Russia. Six years later, such efforts had had no apparent effect on that country. On the contrary, Russian president Vladimir Putin, perhaps in response to perceived provocations by Clinton,[89] was able to exploit internet freedom and openness in the United States to cause unprecedented disruption in its democratic processes, possibly denying her the presidency. The DNC hack, as President Obama noted, was "not particularly sophisticated—this was not some elaborate, complicated espionage scheme."[90] It was a simple phishing operation that extracted email messages which, once made public and churned through social media, caused a public storm. The Russians also weaponized speech through social media accounts in ways that appeared to be designed to advantage Donald Trump. For many Americans, these commonplace tactics called into question the legitimacy of the election and of the democratic system more broadly. The really bad news is that there is little to prevent something like this, or worse, from happening in the next presidential election, this time at the hands of multiple foreign actors.

CONCLUSION: TRADEOFFS

The Trump administration has hollowed out the State Department and has deemphasized human rights and free trade. It is thus doubtful that it will give much support to the internet freedom agenda. But even a future administration more sympathetic to the agenda will need to address its failures to date by acknowledging some uncomfortable realities about the internet and by facing some large tradeoffs. Here are what I think are the three most important ones.

The first set of tradeoffs arise from how the United States promotes its anti-censorship principle abroad. That principle is premised on a commitment to spreading democracy and U.S. constitutional values that has been a lynchpin of American foreign policy since at least World War II, if not earlier. There are many ways to maintain this commitment while rethinking the tactic of meddling in foreign networks to undermine authoritarian governments. The American people are angry about and threatened by Russian cyber interference in the 2016 election. But the Russian government, as well as China's and Iran's governments and others, are angry about and threatened by U.S. intervention in their domestic networks with the ultimate aim of changing their forms of state and society.

Network interventions to promote freedom and democracy are not on the same moral plane as network interventions to disrupt or undermine democracy. But regardless of the morality of the situation, it is fanciful to think that the digitally dependent United States can continue its aggressive cyber operations in other nations if it wants to limit its own exposure to the same.[91] Unless the United States can raise its cyber defenses or improve its cyber deterrence—a dim prospect at the moment—it will need to consider the possibility of a cooperative arrangement in which it pledges to forgo threatening actions in foreign networks in exchange for relief from analogous adversary operations in its networks.[92] The Russian government recently proposed a mutual ban on foreign political interference, including through cyber means.[93] The significant hurdles to such an agreement include contestation over the terms of mutual restraint, a lack of trust, and verification difficulties.[94] These high hurdles are not obviously higher than the hurdles to improving U.S. cyber defenses and cyber deterrence. And yet, no one in the U.S. government appears to be thinking about which sorts of operations the United States might be willing to temper in exchange for relief from the devastating cyber incursions of recent years.[95]

The second set of tradeoffs concern U.S. skepticism about more extensive government regulation of and involvement in domestic networks. The devastating cyber losses that the United States has been suffering result in large part from market failures that only government regulation can correct. The government will also need to consider doing more to police and defend telecommunications channels from cyberattack and cybertheft, just as it polices and defends threats that come via air, space, sea, and land. This might involve coordination with firms to scan internet communications, to share threat information, and to frame a response. And it might require accommodations for encrypted communications. The hazards for privacy from these steps are so extreme as to make them seem impossible today. But there are also serious hazards for privacy from not providing adequate cybersecurity.[96] If the threat to our valuable digital networks becomes severe enough, the American people will insist that the government take steps to protect them and the forms of social and economic life they enable. Our conception of the tradeoffs among different privacy commitments and between privacy and security will adjust.

Finally, U.S. regulators, courts, and tech firms may need to recalibrate domestic speech rules. Tim Wu's essay in this volume proposes some ways to rethink First Amendment law to deal with the pathologies of internet speech.[97] For instance, First Amendment doctrine might be stretched to prevent government officials from inciting attack mobs to drown out disfavored speakers, as President Trump has sometimes appeared to do. Or the doctrine might be tempered, to allow the government to more aggressively criminalize or regulate cyberstalking and trolling, or even to require speech platforms to provide a healthy and fair speech environment. These are bold reforms, but they are also potentially very dangerous. The line between genuine political speech (including group speech) and propaganda and trolling will be elusive and controversial. The effort to ensure a healthy speech environment is even more fraught and will invariably ban or chill a good deal of speech that should be protected. These misgivings do not mean that such modifications are not worth exploring or that current understandings of the First Amendment are sacrosanct. They just mean that here, as with the other tradeoffs, the choices we face are painful.

The Limits of Supply-Side Internet Freedom

David Kaye

JACK GOLDSMITH has written a compelling essay arguing that the U.S. internet freedom agenda has failed. Online freedoms are on a downward trajectory globally. American advocacy for an open and secure internet appears hypocritical in light of Edward Snowden's 2013 revelations of the National Security Agency's activities and the U.S. development and use of offensive cyber capabilities. The contemporary internet, dominated by American social network companies, contributes to a coarsening public discourse, viral disinformation and propaganda, diminished trust in domestic institutions of governance and media, and rampant digital insecurity. Goldsmith has unusual credibility to highlight the persistence of authoritarian interest in retaining control in the digital age, for way back in 2006 he and Tim Wu warned against the era's widespread belief in a utopian borderless internet.[98]

As strong as the essay is, it is limited by what I'd call a supply-side view of internet freedom, according to which its success or failure depends upon American policy, American norms, and America's ability to overcome foreign resistance. The United States, Goldsmith suggests, sought to export valuable goods to others: "freedom technologies" (quoting the George W. Bush administration), democracy, "U.S. constitutional values," and the blessings of "American-style freedom of speech and expression on the global internet." This is the language of supply and, when turned around and placed in the hands of authoritarian regimes, an easy way to smear internet freedom as digital colonialism.

In presenting internet freedom in such supply-driven terms, the essay leaves out the global *demand* for online access, privacy, security, and freedom of expression. True, the U.S. government sought to play an important role in the internet freedom movement, and Goldsmith is certainly correct that U.S. officials have seen the internet at least in part as a tool of a democracy-promoting foreign policy. But the demand for internet freedom exists independently of U.S. policy and its aspiration to open up authoritarian regimes. Indeed, the normative ideals that underlie the global demand for internet access and freedom online are not particularly American—neither inspired nor informed by the U.S. constitutional guarantee of free speech. Ignoring global demand limits how we think about U.S. policy, abroad and at home, and risks distorting the conclusions we draw from the facts of online freedom today.

Goldsmith identifies Secretary of State Hillary Clinton's January 2010 speech on internet freedom[99] as "the most elaborate and mature expression of the American conception of internet freedom." Clinton's speech, he notes, invoked "American traditions from the First Amendment to the Four Freedoms." The speech is a good place to start, but it was also about something more than American values: it was an articulation of internet freedom *as a human right*. Clinton quoted the guarantee in Article 19 of the Universal Declaration of Human Rights that everyone enjoys the right to "to seek, receive and impart information and ideas through any media and regardless of frontiers." And she promised a multilateral approach, in which the United States would pursue an internet freedom resolution at the UN Human Rights Council.[100]

As these parts of Clinton's speech reflected, the global struggle for internet freedom is not just a U.S. struggle with Russia or China or others—although parts of it, such as the battle over disinformation, certainly have geopolitical angles. It is also, and more fundamentally, a set of claims rooted in human rights law. Goldsmith may be right that the U.S. government's hypocrisies make it ill equipped to be an internet freedom leader, but focusing too much on this point distracts both from the need for U.S. reform and from the persistent global demand for internet freedom even in the face of U.S. bad behavior.

If we reorient the internet freedom analysis away from U.S. supply or geopolitical struggle, our accounting of the gains and losses over the past decade may look a bit different, and we may be able to identify additional reforms for the United States to pursue as part of its anti-censorship agenda.[101] It's still a grim picture, for all the reasons Goldsmith recounts. And as the reality of people's lived experiences matters most, the widespread repression of online freedom is indeed a failure—just not an exclusively American one or one that is irreversible.

Yet at the same time, European anger over the power of U.S. internet firms may reflect a paradoxical success of U.S. policy, at least according to the rights-oriented terms of Clinton's speech. Many Europeans, including individual citizens who have been the driving forces behind the right to be forgotten (Spain's Mario Costeja González) and the breakup of the U.S.-EU privacy safe harbor (Austria's Max Schrems), are demanding what they believe they are guaranteed under European and international human rights law.[102] European member state and Commission initiatives against "illegal hate speech" often test the limits of human rights constraints, and they ought to be more carefully calibrated than they are now, but they also advance another set of U.S. policies calling for companies to crack down on terrorist and extremist content online.[103]

When we see that the internet freedom agenda is not a wholly owned operation of the United States, different legal and policy options may open up for U.S. policy-makers who wish to advance it. One set involves continuing to support initiatives at the multilateral level, where civil society representatives and like-minded governments collaborate to develop a normative framework friendly to online human rights demands. The UN Human Rights Council and General Assembly, repeatedly noting that offline rights apply online, have promoted digital security and privacy, condemned internet shutdowns, and championed online protections for journalists, bloggers, NGOs, and others.[104] Hundreds of grassroots organizations around the world have relied on this normative framework in litigation and legislative work as they seek online freedoms in their own political and legal environments. Regional human rights courts and commissions in Europe, Africa, and the Inter-American system have also helped to reinforce human rights online, including through concrete challenges to online repression by governments like Russia's.[105] The governments of the Netherlands, Norway, Sweden, and many other nations continue to devote resources to supporting online freedom activists. Politically, the United States and its allies should continue to pursue a multi-stakeholder approach to internet governance, involving companies, advocates, academics, and others, in venues like the UN's Internet Governance Forum. These efforts have long-term value, laying the groundwork for resistance to authoritarian policies and laws.

Given the immense power wielded by companies in the information and communications technology sector, these companies need to be engaged as well. Corporate policies in this sector have a substantial impact on internet freedom and should be part of any agenda to advance it. Telecommunications, social media, search, and content delivery companies, among many others, have the capacity to mitigate many threats to freedom online. Their own policies should be designed in ways that foster individual rights, especially privacy and freedom of expression.[106]

Human rights approaches can also add some perspective to proposals "to recalibrate domestic speech rules" in the United States, which Goldsmith accurately sees as "potentially very dangerous." Aggressive content regulation by the state, whether by the United States operating under an "obsolete First Amendment"[107] or by the European Union and its member states fearing a loss of control over their public space, may do unnecessary damage to freedom of speech and the internet freedom agenda. In contrast, government disclosure requirements that impose standards on tech companies—drawing from the UN Guiding Principles on Business and Human Rights[108]—may empower users with greater control of their information environment, addressing some of "the pathologies of internet speech" without undermining freedom of expression guarantees (international or domestic).

Some forms of transparency could facilitate approaches to accountability that today hardly exist, providing robust information about how and why companies adopt and enforce content-moderation rules, clarity about processes such as flagging and verification, and usable mechanisms to appeal decisions affecting users. Transparency about rules and processes, including algorithmic ones, may help to ameliorate some of the very deep power discrepancies between the companies and all other relevant actors.[109] Additional reforms might delegate more power to users and to local communities worldwide to deal with hateful content, harassment, false information, and other internet ills.

Overall, a U.S. internet freedom policy rooted in demand rather than supply would be in step with the global interest in identifying threats to online freedom and ways to address them. In May 2018, the nature of that demand showed itself when over 2,500 people gathered in Toronto for the eighth annual RightsCon digital rights conference, 1,000 more people than had gathered for the 2017 RightsCon in Brussels. Civil society representatives organized and dominated proceedings, corporate players actively engaged, and the relatively few governmental actors stayed largely in the background. Nearly 25 percent of the participants came from the developing world, and hundreds more, the organizers tell me, would have attended but for lack of funding. That demand, and responding to it, is where the future of the internet freedom agenda can be found.

Internet Freedom Without Imperialism

Nani Jansen Reventlow
and Jonathan McCully

JACK GOLDSMITH ARGUES that the United States' internet freedom agenda has failed. He does so by offering an overview of the contradictions and conundrums that have frustrated the U.S. government's efforts across the Clinton, Bush, and Obama administrations, and he raises considered observations as to what the potential tradeoffs might look like if a future administration were to pursue this agenda again.

As thoughtful as it is, Goldsmith's essay appears to be premised on the idea that promoting the underlying principles of commercial nonregulation and anti-censorship, as initially envisaged by the Clinton administration in the 1990s, is a legitimate means of achieving internet freedom worldwide. That premise deserves critical scrutiny. This commentary will highlight some of the inherent flaws in the U.S. approach to internet freedom, which may have contributed to its failure as a global policy.

INTERNET FREEDOM: BEYOND FREE SPEECH AND FREE MARKETS

By focusing on commercial nonregulation and anti-censorship, the U.S. government's internet freedom agenda is too narrow in scope to be fully accepted internationally. This approach may reflect the "preferred position" that the principle of free speech and the metaphor of a marketplace of ideas hold in the U.S. constitutional hierarchy,[110] but it fails to sufficiently take into account the other human rights that should be promoted and protected to achieve internet freedom on a global scale.

The two-principle approach identified by Goldsmith sits in stark contrast to the approach adopted by the United Nations Human Rights Council (UNHRC). In July 2016, the UNHRC adopted a resolution affirming the importance of "applying a *comprehensive* human rights–based approach in providing and in expanding access to the Internet."[111] In this document, the UNHRC noted the variety of human rights that are engaged on the internet—from the rights to privacy and freedom of expression to the rights to education and freedom from discrimination—and affirmed that the same rights that are protected offline must be protected online.

Compared to the U.S. government's internet freedom agenda, the approach adopted by the UNHRC has two key strengths bolstering its global legitimacy. First, it builds upon the UN's commitment to developing and codifying international norms through multi-stakeholder, multi-jurisdictional mechanisms, instead of attempting to export domestic values to other jurisdictions. The July 2016 resolution, for example, was jointly submitted to the UNHRC by Brazil, Nigeria, Sweden, Tunisia, Turkey, and the United States, and it was signed by some seventy states.[112]

This does not necessarily mean that every country agreed with the entirety of the text—China and Russia, notably, attempted without success to amend various aspects of the resolution[113]—but it reflects a consensus-based approach to protecting rights and freedoms online. It also clarifies that the international human rights guaranteed by relevant international treaties, including the International Covenant on Civil and Political Rights (ICCPR), apply to the online context.

These international treaties are more promising vehicles than U.S. unilateralism for enhancing protection for online freedom across the globe. The ICCPR has been ratified by 171 countries, which have thereby agreed to be bound by the human rights obligations enshrined in it.[114] To hold states to these standards is to hold them accountable to the global norms they have explicitly agreed to honor, rather than to a vision of internet freedom defined by one particularly powerful state.

Second, the UNHRC approach recognizes that internet freedom is not only (or even primarily) about the right to free speech and a free marketplace of ideas. Instead, it observes that there is a need to respond to technological developments in a way that protects all human rights. This is something that the U.S. internet freedom agenda has failed to appreciate. For example, in her January 2010 speech on internet freedom, Secretary of State Hillary Clinton made reference to privacy but only as a means of promoting free speech.[115] In so doing, she failed to recognize the right to privacy as a fundamental right in and of itself. This failure leads to an inevitable conclusion, one that can also be inferred from Goldsmith's essay, that measures adopted to protect these other human rights in ways that might undermine the principles of commercial nonregulation and anti-censorship are the antithesis of internet freedom. However, this is not always the case.

Consider Europe's new General Data Protection Regulation (GDPR), which places a number of legal obligations on online businesses as to how they may process the personal data of their users. Goldsmith frames the GDPR as contrary to the internet freedom agenda, because it "limit[s] the flow of information across national borders and pressure[s] firms to store data about users in a given country on servers located within that country." What is missing from this framing is the fact that the GDPR is inspired by the European understanding of privacy, which encompasses an individual's right to "informational self-determination" as to how her data is used by third parties.[116] It is difficult to argue that this conception of privacy as a form of informational autonomy does not amount to a type of online freedom. So why shouldn't the promotion and protection of the right to privacy, as envisaged by the GDPR, also form part of the internet freedom agenda, rather than be treated as a threat to it?

COMMERCIAL NONREGULATION AND ANTI-CENSORSHIP: THE INTERNAL CONTRADICTION

The U.S. internet freedom agenda has also failed to grapple with the fact that commercial nonregulation and anti-censorship will not always go hand-in-hand. Although a vast number of countries violate the right to freedom of expression on the internet, government actors are not the only actors policing this environment. Privately owned online platforms exert a remarkable amount of control over what information can or cannot be communicated over their services. By seeking to take a hands-off approach when it comes to regulating these platforms, the internet freedom agenda thus jeopardizes the anti-censorship principle.

With their expansive reach across the world,[117] many U.S.-based online platforms have become the global norm creators for the internet, even though they are generally not subject to U.S. constitutional constraints and do not necessarily fully subscribe to First Amendment principles.

For instance, Facebook's policies have come under fire for being too restrictive of speech.[118] The company's real-name registration requirement, which is arguably incompatible with First Amendment principles protecting anonymous and pseudonymous speech,[119] is legal in the United States but has been successfully challenged before the German courts.[120]

The fact that the U.S. internet freedom agenda seeks to push back against foreign governments that refuse to abide by American notions of free speech, even while refusing to intervene when a powerful U.S. commercial entity threatens free speech, seriously undermines the legitimacy and effectiveness of the policy.

AUTHORITARIAN REGIMES AND INTERNET FREEDOM

Goldsmith gives alarming examples of authoritarian governments imposing measures to censor expression on the internet. It is important to note that these measures are not necessarily a response to (and failure of) the U.S. government's internet freedom agenda. In some jurisdictions where governments have been increasingly violating the right to freedom of expression online, it may simply be a case of enforcement practices catching up with technology.

In a number of jurisdictions, laws that predate the internet are relied on to penalize free speech online. The well-known Kenyan blogger Robert Alai, for instance, was charged in 2014 with having undermined the authority of a public officer after he tweeted about the alleged immaturity of President Uhuru Kenyatta. Those charges were brought pursuant to a law that had been created in 1958 to protect and sustain colonial rule in the country.[121] In other jurisdictions, similarly antiquated laws on false news,[122] sedition[123] and criminal defamation[124] are being used against online speakers. This is despite the fact that these laws have been broadly condemned as being incompatible with international human rights law.[125]

U.S. efforts to promote tools that can circumvent government censorship and allow individuals to communicate through encryption have been important initiatives, but they fail to address the more fundamental problem: the unwillingness of certain countries to respect international human rights law online, and the inability of the international community to hold most violators to account. For the reasons explained above, perhaps the United States should refocus its energies on strengthening the international enforcement of human rights norms, rather than continuing to insist on its own notions of commercial nonregulation and anti-censorship.

CONCLUSION

One of the key failings of the U.S. internet freedom agenda is its refusal to take a truly holistic and global approach to the protection of online freedom. By equating this agenda with the principles of commercial nonregulation and anti-censorship, the United States has neglected the role of other rights and non-state entities in guaranteeing online freedom.

Instead of remaining wedded to this one-sided agenda, the next administration that is interested in truly advancing the free flow of information online should look at international efforts, underpinned by a human rights–based approach, and strive to support those efforts. Of course, this would require coming to terms with the fact that, from a global perspective, the U.S. approach to freedom of speech and expression is an outlier in important respects. Time will tell if the United States can bring its own internet freedom priorities better in line with emerging human rights norms.

NOTES

1. Ira C. Magaziner, *Creating a Framework for Global Electronic Commerce*, Progress & Freedom Found. (July 1999), http://www.pff.org/issues-pubs/futureinsights /fi6.1globaleconomiccommerce.html.
2. *See, e.g.*, Toby Carroll & Ruben Gonzalez-Vicente, *From New Deal to the Art of the Deal: How the Neoliberal Project Led to Trump*, Conversation (Jan. 20, 2017), http://theconversation.com/from-new-deal-to-the-art-of-the-deal-how -the-neoliberal-project-led-to-trump-71576; George Monbiot, *Neoliberalism: The Deep Story That Lies Beneath Donald Trump's Triumph*, Guardian (Nov. 14, 2016), https://www.theguardian.com/commentisfree/2016/nov/14 /neoliberalsim-donald-trump-george-monbiot.
3. *See generally* Samuel Moyn, *Not Enough: Human Rights in an Unequal World* (2018).
4. *See generally* David E. Pozen, *Transparency's Ideological Drift*, 128 Yale L.J. 100 (2018).
5. *See generally* Bernard Harcourt, *The Illusion of Free Markets: Punishment and the Myth of Natural Order* (2012).
6. Jack Goldsmith & Tim Wu, *Who Controls the Internet? Illusions of a Borderless World* (2006).
7. Kate Klonick, *The New Governors: The People, Rules, and Processes Governing Online Speech*, 131 Harv. L. Rev. 1598 (2018).

THE FAILURE OF INTERNET FREEDOM

For comments on the ideas in this essay, I thank Yochai Benkler, Rishabh Bhandari, Adam Klein, David Pozen, Stuart Russell, Tim Wu, Jonathan Zittrain, workshop participants at the Belfer Center's Cyber Security Project and at Harvard's Program on Constitutional Government, and commentators at a "Talks at Google" presentation. I also thank those who commented on the version of this essay that I presented as the Brainerd Currie memorial lecture at Duke Law School on March 6, 2018. I thank Devyani Aggarwal, Andrei Gribakov, and Robert Nelson for excellent research and related assistance.

8. President William J. Clinton & Vice President Albert Gore, Jr., *A Framework for Global Electronic Commerce* (1997), https://clintonwhitehouse4.archives.gov /WH/New/Commerce/read.html; *see also* Ira C. Magaziner, *Creating a Framework for Global Electronic Commerce*, Progress & Freedom Found. (July 1999), http:// www.pff.org/issues-pubs/futureinsights/fi6.1globaleconomiccommerce.html (arguing "against a traditional regulatory role for government").

9. Magaziner, *supra* note 8.

10. *Id.* The most notable stakeholder-based experiment was the internet's naming and numbering system. *See* Management of Internet Names and Addresses, 63 Fed. Reg. 31741 (June 10, 1998).

11. On privacy, for example, the Clinton administration "favored the formation of industry or private sector self-regulation" but acknowledged that "there may be certain cases where, as a backup, government action will be needed" in "very precise ways to address the voids left by self-regulation." Magaziner, *supra* note 8.

12. *Id.*

13. *Clinton's Words on China: Trade Is the Smart Thing*, N.Y. Times (Mar. 9, 2000), https://www.nytimes.com/2000/03/09/world/clinton-s-words-on-china-trade-is-the -smart-thing.html.

14. U.S. Dep't of State, *Global Internet Freedom Task Force* (information released online from Jan. 20, 2001 to Jan. 20, 2009), https://2001-2009.state.gov/g/drl /lbr/c26696.htm. GIFT added an assessment of internet freedom to the State Department's annual human rights report and established the institutional machinery to monitor and protest "serious incidents of Internet repression." U.S. Dep't of State, *Global Internet Freedom Task Force (GIFT) Strategy: A Blueprint for Action* (Dec. 28, 2006) [hereinafter GIFT Blueprint], https://2001-2009.state. gov/g/drl/rls/78340.htm.

15. GIFT Blueprint, *supra* note 14.

16. *See generally* Rebecca MacKinnon, *Consent of the Networked: The Worldwide Struggle for Internet Freedom*, ch. 12 (2012).

17. Secretary of State Hillary Rodham Clinton, *Remarks on Internet Freedom* (Jan. 21, 2010), https://foreignpolicy.com/2010/01/21.

18. Cong. Research Serv., R41837, *Promoting Global Internet Freedom: Government and Industry Initiatives* 2 (2016).

19. *See, e.g.*, Open Technology Fund, *About the Program*, https://www.opentech .fund/about/program (last visited July 18, 2019) (describing how a component of Radio Free Asia supports "research, development, and implementation programs

focused on increasing . . . [a]ccess to the internet, including tools to circumvent website blocks, connection blackouts, and widespread censorship").

20. *See Review of Resources, Priorities, and Programs in the FY 2017 State Department Budget Request: Hearing Before the Subcomm. on W. Hemisphere, Transnat'l Crime, Civilian Sec., Democracy, Hum. Rts., and Global Women's Issues of the S. Comm. on Foreign Relations*, 114th Cong. (2016) (testimony of Assistant Secretary Tom Malinowski), https://www.foreign.senate.gov/imo /media/doc/042616_Malinowski_Testimony.pdf. The figure may be as high as $145 million. *See* U.S. Dep't of State, *Internet Freedom* (archived June 9, 2017), https://web.archive.org/web/20170609001151/https:/www.state.gov/j/drl /internetfreedom.

21. Magaziner, *supra* note 8.

22. Clinton, *supra* note 17.

23. For background, see generally Jack Goldsmith & Tim Wu, *Who Controls the Internet? Illusions of a Borderless World* (2006).

24. *See id.* at chs. 3, 10. The United States relinquished this control in 2016. *See* ICANN, *Stewardship of IANA Functions Transitions to Global Internet Community as Contract with U.S. Government Ends* (Oct. 1, 2016), https://www .icann.org/news/announcement-2016-10-01-en.

25. *See* Goldsmith & Wu, *supra* note 23, at ch. 6.

26. *Id.* at chs. 1, 10.

27. *See* Samuel J. Rascoff, *The Norm Against Economic Espionage for the Benefit of Private Firms: Some Theoretical Reflections*, 83 U. Chi. L. Rev. 249 (2016).

28. *See, e.g.,* Julie Hirschfeld Davis, *Hacking of Government Computers Exposed 21.5 Million People*, N.Y. Times (July 9, 2015), https://www.nytimes.com /2015/07/10/us/office-of-personnel-management-hackers-got-data-of-millions .html; Franz-Stefan Gady, *New Snowden Documents Reveal Chinese Behind F-35 Hack*, Diplomat (Jan. 27, 2015), https://thediplomat.com/2015/01/new-snowden -documents-reveal-chinese-behind-f-35-hack.

29. Josh Rogin, *NSA Chief: Cybercrime Constitutes the "Greatest Transfer of Wealth in History,"* Foreign Pol'y (July 9, 2012), https://foreignpolicy.com/2012/07/09/nsa -chief-cybercrime-constitutes-the-greatest-transfer-of-wealth-in-history.

30. Clinton, *supra* note 17.

31. *Id.*

32. *Id.*

33. *Id.*

34. *See* Alexander Klimburg, *The Darkening Web: The War for Cyberspace* 104–10, 211–12, 327–28 (2017).

35. Mark Landler & Brian Stelter, *Washington Taps Into a Potent New Force in Diplomacy*, N.Y. Times (June 16, 2009), https://www.nytimes.com/2009/06/17 /world/middleeast/17media.html.

36. Evgeny Morozov, *The Net Delusion: The Dark Side of Internet Freedom* 10 (2011).

37. *Id.* at 236.

38. Secretary of State Hillary Rodham Clinton, *Remarks on Internet Freedom* (Feb. 15, 2011), https://www.eff.org/files/filenode/clinton_internet_rights_wrongs _20110215.pdf.

39. *See* Joseph Marks, *Hillary Clinton: "Internet Freedom" Activist?*, Politico (Aug. 10, 2015), https://www.politico.com/story/2015/08/hillary-clinton-2016 -internet-freedom-121229.

40. Shane Harris & John Hudson, *Not Even the NSA Can Crack the State Dept's Favorite Anonymous Network*, Foreign Pol'y (Oct. 4, 2013), https://foreignpolicy. com/2013/10/04/not-even-the-nsa-can-crack-the-state-depts-favorite-anonymous -network.

41. *See* Memorandum from Secretary of Defense, Establishment of a Subordinate Unified U.S. Cyber Command Under U.S. Strategic Command for Military Cyberspace Operations (June 23, 2009), https://fas.org/irp/doddir/dod/secdef -cyber.pdf.

42. Shane Harris, *The Cyberwar Plan, Not Just a Defensive Game*, Nextgov (Nov. 13, 2009), https://www.nextgov.com/cybersecurity/2009/11/the-cyberwar -plan-not-just-a-defensive-game/45303.

43. *Id.*

44. *See* Robert Booth & Julian Borger, *US Diplomats Spied on UN Leadership*, Guardian (Nov. 28, 2010), https://www.theguardian.com/world/2010/nov/28 /us-embassy-cables-spying-un.

45. Clinton, *supra* note 17.

46. David E. Sanger. *Obama Order Sped Up Wave of Cyberattacks Against Iran*, N.Y. Times (June 1, 2012), https://www.nytimes.com/2012/06/01/world/middleeast /obama-ordered-wave-of-cyberattacks-against-iran.html.

47. *Id.*

48. *Id.*

49. *See generally Snowden Revelations*, Lawfare, https://lawfareblog.com/snowden -revelations (last visited July 18, 2019) (compiling revelations by Snowden).

50. These revelations concerned collection primarily under Section 702 of the Foreign Intelligence Surveillance Act.

51. Leon Spencer, *Snowden Docs Reveal NSA Digital Warfare Capabilities*, ZDNet (Jan. 19, 2015), https://www.zdnet.com/article/snowden-docs-reveal-nsa -digital-warfare-capabilities.

52. Eileen Donahue, *Brazil as the Global Guardian of Internet Freedom?*, Hum. Rts. Watch (Feb. 13, 2015), https://www.hrw.org/news/2015/02/13/brazil-global -guardian-internet-freedom.

53. *See, e.g.*, Damian Paletta, *How the U.S. Fights Encryption — and Also Helps Develop It*, Wall St. J. (Feb. 22, 2016), https://www.wsj.com/articles /how-the-u-s-fights-encryptionand-also-helps-develop-it-1456109096.

54. *See, e.g.*, Alex Marthews & Catherine Tucker, Government Surveillance and Internet Search Behavior (Feb. 17, 2017) (unpublished manuscript), https:// ssrn.com/abstract=2412564; Jonathon W. Penney, *Chilling Effects: Online Surveillance and Wikipedia Use*, 31 Berkeley Tech. L.J. 117 (2016); Elizabeth Stoycheff, *Under Surveillance: Examining Facebook's Spiral of Silence Effects in the Wake of NSA Internet Monitoring*, 93 Journalism & Mass Comm. Q. 296 (2016).

55. In addition to the developments recounted in this essay, see, for example, Ron Deibert, *The Geopolitics of Cyberspace After Snowden*, Current History,

Jan. 2015, at 9; Asaf Lubin, *A New Era of Mass Surveillance Is Emerging Across Europe*, Just Security (Jan. 9, 2017), https://www.justsecurity.org/36098/era -mass-surveillance-emerging-europe; Charles Maynes, *Snowden Revelations Lead Russia to Push for More Spying on Its Own People*, PRI (Dec. 4, 2013), https:// www.pri.org/stories/2013-12-04/russia-uses-snowden-excuse-step-spying-its-own -people; Tatevik Sargsyan, *Data Localization and the Role of Infrastructure for Surveillance, Privacy, and Security*, 10 Int'l J. Comm. 2221 (2016).

56. *See* Gary King et al., *How Censorship in China Allows Government Criticism but Silences Collective Expression*, 107 Am. Pol. Sci. Rev. 1 (2013).

57. *See* Furio Fu, *The List of Blocked Websites in China*, Sapore di Cina (Jan. 10, 2018), https://www.saporedicina.com/english/list-of-blocked-websites-in-china.

58. *See* Radio Free Asia, *China to Block Overseas VPN Services from End of March* (Jan. 31, 2018), https://www.rfa.org/english/news/china/china-to-block-overseas -vpn-services-from-end-of-march-01312018102313.html.

59. *See, e.g.,* Simon Denyer, *China's Scary Lesson to the World: Censoring the Internet Works*, Wash. Post (May 23, 2016), https://www.washingtonpost.com /world/asia_pacific/chinas-scary-lesson-to-the-world-censoring-the-internet -works/2016/05/23/413afe78-fff3-11e5-8bb1-f124a43f84dc_story.html; Simon Denyer, *The Walls Are Closing In: China Finds New Ways to Tighten Internet Controls*, Wash. Post (Sept. 27, 2017), https://www.washingtonpost.com/world /asia_pacific/the-walls-are-closing-in-chinafinds-new-ways-to-tighten-internet -controls/2017/09/26/2e0d3562-9ee6-11e7-b2a7-bc70b6f98089_story.html; John Leonard, *China's Great Firewall: How It Works and What It Reveals About China's Plans*, V3 (Apr. 23, 2018), https://www.v3.co.uk/v3-uk/analysis/3030741 /chinas-great-firewall-how-it-works-and-what-it-reveals-about-chinas-plans.

60. *See* Chris Mirasola, *Understanding China's Cybersecurity Law*, Lawfare (Nov. 8, 2016), https://www.lawfareblog.com/understanding-chinas-cybersecurity -law; Samm Sacks & Paul Triolo, *Shrinking Anonymity in Chinese Cyberspace*, Lawfare (Sept. 25, 2017), https://www.lawfareblog.com/shrinking-anonymity -chinese-cyberspace.

61. *See* Chris Mirasola, *China's New Guidance Further Restricts the Transfer of Digital Information*, Lawfare (Apr. 17, 2017), https://www.lawfareblog.com /chinas-new-guidance-further-restricts-transfer-digital-information.

62. *See, e.g.,* Tim Bradshaw, *Apple Drops Hundreds of VPN Apps at Beijing's Request*, Financial Times (Nov. 21, 2017), https://www.ft.com/content/ad42e536-cf36 -11e7-b781-794ce08b24dc; Stephen Nellis & Cate Cadell, *Apple Moves to Store iCloud Keys in China, Raising Human Rights Fears*, Reuters (Feb. 24, 2018), https://www.reuters.com/article/us-china-apple-icloud-insight/apple-moves-to -store-icloud-keys-in-china-raising-human-rights-fears-idUSKCN1G8060.

63. Clinton, *supra* note 17.

64. *See* Phred Dvorak & Yasufumi Saito, *Silicon Valley Powered American Tech Dominance—Now It Has a Challenger*, Wall St. J. (Apr. 12, 2018), https://www .wsj.com/articles/silicon-valley-long-dominated-startup-fundingnow-it-has-a -challenger-1523544804; Joanna Glasner, *US Early-Stage Investment Share Shrinks as China Surges*, TechCrunch (Apr. 16, 2018), https://techcrunch .com/2018/04/16/us-early-stage-investment-share-shrinks-as-china-surges.

65. *See, e.g., America v. China: The Battle for Digital Supremacy*, Economist (Mar. 15, 2018), https://www.economist.com/news/leaders/21738883-americas -technological-hegemony-under-threat-china-battle-digital-supremacy; *In Fintech, China Shows the Way*, Economist (Feb. 25, 2017), https://www .economist.com/news/finance-and-economics/21717393-advanced-technology -backward-banks-and-soaring-wealth-make-china-leader; Gabriel Wildau & Leslie Hook, *China Mobile Payments Dwarf Those in US as Fintech Booms, Research Shows*, Fin. Times (Feb. 13, 2017), https://www.ft.com/content/00585722 -ef42-11e6-930f-061b01e23655.

66. *See China's Internet Giants Go Global*, Economist (Apr. 20, 2017), https://www .economist.com/business/2017/04/20/chinas-internet-giants-go-global.

67. Ron Deibert, *Authoritarianism Goes Global: Cyberspace Under Siege*, J. Democracy, July 2015, at 64, 64.

68. Freedom House, *Freedom on the Net 2017: Manipulating Social Media to Undermine Democracy* (2017), https://freedomhouse.org/report/freedom-net /freedom-net-2017.

69. *Id.*

70. Mathias Döpfner, An Open Letter to Eric Schmidt (Apr. 16, 2014), available at http://www.axelspringer.de/dl/433625/LetterMathiasDoepfnerEricSchmidt.pdf.

71. *See, e.g.*, Mark Scott, *E.U. Rules Look to Unify Digital Market, but U.S. Sees Protectionism*, N.Y. Times (Sept. 13, 2016), https://www.nytimes.com/2016/09/14 /technology/eu-us-tech-google-facebook-apple.html.

72. *See* Ali Breland, *Apple Pays First Batch of $15.3B Back Taxes to Ireland*, Hill (May 18, 2018), https://thehill.com/policy/technology/388359-apple-pays-first -batch-of-back-taxes-to-ireland.

73. *See* Larry Downes, *GDPR and the End of the Internet's Grand Bargain*, Harv. Bus. Rev. (Apr. 9, 2018), https://hbr.org/2018/04/gdpr-and-the-end-of-the -internets-grand-bargain.

74. *See* Sarah Gordon & Aliya Ram, *Information Wars: How Europe Became the World's Data Police*, Fin. Times (May 20, 2018), https://www.ft.com/content /1aa9b0fa-5786-11e8-bdb7-f6677d2e1ce8.

75. For discussion of other such regulations, see Anupam Chander & Uyên P. Lê, *Data Nationalism*, 64 Emory L.J. 677 (2015).

76. *See generally* Rachel F. Fefer et al., Cong. Research Serv., R44565, *Digital Trade and U.S. Trade Policy* 12–19 (2018).

77. *See, e.g., CFIUS Intervenes in Broadcom's Attempt to Buy Qualcomm*, Economist (Mar. 8, 2018), https://www.economist.com/news/business/21738398-powerful -committee-top-american-officials-becomes-more-intrusive-cfius-intervenes; Martin Giles, *CFIUS: The Powerful Sheriff Policing US Tech's Megadeal*, MIT Tech. Rev. (Mar. 9, 2018), https://www.technologyreview.com/s/610455 /cfius-the-powerful-sheriff-policing-us-techs-megadeal. In recent years, CFIUS has vetoed Broadcom's attempted takeover of Qualcomm, Ant Financial's attempted takeover of MoneyGram, Fujian Grand Chip Investment Fund's attempted takeover of the U.S. business of German semiconductor company Aixtron SE, and the attempted takeover of Lattice Semiconductor by a U.S. private equity firm funded by the Chinese government.

78. *See China's Protectionism Comes Home to Roost*, Fin. Times (Jan. 3, 2018), https://www.ft.com/content/14196546-f098-11e7-ac08-07c3086a2625.

79. *See, e.g.*, Kati Suominen, *Where the Money Is: The Transatlantic Digital Market*, Ctr. for Strategic & Int'l Stud. (Oct. 12, 2017), https://www.csis.org/blogs/future-digital-trade-policy-and-role-us-and-uk/where-money-transatlantic-digital-market ("In 2015, the U.S. had a $161.5 billion trade surplus in digitally-deliverable services.").

80. This is the major theme of Goldsmith & Wu, *supra* note 23.

81. Clinton, *supra* note 17.

82. Exec. Office of the President, *Federal Cybersecurity Risk Determination Report and Action Plan* 15 (2018), https://www.whitehouse.gov/wp-content/uploads/2018/05/Cybersecurity-Risk-Determination-Report-FINAL_May-2018-Release.pdf.

83. Gus Hunt, *Cyber Moonshot: The Time Has Come*, Accenture Security Blog (Oct. 24, 2017), https://www.accenture.com/us-en/blogs/blogs-cyber-moonshot-time-come.

84. *Id.*

85. *See, e.g.*, Tyler Moore, *The Economics of Cybersecurity: Principles and Policy Options*, 3 Int'l J. Critical Infrastructure Protection 103 (2010).

86. *Full Transcript: President Obama's Final End-of-Year Press Conference*, Politico (Dec. 16, 2016) [hereinafter Obama Transcript], https://www.politico.com/story/2016/12/obama-press-conference-transcript-232763.

87. *See, e.g.*, Cass R. Sunstein, *#Republic: Divided Democracy in the Age of Social Media* 252 (2017) (stressing "the serious problems for individuals and societies alike that are likely to be created by the practice of self-insulation").

88. For a good summary, see Tim Wu's essay in this volume.

89. *See* Fiona Hill, *3 Reasons Russia's Vladimir Putin Might Want to Interfere in the US Presidential Elections*, Vox (July 27, 2016), https://www.vox.com/2016/7/27/12304448/putin-elections-dnc-hack; Josh Meyer, *DNC Email Hack: Why Vladimir Putin Hates Hillary Clinton*, NBC News (July 26, 2016), https://www.nbcnews.com/news/us-news/why-putin-hates-hillary-clinton-n617236.

90. Obama Transcript, *supra* note 86.

91. *See* Jack Goldsmith, *Contrarian Thoughts on Russia and the Presidential Election*, Lawfare (Jan. 10, 2017), https://www.lawfareblog.com/contrarian-thoughts-russia-and-presidential-election.

92. *Id.*

93. *See* John Hudson, *How Putin Hoped to Make Up with Us*, BuzzFeed News (Sept. 12, 2017), https://www.buzzfeed.com/johnhudson/russia-sought-a-broad-reset-with-trump-secret-document-shows; John Hudson, *No Deal: How Secret Talks with Russia to Prevent Election Meddling Collapsed*, BuzzFeed News (Dec. 8, 2017), https://www.buzzfeed.com/johnhudson/no-deal-how-secret-talks-with-russia-to-prevent-election.

94. *See* Jack Goldsmith, *Cybersecurity Treaties: A Skeptical View*, Hoover Inst. (Mar. 9, 2011), http://media.hoover.org/sites/default/files/documents/FutureChallenges_Goldsmith.pdf; Jack Goldsmith, *On the Russian Proposal for Mutual Noninterference in Domestic Politics*, Lawfare (Dec. 11, 2017)

[hereinafter Goldsmith, *On the Russian Proposal*], https://www.lawfareblog.com /russian-proposal-mutual-noninterference-domestic-politics.

95. See Goldsmith, *On the Russian Proposal, supra* note 94.

96. See David E. Pozen, *Privacy-Privacy Tradeoffs*, 83 U. Chi. L. Rev. 221, 235–36 (2016). For an argument that encryption backdoors and related proposals are bad for all stripes of privacy, including privacy compromised by bad cybersecurity, see Susan Landau, *Listening In: Cybersecurity in an Insecure Age* (2017).

97. Wu, this volume.

THE LIMITS OF SUPPLY-SIDE INTERNET FREEDOM

98. Jack Goldsmith & Tim Wu, *Who Controls the Internet? Illusions of a Borderless World* (2006).

99. Secretary of State Hillary Rodham Clinton, *Remarks on Internet Freedom* (Jan. 21, 2010), https://foreignpolicy.com/2010/01/21/internet-freedom.

100. Secretary Clinton followed through. See Human Rights Council Res., *The Promotion, Protection and Enjoyment of Human Rights on the Internet*, U.N. Doc. A/HRC/RES/20/8 (July 16, 2012), https://ap.ohchr.org/documents/dpage_e.aspx?si =A/HRC/RES/20/8. For the most recent Council resolution, see Human Rights Council Res., *The Promotion, Protection and Enjoyment of Human Rights on the Internet*, U.N. Doc. A/HRC/RES/32/13 (July 18, 2016), https://ap.ohchr.org /documents/dpage_e.aspx?si=A/HRC/RES/32/13.

101. Thus far, it appears that the State Department's support for internet freedom policies and priorities developed during the Obama administration are continuing. Anticipated funding for the Bureau of Democracy, Human Rights, and Labor's global programs, including internet freedom programs, held fairly steady in fiscal years 2018 and 2019. See U.S. Dep't of State, *Congressional Budget Justification: Fiscal Year 2018*, at 289 (2017), https://www.state.gov/documents/organization /271013.pdf; U.S. Dep't of State, *Congressional Budget Justification: Fiscal Year 2019*, at 97 (2018), https://www.state.gov/documents/organization/277155.pdf.

102. See Case C-131/12, Google Spain SL v. Agencia Española de Protección de Datos, 2014 E.C.R. 317; Case C-362/14, Schrems v. Data Prot. Comm'r, 2015 E.C.R. 650.

103. See David Kaye, *How Europe's New Internet Laws Threaten Freedom of Expression*, Foreign Aff. (Dec. 18, 2017), https://www.foreignaffairs.com/articles /europe/2017-12-18/how-europes-new-internet-laws-threaten-freedom-expression.

104. See *supra* note 100; *see also* U.N. General Assembly Third Comm. Res., *The Safety of Journalists and the Issue of Impunity*, U.N. Doc. A/C.3/72/L.35 (Oct. 30, 2017), https://undocs.org/A/C.3/72/L.35 (noting that rights offline apply online as well).

105. See OOO Flavus v. Russia, App. No. 12468/15 (Eur. Ct. H.R. communicated Aug. 30, 2017) (pending case involving Russian government blocking of websites on grounds of "extremism"); *see also* Intervention by U.N. Special Rapporteur on the Promotion and Protection of the Right to Freedom of Opinion and Expression, OOO Flavus v. Russia, App. No. 12468/15 (Eur. Ct. H.R. Jan. 11, 2018), https://freedex.org/wp-content/blogs.dir/2015/files/2018/05/Flavus-OOO -SR-intervention.pdf; *Civil Society to European Court: Russia Website Blocking of "Extremist" Material Violates Freedom of Expression*, ARTICLE 19 (Feb. 6, 2018),

https://www.article19.org/resources/civil-society-european-court-russia-website
-blocking-extremist-material-violates-freedom-expression.

106. *See* Human Rights Council, *Report of the Special Rapporteur on the Promotion and Protection of the Right to Freedom of Opinion and Expression*, U.N. Doc. A/HRC/38/35 (Apr. 6, 2018) [hereinafter Content Regulation Report], https:// ap.ohchr.org/documents/dpage_e.aspx?si=A/HRC/38/35; Human Rights Council, *Report of the Special Rapporteur on the Promotion and Protection of the Right to Freedom of Opinion and Expression*, U.N. Doc. A/HRC/35/22 (Mar. 30, 2017), https://ap.ohchr.org/documents/dpage_e.aspx?si=A/HRC/35/22; Human Rights Council, *Report of the Special Rapporteur on the Promotion and Protection of the Right to Freedom of Opinion and Expression*, U.N. Doc. A/HRC/32/38 (May 11, 2016), https://ap.ohchr.org/documents/dpage_e.aspx?si=A/HRC/32/38.

107. Wu, this volume.

108. Office of the U.N. High Comm'r for Human Rights, *Guiding Principles on Business and Human Rights: Implementing the United Nations "Protect, Respect and Remedy" Framework* (2011), http://www.ohchr.org/Documents/Publications /GuidingPrinciplesBusinessHR_EN.pdf.

109. *See* Content Regulation Report, *supra* note 106, at 16–20; *see also* David E. Pozen, *Transparency's Ideological Drift*, 128 Yale L.J. 100, 163 (2018) (urging that transparency policy "[c]onnect[] asymmetries of information to asymmetries of power").

INTERNET FREEDOM WITHOUT IMPERIALISM

110. *See, e.g.*, *Murdock v. Pennsylvania*, 319 U.S. 105, 115 (1943).

111. Human Rights Council Res., *The Promotion, Protection and Enjoyment of Human Rights on the Internet*, U.N. Doc. A/HRC/RES/32/13 (July 18, 2016), https:// ap.ohchr.org/documents/dpage_e.aspx?si=A/HRC/RES/32/13 (emphasis added).

112. *See* Penelope Andrews, *South Africa's Vote Against Internet Freedom Tarnishes Its Global Image*, Conversation (July 14, 2016), https://theconversation.com /south-africas-vote-against-internet-freedom-tarnishes-its-global-image-62112.

113. *See* Natasha Lomas, *UN Agrees to Adopt Expanded Resolution on Online Speech Rights*, TechCrunch (July 1, 2016), https://techcrunch.com/2016/07/01 /un-agrees-to-adopt-expanded-resolution-on-online-speech-rights.

114. *See* Office of the U.N. High Comm'r for Human Rights, *Status of Ratification Interactive Dashboard*, http://indicators.ohchr.org.

115. Secretary of State Hillary Rodham Clinton, *Remarks on Internet Freedom* (Jan. 21, 2010), https://foreignpolicy.com/2010/01/21/internet-freedom.

116. *See, e.g.*, *Satakunnan Markkinapörssi Oy & Satamedia Oy v. Finland*, App. No. 931/13 (Eur. Ct. H.R. June 27, 2017), https://lovdata.no/static/EMDN/emd -2013-000931-2.pdf; *Benedik v. Slovenia*, App. No. 62357/14 (Eur. Ct. H.R. Apr. 24, 2018), http://hudoc.echr.coe.int/eng?i=001-182455.

117. *See* Alexa, *The Top 500 Sites on the Web*, https://www.alexa.com/topsites.

118. *See, e.g.*, Leigh Alexander, *Facebook's Censorship of Aboriginal Bodies Raises Troubling Ideas of "Decency,"* Guardian (Mar. 23, 2016), https://www.theguardian .com/technology/2016/mar/23/facebook-censorship-topless-aboriginal-women; Stephany Bai, *The First Amendment and Social Media: The Rules Just Don't Apply,*

Teen Vogue (Dec. 29, 2017), https://www.teenvogue.com/story/first-amendment -social-media; Nikki Williams, *Facebook Unfriends Free Speech*, Ctr. for Digital Ethics & Pol'y (Feb. 8, 2016), https://www.digitalethics.org/essays/facebook -unfriends-free-speech.

119. *See, e.g., McIntyre v. Ohio Elections Comm'n*, 514 U.S. 334 (1995).

120. *See* April Glaser, *Why Some Americans Are Cheering Germany for Taking on Facebook's Policy that You Need to Use Your Real Name*, Slate (Feb. 17, 2018), https://slate.com/technology/2018/02/why-some-americans-are-cheering-germany -for-taking-on-facebooks-real-name-policy.html.

121. Robert Alai has since successfully challenged the law on constitutional grounds. *See Alai v. Hon. Att'y Gen.*, Petition No. 174 of 2016, High Ct. of Kenya (Mwita, J.) (Apr. 26, 2017), http://kenyalaw.org/caselaw/cases/view/135467.

122. *See Bahrain: Exonerate, Free Nabeel Rajab*, Human Rts. Watch, https://www.hrw .org/news/2018/06/03/bahrain-exonerate-free-nabeel-rajab.

123. *See Prominent Malaysian Blogger Arrested Under Sedition Act for Social Media Post*, Straits Times (July 15, 2015), https://www.straitstimes.com/asia/se-asia /prominent-malaysian-blogger-arrested-under-sedition-act-for-social-media-post; Patpicha Tanakasempipat, *Thai Journalist Accused of Sedition Says Charge Creates "Chilling Effect,"* Reuters (Aug. 4, 2017), https://www.reuters.com/article /us-thailand-rights-idUSKBN1AK11B.

124. *See* Andrew Downie, *In Brazil, Outdated Defamation Laws and Costly Court Cases Used to Pressure Critics*, Comm. to Protect Journalists Blog (Apr. 6, 2017), https://cpj.org/blog/2017/04/in-brazil-outdated-defamation-laws-and-costly-cour .php; *Nigerian Blogger, Publisher Jailed on Defamation Charges*, Comm. to Protect Journalists (Mar. 24, 2017), https://cpj.org/2017/03/nigerian-blogger-publisher -jailed-on-defamation-ch.php.

125. *See, e.g.*, U.N. Special Rapporteur on Freedom of Opinion and Expression et al., *Joint Declaration on Freedom of Expression and "Fake News," Disinformation and Propaganda* (Mar. 3, 2017), https://www.osce.org/fom/302796?download=true; *see also* U.N. Human Rights Comm., *General Comment No. 34*, U.N. Doc. CCPR/C/GC/34 (Sept. 12, 2011), http://www2.ohchr.org/english/bodies/hrc /docs/gc34.pdf.

6

CRISIS IN THE ARCHIVES

David E. Pozen

CRITICS OF THE EXECUTIVE branch's information control practices tend to focus on the here and now. They argue that overclassification of national security–related documents undermines democratic self-rule.[1] They inveigh against delays and denials in the implementation of the Freedom of Information Act.[2] They condemn regulations that "incorporate by reference" materials developed by industry groups.[3] They worry about the growing use of black box algorithms,[4] criminal leak investigations,[5] and secret waivers for former lobbyists turned political appointees.[6] All of these critiques raise important issues, even if they sometimes understate the transparency that exists—U.S. administrative agencies "are some of the most extensively monitored government actors in the world"[7]—or overstate the benefits of sunlight.[8]

One of the executive's most worrisome information control practices has received relatively little attention, perhaps because it requires taking a longer view. Over the last several decades, as Matthew Connelly explains in his essay, our national archives have been quietly falling apart. FOIA backlogs look like a Starbucks queue compared to the 700,000 cubic feet of records at the National Archives and Records Administration's research facility in Maryland that were unprocessed as of 2013. The Public Interest Declassification Board recently estimated that it would take a year's work by 2 million declassifiers to review the amount of data that a single intelligence agency now produces in eighteen months.[9]

The U.S. government's entire system for organizing, conserving, and revealing the record of its activities, Connelly maintains, is on the verge of collapse; a "digital dark age" awaits us on the other side. His is less a story about excessive information control than a story about the *absence* of information control. Archivists simply have not been able to cope with the flood they face. The negative consequences extend far beyond the professional study of history, as Democrats learned in the summer of 2018 when NARA announced that it was incapable of reviewing and releasing all of Brett Kavanaugh's papers before the Senate voted on his nomination to the Supreme Court.[10]

How did this crisis in the archives develop, and what might be done to mitigate it? Woefully inadequate appropriations and "dubious management decisions" bear some of the blame, according to Connelly. When the ratio of spending on the classification and protection of national security secrets to spending on their declassification exceeds 99 to 1, the historical record is bound to suffer. But the deeper cause of the crisis, Connelly suggests, lies in the exponential growth of government records, particularly electronic records. In a world where the State Department generates 2 billion emails each year—all of which need to be screened for sensitive personal and policy details prior to disclosure through any official process—the traditional tools of archiving cannot possibly keep up.

Maybe the tools ought to be updated for the age of "big data," then. Connelly has collaborated extensively with data scientists on the problems he highlights,[11] and he argues that sophisticated use of computational methods, from topic modeling to traffic analysis to predictive coding, could go a long way toward rationalizing records management and accelerating declassification. If these techniques were to be combined with bigger budgets for archivists and greater will to curb classification, NARA might one day make good on its aspiration to ensure "continuing access to the essential documentation of the rights of American citizens and the actions of their Government."[12] There is something intuitively appealing about this vision: digital technologies got us into this mess, and now they ought to help get us out of it. Connelly's diagnosis of information overload and political neglect is so stark, however, that one wonders whether any such reforms will prove adequate to the challenge.

Three response pieces recast this challenge in a somewhat different light. The Archivist of the United States, David Ferriero, emphasizes steps NARA is taking to digitize its holdings, enhance public access to them, and enforce government recordkeeping requirements. Ferriero does not dispute that "the country would be well served" by greater funding for the agency he leads, but he suggests that progress is being made even within severe budgetary constraints.

Elizabeth Goitein largely endorses Connelly's reform proposals but urges that they be pushed further in the area of national security information. Drawing on extensive research and advocacy she has done as codirector of the Brennan Center for Justice's Liberty and National Security Program, Goitein offers a suite of specific recommendations, from tightening the substantive criteria for classification to requiring federal agencies to spend certain amounts on declassification to subjecting officials who engage in serious overclassification to mandatory penalties.

Finally, Kirsten Weld raises critical questions about Connelly's characterization of the problem and urges that his reform proposals be pushed *much* further. Weld points out that the records maintained by NARA represent just a "slice" of U.S. history, albeit an important one, and that the government's management of that slice has always been bound up with larger political struggles. The true source of the crisis at NARA, Weld submits, is not the rise of electronic records or the politicization of transparency but "the dismantling of the postwar welfare state and the concomitant ascendance of neoliberal governance." To address the crisis, accordingly, technical fixes are bound to be insufficient. Nothing short of "a sea change in the federal government's priorities" and "a massive reinvestment in the public sphere" will do.

A crisis in the National Archives, all of the authors agree, is a crisis in American democracy. It is certainly not the only one we face, and it may not be the most acute, but preserving a record of our collective history arguably has a kind of epistemic priority. As we fight for our democratic future, the essays in this chapter remind us to fight for the institutions that help us understand how we arrived at the perilous present.

State Secrecy, Archival Negligence, and the End of History as We Know It*

Matthew Connelly

NO MATTER how heated a political debate, the bitterest of adversaries can usually agree on one thing: someday, historians will look back, judge the rights and wrongs, and render an informed verdict. What reporters and pundits say, after all, is only the first draft of history, and they do not have access to all the relevant information—especially when much of it is classified. It takes time for events to play out, for passions to cool, and for the protagonists to leave the stage. Researchers also need full access to the documentary record. True, history may be written by the winners. But if records survive and people still care about the past, we trust that eventually the truth will out.

History has often served as the ultimate court of appeal when other courts fail to uphold constitutional rights. Although eugenicists convinced eight justices of the U.S. Supreme Court in 1927 that the "feeble-minded" Carrie Buck could be compelled to undergo sterilization,[13] the patient work of scholars has shown that she was a victim of class prejudice.[14] Similarly, it took almost three-quarters of a century before the *Korematsu* decision allowing the internment of Japanese Americans was officially repudiated.[15] But long before, it had become a textbook example of how whole communities can lose their rights because of fear and racism.[16] And while efforts to defend the free speech of alleged communist "subversives" failed in a number of mid-twentieth-century cases,[17] scholars have made the Red Scare and McCarthyism object lessons in how important it is to protect unpopular speech when the nation is under threat.[18] History can supply a nearly limitless source of insight into how our government and Constitution actually work—or fail to work. As Chief Justice Earl Warren wrote in 1957: "Teachers and students must always remain free to inquire, to study and to evaluate, to gain new maturity and understanding; otherwise our civilization will stagnate and die."[19]

But while history is our last chance to redeem constitutional liberties, it is hardly our best chance, and our chances keep getting worse. A faith in history assumes that there will be a historical record for scholars to examine. This assumption, in turn, is based on many other assumptions, starting with the idea that decision-makers will treat their records as public records, not classify them without cause, and certainly not destroy or delete them. Departments and agencies must keep these records organized on stable media and eventually entrust them to the National Archives. Archivists have to be able to identify the records that merit preservation, withhold only those containing still-sensitive national security or personal information, and put everything else on open archival shelves or on the internet—complete with finding aids to guide researchers. It is only then that we can start gaining that "maturity and understanding" and finally learn what the government has done in our name.

In fact, none of these assumptions is likely to prove valid. While politicians will continue to appeal to history when convenient, they have so neglected the National Archives and so failed to control official secrecy that future historians will have a hard time proving anything at all. It is a true crisis, one that has not garnered more public notice because we tend to pay attention only to that first link in the chain: the excessive secrecy of current officeholders, or at least officeholders from the opposing party. But that is only the beginning of our problems. The other factors contributing to the crisis are metastasizing slowly, quietly, in record centers, archives, and libraries. We will not be fully aware of what is being lost for decades to come, if ever. But the effects are already manifest in a range of scandals that have poisoned political discourse, from the destruction of interrogation videos by the Central Intelligence Agency (CIA) to the Internal Revenue Service's inability to produce emails related to the treatment of conservative groups to Secretary of State Hillary Clinton's decision to use a private server for official communications.

Government transparency was once a bipartisan cause, championed by both the left and the right. But each of these scandals was intensely polarizing, to the point that it is becoming impossible to protest such behaviors without being dismissed as politically motivated. What may be even worse is when we are *not* scandalized by even more obviously outrageous conduct, such as the recent revelation that President Donald Trump routinely rips up his papers into tiny little pieces in violation of the Presidential Records Act, and that he fired the career government records managers who had been painstakingly taping them back together.[20] As long as we fail to see what all of these things have in common, we will keep missing the bigger picture. How will history judge a generation of government officials who not only insist on working in secrecy but also fail to protect, or even destroy, the record of their actions?

To understand how we arrived at this crisis, we have to go back in time. We need to trace two long-term developments: the growth of a postwar national secrecy complex and the simultaneous creation of a system of laws and institutions to organize and preserve official records. The first of these developments gets far more attention. But state secrecy in the United States has always been intertwined with—and to some extent legitimated by—state archiving. Over the past three decades, however, the exponential growth in state secrecy and the neglect of state archives have imperiled the whole system for organizing, protecting, preserving, and revealing the historical record. If this system collapses, America's commitment to learning from its history will become a thing of the past, because the past itself will be impossible to recover.

ARCHIVES AND THE CURRENCY OF SECRECY

Americans typically visit at most one archive and do so as tourists: the National Archives on the Mall in Washington, D.C. The impressive neoclassical facade has the aura of antiquity. In fact, the building did not open until 1935, the year after Congress established the National Archives and Records Administration (NARA). Until then, every government department managed (or mismanaged) its own records, no matter how old. The State Department had responsibility for the papers of the Continental Congress, so even the Declaration of Independence suffered from wet press-copying, direct sunlight, and botched repairs with glue and scotch tape.[21] The original, signed Constitution was lost for decades before it was found in a closet folded up in a small tin box.[22]

These documents are so faded as to be scarcely legible, but they are now displayed in the National Archives rotunda in a row of bulletproof encasements filled with argon gas. For some visitors, the physical security may be more impressive than the documents themselves. At the first hint of danger, any one of the guards can activate a mechanism that lowers them into a custom-built armored vault. It is designed to withstand the blast of a nuclear bomb.[23]

Standing before these documents creates mixed feelings. There is a sense of democratic transparency, as all the world can see the physical manifestation of American popular sovereignty. But at the same time, one senses an acute vulnerability. These documents have barely survived and could still disintegrate or disappear.

Government archives and records centers have always been like this. They afford a glimpse of the state's inner workings. But access can be withdrawn, documents can be destroyed, and far more is hidden than what is put on display. When the documents are digital and concern sensitive matters, that sense of vulnerability is even more acute. Instead of glass cases in the National Archives, we have to imagine repositories such as the server farms operated by the National Security Agency or the National Reconnaissance Office, where enormous volumes of data can be stored, mined, and instantly deleted. We can only guess at how such data are managed because we don't have a window to look into what these agencies are actually doing. The intelligence community was built to look at *us*—all of us, around the world—recording what it sees for purposes that may not be revealed until years or decades into the future, if ever.

For its first 150 years, the U.S. government kept few official secrets, which is why it hardly bothered to keep archives. Other countries routinely intercepted the mail and operated "black chambers" to decode encrypted communications.[24] But the U.S. government had no such capacity. Mail tampering was expressly prohibited by law—indeed, it was punishable by death until the late 1800s.[25] After the first generation of revolutionaries passed from the scene, even American diplomats sent nearly all their dispatches in the clear.[26] Beginning in 1861, the State Department began to publish normally secret communications with other states on an annual basis. President Lincoln believed that this kind of radical transparency would show the world that the Union deserved support in its fight against the Confederacy.[27]

It was not until 1882 that the United States established its first foreign intelligence agency, the Office of Naval Intelligence. This office grew out of the Navy Department Library, which collected reports from naval attachés posted abroad.[28] It was only when the United States entered World War I that the Navy and Army both borrowed the British practice of systematically classifying sensitive information as "confidential" or "secret," and at the same time began to upgrade their cryptological capabilities.[29] Shortly afterward, a former librarian, J. Edgar Hoover, began to assemble and organize surveillance files as director of the new Federal Bureau of Investigation (FBI).

But the U.S. apparatus for producing secret information was still puny in comparison to those of other great powers. The State Department continued to mark documents "confidential" or "private" almost at random, and in 1929, Secretary of State Henry Stimson shut down the department's cryptologic group on the grounds that "gentlemen do not read each other's mail."[30] There was no central agency to coordinate intelligence work. Nor was there a central archive to organize and preserve government information. In the 1930s, half a century after other great powers had created national archives, federal workers for the first time started to inventory the holdings of U.S. departments and agencies. They found War Department papers moldering in piles in the White House garage.[31]

Like so much else, this changed with the New Deal. Congress passed the National Archives Act in 1934, and President Franklin Roosevelt appointed the first Archivist of the United States. Proliferating agencies and departments produced exponential growth in government papers. By 1930, the federal government had accumulated less than half as many records as it would generate just in the ten years leading up to its entry in World War II.[32] Starting with the General Disposal Act of 1939, and continuing with the Federal Records Acts of 1943 and 1950, the National Archives was authorized to decide what should be saved. As Roosevelt's second archivist, Solon Buck, explained, "the chief reason for destroying is to save": without "weeding out useless papers," there could be no recognition or preservation of records of lasting value.[33]

Crucially, Congress made it unlawful to "alienate[] or destroy[]" any U.S. government records except in accordance with procedures established by the Archivist.[34] Even if individual employees would continue to keep their personal records to themselves, the thinking went, contemporaneous archiving systems would remove any temptation to rewrite the official record. Roosevelt so believed in the importance of archives that he created the first presidential library in 1941, offering these words when it was dedicated at his estate in Hyde Park:

> To bring together the records of the past and to house them in buildings where they will be preserved for the use of men and women in the future, a Nation must believe in three things. It must believe in the past. It must

believe in the future. It must, above all, believe in the capacity of its own people so to learn from the past that they can gain in judgment in creating their own future.[35]

Roosevelt also believed in secrecy, however. He was the first president to issue an executive order systematizing the national security–related information that would be withheld from the public.[36] Wartime, moreover, revealed that archives themselves could contribute to national security. While the Declaration of Independence and the Constitution were shipped off to Fort Knox for safekeeping during World War II, archivists set to work finding detailed maps of German and Japanese cities for target intelligence.[37] Meteorological records were required for preparing amphibious landings. State Department papers from prior international negotiations were important in planning postwar settlements. Roosevelt also created the Office of Strategic Services (OSS), the precursor to the CIA. The OSS cordoned off parts of the National Archives building so that it could use the collection in secrecy.[38]

State archiving and state secrecy thus grew together out of the same ground and for some of the same reasons. Archives provided a place where secrets could be safely stored, and sometimes destroyed, but always with the idea that the most important secrets would be preserved, both as working memory for "the official mind" and for the judgment of posterity.

At the start, it was not obvious that secrecy would overpower archiving. For instance, President Roosevelt expected that the War Department would only sublet the Pentagon—after the end of hostilities, these 2 million square feet were to be turned over to the National Archives for the storage of valuable papers.[39] President Truman abolished the OSS, worried that a powerful intelligence agency might be used against Americans, and initially replaced it with a small group that merely coordinated the information flowing to the president.[40]

Ultimately, though, the war not only led to the creation of a permanent military-industrial complex; it also created what Senator Daniel Patrick Moynihan later called a "culture of secrecy."[41] On the ground that loose lips could sink ships, information was shared only on a "need to know" basis. Stamping a document "secret" made it currency that could be exchanged for other assets.[42] By 1944, so much was secret that a new classification was created, "top secret." The entire Manhattan Project was deemed a top secret, and it became the model for how to compartmentalize information.[43]

Inevitably, the currency of secrecy became debased. In 1956, during another decade of exponential growth in federal records, a Department of Defense study found that "overclassification has reached serious proportions."[44] Excessive secrecy hindered public accountability and made it harder to protect real secrets, even as it led officials to undervalue open sources. By 1961, the National Archives had taken custody of almost 100,000 cubic feet of classified records.[45] A series of high-level panels, right down to Moynihan's own 1997 Commission on Protecting and Reducing Government Secrecy, came to the same conclusion: officials found classifying information to be safe, easy, and expedient, whereas bucking the system to reduce secrecy was risky, complicated, and unrewarding.[46]

Overclassification has therefore long been notorious. But the costs are not limited to reducing accountability in the here and now. The more information is classified, the greater the cumulative burden of secrecy weighs on us for decades to come.

THE ILLUSION OF REFORM

Almost every president since Roosevelt has promised to make the government more transparent. When he tightened the security classification system, Truman claimed that in the long run his order would make more information available to the public, rather than less.[47] Even President Nixon promised "to lift the veil of secrecy which now enshrouds altogether too many papers written by employees of the Federal establishment."[48] These presidents follow the same basic playbook, pledging to "automatically" release the secrets of previous administrations after a fixed period of time, typically ten or twenty-five years; to reduce the number of people who are allowed to classify information; and to reduce the amount of information that is classified at the highest level.[49]

These reforms aspire to prevent the debasement of the currency of secrecy. But every president has allowed lots of exceptions to "automatic" declassification. And no Congress has made significant resources available for reviewing the massive backlog of classified information. Reform has always failed in the face of unrelenting inflationary pressure coming from the other direction.

Take automatic and systematic declassification, whereby presidents try to open up the secrets of their predecessors. This is the main route by which most classified documents are declassified: some 44 million pages in fiscal year 2016.[50] But some 59 million more pages were withheld that year under automatic and systematic declassification, even though most were decades old.[51] Any department that claims an "equity" in a document can block its release. And this does not even account for all the papers exempt from automatic review. For instance, bureaucrats reportedly decided that more than 90 percent of classified documents fell under the many exemptions allowed by President Carter's executive order.[52] Executive orders have long allowed any record that might reveal intelligence sources and methods to be excluded from automatic review.[53] Even when it comes to the relatively innocuous work of research and analysis, the CIA still withholds 80 to 90 percent of the documents from the Cold War era that are reviewed for automatic declassification.[54] The CIA is also notorious for blocking the release of documents by other departments and agencies, but it is not the only one. The Department of Energy, for instance, has broad powers to keep documents classified if they might contain information related to nuclear weapons. It requires page-by-page review, and it double-checks the work of other departments.[55] So there is nothing automatic about automatic declassification.

Congress and the president sometimes direct that materials not yet accessioned to the National Archives undergo review for "discretionary" declassification. This can serve the laudable goal of advancing more immediate accountability, as when the Obama administration decided to disclose the intelligence agencies' budgets[56] and the size of the U.S. nuclear stockpile.[57] It can likewise support "truth and reconciliation" efforts, as occurred with the declassification of records on U.S. support for military dictatorships in Latin America.[58]

But discretionary declassification can also be weaponized to discredit opponents and preserve the prerogatives of whoever occupies the White House. This could be seen in the recent release (in full) of Senate Republicans' memorandum attacking the Obama administration's investigation of the Trump campaign, and even more so in the (heavily redacted) Democratic rebuttal.[59] This is an old story. Former vice president Dick Cheney criticized President Obama for releasing legal memoranda that detailed "enhanced interrogation" techniques without simultaneously declassifying documents that allegedly showed how these techniques produced valuable intelligence.[60] And decades ago, President Nixon put his "plumbers" in charge of declassifying documents on the 1961 invasion of the Bay of Pigs in order to discredit the Kennedys.[61]

Similarly, reducing the number of people in the federal bureaucracy who classify information may serve the interests of the president and the president's political appointees by helping them to centralize control of secrecy, without necessarily having any effect on the overall amount of secret-keeping. For instance, Obama promised on his first day as president to have the most transparent administration ever,[62] and during his first term he reduced the number of people with "original classification authority"— the only people who can decide that some new item or category of information must be kept secret—from 4,109 in fiscal year 2008[63] to 2,326 in fiscal year 2012.[64] But many more people can still classify documents that are related to previously classified subjects or that contain information falling into an approved category. According to the government's Information Security Oversight Office (ISOO), the number of "derivative" classification actions more than quadrupled during the same period, from approximately 23 million in 2008[65] to over 95 million in 2012.[66] In other words, three times a second, every second, some government official decided that what he or she was working on had to be shielded from public scrutiny until years or decades into the future.

The Obama administration also carried out more prosecutions for leaks to the media than all preceding administrations put together. It is not clear why. One possibility is that new technology made it easier to catch leakers; another centers on the creation in 2006 of a National Security Division within the Justice Department.[67] But whatever the cause, the effect may be to further reinforce the president's power to decide what ought to be kept secret and what ought to be revealed. Conversely, penalties for overclassification are almost never applied,[68] even though the Interagency Security Classification Appeals Panel (ISCAP) has found hundreds of cases in which officials have wrongly denied the public access to government information.[69]

In this otherwise dreary history, the Freedom of Information Act (FOIA) would appear to show what real reform looks like, given that hundreds of thousands of requests for federal agency records are processed under FOIA each year. President Lyndon B. Johnson was deeply suspicious of FOIA, but he reluctantly signed it anyway. Many in his administration did not think it would make any practical difference when it came to classified information.[70] Indeed, the original 1966 law turned out to be a "relatively toothless beast" more generally,[71] revealing a fundamental flaw: rather than regulating official secrecy at the source, FOIA placed the burden on the individual to know which secrets should be revealed and to seek their release on a case-by-case basis.[72]

Even after Congress strengthened FOIA in 1974, FOIA has proven to be a notoriously slow and unwieldy instrument in those areas where official secrecy is most likely to be abused. With exceedingly rare exceptions—what some call "legal unicorns"[73]—judges accept at face value agencies' refusals to release documents for national security reasons, all but abdicating the role Congress gave them.[74] In 2016, Congress passed a FOIA Improvement Act that included some useful features, such as requiring that agencies post frequently requested records on the internet. But Congress did not appropriate any new funds to meet these mandates.[75] As of fiscal year 2015, the federal government was spending $480 million annually complying with FOIA requests, more than NARA's entire budget.[76] And whereas FOIA's original advocates were journalists and it is commonly assumed that FOIA requests are intended to serve the public interest,[77] most of this money constitutes corporate welfare. At numerous agencies, well over two-thirds of the FOIA requests are submitted by corporate requesters, including a slew of companies that aggregate information extracted from regulatory or contracting agencies and then keep it secret from everyone except paying customers.[78]

FOIA can still be a useful workaround for the historian when all else fails, but it is inefficient and it diverts resources and attention that might otherwise go toward constructing a more rational declassification system. Even high-profile victories can make the public believe that their government is more open and accountable than it really is. Rather than help secure the historical record, FOIA may have legitimated and strengthened the president's all-but-exclusive control over classified information, the bedrock of our national secrecy complex.[79]

Leaks to the press can be seen as another strategy for coping with overclassification.[80] Here again, though, the White House maintains its monopoly on the licit use of state secrets, as high-level officials speaking on behalf of the president are almost never prosecuted and as ambiguously authorized "pleaks" and "plants" allow such officials to shape the public record while maintaining plausible deniability.[81] Wiki-sized leaks by transparency vigilantes are no solution either. Even aside from the potentially catastrophic costs to innocent victims, these leaks, too, only represent a relatively small and biased sample of the historical record. Moreover, researchers have a hard time knowing what to do with this kind of data because they usually cannot tell what it actually represents, or even whether it is authentic. At the same time, fears of vigilante leaks and hacks serve to justify ever more spending to protect classified information.

To be sure, both FOIA and unofficial disclosures can form useful parts of a larger transparency ecosystem.[82] But manure and decaying carcasses can also help other things grow. We need to think harder about how both FOIA and unofficial disclosures have nourished and strengthened the growth of the national secrecy complex, while the slender vine of state archiving withers in the darkness.

THE CURRENT CRISIS

In recent years, three trends have converged to create a true crisis for the U.S. historical record. The first is that a decline in appropriations and dubious management decisions have decimated the cadre of experienced archivists. NARA's annual budget dropped by nearly a quarter in inflation-adjusted terms during the Obama administration, to around $375 million.[83] Attrition is also changing the composition of NARA's workforce. In the past, newly hired archivists trained under senior colleagues while gaining deep knowledge of a particular group of records. In recent years, new hires have instead been trained in information management and rotated from one collection to the next, never long enough to acquire mastery. Archivists who previously advised researchers or processed new collections have been reassigned to serve senior management or to staff high-profile digitization projects. Once this institutional memory was lost, it was lost forever.

The result is that morale at NARA is among the worst in the entire federal government. In surveys of employee job satisfaction at government departments and agencies, NARA now routinely ranks among the unhappiest workplaces.[84] "It is so difficult," the president of the NARA workers' union has explained, "it's like trying to fight an octopus in a cave, underground, that has just squirted you with ink."[85]

At NARA's largest research facility, Archives II in College Park, Maryland, there were just forty-one archivists remaining as of 2013—the last time NARA's inspector general audited the processing of paper records—to work through over 700,000 cubic feet of unprocessed records.[86] At the presidential libraries, the situation is even worse. Archivists in these libraries had not processed the majority of the paper records they had received, and they estimated it would take decades to reduce the backlog.[87] The inspector general's audit did not even attempt to quantify the backlog of electronic records, except to note that the volume of electronic records has "grown exponentially" since the Reagan administration, that as of 2012 the presidential libraries held over 300 million "logical data records," and that over 95 percent of these records are believed to remain unprocessed.[88] It "boggles the mind," admitted William Mayer, NARA's executive for research services, in 2014.[89] Referring to the final scene from *Raiders of the Lost Ark*, which shows how a crate stamped "top secret" would be lost among thousands of other crates in a cavernous warehouse, Mayer said he has come to realize that "Spielberg got it right!"[90]

This brings us to the second trend: the growth in the sheer volume of records that need to be reviewed for national security information. In recent years, the reported number of classification decisions has stabilized, at around 55 million annually.[91] This is self-reported data, from officials who have been told to stop classifying so much. Even so, between 2007 and 2016 over 630 million classification decisions were taken overall,[92] covering an incalculable number of documents, emails, PowerPoint presentations, and audio/video recordings.

The amount of money the government spends each year to keep this information secure provides the most tangible way to measure the growth of national security secrecy and the threat it poses to the historical record. In the three years following Edward Snowden's disclosures in 2013, government spending on such items as physical and personnel security, training, and "technical surveillance countermeasures" increased by 45 percent, to almost $17 billion per year.[93] If we had a "ministry of secrets," its budget would now be bigger than that of the Department of Commerce or the Department of the Interior. Spending on declassification, on the other hand, was less than $109 million in fiscal year 2016, notwithstanding the massive increase in the amount of classified information requiring review.[94]

So while the Obama administration promised to strike a "careful balance between protecting essential secrets and ensuring the release of once sensitive information to the public as quickly and as fully as possible,"[95] the actual "balance" is tipped toward secrecy by more than 99 to 1. And it keeps tilting further in the wrong direction. The share devoted to declassification is one-tenth as high as it was back in 1999, when spending on information security was less than a fourth of what it is now and spending on declassification was more than two times *greater* than it is now.[96]

The collapse in funding for declassification and the growth in the number of classified documents that require review have had a predictable impact on the amount of information released to the public. For a period in the late 1990s, approximately 200 million pages of documents were being declassified each year.[97] But between 2007 and 2016 (the last year for which we have data), this number averaged 31 million.[98] The last two years saw a slight recovery, with 37 and 44 million pages declassified in 2015 and 2016, respectively.[99] But the percentage of pages withheld (out of the total number of pages reviewed for declassification) also increased in those years, to over 57 percent, the highest level ever recorded.[100]

People can try to force the release of records right away by filing FOIA requests. But even apart from the special difficulties raised by requests for classified records—which are often released in extensively redacted form if they are released at all—there is also a massive and growing FOIA backlog throughout the executive branch. In 2009, President Obama ordered all departments with significant FOIA backlogs to reduce them "by 10 percent each year."[101] As of 2015, fourteen of fifteen cabinet departments had failed to meet this goal, and the average annual backlog across all federal departments had *increased* by over 8 percent.[102] The two worst offenders were the State Department and the Department of Homeland Security.[103] Moreover, it seems that many departments have reduced their backlogs simply by asking requesters if they are still interested, and then closing cases when they don't receive an immediate response.[104]

The third trend involves the shift from paper documents to digital data—really big data—and it is the one that may finally bring about a collapse. As the nonpartisan Public Interest Declassification Board warned in 2012: "The expected growth of electronic records will create new backlogs almost incomprehensible in size."[105] State Department historians have started to call it the "Big Bang." While many were amazed at the 250,000 diplomatic cables released by WikiLeaks in 2010 and 2011, these cables represented less than 1 percent of the 27 million records amassed in the State Department's Central Foreign Policy Files between 1973 and 2006.[106] But the real growth is in new media. It is estimated that the State Department is generating 2 *billion* emails every single year.[107]

Imagine for a moment that just 3 percent of these records were retained, roughly the same proportion of paper records that have historically been retained by the National Archives. What would it take to screen 60 million emails for national security and personal information? We can get a preview by looking at how long it took the State Department to process former secretary Hillary Clinton's emails, which totaled some 54,000 messages. With a federal judge and Clinton herself urging rapid review, the government gave it top priority. A large team was assembled, with dozens of officials focusing on this one task. Still, it took about nine months to review nearly all the emails Clinton turned over and to release them to the public.[108] How long would it take to review one year's worth of State Department emails with the same urgency and the same staffing, assuming we wanted to retain roughly the same 3 percent of those emails as historically significant? More than 830 years.[109]

The State Department probably does a better job preserving its records than most of the government. It has about fifty full-time historians. Unique among federal agencies, the State Department has a congressional mandate to publish a documentary record of U.S. foreign relations.[110] Congress also created an external Historical Advisory Committee that meets regularly and reviews archival practices.[111] Contrast this with what we know (or don't know) about the rest of the federal bureaucracy. According to the Public Interest Declassification Board, a bipartisan body created by Congress to promote public access, a single (unnamed) intelligence agency produces a petabyte of classified information every eighteen months.[112] A petabyte equals approximately 20 million four-drawer file cabinets filled with textual documents. The board notes that, using current declassification methods, 2 million employees would have to work full time to review this many documents each year.[113] The fact that most intelligence records likely do not come in text form but rather as remote sensing data, communications intercepts, and so on makes this challenge qualitatively greater. It is utterly new, something that an understaffed and demoralized National Archives and an outmoded declassification system cannot possibly cope with.

A DIGITAL DARK AGE

Historians once hoped that digital sources, accessed via the internet, would democratize historical research and make it accessible to a broader audience.[114] Instead, the United States may be entering what's been called a digital dark age.[115] As discussed above, digitization has led to an exponential increase in the volume of government records and to crushing new burdens for government archivists. But historians also need to worry about the deliberate erasure of electronic records, as when CIA official Jose Rodriguez ordered the destruction of videotapes showing how suspected terrorists were subjected to repeated waterboarding.[116] We also need to consider how darkness can fall for reasons that are more banal than evil, including overzealous pruning of archives and "bit rot," the loss of data on outmoded software and hardware. And even when electronic records survive and can be accessed, we need to confront a host of challenges raised by reviewing such records for sensitive information and using them for historical research.

Start with the unauthorized loss or destruction of federal records. The National Archives is currently investigating twenty-five cases, many involving government officials using private email or encryption services like Signal.[117] This is the first time NARA has reported such investigations. But bureaucrats have been trying to delete incriminating emails since they first began sending them. In 1989, it took a last-minute lawsuit to prevent President Reagan's outgoing National Security Council (NSC) from destroying all of its electronic messages, on the same system that had enabled investigators to uncover the Iran-Contra scandal.[118] After years of litigation, the district court eventually ruled that the government had to preserve these messages, including their metadata (the subject line, from/to fields, and so on).[119] Much of the value in electronic records comes from being able to use metadata to analyze them in the aggregate.

At that point, a whole new set of problems emerged. Recovering the NSC emails from 150 hard drives almost overwhelmed NARA's technical capabilities. Torn tapes had to be spliced, creases ironed out, and moisture baked off in ovens.[120] So how would today's NARA, with a significantly smaller budget, cope with a vastly larger data dump of DOS-era software and decades-old hardware? As it is, NARA's information technology infrastructure is inadequate for the existing workload. Back in 2013, the agency's inspector general found that it could not assure the long-term preservation of electronic records.[121] More recently, the inspector general reported that management is continuing to use legacy systems for declassification and redaction that were already due for replacement five years ago; NARA does not even have a process in place to determine the age of these systems.[122] The agency is developing a new Electronic Records Archive, but assessment of how it could be adapted to classified records "is still in the earliest stages."[123]

Nevertheless, all federal departments and agencies were ordered in 2012 to switch from paper to electronic archives by 2019.[124] Forty years too late, NARA's strategic plan calls for coordination so that these departments and agencies can deliver the data in a form NARA will be able to preserve and process.[125] We can already see what is likely to happen by examining how NARA dealt with some of the first electronic records that came its way: the State Department's Central Foreign Policy Files. In 2007, archivists decided it would be impossible to review all 27 million records in these files to determine what to preserve permanently.[126] They began to experiment with sampling. In the case of records related to passports, visas, and citizenship, for instance, they looked at 200 documents out of almost 6 million, or 0.003 percent. They did not actually have a random sample, and in most cases they did not even read the full sample before deciding that a whole class of records should be permanently deleted. Diplomatic cables on cultural diplomacy, educational exchanges, international sport, and scientific cooperation are now among the permanent gaps in the historical record.

Records managers and archivists have always had to "weed" or "prune" routine documents and duplicate documents to make room on archival shelves. But these State Department records were small text files, millions of which easily fit on a single hard drive. Moreover, seemingly mundane records can present remarkable opportunities for research using contemporary data-mining techniques. With millions of cables on passports and visas, for instance, researchers might have been able to develop a vastly more sophisticated understanding of global migration. This opportunity is now lost forever.

Even before archivists began deleting files, the text of more than 7 percent of the cables for the years 1973 to 1978 had been lost for reasons the State Department still cannot explain. A much higher proportion of secret cables—22 percent—and cables from particular periods went missing.[127] Gone are the majority of telegrams from the beginning of December 1975, when President Ford and Secretary of State Kissinger acquiesced in General Suharto's murderous invasion of East Timor. We are also missing almost all records from the end of March 1976, when the U.S. government supported a military coup that started a civil war in Argentina. Gone, too, are the messages from June 1976, a period that included the Soweto uprising against apartheid and the Israeli raid on Entebbe.

Of the remaining files, the government is still withholding a large and growing percentage from the public. This includes virtually all the top secret cables, some of which are now almost half a century old. State Department officials have told me that declassifiers don't have access to hardware that is considered sufficiently secure. Yet most of the withheld records were never classified to begin with, which suggests that they are being withheld because they are thought to contain "personally identifiable information." Ironically, the government's solicitous regard for decades-old addresses and phone numbers means that we may never learn the full story of how it conducted surveillance programs. Operation Boulder, for example, subjected tens of thousands of visa applicants to FBI investigation between 1973 and 1975 merely because they had Arabic-sounding last names.[128] That history might have proved instructive after 9/11, but the vast majority of these Boulder records are still unavailable to researchers.

Millions of electronic records from the State Department Central Foreign Policy Files *have* been preserved and released, and we can use keyword searching to retrieve them.[129] This is a powerful tool, but it is a poor substitute for a finding aid, which knowledgeable archivists create to provide detailed descriptions of the scope and content of historical collections. In a classic study, researchers found that people miss four out of five relevant records because they do not—and cannot—know all the keywords to use.[130] Even when researchers do find something, what then? Historians have long sought to read documents in the same way our subjects did, in the context of related materials organized in files. Only in that way can we understand how they viewed the world. In that sense, all of these diplomatic cables are now lost, floating in cyberspace.

It is not just the cables. In 1974, the State Department began microfilming paper records in the Central Foreign Policy Files and storing copies in the same electronic system, destroying the originals as well as the physical filing system. We can only order these records in the NARA reading room at College Park. But they come in a box filled with otherwise random printouts. What else might the Secretary of State have been looking at or dealing with when he held that document in his hands? It is almost impossible now to tell.

This crisis in the archives is not, therefore, just a threat for the future. It is a depressing everyday reality for the scholar of recent history. In the place of an archivist, we have a search box. Instead of finding aids, we have an FAQ webpage. Rather than gaining a sense of context and the possibility of drawing serendipitous connections, we experience vertigo, with millions of documents effectively dumped on the ground, left for us to pick through and trip over.

This is how the government treats what all agree is one of the core collections recording our national and global history, a collection that is protected by the State Department's Office of the Historian and subject to robust oversight by a congressionally mandated advisory committee. What will happen to the millions and eventually billions of emails and other records produced by every other department and agency, records that might not have the same relevance to national security but might ultimately prove even more important?

Recently, a group of scholars gathered to consider the state of historical knowledge about just one part of our collective past, the space program. Inspiring stories like the film *Hidden Figures* have shown that, decades later, we still have much to learn about what was already celebrated as one of the greatest achievements in the history of life on earth. But in fact, the assembled historians and archivists found that, when the space program first began, officials at the National Aeronautics and Space Administration (NASA) seemed not to care whether they preserved a historical record. So great are the gaps, it is unclear whether any archivist was around when the program first reached into space, sent humans to the moon, and probed the universe beyond. Even now, NASA archivists must "constantly" justify the need for their work to agency leaders and find themselves increasingly overwhelmed by the challenge of saving digital records.[131] Will future generations of Americans travel to the stars without even knowing how we got there?

WHAT CAN BE DONE?

Martin Luther King Jr. famously said that "the arc of the moral universe is long but it bends toward justice."[132] The context makes clear that King— who was actually quoting another minister—was not talking about current events but divine judgment in the hereafter. The only part of that universe now visible to humans is what we call history. "Evil may so shape events that Caesar will occupy a palace and Christ a cross," King wrote a decade earlier, "but one day that same Christ will rise up and split history into A.D. and B.C., so that even the life of Caesar must be dated by His name."[133]

We do not need to wait for future historians, or God, to judge those rulers who try to bend historical scholarship to their own ends or bend the historical record toward oblivion. Americans need to ask themselves right now why we have allowed our elected officials to neglect their most basic duty: to preserve a record of what they do in our name.

Even rulers who do not care about how they are judged should recall that other governments, some more cynical than ours, have much longer memories. They know how to use history not just to learn from the past but to confuse and embarrass their enemies, as when Vladimir Putin recently accused the United States of breaking a promise not to extend NATO into Eastern Europe.[134] Was he right? Or how about the Iranian nuclear program: was it fair for Mahmoud Ahmadinejad to say that we only opposed it when the Iranian government was no longer our ally?[135] And what exactly is the commitment past U.S. presidents made to defend Taiwan in a conflict with China? If you don't know the answer to these questions, that is precisely the problem. As President Roosevelt realized, preserving institutional memory is not just essential for democratic accountability. It is a matter of national security.

So too is gaining control over official secrecy. When everything is secret, nothing is truly secure.[136] A culture of extreme secrecy breeds contempt, and sometimes revolt. This is a lesson we should learn from Daniel Ellsberg, Chelsea Manning, and Edward Snowden. Rightly or wrongly, each one felt that he or she owed fellow citizens a full account of official lies and misconduct. Rather than seeing the almost constant leaking from the Trump administration as an aberration, it may instead represent the culmination of a crisis that is decades in the making. And if we cannot find a way to restore control, how will any future president ever again be able to act "with secrecy and despatch," as Alexander Hamilton put it, when our national security depends on it?[137]

We therefore need to quickly take some commonsense steps, while also starting to think about more radical measures commensurate with the even more immense challenges to come.

1. Congress must raise NARA's funding to match its mission. Among federal departments and agencies, NARA is more like the Department of Veterans Affairs (VA) than the Department of Education. Its budget cannot grow and shrink depending on policy preferences any more than the VA can stop caring for wounded warriors once any given war comes to an end. Both must cope with a cumulative legacy, including conflicts and covert operations that occurred decades ago. If NARA does not have adequate resources, then the hard-won lessons of the past will never be preserved, and we will be paying for yet more national traumas. A billion-dollar budget for the National Archives—roughly half the cost of a single Navy destroyer— would be a cheap insurance policy against repeating trillion-dollar mistakes.

2. NARA must adapt archival practices to the era of big data. As NARA has acknowledged, electronic records are the agency's "single greatest challenge and opportunity."[138] Meeting this challenge does not necessarily mean diverting resources to digitizing paper collections. Why do that when we are already losing *born-digital* collections to bit rot? Meeting this challenge begins, instead, with the realization that data-mining will be an increasingly important method of historical research and taking this into account when archivists appraise whether records merit preservation. If archivists use statistical sampling, they should use rigorous methods and ensure they have a randomized sample. And if they delete a collection, they should at least preserve the sample, so future researchers will know what they are missing.

3. The rest of us must stop treating each new scandal about archival neglect or destruction as just another opportunity to score political points. All of us pay a price when public officials disregard the most basic requirements of democratic accountability. To be sure, Democrats paid the biggest price when Hillary Clinton used a private email server for official business and had her lawyers delete messages they deemed personal years after the fact. Instead of an honest reckoning, one that would acknowledge her understandable fear that her personal emails might be sought through FOIA, Clinton and her defenders continue to insist it was all just a big distraction from "the real issues."[139] But according to the Justice Department inspector general's report, one of the reasons she was not prosecuted for the concealment, removal, or destruction of records is because the relevant law has "never been used to prosecute individuals for attempting to avoid Federal Records Act requirements."[140]

On the other hand, Clinton's defenders were right to be furious when FBI director James Comey claimed she was "extremely careless" because a small fraction of her communications were later deemed to require classification.[141] Every day, government officials disagree about what information is truly sensitive—usually without even realizing it, as when they release two versions of the same document with different redactions.[142] While FBI agents were investigating Clinton for how she handled information that may or may not have been sensitive, they repeatedly handed sensitive information to reporters. Comey himself used private email for official business and leaked to the press.[143]

President Trump's habit of tearing up presidential records into little pieces[144] is only the most extreme example—so far—of a degenerative process that has been decades in the making. The more examples we have of both Democrats and Republicans ignoring their responsibility to preserve historical records, the more obvious it should be that no issue could be more real or worthy of bipartisan attention.

4. **The executive branch must establish a standard of professional responsibility for classifiers and declassifiers and prioritize the protection of truly sensitive information.** All the way back in 1955, Senator Hubert Humphrey complained that the government was making a massive investment in official secrecy without establishing what, exactly, had to be kept secret.[145] More than sixty years later, it is high time the government used part of the $17 billion it spends each year on information security to identify with greater care the information that officials agree requires safeguarding and—no less important—to identify information that has been improperly withheld. Academics have carried out hundreds of studies on "intercoder agreement" regarding myriad topics, few as important as this one. This kind of research is the only way to establish a reasonable standard for recognizing truly sensitive information, and for inculcating in classifying and declassifying officials a set of shared norms of professional responsibility.

Against the status quo of rampant overclassification, government commissions have repeatedly recommended a more rational, risk-management approach to protecting sensitive information. Even when it comes to nuclear weapons, the government's design goal is not to make accidents impossible—that standard would itself be impossible and would stand in the way of the more practical goal of minimizing risk.[146] But the executive branch's classification and declassification practices too often ignore this basic principle. Congressional statutes may also require rewriting, or at least reinterpretation, starting with the Kyl-Lott Amendment to the 1999 Defense Appropriations Act. Under Kyl-Lott, millions of records—even a serviceman's application to marry a Vietnamese citizen—continue to be reviewed page by page to ensure that none has information useful for building a nuclear weapon.[147] Watchdog groups have repeatedly found that this irrational, zero-risk approach to declassification severely slows down the process while also allowing dangerous information to slip through and sit on the open shelves of the National Archives, including sabotage manuals and recipes for manufacturing explosives.[148]

5. **The executive branch must employ data-science techniques to mitigate information overload and to identify state secrets and personal information.** How can officials cope with millions upon millions of

electronic records and prioritize those that really do require close scrutiny and safe handling? This basic challenge is not unique to the executive branch. It is analogous to the discovery process in large-scale litigation. Defense attorneys and data scientists have devised techniques for automatically identifying records responsive to a plaintiff's subpoena and for segregating records that are privileged because they contain attorney-client communications, trade secrets, or personal information.[149] Plaintiffs, for their part, have developed methods to find suspicious patterns in electronic communications.[150] As historians confront ever larger corpora, they too are starting to team up with data scientists to develop machine learning and natural language processing techniques, such as "topic modeling" large collections of declassified records to identify anomalous language, using traffic analysis to identify bursts of activity indicative of important events, and training algorithms to automatically classify sensitive and non-sensitive communications.[151]

We can use these and other techniques to begin to build a "declassification engine." Once we have established the reliability of human classifiers and declassifiers, we will know the standard these algorithms have to meet or beat. And if we can capture and store the information that officials are generating every time they release or redact a record, we can start using this data to train algorithms to help human reviewers focus on the records that are most likely to contain sensitive information.[152] The Public Interest Declassification Board has urged pilot projects to automate and streamline declassification. But so far, this has remained an unfunded mandate, and there is "little evidence that Executive departments and agencies are employing or developing the technologies needed to meet these objectives."[153]

CONCLUSION: THE JUDGMENT OF HISTORY

In the short term, these commonsense measures could prevent a collapse in the system for keeping our government accountable. But over the longer run, we will need to consider truly creative solutions for preserving both government transparency and legitimate state secrets in the era of big data. For instance, if secrecy is a kind of currency, then perhaps officials should not be able to mint new secrets—measurable by the number of "original classifications" recorded each year—without at the same time declassifying a comparable number of old secrets. If officials are found to have wrongly withheld information from the public, as often happens when their decisions are reviewed, it could be treated with the same severity as an unauthorized disclosure. And if the executive branch cannot reform itself and courts continue to abdicate their responsibility, Congress might consider creating an independent body, akin to the Federal Reserve, with a mandate to control official secrecy and safeguard the public record.

Historians are awakening to the danger, but we cannot do much on our own. History is bigger and more important than the historical profession. The judgment of history, the very survival of history, depends on the work of records managers, archivists, cabinet officers, members of Congress, judges, and countless ordinary citizens committed to preserving and learning from the past.

To think we can all come together to preserve the record of our times may seem naïve, but here again, we can and must learn from history. When, in the 1960s, Pennsylvania Station fell to the wrecking balls and the Cuyahoga River caught fire because it had become clogged with oil and debris, national movements rose up and passed laws to preserve landmarks and protect the environment. The danger facing the National Archives is no less grave, and to secure the historical record we need a national movement energized with similar passion and dedication. It is never naïve to let the past be our guide.

A Response from the National Archives

David S. Ferriero

MATTHEW CONNELLY'S thoughtful essay describes many of the major challenges we face at the National Archives, as we continue to transition from an analog to a digital archives while struggling to make the most of the limited resources available to us. He clearly understands how important our work is to the function of our democracy and to the preservation of our nation's heritage. We take our mission very seriously and, despite the challenges outlined in the essay, are doing all we can to preserve and provide access to all the records in our holdings.

We launched a new strategic plan in 2018 to guide our work and to drive change across all of the federal government. In June 2019, we announced policies and processes to support federal agencies' transition to fully electronic recordkeeping. By December 31, 2022, we will, to the fullest extent possible, no longer accept transfers of permanent or temporary records in analog formats and will accept records only in electronic format and with appropriate metadata. I am very happy to say that this strategic goal was endorsed by the president's reform plan, "Delivering Government Solutions in the 21st Century," and that our reform proposal, "Transition to Electronic Government," was included in the president's plan.

Our strategic plan's other goals include processing 82 percent of our holdings to enable discovery and access by the public by 2021; digitizing 500 million pages of records and making them available online by 2024; providing digital, next-generation finding aids to 95 percent of our holdings by 2025; and having 1 million records enhanced by citizen contributions in our online catalog by 2025.

To achieve these goals, we are recruiting a data scientist to help us cope with the challenges and make the most of the opportunities presented by "Big Data." This person will help us create connections between disparate sets of data, enabling faster, easier, and more efficient search of our holdings. The data scientist will be focused both internally and externally, looking out across the totality of our data and finding better ways to make it available and put it to work. These efforts will allow us to leverage data to provide better access to our records for the American people and simultaneously improve our business processes to provide improved customer service. This is one example of how we are building our future through our people so that we can meet our goals to make access happen, connect with customers, and maximize our value to the nation, as outlined in our strategic plan. The entire plan is available online at archives.gov.

On the topic of secrecy, the National Archives remains firmly committed to providing the fullest possible access to declassified government records, while vigilantly safeguarding information that is not yet appropriate for release. In addition, our Information Security Oversight Office leads the government's efforts to oversee the management of classified and controlled unclassified information. We provide staff support to the Public Interest Declassification Board, which advises the president on issues pertaining to national classification and declassification policy, and also to the Interagency Security Classification Appeals Panel, which provides a forum for further review of classification decisions for the public as well as users of the classification system.

Regarding the issue of archival neglect, we take our responsibilities seriously and are vigilant to ensure that government agencies are meeting their recordkeeping requirements. We take quick action when we see examples that concern us, working within the framework of the Presidential and Federal Records Acts.

Finally, on the topic of our funding levels, we agree that the country would be well served to invest in its National Archives and in the care of its federal government records. However, we understand that every presidential administration attempts to make the most effective use of available funds in proposed budgets, and that hard decisions must always be made during budget negotiations in Congress. As we have always done, we will continue to do the very best we can with the resources that we are given.

Professor Connelly's analysis and recommendations are thought-provoking and well informed. I commend him for taking on some tough topics and providing cogent arguments. I look forward to seeing the discussions that I am sure will be sparked by his essay. And we very much welcome everyone to come visit the National Archives Building on the Mall in Washington, D.C., where you can see the very faded original Declaration of Independence, but also the very legible Constitution and Bill of Rights.

Rescuing History (and Accountability) from Secrecy

Elizabeth Goitein

MATTHEW CONNELLY'S essay on state secrets and archival negligence offers a fascinating new lens on an old problem. The literature on national security secrecy tends to focus on the threat it poses to democratic accountability and participation. I have spent years thinking and writing about excessive government secrecy, and yet I had never considered the issue from the perspective of an archivist or historian.

Connelly describes numerous challenges to modern recordkeeping, ranging from the problem of "bit rot" (loss of data resulting from outmoded software or hardware) to the inadequacy of keyword searches as a substitute for finding aids. But one challenge that particularly concerns him is the government's generation of a massive amount of classified material coupled with an ineffective system for declassifying it. I will limit myself to commenting on this aspect of his essay, since the rest of it goes beyond my expertise.

Connelly aptly conveys the scope of problem—both how long it has existed and how massive it is. He outlines the skewed incentives that lead officials to classify documents unnecessarily and in ever-increasing numbers. He shows that the pace of declassification has fallen far behind the pace of classification, creating a growing and potentially insurmountable backlog. He makes a convincing case that our system of historical recordkeeping is in critical condition, due to classification-related problems as well as other causes, and that if this system collapses, "America's commitment to learning from its history will become a thing of the past, because the past itself will be impossible to recover."

Although they are understandably not Connelly's focus, it's worth highlighting some of the more commonly cited and immediate harms of overclassification. Depriving people of information about the government's policies or activities impedes their ability to engage in informed debate and to cast informed votes. Overclassification thus damages the most basic mechanisms of democracy. It also undermines the rule of law, as the government cannot be held accountable for violations that are concealed from the public. And it subverts the constitutional system of checks and balances, making it more difficult in myriad ways for Congress and the courts to provide meaningful oversight.

Connelly proposes several solutions, all of which have merit. He leads with the issue of resources, exhorting Congress to increase funding for the National Archives and Records Administration. Funding is a dry subject, and legal and policy experts usually stick to sexier remedies—things like curbing executive privilege or beefing up judicial review. But as Joe Biden has said, "Don't tell me what you value. Show me your budget, and I'll tell you what you value."[154] Connelly is to be commended for understanding the critical importance of funding to this issue. I would expand on his recommendation and urge Congress to earmark funding for agencies' own declassification efforts or to require agencies to spend a certain percentage of their information security budgets on declassification. As Connelly points out, the ratio of declassification spending to classification spending has decreased dramatically in recent years.

Connelly also recommends that the executive branch use data-science techniques, such as machine learning, to build a "declassification engine"—in lay terms, computer programs that could help identify sensitive information for purpose of speeding up declassification review. A CIA pilot project in this area showed promising results,[155] but Congress hasn't allocated the necessary funding to follow up. I agree with Connelly's recommendation, with one caveat. It is critical that automated technology *not* be used to make decisions about whether to classify information in the first instance (as some have proposed).[156] When "trained" with information that has already been classified, computers can identify documents that contain roughly the same information—a convenient aid to declassification. But initial determinations of whether national security would be harmed by the disclosure of information are inherently subjective, requiring careful thought and judgment.

As for derivative declassification—the practice of classifying documents on the ground that they contain previously classified information—automation might seem useful in theory, but it could be disastrous in practice. Computer programs would occasionally make mistakes, especially in the beginning.

Given that officials always err on the side of classification, they would likely correct a computer program's false negatives but not its false positives. The "machine learning" function would then internalize, perpetuate, and magnify the human tendency toward overclassification.

I would add two other recommendations in the area of declassification. Connelly mentions so-called automatic, systematic, and discretionary declassification, but he leaves out the fourth way in which records may be declassified: mandatory declassification review (MDR). Under MDR, members of the public can submit requests to agencies to declassify particular documents. They can appeal denials, first within the agency and then to the Interagency Security Classification Appeals Panel. The rate of declassification under MDR is orders of magnitude higher than under the Freedom of Information Act: more than 90 percent of requested documents are declassified either in whole or in part.[157] But MDR is underfunded, understaffed, and notoriously slow. Again, Congress should dedicate more funding in this area. In addition, agencies should create an expedited review track—similar to the expedited review track that exists in FOIA—when the requested records address a matter of significant public interest.

To the four existing declassification mechanisms, I would add a fifth. All classified documents must be marked with a declassification date. In 2017, most documents were classified for periods of ten years or less.[158] Yet incredibly, there is no regular system for performing declassification reviews before "automatic" declassification kicks in at twenty-five years. Unless someone happens to request a document through FOIA or MDR, it is likely to remain classified even though its declassification date came and went years ago. Going forward, classified documents should be electronically tagged to generate a prompt when the document reaches its declassification date, triggering a requirement to review. This would not only make more information available to the public sooner but also reduce the burden on the automatic review process that is triggered at the twenty-five-year mark.[159]

Even with these reforms, though, declassification will never be able to keep up unless we reduce the amount of classified information pouring into the system. Connelly alludes to this, and he notes the need to adopt "a more rational, risk-management approach to protecting sensitive information." He is correct, but the executive branch needs more than an attitude adjustment: it needs narrower and more specific criteria for classification. The executive order that currently governs classification contains no definition of national security nor any examples of harm that would justify classification.[160] Moreover, the categories of classifiable information listed in the order are far too broad. For instance, they include "intelligence sources or methods" writ large, even though intelligence agencies often rely on open sources and many of their methods are well known. The categories also include "foreign relations or foreign activities of the United States," which encompasses much of what we read in the newspaper every day. While it's true that officials need a fair amount of discretion in making assessments of national security harm, that discretion should not be virtually unfettered. I would like to see a White House–led commission of senior agency officials charged with tightening the criteria for classification and providing a definition of "damage to the national security" that sets an appropriately high bar.

The new criteria also should expand on the categories of information that may *not* be classified. In recent years, the government has advanced a dangerous new argument that information may be classified if our enemies could use it as anti-U.S. propaganda. The government has used this argument to shield photos and videos of Guantánamo detainees, for instance.[161] Of course, the worse the U.S. government's conduct, the more likely our enemies could use it to generate anti-U.S. sentiment. Although the executive order on classification prohibits classifying information to "conceal violations of law," the government's theory provides a convenient workaround: it could simply claim that its motive is not to hide misconduct but to deny our enemies a propaganda opportunity. The resulting ability to classify the government's worst abuses endangers core accountability and rule-of-law principles. New classification criteria should make clear that concerns about propaganda are not a legitimate basis for classification.

They should also rein in the practice of secret law. Increasingly, the executive branch is classifying rules and legal interpretations that set binding standards for government conduct. This secret body of law includes not only Office of Legal Counsel opinions—perhaps the best-known source of secret law—but also presidential directives, intelligence agencies' rules and regulations, and unpublished international agreements that have the force of treaties. As I explained in a 2016 Brennan Center report, classifying legal authorities raises serious constitutional questions and leads to distinct democratic harms.[162] Executive branch officials should not have the option of classifying pure legal analysis or legal standards.

Whatever the applicable limits on classification, officials will continue to exceed them until the incentives change. In his conclusion, Connelly suggests that in the longer run, it might become necessary for agencies to treat the wrongful withholding of information as seriously as they treat unauthorized disclosures. I agree, except that I wouldn't wait. Agencies should act now to implement systems for holding officials accountable for overclassification. Classifiers should be required to document their reasoning (the National Geospatial-Intelligence Agency already does this, according to a recent report of the government office that oversees classification policy[163]). Agencies should then conduct periodic spot audits, reviewing classification decisions and the supporting documentation. Officials found to engage in intentional, negligent, or routine overclassification should be subject to mandatory penalties. Conversely, officials should be granted "safe harbor" for good-faith decisions not to classify information. Agencies might also consider giving small cash awards to employees who bring successful challenges to classification decisions.[164]

Finally, the entire classification system rests on the premise that shielding information is an effective method of protecting national security. Given the practical difficulties with securing data in the digital era, it might be time to rethink this premise. Indeed, experts have already begun to question the utility of secrecy. In a 2005 memo, Defense Secretary Donald Rumsfeld concluded that "the United States Government is incapable of keeping a secret. If one accepts that, and I do, that means that the U.S. Government will have to craft policies that reflect that reality."[165] In 2011, a distinguished group of national security officials and experts convened a workshop to discuss how the United States might revamp its national security strategies for a world where data hacks and "insider threats" arguably make secrecy unsustainable.[166] Reversing the secrecy-obsessed mindset that has permeated the national security state since its inception is easier said than done. But it might prove crucial to our security. We would never place our faith in, say, a missile defense system that performed as poorly as the secrecy system does today.

Of course, there is no chance that the Trump administration will take up any of these proposals and little chance that a future one will pursue more than incremental change. Executive branch officials are far too committed to the secrecy system and unlikely to embrace limits on their own authority. Accordingly, my final recommendation picks up on a point that Connelly touches on in his conclusion: Congress must end its decades of abdication in this area. There are constitutional dimensions to the president's power to classify information, but it does not follow that Congress is powerless. It has acted boldly in the past. FOIA, for instance, authorizes judges to overturn presidential classification decisions, although they almost never do so. Many of the reforms sketched above could be mandated or incentivized by Congress. This Congress, or a future one, should flex its constitutional muscle and exert some control over the runaway classification regime. That would be a win for democracy, the rule of law, and—as Connelly has shown—history.

Archiving as Politics in the National Security State

Kirsten Weld

IN ONE SENSE, Matthew Connelly gives history and historians too much credit. He presents history as "the ultimate court of appeal" when states violate citizens' rights, a sobering thought for those of us who like to think of ourselves as rights-bearing subjects in the here and now. The professional study of the past is, Connelly argues, "our last chance to redeem constitutional liberties," in that it allows historians to render "an informed verdict" about "the truth" after the fact—a capacity severely threatened in the United States by the multifaceted crisis afflicting the National Archives and Records Administration (NARA). I am sympathetic to this juridical take on the historian's role: the notion that she should assign blame, serve as her society's conscience, and identify abuses of state power. But it overestimates the patience of those who await judgment, misses the fact that cases like *Buck v. Bell* and *Korematsu v. United States* were overruled in "the court of history" less because of new archival discoveries than because of shifts in societal attitudes toward eugenics and racial internment, and elides the marginality of the conditions in which most historians ply their trade. Our ability to contextualize may be great, but our success rate in winning accountability from authorities may more closely resemble the dwindling share of university faculty positions that still pay a living wage.

In another sense, though, Connelly gives history and historians too *little* credit. If the reforms he recommends are not brought to fruition, he warns, "future historians will have a hard time proving anything at all." We risk "the very survival of history" by allowing the U.S. government to overclassify, neglect, and destroy its records. In fact, we are told, we face nothing less than "the end of history as we know it," a dystopian future in which "the past itself will be impossible to recover." Yet social historians have long shown that the past cannot be and never has been interpreted using state archives alone. These records steer our gaze toward the white, the male, the wealthy, the influential. Moreover, we have always had to fight for access to them, and that access has always been partial at best. But we are resourceful. We have long worked outside government collections to construct more complete and representative accounts of the past, using sources from social movements, religious bodies, unions, nongovernmental organizations, businesses, and individual historical actors both within and beyond U.S. borders. So, as we do the crucial work of advocating for archival declassification and preservation, let us not conflate capital-H History with the particular slice of it NARA is mandated to protect.

That slice is an uncommonly large and important one, however, and Connelly is absolutely correct to sound the alarm about the dangers it faces. Apt is the analogy of climate change: a disaster long in the making whose immense dimensions are difficult to comprehend, yet one we may have the ability to reverse if we act boldly and if we act now. Connelly is also correct to insist that historians must push for government transparency and archival access, and that we cannot do it alone. Instead, he argues, "we need a national movement energized with . . . passion and dedication." Such a movement would require building a mass constituency around the principle that we have a right to know what our governments do in our name, and around the fact that this right depends on public access to government records. To get there, we will need a much bolder and more radical vision than the one Connelly proposes.

* * *

The idea that a government should preserve and democratize its documentary production dates to the French Revolution.[167] Not two weeks after the storming of the Bastille, the new National Assembly created the first-ever national archives, aiming to centralize the keeping of state records and guarantee that the public could consult them. Ever since, creating and maintaining national archives has been a central task of state formation around the world, useful both for those institutions' symbolic power and for the all-too-material power exercised via the creation, consultation, classification, and accessibility of the records they contain. As I have written elsewhere, how states regulate archival access says a great deal about their relationship to those they govern.[168] Winning any significant change in how a state treats its archives thus requires nothing less than a revision of the social contract. For France, that involved the overthrow of the corrupt *ancien régime*. What will it take in the contemporary United States?

Revealingly, it was not until 1934 that the United States, where mistrust of federal overreach has been an enduring axiom of political life, established its own national archives. The New Deal's proliferation of new government agencies meant the proliferation of new records-creating entities, and the Roosevelt administration set professional norms for the appraisal and safeguarding of their materials. This was, Connelly suggests, a rich moment of potential for American democracy. Legal checks were instituted to prevent the inappropriate destruction of government records, substantial institutional resources and muscle were devoted to the task, and Roosevelt himself extolled the value of archives and recordkeeping to the national project. Official secrecy was to be used judiciously, in the interests of national security.

As with the fruits of New Deal liberalism more generally, however, the democratic promise of the postwar moment with regard to archiving was in many respects limited, not least because, as in so many other remits of U.S. history, the country's drive to expansion and empire undermined the integrity of its stated ideals. The story of government secrets is a story of war and imperialism. Well before the founding of NARA, the federal government developed massive intelligence-gathering and covert surveillance capabilities in its occupation of the Philippines. As World War I wound down, the United States repatriated the extraconstitutional information-gathering apparatus developed abroad for use against domestic dissidents.[169] The advent of the Second World War offered Roosevelt justification for systematizing the classification of national security–related information for the first time. The close relationships the U.S. government built during that same period with foreign police and militaries, whose information-gathering capacities it would soon pay handsomely to fortify, allowed it to vacuum up enormous amounts of global intelligence, as well as to make that expertise available to local law enforcement for use policing U.S. residents. The Central Intelligence Agency and the National Security Agency were founded in 1947 and 1952, respectively, thereby institutionalizing both covert action and the production of archival materials that were sensitive by definition. The rise of the military-industrial complex, and what we might politely call the foreign policy misadventures of the United States during the Cold War, ensured that secrecy would triumph over transparency. That state of affairs continues to this day, its scale grossly exacerbated by the digital turn.

Since the archival politics of states reflect deeper truths about how rulers and ruled relate to each other, it is unsurprising that the dismantling of the postwar welfare state and the concomitant ascendance of neoliberal governance has had consequences for the nation's recordkeeping. One fascinating detail in Connelly's essay is the observation that the instrument most commonly associated with government transparency, the federal Freedom of Information Act (FOIA), has been largely captured by corporate America. FOIA was won in large part by journalists in 1966; Congress strengthened the legislation somewhat in 1974 under intense public pressure regarding Vietnam and Watergate.[170] Since then, however, not only has the program been progressively starved of compliance funds by Congress, but, Connelly notes, the resources allocated to fulfilling FOIA requests essentially represent corporate welfare, given that at some regulatory agencies well over two-thirds of requests are filed by private companies extracting information for their own profit. Even more so than FOIA, the state's commitment to ensuring archival access has been the victim of willful neglect. Congress has slashed NARA's budget and staff, even as the volume of records needing an archivist's review for classification purposes has massively expanded. The result has been a perfect storm: vaster and vaster amounts of digital records but a gutted institutional capacity to process them, yielding gigantic backlogs and, hence, growing state secrecy and impunity. If we learn a lot about a state by looking at how it handles its archives, then it is hard to avoid concluding from this assessment that the United States is not a true democracy.

* * *

To address the situation, Connelly suggests a series of reforms, including increased funding for NARA, a revamped approach to information security on the federal government's part, and the use of data mining to manage the proliferation of records. To get the job done, Connelly argues that we must transcend politics. He claims that government transparency "was once a bipartisan cause, championed by both the left and the right," and that we "must stop treating each new scandal about archival neglect or destruction as just another opportunity to score political points." But the idea that some kind of nonpartisan golden age of U.S. government openness once reigned is false. So too is the hope that today's national security state, sustained precisely by bipartisan consensus and deeply enmeshed in what Samuel Moyn has called the "forever war," will cede control over classification protocols without a fight.[171] The crisis at NARA is not one of technical capacity. It is one of politics.

After all, archival access is power. Moments of increased government openness, whether in the United States or anywhere else, are rarely volunteered by those in charge. Instead, they are forged through struggle. That NARA was part of the New Deal is not an incidental detail of its history. The New Deal order, as Steve Fraser and Gary Gerstle have shown, was no act of liberal charity but was won via conflict: namely, the hard work of organizing and mobilization by the left, including the Communist Party, for economic, racial, and social justice.[172] That order was methodically dismantled over decades by committed ideological conservatives who advanced a very different vision of the ideal relationship between society and state. For all its weaknesses, FOIA, similarly, would not exist if journalists and other civil society groups had not waged an uphill battle for it. And most of the publicly available government records documenting U.S. covert activity in places like Indonesia, Vietnam, Iran, Guatemala, Chile, Angola, and Cuba—to say nothing of the policing of the home front—have been pried from the federal government, not proffered by it. These victories were won from below by committed leftists, not ceded from above by elite liberals. The problems at NARA will not be solved by us asking nicely. Instead, we need to tackle the country's grave problems of power and governance.

This is not to discount Connelly's suggestions for reform, which are sound and sensible. Congress should absolutely raise NARA's funding to match its mission, federal agencies should certainly declassify far more than they do, and NARA must adapt its practices to the age of big data. Conveniently, the forever war has led our intelligence agencies to develop state-of-the-art data-mining programs like Real Time Regional Gateway (RTRG) and PRISM, which means that Connelly's recommendation that NARA integrate data mining into the declassification process should, technically speaking, be easy to implement. We know about RTRG and PRISM thanks only to Edward Snowden, however, and it is worth asking: absent any meaningful devolution of power from the national security state, and given the extant domination of the FOIA system by corporations seeking to game the regulatory system, whose purposes would more data mining at NARA serve? Pushing for a technical fix without a political one is a risky game indeed.

In an era in which the rest of the public sector is being systematically defunded, deregulated, privatized, or shuttered outright, we cannot expect to save NARA except as part of a broader agenda for social change. (The devastating recent fire at Brazil's National Museum illustrates all too well how government austerity threatens historical preservation.[173]) That broader agenda must articulate the essential link between the technocratic remit of archival access protocols and a far more robust set of demands for transforming the relationship between society and state. After all, if it is government accountability we are after, we must concede that even a complete overhaul of the declassification process would only get us a small part of the way there.

What we need instead is accountability for the shredding of the U.S. social contract over the last four decades. We live in a time of gerrymandering, felon disenfranchisement, mass incarceration, runaway corporate greed, and soaring socioeconomic inequality. The commons have been eviscerated by design. The U.S. military has active-duty troops stationed in more than 150 countries and an annual budget approaching a trillion dollars, while our elderly stock shelves in Amazon warehouses because they cannot afford to retire, and our families lose their homes because they cannot pay their medical bills.[174] Here, the analogy to climate change is relevant once more: if we wish to forestall its devastating effects, we will not succeed by focusing our energies on one sole polluter or one sole resource. Instead, as Naomi Klein writes, "the real solutions to the climate crisis are also our best hope of building a much more enlightened economic system—one that closes deep inequalities, strengthens and transforms the public sphere, generates plentiful, dignified work and radically reins in corporate power."[175] I submit here that the same must be said about the archival crisis Connelly diagnoses. To do otherwise would be to rearrange the deck chairs on the Titanic.

So, yes, let us come together and save NARA. But we cannot stop there. We must demand a sea change in the federal government's priorities, which we will only win through concerted political struggle and a major redistribution of power in our society. We must push for a massive reinvestment in the public sphere, not just at the National Archives but across government agencies. We must build coalitions around the fact that archival preservation and democratic activism are one and the same. And we must fight not just to declassify the forever war but to end it.

NOTES

1. *See, e.g.,* Elizabeth Goitein & David M. Shapiro, Brennan Ctr. for Justice, *Reducing Overclassification Through Accountability* (2011), https://www.brennancenter.org/sites/default/files/legacy/Justice/LNS/Brennan_Overclassification_Final.pdf.
2. *See, e.g.,* Staff of. H. Comm. on Oversight & Gov't Reform, 114th Cong., *FOIA Is Broken: A Report* (Comm. Print 2016).
3. *See, e.g.,* Nina A. Mendelson, *Private Control over Access to the Law: The Perplexing Federal Regulatory Use of Private Standards,* 112 Mich. L. Rev. 737 (2014); Peter L. Strauss, *Private Standards Organizations and Public Law,* 22 Wm. & Mary Bill Rts. J. 497 (2013).
4. *See, e.g.,* Frank Pasquale, *The Black Box Society: The Secret Algorithms That Control Money and Information* (2015).
5. *See, e.g.,* Leonard Downie Jr. with Sara Rafsky, Comm. to Protect Journalists, *The Obama Administration and the Press: Leak Investigations and Surveillance in Post-9/11 America* (2013), https://cpj.org/reports/us2013-english.pdf.
6. *See, e.g.,* Eric Lipton, *Top Ethics Officer Challenges Trump over Secret Waivers for Ex-Lobbyists,* N.Y. Times (May 1, 2017), https://www.nytimes.com/2017/05/01/us/politics/top-ethics-officer-challenges-trump-over-secret-waivers-for-ex-lobbyists.html.
7. Jacob E. Gersen & Anne Joseph O'Connell, *Hiding in Plain Sight? Timing and Transparency in the Administrative State,* 76 U. Chi. L. Rev. 1157, 1161 (2009).
8. *See generally* David E. Pozen, *Transparency's Ideological Drift,* 128 Yale L.J. 100 (2018).
9. *See* Pub. Interest Declassification Bd., *Transforming the Security Classification System* 17 (2012), https://www.archives.gov/files/declassification/pidb/recommendations/transforming-classification.pdf ("Under the current declassification model, it is estimated that . . . one intelligence agency would, therefore, require *two million employees* to review manually its one petabyte of information each year. Similarly, other agencies would hypothetically require millions more employees just to conduct their reviews.").
10. *See* Charles S. Clark, *National Archives Plays Unusual Role in Kavanaugh Nomination Battle,* Gov't Executive (Aug. 22, 2018), https://www.govexec.com/oversight/2018/08/national-archives-plays-unusual-role-kavanaugh-nomination-battle/150744.
11. *See generally* History Lab, http://www.history-lab.org (last visited July 18, 2019).
12. *About the National Archives of the United States,* Nat'l Archives, https://www.archives.gov/publications/general-info-leaflets/1-about-archives.html (last visited July 18, 2019).

STATE SECRECY, ARCHIVAL NEGLIGENCE, AND THE END OF HISTORY AS WE KNOW IT

This essay started as a collaboration with David Allen and Richard Immerman. I am greatly in their debt, both for their many substantive contributions and for graciously allowing me to carry the project through to completion. I am also grateful to David Pozen for making extremely judicious edits and for sharing his expansive knowledge of the subject. Finally, while parts of this essay are critical of contemporary archival practices, I could not have written it if archivists had not been so open and honest about the extraordinary challenges they have had to face with extremely limited resources.

13. *Buck v. Bell*, 274 U.S. 200, 205 (1927).

14. *See, e.g.*, Adam Cohen, *Imbeciles: The Supreme Court, American Eugenics, and the Sterilization of Carrie Buck* (2016); Daniel J. Kevles, *In the Name of Eugenics: Genetics and the Uses of Human Heredity* 110–12, 329–30 (1995).

15. *See Trump v. Hawaii*, 138 S. Ct. 2392, 2423 (2018) (stating that *Korematsu v. United States*, 323 U.S. 214 (1944), "was gravely wrong the day it was decided, has been overruled in the court of history, and . . . has no place in law under the Constitution" (internal quotation marks omitted)).

16. There are many teaching guides. *See, e.g.*, Digital Pub. Libr. of Am., *Japanese American Internment During World War II*, https://dp.la/primary-source -sets/japanese-american-internment-during-world-war-ii (last visited July 18, 2019).

17. *See, e.g.*, *Communist Party of the U.S. v. Subversive Activities Control Bd.*, 367 U.S. 1 (1961); *Dennis v. United States*, 341 U.S. 494 (1951).

18. *See, e.g.*, Griffin Fariello, *Red Scare: Memories of the American Inquisition* (2008); Geoffrey R. Stone, *Free Speech in the Age of McCarthy: A Cautionary Tale*, 93 Calif. L. Rev. 1387 (2005).

19. *Sweezy v. New Hampshire*, 354 U.S. 234, 250 (1957).

20. *See* Annie Karni, *Meet the Guys Who Tape Trump's Papers Back Together*, Politico (June 10, 2018), https://www.politico.com/story/2018/06/10/trump-papers -filing-system-635164.

21. U.S. Nat'l Archives, *The Declaration of Independence: A History*, https://www .archives.gov/founding-docs/declaration-history (last visited July 18, 2019).

22. *See* Michael Kammen, *A Machine That Would Go of Itself: The Constitution in American Culture* 127 (2017 ed.).

23. *See* Elliott Carter, *National Archives Vault*, Atlas Obscura, https://www .atlasobscura.com/places/national-archives-vault (last visited July 18, 2019).

24. *See generally* David Kahn, *The Codebreakers: The Comprehensive History of Secret Communication from Ancient Times to the Internet* 157–88 (1996).

25. *See* Edward L. Hammer, Note, *A Functional View of the Rule of Lenity: Does Theft of Misaddressed Mail Violate the Federal Mail Theft Statute?*, 58 Fordham L. Rev. 215, 221 n.36 (1989).

26. On the declining use of encryption, see the data in Ralph E. Weber, *Masked Dispatches: Cryptograms and Cryptology in American History, 1775–1900*, at 68–69 (2002).

27. *See* Aaron W. Marrs, *The Civil War Origins of the FRUS Series, 1861–1868*, in *Toward "Thorough, Accurate, and Reliable": A History of the* Foreign Relations of the United States *Series* 17 (William B. McAllister et al., eds., 2015), https:// s3.amazonaws.com/static.history.state.gov/frus-history/ebooks/frus-history.pdf.

28. *See* Captain Wyman H. Packard, *A Century of U.S. Naval Intelligence* 1–4 (1996), http://ibiblio.org/pha/A%20CENTURY%20OF%20US%20NAVAL %20INTELLIGENCE.pdf.

29. *See* 1 Arvin S. Quist, *Security Classification of Information: Introduction, History, and Adverse Impacts* 9, 14, 23–27 (2002), https://fas.org/sgp/library/quist/chap_2 .pdf.

30. David Kahn, *Cryptology Goes Public*, 58 Foreign Aff. 141, 142 (1979); *see also* The History of Security Classification, Brownell Papers, Eisenhower Presidential Library, Box 184.

31. *See* Tom Ryan, *Survey of Federal Archives*, U.S. Nat'l Archives: Pieces of History (Oct. 6, 2014), https://prologue.blogs.archives.gov/2014/10/06/survey -of-federal-records.

32. James Gregory Bradsher, *An Administrative History of the Disposal of Federal Records, 1789–1949*, Provenance, J. Society Georgia Archivists (Fall 1985), https://digitalcommons.kennesaw.edu/cgi/viewcontent.cgi?referer=&httpsredir =1&article=1307&context=provenance, at 9.

33. *Id.* at 13.

34. *E.g.*, Records Disposal Act of 1943, Pub. L. No. 78–115, § 15, 57 Stat. 380, 383.

35. Cynthia M. Koch & Lynn A. Bassanese, *Roosevelt and His Library*, Prologue Mag. (Summer 2001), https://www.archives.gov/publications/prologue/2001 /summer/roosevelt-and-his-library-1.html. On Roosevelt's role in shaping the National Archives and the presidential library system, see Bob Clark, *FDR, Archivist*, Prologue Mag. (Winter 2006), https://www.archives.gov/publications /prologue/2006/winter/fdr-archivist.html.

36. Exec. Order No. 8381, 3 C.F.R. 634 (1938–1943).

37. *See* Anne Bruner Eales, *Fort Archives: The National Archives Goes to War*, Prologue Mag. (Summer 2003), https://www.archives.gov/publications/prologue /2003/summer/fort-archives-1.html; Milton Gustafson, *Travels of the Charters of Freedom*, Prologue Mag. (Winter 2002), https://www.archives.gov/publications /prologue/2002/winter/travels-charters.html.

38. *See* James Worsham, *Our Story: How the National Archives Evolved over 75 years of Change and Challenges*, Prologue Mag. (Summer 2009), https://www.archives .gov/publications/prologue/2009/summer/history.html.

39. *See* Eales, *supra* note 37.

40. *See The CIA Under Harry Truman*, at xii–xiv (Michael Warner, ed., 1994), https:// www.cia.gov/library/center-for-the-study-of-intelligence/csi-publications/books -and-monographs/the-cia-under-harry-truman/pdfs/Preface.pdf.

41. Daniel Patrick Moynihan, *Secrecy: The American Experience* 154 (1998).

42. *See id.* at 73.

43. *See* Alex Wellerstein, Knowledge and the Bomb: Nuclear Secrecy in the United States, 1939–2008, at 58–91 (2010) (unpublished Ph.D. dissertation, Harvard University) (on file with author).

44. Dep't of Def. Comm. on Classified Info., Report to the Secretary of Defense by the Committee on Classified Information 6 (1956), http://bkofsecrets.files .wordpress.com/2010/07/coolidge_committee.pdf.

45. Arthur M. Schlesinger Memorandum for McGeorge Bundy, Mar. 20, 1961, John F. Kennedy Presidential Library, Papers of Arthur M. Schlesinger, Jr., Box WH-12.

46. *See generally* Comm'n on Protecting and Reducing Gov't Secrecy, Report, S. Doc. No. 105–2 (1997), https://www.gpo.gov/fdsys/pkg/GPO-CDOC-105sdoc2 /content-detail.html.

47. Letter from Joseph Short, White House Press Sec'y, to George Todt, Nov. 7, 1951, Harry S. Truman Presidential Library, White House Official Files, Box 1069.
48. Richard Halloran, *President Orders Limit on Labeling of Data as Secret*, N.Y. Times (Mar. 9, 1972), https://www.nytimes.com/1972/03/09/archives/president-orders-limit-on-labeling-of-data-as-secret-calls-for.html.
49. For public announcements of such policies, see, for example, *Text of White House Statement and Executive Order Promulgating New Security Code*, N.Y. Times (Nov. 7, 1953), https://www.nytimes.com/1953/11/07/archives/text-of-white-house-statement-and-executive-order-promulgating-new.html; *President Eases Code on Secrecy; Order Defense Documents Reclassified at Intervals*, N.Y. Times (Sept. 21, 1961), https://www.nytimes.com/1961/09/21/archives/president-eases-code-on-secrecy-order-defense-documents.html; and Martin Tolchin, *President to Issue Order to Liberalize Rule on Secret Data*, N.Y. Times (June 29, 1978), https://www.nytimes.com/1978/06/29/archives/president-to-issue-order-to-liberalize-rule-on-secret-data-change.html. President Reagan was an exception, explicitly ordering steps to make it harder to release information. *See* Howell Raines, *Reagan Order Tightens the Rules on Disclosing Secret Information*, N.Y. Times (Apr. 3, 1982), https://www.nytimes.com/1982/04/03/us/reagan-order-tightens-the-rules-on-disclosing-secret-information.html.
50. Info. Security Oversight Off., *2016 Report to the President* 1 (2017), https://www.archives.gov/files/isoo/reports/2016-annual-report.pdf.
51. *Id.*
52. *See* Neil A. Lewis, *New Proposal Would Automatically Limit Secrecy*, N.Y. Times (Sept. 30, 1993), https://www.nytimes.com/1993/09/30/us/new-proposal-would-automatically-limit-secrecy.html.
53. *See, e.g.*, Exec. Order No. 13,526, § 3.3(b)(1), 75 Fed. Reg. 707, 714–15 (Dec. 29, 2009).
54. The Information Security Oversight Office no longer provides a comparative breakdown of automatic declassification rates by department and agency, but for the most recent such data, see Info. Security Oversight Off., *2014 Report to the President* 8 (2015), https://www.archives.gov/files/isoo/reports/2014-annual-report.pdf.
55. *See* Steven Aftergood, *Openness and Secrecy at the Department of Energy After the China Espionage Investigations*, 53 J. Fed'n Am. Scientists (Jan./Feb. 2000), https://fas.org/faspir/v53n1a.htm.
56. *See* Off. of Mgmt. & Budget, *National Intelligence Program: The Federal Budget Fiscal Year 2012*, https://obamawhitehouse.archives.gov/omb/factsheet_department_intelligence (last visited July 18, 2019).
57. *See* Mary Beth Sheridan & Colum Lynch, *Obama Administration Discloses Size of Nuclear Arsenal*, Wash. Post (May 4, 2010), http://www.washingtonpost.com/wp-dyn/content/article/2010/05/03/AR2010050302089.html.
58. *See* Peter Kornbluh, *Chile and the United States: Declassified Documents Relating to the Military Coup, September 11, 1973*, Nat'l Security Archive Elec. Briefing Book No. 8, https://nsarchive2.gwu.edu//NSAEBB/NSAEBB8/nsaebb8i.htm (last visited July 18, 2019).
59. *See* Nicholas Fandos, *2 Weeks After Trump Blocked It, Democrats' Rebuttal of G.O.P. Memo Is Released*, N.Y. Times (Feb. 24, 2018), https://www.nytimes.com/2018/02/24/us/politics/democratic-memo-released-fbi-surveillance-carter-page.html.

60. *See* Ewen MacAskill & Robert Booth, *Senior Bush Figures Could Be Prosecuted for Torture, Says Obama*, Guardian (Apr. 21, 2009), https://www.theguardian.com /world/2009/apr/21/cheney-obama-cia-torture-memos.

61. Memorandum from Tom Latimer, Nat'l Security Staff, to Alexander M. Haig, Oct. 8, 1971, U.S. National Archives, College Park, MD, Documents of the National Security Council, 8th Supplement NSSM 113 Memo, reproduced in ProQuest History Vault, Folder 000076-011-0512.

62. Transparency and Open Government: Memorandum for the Heads of Executive Departments and Agencies, 74 Fed. Reg. 4685 (Jan. 21, 2009).

63. Info. Security Oversight Off., *2008 Report to the President* 1 (2009), https://fas.org /sgp/isoo/2008rpt.pdf.

64. Info. Security Oversight Off., *2012 Annual Report to the President* 1 (2013), https://fas.org/sgp/isoo/2012rpt.pdf.

65. Info. Security Oversight Off., *supra* note 63, at 1.

66. Info. Security Oversight Off., *supra* note 64, at 1.

67. *See* David E. Pozen, *The Leaky Leviathan: Why the Government Condemns and Condones Unlawful Disclosures of Information*, 127 Harv. L. Rev. 512, 629–31 (2013).

68. *See* Elizabeth Goitein & David M. Shapiro, Brennan Ctr. for Justice, *Reducing Overclassification Through Accountability* 27–30 (2011), https://www.brennancenter .org/sites/default/files/legacy/Justice/LNS/Brennan_Overclassification_Final.pdf.

69. From May 1996 to September 2015, ISCAP affirmed the classification of 605 challenged documents and declassified 1,802 documents in part or in their entirety. Info. Security Oversight Off., *2015 Report to the President* 28 (2016), https://www.archives.gov/files/isoo/reports/2015-annual-report.pdf.

70. *See* Sam Lebovic, *How Administrative Opposition Shaped the Freedom of Information Act*, in *Troubling Transparency: The History and Future of Freedom of Information* 13, 20 (David E. Pozen & Michael Schudson, eds., 2018) ("In the lead-up to FOIA's passage, there was remarkably little concern that FOIA would interfere with national security secrecy.").

71. Antonin Scalia, *The Freedom of Information Act Has No Clothes*, Regulation, Mar./Apr. 1982, at 14, 15.

72. *See* David E. Pozen, *Freedom of Information Beyond the Freedom of Information Act*, 165 U. Pa. L. Rev. 1097, 1100–01 (2017) (discussing FOIA's "reactionary," request-driven character); *id.* at 1122 ("Rather than seek to revamp the classification process, . . . Congress opted in the end for the indirect FOIA model and the pointillistic resolution of secrecy disputes on a case-by-case basis.").

73. David McCraw, *FOIA Litigation Has Its Own Rules, but We Deserve Better*, Just Security (Mar. 15, 2016), https://www.justsecurity.org/29974/foia-litigation -rules-deserve.

74. *See* Pozen, *supra* note 72, at 1118–23.

75. *See* U.S. Dep't Just.: Off. of Info. Pol'y, *OIP Summary of the FOIA Improvement Act of 2016* (Aug. 17, 2016), https://www.justice.gov/oip/oip -summary-foia-improvement-act-2016.

76. Pozen, *supra* note 72, at 1122 & n.145.

77. *Id.* at 1116–17.

78. *See* Margaret B. Kwoka, *FOIA, Inc.*, 65 Duke L.J. 1361, 1376–401 (2016).

79. *See* Pozen, *supra* note 72, at 1122 ("Not only did FOIA's legislative sponsors fail to solve or even seriously confront the overclassification problem when they empowered private parties to bring lawsuits in pursuit of specific records, but they also helped to entrench and legitimate the emerging classification system.").

80. *See* Pozen, *supra* note 67, at 581–82.

81. *See id.* at 559–73.

82. *See generally* Seth F. Kreimer, *The Freedom of Information Act and the Ecology of Transparency*, 10 U. Pa. J. Const. L. 1011 (2008).

83. In fiscal year 2009, NARA's total budgetary authority amounted to $447,435,000, compared to 374,865,000 in fiscal year 2016, a 16 percent decline in absolute terms. *See* NARA, *2010 Performance Budget Congressional Justification*, at I-1 (2010), https://www.archives.gov/files/about/plans-reports /performance-budget/2010/2010-performance-budget.pdf; NARA, *FY 2018 Congressional Justification* 3 (2017), https://www.archives.gov/files/about /plans-reports/performance-budget/fy-2018-performance-budget.pdf.

84. *See, e.g.*, U.S. Off. of Personnel Mgmt., *2012 Federal Employee Viewpoint Survey Results* 46–49 (2012), https://www.opm.gov/fevs/archive/2012files/2012 _Government_Management_Report.PDF (reporting 2012 survey results showing that, across dozens of federal agencies, NARA employees had the lowest "job satisfaction" and "global satisfaction" levels).

85. Yuki Noguchi, *Furloughs Only the Latest Blow to Federal Worker Morale*, NPR (May 9, 2013), https://www.npr.org/2013/05/09/182019098/furloughs-only -the-latest-blow-to-federal-worker-morale (brackets omitted).

86. NARA Off. of Inspector Gen., *Audit of Processing of Textual Records* 13 tbl.3 (2013), https://www.archives.gov/files/oig/pdf/2013/audit-report-13-14.pdf.

87. *Id.* at 12 & tbl.2; *see also id.* at 12 ("At the current pace NARA may never get through the processing backlog if no changes are made to the presidential libraries processing program.").

88. *Id.* at 16 & tbl.5.

89. William A. Mayer, Remarks at Ctr. for Research Libraries Conference on Leviathan: Libraries and Government Information in the Age of Big Data (Apr. 24, 2014), https://www.youtube.com/watch?v=6x1UQLccKNw.

90. *Id.*

91. *See* Info. Security Oversight Off., *supra* note 50, at 5 (reporting 52.8 million derivative classification decisions in FY 2015 and 55.2 million in FY 2016). The overwhelming majority of classification decisions are "derivative" rather than "original" in nature. *See id.* at 3–5.

92. *Id.* at 5.

93. *Id.* at 29–30.

94. *Id.* at 29.

95. William H. Leary, *Promoting Openness and Accountability by Making Classification a Two-Way Street*, White House Blog (Dec. 29, 2009), http://thewhitehouseblogus.blogspot.com/2009/12/promoting-openness-and -accountability.html.

96. *See* Info. Security Oversight Off., *2013 Report to the President* 21 (2017), https:// www.archives.gov/files/isoo/reports/2013-annual-report.pdf.

97. *See* Info. Security Oversight Off., *2000 Report to the President* 20 (2001), https://www.archives.gov/files/isoo/reports/2000-annual-report.pdf (reporting that 196 million pages were declassified in FY 1996, 204 million pages in FY 1997, and 193 million pages in FY 1998).

98. *See* Info. Security Oversight Off., *supra* note 50, at 9.

99. *Id.*

100. *Id.*

101. Memorandum from Peter R. Orszag, Director, Off. of Mgmt. & Budget, to the Heads of Exec. Dep'ts & Agencies 3 (Dec. 8, 2009), https://obamawhitehouse.archives.gov/sites/default/files/omb/assets/memoranda_2010/m10-06.pdf.

102. Swetha Kareti, *HHS Only Department to Meet Obama's FOIA Backlog Reduction Order*, Unredacted (Feb. 9, 2017), https://unredacted.com/2017/02/09/hhs-only-department-to-meet-obamas-foia-backlog-reduction-order.

103. *Id.*

104. *See* Adam Marshall, *Agencies Want to Know: Are You Still Interested?*, News Media & L. (Fall 2014), https://www.rcfp.org/browse-media-law-resources/news-media-law/news-media-and-law-fall-2014/agencies-want-know-are-you-st.

105. Pub. Interest Declassification Bd., *Transforming the Security Classification System* 19 (2012), https://www.archives.gov/files/declassification/pidb/recommendations/transforming-classification.pdf.

106. David Langbart et al., Appraisal of Records Covered by N1-59-07-3-P (June 4, 2007) (on file with author).

107. William McAllister, *The Documentary Big Bang, the Digital Records Revolution, and the Future of the Historical Profession*, Passport (Sept. 2010), https://shafr.org/sites/default/files/Sept-2010-v10.pdf, at 12.

108. *See generally* U.S. Dep't of State, *Secretary Clinton Emails*, https://foia.state.gov/Search/Collections.aspx (last visited July 18, 2019).

109. If it takes nine months to review 54,000 emails, then at that rate reviewing 3 percent of 2 billion emails would take 833.3 years.

110. 22 U.S.C. §§ 4351–57 (2012); *see* William B. McAllister & Joshua Botts, *Introduction, in Toward "Thorough, Accurate, and Reliable": A History of the Foreign Relations of the United States Series, supra* note 27, at 1, 1–2 (discussing this statutory mandate).

111. *See* 22 U.S.C. § 4356.

112. Pub. Interest Declassification Bd., *supra* note 105, at 17.

113. *Id.*

114. *See, e.g.*, Roy Rosenzweig, *The Road to Xanadu: Public and Private Pathways on the History Web*, 88 J. Am. Hist. 548 (2001).

115. Terry Kuny, A Digital Dark Ages? Challenges in the Preservation of Electronic Information (1997) (unpublished manuscript), https://archive.ifla.org/IV/ifla63/63kuny1.pdf.

116. *See* Tim Golden, *Haspel, Spies and Videotapes*, ProPublica (May 9, 2018), https://www.propublica.org/article/haspel-spies-and-videotape.

117. *See* U.S. Nat'l Archives, *Unauthorized Disposition of Federal Records*, https://www.archives.gov/records-mgmt/resources/unauthorizeddispositionoffederalrecords (last updated July 10, 2018).

118. *See* David A. Wallace, Preserving the U.S. Government's White House Electronic Mail: Archival Challenges and Policy Implications 2–7 (1998) (unpublished manuscript), http://www.ercim.eu/publication/ws-proceedings /DELOS6/wallace.pdf.

119. *See id.* at 5–6.

120. *Id.* at 12–13.

121. *See* NARA Off. of Inspector Gen., *Audit of the Electronic Records Archives System's Ability to Preserve Records* 24–25 (2013), https://www.archives.gov/files /oig/pdf/2013/audit-report-13-03.pdf.

122. NARA Off. of Inspector Gen., *Audit of NARA's Legacy Systems* 7–9 (2018), https://www.archives.gov/files/audit-of-naras-legacy-systems-oig-report-no -18-aud-06.pdf.

123. NARA Off. of Inspector Gen., *NARA's Electronic Records Archives 2.0 Project* 11 (2017), https://www.archives.gov/files/oig/reports/audit-report-17-AUD-15.pdf.

124. Memorandum from Jeffery D. Zients, Acting Dir., Off. of Mgmt. & Budget, to David S. Ferriero, Archivist of NARA (Aug. 24, 2012), https://www.archives.gov /files/records-mgmt/m-12-18.pdf.

125. U.S. Nat'l Archives, *Fiscal Year 2014–2018 Strategic Plan* 2 (2014), https:// www.archives.gov/files/about/plans-reports/strategic-plan/2014/nara-strategic -plan-2014-2018.pdf. The "initiatives" identified in NARA's 2014 strategic plan should have been initiated in 1974, when the State Department adopted a central filing system based on electronic records.

126. Langbart et al., *supra* note 106.

127. *See* Renato Rocha Souza et al., Using Artificial Intelligence to Identify State Secrets 15–17 (2016) (unpublished manuscript), https://arxiv.org/ftp/arxiv /papers/1611/1611.00356.pdf; NARA, *Frequently Asked Questions (FAQ): Record Group 59: General Records of the Department of State Central Foreign Policy File, 1973–1979*, at 6–7 (2014), https://www.archives.gov/files/research/foreign-policy /state-dept/rg-59-central-files/faqs.pdf.

128. *See* Pamela E. Pennock, *From 1967 to Operation Boulder: The Erosion of Arab Americans' Civil Liberties in the 1970s*, 40 Arab Stud. Q. 41 (2018).

129. NARA, Wars/International Relations: Diplomatic Records, https://aad.archives. gov/aad/series-list.jsp?cat=WR43 (last visited July 18, 2019).

130. David C. Blair & M.E. Maron, *An Evaluation of Retrieval Effectiveness for a Full-Text Document-Retrieval System*, 28 Comm. ACM 289 (1985).

131. Zoë Jackson, *Archiving the Final Frontier: Preserving Space History for the Future*, Perspectives on Hist. (May 1, 2018), https://www.historians.org/publications-and -directories/perspectives-on-history/may-2018/archiving-the-final-frontier -preserving-space-history-for-the-future.

132. Martin Luther King, Jr., *Where Do We Go from Here?*, in *A Testament of Hope: The Essential Writings and Speeches of Martin Luther King, Jr.* 245, 252 (James M. Washington, ed., 1986).

133. Martin Luther King, Jr., *Facing the Challenge of a New Age*, in *id.* at 135, 141.

134. *See* Mary Elise Sarotte, *A Broken Promise? What the West Really Told Moscow About NATO Expansion*, Foreign Aff. (Sept./Oct. 2014), https://www.foreignaffairs .com/articles/russia-fsu/2014-08-11/broken-promise.

135. *See* Abbas Milani, *The Shah's Atomic Dreams*, Foreign Pol'y (Dec. 29, 2010), https://foreignpolicy.com/2010/12/29/the-shahs-atomic-dreams.

136. *Cf.* N.Y. *Times Co. v. United States*, 403 U.S. 713, 729 (1971) (Stewart, J., concurring) ("[W]hen everything is classified, then nothing is classified, and the system becomes one to be disregarded by the cynical or the careless, and to be manipulated by those intent on self-protection or self-promotion.").

137. *The Federalist* No. 70, at 424 (Alexander Hamilton) (Clinton Rossiter, ed., 1961).

138. U.S. Nat'l Archives, *supra* note 125, at 2.

139. Hillary Rodham Clinton, *What Happened* 289, 309 (2017).

140. Off. of Inspector Gen., U.S. Dep't of Justice, A *Review of Various Actions by the Federal Bureau of Investigation and Department of Justice in Advance of the 2016 Election* 257 (2018), https://www.justice.gov/file/1071991/download.

141. Statement by FBI Director James B. Comey on the Investigation of Secretary Hillary Clinton's Use of a Personal E-Mail System, FBI Nat'l Press Off. (July 5, 2016), https://www.fbi.gov/news/pressrel/press-releases/statement-by-fbi-director -james-b-comey-on-the-investigation-of-secretary-hillary-clinton2019s-use-of -a-personal-e-mail-system.

142. *See* Matthew Connelly & Rohan Shah, *Here's What Data Science Tells Us About Hillary Clinton's Emails*, Wash. Post (Nov. 2, 2016), https://www.washingtonpost. com/news/monkey-cage/wp/2016/11/02/heres-what-data-science-tells-us-about -hillary-clintons-emails; *see also* Pozen, *supra* note 67, at 611 (discussing problems of "pervasive uncertainty" that have "always dogged the classification system").

143. *See* Matt Apuzzo, *Report Criticizes Comey but Finds No Bias in F.B.I. Decision on Clinton*, N.Y. Times (June 14, 2018), https://www.nytimes.com/2018/06/14/us /politics/fbi-inspector-general-comey-trump-clinton-report.html.

144. *See supra* note 20 and accompanying text.

145. *See* Comm'n on Protecting and Reducing Gov't Secrecy, *supra* note 46, at XXXII, 48.

146. *See* Eric Schlosser, *Command and Control: Nuclear Weapons, the Damascus Incident, and the Illusion of Safety* 170–72 (2013).

147. *See* James David, *Can We Finally See Those Records? An Update on the Automatic/ Systematic Declassification Review Program*, 76 Am. Archivist 415, 422–27 (2013); Justin Elliott, *U.S. Secrecy System "Literally out of Control,"* Salon (Jan. 31, 2012), https://www.salon.com/2012/01/31/u_s_secrecy_system_literally_out_of_control; Fed. of Am. Scientists, *Congress Halts Automatic Declassification*, https://fas.org/sgp /congress/hr3616am.html (last visited July 18, 2019).

148. Matthew M. Aid, *Declassification in Reverse*, Nat'l Security Archive (Feb, 21, 2016), https://nsarchive2.gwu.edu/NSAEBB/NSAEBB179.

149. *See generally* Christina T. Nasuti, *Shaping the Technology of the Future: Predictive Coding in Discovery Case Law and Regulatory Disclosure Requirements*, 93 N.C. L. Rev. 222 (2014).

150. Data scientists typically do this work as consultants, applying anomaly detection techniques that have been developed (and published) using nonproprietary data. For an example of what is possible using emails from former Enron employees, see Erin S. Crabb, *"Time for Some Traffic Problems": Enhancing E-Discovery and Big Data Processing Tools with Linguistic Methods for Deception Detection*, 9 J. Digital Forensics, Security & L. 167 (2014).

151. *See, e.g.,* Allison J.B. Chaney et al., *Detecting and Characterizing Events,* Proceedings of the 2016 Conference on Empirical Methods in Natural Language Processing (2016), http://ajbc.io/projects/papers/ChaneyWallachConnelly Blei2016.pdf; Yuanjun Gao et al., Mining Events with Declassified Diplomatic Documents (Dec. 21, 2017) (unpublished manuscript), https://arxiv.org/pdf /1712.07319.pdf; Souza et al., *supra* note 127.

152. A rare example of a structured experiment assessing the reliability of review for sensitivity demonstrated in 2017 that even the same reviewer can be inconsistent and inaccurate, and that technologically assisted review achieves better results. Gordon V. Cormack & Maura R. Grossman, *Navigating Imprecision in Relevance Assessments on the Road to Total Recall: Roger and Me,* Proceedings of SIGIR '17 (2017), https://judicialstudies.duke.edu/sites/default/files/centers/judicialstudies /panel-1_navigating_imprecision_in_relevance_assessments_on_the_road.pdf.

153. Pub. Interest Declassification Bd., *supra* note 105, at 1; *see also id.* at 4–5, 25–27 (discussing how technology can "aid classification and declassification").

RESCUING HISTORY (AND ACCOUNTABILITY) FROM SECRECY

154. *Biden's Remarks on McCain's Policies,* N.Y. Times (Sept. 15, 2018), https://www .nytimes.com/2008/09/15/us/politics/15text-biden.html.

155. *See* Adam Mazmanian, *IT Tools Can Help Declassification Backlog, but Is There Funding?,* FCW (June 25, 2015), https://fcw.com/articles/2015/06/25/declassification -and-tech.aspx.

156. *See, e.g.,* U.S. Nat'l Archives, *Using Technology to Improve Classification and Declassification,* Transforming Classification (Mar. 14, 2011), https://transforming -classification.blogs.archives.gov/2011/03/14/using-technology-to-improve -classification-and-declassification.

157. *See* Info. Security Oversight Off., *2017 Report to the President* 16–17 (2018), https://www.archives.gov/files/isoo/reports/2017-annual-report.pdf.

158. *Id.* at 44.

159. I proposed this measure, along with others discussed here, in a short white paper solicited by the Public Interest Declassification Board, a presidential advisory group. *See* Elizabeth Goitein, *Eight Steps to Reduce Overclassification and Rescue Declassification,* Transforming Classification (Dec. 5, 2016), https://transforming-classification.blogs.archives.gov/2016/12/05/eight-steps-to -reduce-overclassification-and-rescue-declassification-by-elizabeth-goitein -the-brennan-center-for-justice.

160. Exec. Order No. 13,526, 3 C.F.R. § 298 (2010).

161. *See* Elizabeth Goitein, *The US Government's Secrecy Problem Just Got Worse,* Al Jazeera Am. (Oct. 17, 2013), http://america.aljazeera.com/articles/2013/10/17 /government-secrecyoverclassificationmohammedalqhatani.html.

162. Elizabeth Goitein, Brennan Ctr. for Justice, *The New Era of Secret Law* (2016), https://www.brennancenter.org/sites/default/files/publications/The_New_Era_of _Secret_Law.pdf.

163. Info. Security Oversight Off., *supra* note 157, at 12–13.

164. These proposals are explained in more detail in another Brennan Center report. Elizabeth Goitein & David M. Shapiro, Brennan Ctr. for Justice, *Reducing*

Overclassification Through Accountability (2011), https://www.brennancenter.org /sites/default/files/legacy/Justice/LNS/Brennan_Overclassification_Final.pdf.

165. Donald Rumsfeld, U.S. Government Incapable of Keeping a Secret (Nov. 2, 2005), available at https://fas.org/sgp/bush/rum110205.pdf.

166. *See* Am. Bar Ass'n Standing Comm. on Law and Nat'l Security, *No More Secrets: National Security Strategies for a Transparent World* (2011), https://www .americanbar.org/content/dam/aba/administrative/law_national_security/no _more_secrets2.authcheckdam.pdf.

ARCHIVING AS POLITICS IN THE NATIONAL SECURITY STATE

167. Stefan Berger, *The Role of National Archives in Constructing National Master Narratives in Europe*, 13 Archival Sci. 1 (2013); Jennifer S. Milligan, *"What Is an Archive?"* in the History of Modern France, in *Archive Stories: Facts, Fictions, and the Writing of History* 159 (Antoinette Burton, ed., 2005).

168. Kirsten Weld, *Paper Cadavers: The Archives of Dictatorship in Guatemala* (2014).

169. Alfred W. McCoy, *Policing America's Empire: The United States, the Philippines, and the Rise of the Surveillance State* (2009).

170. To bolster FOIA in 1974, Congress had to override a presidential veto from Gerald Ford, who had originally wanted to sign the legislation but was dissuaded from doing so by his chief of staff and the chief of staff's deputy, who opposed judicial review of certain classified documents. Three decades later, that chief of staff and his deputy—Donald Rumsfeld and Dick Cheney—would preside over the U.S. invasions of Iraq and Afghanistan. *See* Andrew Glass, *House Overrides FOIA Veto, Nov. 20, 1974*, Politico (Nov. 20, 2014), https://www.politico.com /story/2014/11/house-overrides-freedom-of-information-act-expansion -veto-113032. On the "reactionary" nature of FOIA and its flawed original design, see David E. Pozen, *Freedom of Information Beyond the Freedom of Information Act*, 165 U. Pa. L. Rev. 1097 (2017).

171. Samuel Moyn, *Civil Liberties and Endless War*, Dissent (Fall 2015), https://www .dissentmagazine.org/article/civil-liberties-and-endless-war.

172. *The Rise and Fall of the New Deal Order, 1930–1980* (Steve Fraser & Gary Gerstle, eds., 1990).

173. Jonathan Watts, Dom Phillips & Sam Jones, *Brazil National Museum Blaze in Rio Blamed on Austerity*, Guardian (Sept. 3, 2018), https://www.theguardian.com /world/2018/sep/03/brazils-national-museum-blaze-blamed-on-austerity-cuts -amid-olympics-spending.

174. Jeff Stein, *US Military Budget Inches Closer to $1 Trillion Mark, as Concerns over Federal Deficit Grow*, Wash. Post (June 19, 2018), https://www.washingtonpost .com/news/wonk/wp/2018/06/19/u-s-military-budget-inches-closer-to-1-trillion -mark-as-concerns-over-federal-deficit-grow.

175. Naomi Klein, *Capitalism vs. the Climate*, Nation (Nov. 9, 2011), https://www .thenation.com/article/capitalism-vs-climate.

7

AUTHORITARIAN CONSTITUTIONALISM IN FACEBOOKLAND

David E. Pozen

IN AN IMPORTANT 2018 ARTICLE, Kate Klonick described social media platforms like Facebook as the "New Governors" of online speech.[1] These platforms operate with significant legal discretion. Because of the state action doctrine, they are generally assumed to be beyond the reach of the First Amendment. Because of Section 230 of the Communications Decency Act, they enjoy broad immunity from liability for the user-generated content posted on their sites. Nevertheless, Klonick showed in her article, these platforms have created intricate rules for determining whether and how to limit the circulation of material that is arguably offensive or obscene, rules that in some respects appear to track U.S. free speech norms. By studying internal Facebook documents and interviewing employees, Klonick began to illuminate the mysterious world of social media content moderation.

Klonick now pushes this project further. In this volume's final principal essay, she investigates Facebook's use of the "public figure" and "newsworthiness" concepts in its content moderation decisions. Again drawing heavily on interviews, Klonick recounts how Facebook policy-makers first turned to the public figure concept in an effort to preserve robust debate on matters of widespread concern while cracking down on the cyberbullying of "private" individuals. Newsworthiness, meanwhile, emerged over time as a kind of all-purpose free speech safety valve, invoked to justify keeping up content that would otherwise be removable on any number of grounds. Defining public figures and newsworthiness in an attractive yet administrable manner has been a constant challenge for Facebook. The relevant First Amendment case law is no model of clarity and, even if it were, translating it to a platform of Facebook's scale would be far from straightforward. Klonick walks us down the somewhat mazy path the company has traveled to arrive at its current approach.

Klonick's essay offers many intriguing observations about Facebook's "free speech doctrine" and its relationship to First Amendment law and communications torts. Through vivid examples, the essay also brings to life some of the defining dilemmas the company has faced. But if we step back from the details, how should we understand the overall content moderation regime that Klonick is limning?

At one point in the essay, Klonick proposes that we think of it as "a common law system," given the way Facebook's speech policies evolve "in response to new factual scenarios that present themselves and in response to feedback from outside observers." The common law analogy is appealing on several levels. It highlights the incremental, case-by-case development that some of these policies have undergone, and it implies a certain conceptual and normative integrity, an immanent rationality, to this evolutionary process. Facebook's free speech doctrine, the common law analogy might be taken to suggest, has been working itself pure.[2]

Common law systems are generally understood to involve (1) formally independent dispute resolution bodies, paradigmatically courts, that issue (2) precedential, (3) written decisions. As Klonick's essay makes clear, however, Facebook's content moderation regime contains none of these features. The regulators and adjudicators are one and the same, and the little we know about how speech disputes get resolved and speech policies get changed at Facebook is thanks in no small part to Klonick's own sleuthing.

A very different analogy thus seems equally available: perhaps Facebook's content moderation regime is less like a common law system than like a system of authoritarian or absolutist constitutionalism. Authoritarian constitutionalism, as Alexander Somek describes it, accepts many governance features of constitutional democracy "with the noteworthy exception of . . . democracy itself."[3] The absence of meaningful democratic accountability is justified "by pointing to a goal—the goal of social integration"—whose attainment would allegedly "be seriously undermined if co-operation were sought with [the legislature] or civil society."[4] Absolutist constitutionalism, in Mark Tushnet's formulation, occurs when "a single decisionmaker motivated by an interest in the nation's well-being consults widely and protects civil liberties generally, but in the end, decides on a course of action in the decisionmaker's sole discretion, unchecked by any other institutions."[5]

The analogy to authoritarian/absolutist constitutionalism calls attention to the high stakes of Facebook's regulatory choices and to the awesome power the company wields over its digital subjects as a "sovereign" of cyberspace.[6]

It also foregrounds the tension between Facebook's seemingly sincere concern for free speech values and its explicit aspiration to make users feel socially safe and "connected" (and hence to maximize the time they spend on the site), a tension that is shaped by market forces but ultimately resolved by benevolent leader and controlling shareholder Zuckerberg.

There is a jarring scene in Klonick's essay, in which a photograph from the Boston Marathon bombing that is "graphically violent" within the meaning of Facebook's rules is dutifully taken down by content moderators, only to be put back up by unnamed executives on account of its newsworthiness. These executives may have had good intentions, and they may even have made the right call. The episode is nonetheless a reminder of the potential for arbitrary and cynical assertions of authority from on high in Facebookland—and of the potential disconnect between the policies that Facebook adopts and the policies that a more democratic alternative would generate.

Systems of authoritarian constitutionalism and absolutist constitutionalism are not lawless. But their commitment to civil liberties and the public interest is contingent, instrumental, fragile. If one of these models supplies the most apt analogy for Facebook's regulation of online speech, then the crucial tasks for reformers might well have less to do with refining the company's content moderation rules than with resisting its structural stranglehold over digital media.

Three commentaries identify additional concerns raised by Facebook's content moderation practices. Enrique Armijo argues that First Amendment law on public figures can and should be embraced by Facebook and Twitter, but that constitutional protections for anonymous speech become far more frightening when exported to these platforms. To the extent that First Amendment law has predisposed platform architects to be tolerant of anonymous speech, Armijo suggests, it has led them disastrously astray.

Amy Gajda points out that Facebook's newsworthiness determinations have the potential to affect not only millions of Facebook users, at great cost to privacy values, but also an untold number of journalists. Given courts' unwillingness to define newsworthiness when reviewing privacy claims, Facebook's Community Standards could become a touchstone in future media litigation unless and until judges become more assertive in this area.

Finally, Sarah Haan reminds us that Facebook's decisions about how to regulate speech are inevitably influenced by its profit motive. Indeed,

Facebook admits as much.[7] Maintaining a prosocial expressive environment, Haan observes, is difficult and expensive, and there is little reason to expect Facebook to continue to privilege the preferences of American customers as its business model becomes increasingly focused on other parts of the globe. For those of us who worry about the recent direction of U.S. free speech doctrine,[8] Haan's prediction of a future Facebook less beholden to First Amendment ideology is also an invitation to imagine new approaches to online content moderation and social media regulation.

Facebook v. Sullivan

Kate Klonick*

IN AUGUST 2017, shortly after the Unite the Right rally in Charlottesville, Virginia, a post began circulating on Facebook about Heather Heyer, the woman who was killed while protesting the rally.[9] "Heather Heyer, Woman Killed in Road Rage Incident was a Fat, Childless 32-Year-Old Slut" was shared over 65,000 times.[10] To some Facebook users, the post seemed like obvious hate speech that violated the company's Community Standards and therefore ought to be deleted. To other users, it might have seemed like controversial but permissible commentary on a person whose tragic death had turned her into a public figure. Ultimately, Facebook hedged. The company announced that the post would generally be removed because it originated from the neo-Nazi website *Daily Stormer*, but that the post could still be shared if accompanied by a condemnatory caption.[11]

As this episode reflects, the United States now has two systems to adjudicate disputes arising from harmful speech about other people. The first is older and more familiar: the tort system in which judges resolve claims brought under state defamation and privacy law. The second is newer and less well understood: the content moderation policies and practices of private platforms such as Facebook. These platforms are not, as a general rule, bound by the First Amendment. Yet as this episode also reflects, they have come to rely on some of the same concepts used by courts to resolve tensions between regulating harmful speech and preserving free expression, including the concepts of "public figures" and "newsworthiness."

This essay analyzes Facebook's use of these concepts and the implications for online speech. It begins with a brief summary of the Supreme Court cases that introduced the concepts, with an eye toward the underlying First Amendment theory. It then looks to Facebook's moderation of user speech, discussing how and why exceptions for public figures and newsworthiness were carved out. In developing and applying these exceptions, Facebook has adopted much of the Court's reasoning for creating First Amendment limits to tort liability in cases involving public figures and matters of public concern.

Drawing on this analysis, I argue that comparing these systems reveals three main points that can help both courts and platforms going forward. First, Facebook's partial reliance on online news sources and news aggregators to make public figure determinations runs into many of the same critiques leveled at judges who defer to the media in determining newsworthiness. In some circumstances, this results in Facebook keeping up harmful speech about users who have compelling reasons for wanting the speech taken down. Moreover, these aggregators cannot adequately take into account the localized newsworthiness or public figures in smaller communities, and they therefore threaten to overcensor certain other types of speech.

Second, factual situations arising in the unique environment of online culture reveal—for perhaps the first time since the Court imagined them in 1974—the existence of "truly involuntary public figures."[12] The internet has eroded some of the traditional reasons for specially protecting speech concerning public figures, based on the assumption that people become public figures by choice and that, as public figures, they have greater access to channels of rebuttal. These assumptions are becoming increasingly outdated in the digital age, given the dynamics of online virality and notoriety and given the ubiquity of channels for engaging in counterspeech.

Finally, comparing these systems reveals something significant about Facebook's role in society. Whereas courts apply the concept of newsworthiness to resolve private disputes and newspapers apply the concept to decide what to print, platforms like Facebook rely on it for both tasks. Like a court, Facebook responds to claims involving allegedly defamatory, hateful, or otherwise harmful speech. Like a media company, Facebook curates content and decides which sorts of statements reach a large audience and which don't. From the perspective of its users, Facebook functions as a speech regulator, adjudicator, and publisher all at the same time.

Ultimately, Facebook must determine whose interests it wants to prioritize and what theory of free expression will animate the speech standards it sets. I conclude by suggesting that Facebook's approach ought to vary depending on context. When Facebook acts more like a court in evaluating individual claims of harmful speech, the company should focus on threats to individual users. In contrast, when Facebook acts more like the press in evaluating general newsworthiness exceptions, the company should err on the side of allowing as much content as possible to stay up.

"PUBLIC FIGURES" AND "MATTERS OF PUBLIC INTEREST" IN COMMUNICATIONS TORTS

On March 29, 1960, L. B. Sullivan, an elected commissioner of Montgomery, Alabama, sued the *New York Times* for defamation after the newspaper published an advertisement criticizing the way in which police in Montgomery had treated civil rights demonstrators. Writing for the Court in *New York Times Co. v. Sullivan*,[13] Justice William Brennan explained that while the ad did contain false statements, criticism of government was at the core of the speech protected by the First Amendment. Public officials alleging defamation, accordingly, must prove that the offending statement was made with "'actual malice'—that is, with knowledge that [the statement] was false or with reckless disregard of whether it was false or not."[14] In deciding that constitutional values of free speech outweighed liability for harmful speech in the absence of such malice, the Court identified two main concerns: the democratic imperative of protecting "debate on public issues" and the practical ability of "public officials" to rebut remarks made against them.[15]

Today, *Sullivan* is frequently described as a case about "public officials" or "public figures." This characterization is somewhat misleading. To a significant extent, the public figure doctrine has come to focus on whether speech relates to debate on public issues, reflecting the *Sullivan* Court's overriding concern with what Brennan called a "profound national commitment to the principle that debate on public issues should be uninhibited, robust, and wide-open."[16] The result is that the inquiry into whether a tort plaintiff is a public figure is now essentially an element of a larger inquiry into whether the speech in question is sufficiently a matter of public concern.

The *Sullivan* Court itself gave little guidance on the meaning of "public official."[17] Just a few years after *Sullivan*, in the 1967 case *Time, Inc. v. Hill*, the Court applied "the First Amendment principles pronounced in [*Sullivan*]" to a privacy suit brought against *Life Magazine*.[18] Stressing that "freedom of discussion . . . must embrace all issues about which information is needed,"[19] the *Hill* Court declined to rely on "the distinction which has been suggested between the relative opportunities of the public official and the private individual to rebut defamatory charges."[20] In *Hill*, one sees the Court begin to move away from the "public official" concept in justifying its use of the First Amendment to limit libel, privacy, and related tort claims. Instead, the justices were concerned with preserving debate on "matters of public interest,"[21] broadly defined, and to that end they "declared an expansive view of the First Amendment as protection for all newsworthy material."[22] *Hill* signaled that virtually any matter that would be considered of public concern in a defamation action would be considered newsworthy in a privacy tort action and vice versa.[23]

The Court continued to move away from the "public official" concept in subsequent defamation cases. Later that same year, in *Curtis Publishing Co. v. Butts*,[24] the Court extended First Amendment protection to media reports concerning plaintiffs who were not government officials but who were nonetheless sufficiently prominent in their communities to be considered public figures. Four years later, in *Rosenbloom v. Metromedia, Inc.*, a plurality of the Court attempted to extend *Sullivan* to all matters of public concern, regardless of whether the plaintiff was a public or private figure.[25] Writing for the plurality, Justice Brennan reasoned that a matter "of public or general interest . . . cannot suddenly become less so merely because a private individual is involved, or because in some sense the individual did not 'voluntarily' choose to become involved."[26] To "honor the commitment to robust debate on public issues . . . embodied in the First Amendment," in Brennan's view, the *Sullivan* rule should be applied "to all discussion and communication involving matters of public or general concern, without regard to whether the persons involved are famous or anonymous."[27]

Rosenbloom's doctrinal simplicity—if the jettisoning of the "public figure" notion for the equally ambiguous notion of the "public interest" can be considered simplicity—was short-lived. In the 1974 case *Gertz v. Robert Welch, Inc.*, the majority expressly rejected the extension of *Sullivan* to private defamation plaintiffs.[28] Yet despite disavowing Justice Brennan's approach in *Rosenbloom*, the *Gertz* Court's reconstruction of the public figure concept nonetheless incorporated some of its logic. The Court imagined at least two, and perhaps three,[29] types of public figures: (1) general public figures, (2) limited-purpose public figures, and (3) involuntary public figures. General public figures are those who "occupy positions of such persuasive power and influence that they are deemed public figures for all purposes."[30] Limited-purpose public figures "thrust themselves to the forefront of particular public controversies in order to influence the resolution of the issues involved."[31] Notably, the Court left the third (questionable) category particularly undefined, opining that the "instances of truly involuntary public figures must be exceedingly rare."[32]

Although now glossed with a new taxonomy, the Court's basic rationale for affording constitutional protection to speech concerning public figures remained much the same as the rationale suggested in *Sullivan*. The powerful and notorious—be they so from wealth, fame, or public office—have greater access to counterspeech than private individuals. At the same time, the power, fame, or celebrity of such figures makes their behaviors inherently a matter of public interest, just as the behaviors of someone who thrusts herself into a public controversy are inherently a matter of public interest. And the First Amendment must protect robust public debate on all such matters.

FACEBOOK'S FREE SPEECH DOCTRINE

For Facebook, the idea of making exceptions for newsworthy speech or speech concerning public figures did not arise from tort litigation but rather from the company's efforts to deal with situations in which one user alleges that another user's speech has violated Community Standards. Community Standards are Facebook's public rules about the types of speech that users may post on the platform. Because huge amounts of user content are posted each day, Facebook cannot proactively police all speech violations and must rely to a large extent on users to flag speech that might be in violation. The flagged speech is then reviewed by human content moderators—individuals trained to apply Facebook's rules and determine whether the reported speech actually runs afoul of them. Speech that is found to be in violation is removed. The rest stays up.[33]

Somewhat like a common law system, Facebook updates its Community Standards and the internal guidelines used by moderators, both in response to new factual scenarios that present themselves and in response to feedback from outside observers. The first iterations of the Community Standards and content moderation policies were created in 2009 largely by Dave Willner, who was then part of the Site Integrity Operations team. Willner later trans-ferred to a team focused on "organic" content (user-generated content, as opposed to advertising or commercial content) under Jud Hoffman, who joined Facebook in 2010 as global policy manager. Hoffman and Willner were the principal players in a six-person group established to formalize and consolidate the informal rules that Facebook's content moderators had been using, thereby enhancing their consistency and transparency.

FACEBOOK'S PUBLIC FIGURE EXCEPTION FOR BULLYING

Whereas *Sullivan*'s public figure doctrine grew out of claims of defama-tion, both Hoffman and Willner describe Facebook's concept of public figures as emerging from claims about bullying.[34] In 2009, Facebook was facing heavy pressure from anti-cyberbullying advocacy groups to do more to prevent kids from being bullied online.[35] The problem, however, was that traditional academic definitions of bullying seemed impossible to translate to online content moderation. "How do we write a rule about bullying?" recounts Willner. "What is bullying? What do you mean by that? It's not just things that are upsetting; it's defined as a pattern of abusive or harassing unwanted behavior over time that is occurring between a higher power [and] a lower power. But that's not an answer to the problem that resides in the content—you can't determine a power differential from looking at the content. You often cannot even do it from looking at their profiles."[36]

The apparent impossibility of employing a traditional definition of bul-lying meant that Facebook had to make a choice. It could err on the side of keeping up potentially harmful content, or it could err on the side of removing all potential threats of bullying, even if some of the removed con-tent turned out to be benign. Faced with intense pressure from advocacy groups and media coverage on cyberbullying, Facebook opted for the latter approach but with a caveat. The new presumption in favor of taking down speech reported to be bullying would apply only to speech directed at pri-vate individuals. "What we said was, 'Look, if you tell us this is about you, and you don't like it, and you're a private individual, you're not a public figure, then we'll take it down,'" said Hoffman. "Because we can't know whether all of those other elements [of bullying] are met, we had to just make the call to create a default rule for removal of bullying."[37]

Although he denies borrowing directly from the First Amendment public figure doctrine, Hoffman's justification for creating this exception tracks the reasoning of *Sullivan* and subsequent cases in treating certain targets of allegedly harmful speech differently on account of their public status and the public interest in their doings. According to Hoffman, this approach reflected Facebook's mission statement, which at that time was "Make the world more open and connected." "Broadly, we interpreted 'open' to mean 'more content.' Yes, that's a bit of a free speech perspective, but then we also had a concern with things like bullying and revenge porn," Hoffman recalls. "But while trying to take down that bad content, we didn't want to make it impossible for people to criticize the president or a person in the news. It's important there's a public discussion around issues that affect people, and this is how we drew the line."[38]

In trying to resolve these dilemmas, Hoffman and his colleagues sought to "focus on the mission" of Facebook rather than adopt "wholesale . . . a kind of U.S. jurisprudence free expression approach."[39] They quickly realized, however, that the mission had to be balanced against competing interests such as users' safety and the company's bottom line. While Hoffman and Willner were at Facebook, the balance was often struck in favor of "leaving content up," but they were always searching for new ways to address concerns about harmful speech. "We felt like Facebook was the most important platform for this kind of communication, and we felt like it was our responsibility to figure out an answer to this," says Hoffman.[40]

The policy required a new way of determining if someone was a public figure. Facebook told its moderators that when reviewing a piece of content flagged for bullying, they should use Google News.[41] If the user who was the subject of the allegedly bullying content came up in a Google News search, she would be considered a public figure—and the content would be kept up.

By tying the public figure determination to the algorithmic calculations of Google News, Facebook sought to maintain vibrant discussion on matters of public concern while creating a temporal constraint on the "limited-purpose public figure" concept, as individuals who had thrust themselves (or been thrust by circumstance) into a particular public controversy would likely remain in Google News search results only as long as the controversy was topical and newsworthy. For this reason, Willner reflects, "calling the exception [an exception for] 'public figures' was probably a mistake. A more accurate way of thinking about it is as a newsworthy person."[42]

Despite the arguable conflation of "public figure" and "newsworthiness" occasioned by relying on Google News, both Hoffman and Willner were opposed to the idea of a general exception to the Community Standards that would prevent any "newsworthy" piece of content from being taken down. Facebook's approach to this issue would develop on a slightly different track.

FACEBOOK'S GENERAL NEWSWORTHINESS EXCEPTION

For most of the history of Facebook's content moderation, no exceptions were made for content that violated Community Standards but was newsworthy. Overtly sexual, graphically violent, or "extremist" content would be taken down regardless of whether it had cultural or political significance as news. This was a deliberate choice made by Hoffman and Willner. But this policy came under increasing pressure.

Members of the policy team recall an incident in 2013 concerning a graphic picture from the Boston Marathon bombing as a turning point toward the creation of an exception for newsworthy content. The image in question was of a man in a wheelchair being wheeled away with one leg ripped open below the knee to reveal a long, bloody bone. The picture had three versions. One was cropped so that the leg was not visible. A second was a wide-angle shot in which the leg was visible but less obvious. The third, and most controversial, version clearly showed the man's "insides on the outside"—the content moderation team's shorthand rule for when content was graphically violent. Despite being published in multiple media outlets, Facebook policy dictated that any links to or images of the third version of the picture must be removed.[43] "Philosophically, if we were going to take the position that [insides on the outside] was our definition of gore and we didn't allow gore, then just because it happened in Boston didn't change that," remembers one of the team members on call that day.[44] Policy executives at Facebook disagreed, however, and reinstated all such posts on the grounds of newsworthiness.

For some members of the policy team, who had spent years trying to create administrable rules, the imposition of such an exception seemed a radical departure from the company's commitment to procedural consistency. Some of their reasoning echoes the *Gertz* Court's rationale for reining in *Rosenbloom*.[45] In his opinion for the Court in *Gertz*, Justice Lewis Powell worried openly about allowing "judges to decide on an *ad hoc* basis which publications address issues of 'general or public interest' and which do not."[46]

Many at Facebook worried similarly that "newsworthiness as a standard is extremely problematic. The question is really one of 'newsworthy to whom?' and the answer to that is based on ideas of culture and popularity."[47] The result, some feared, would be a mercurial exception that would, moreover, privilege American users' views on newsworthiness to the potential detriment of Facebook's users in other countries.

Although there were other one-off exceptions made for incidents like the Boston Marathon bombing, Facebook's internal content moderation policies continued to have no general exception for newsworthiness until September 2016, when a famous Norwegian author, Tom Egeland, posted a well-known historical picture to his Facebook page. The photograph, "The Terror of War," depicts a nine-year-old Vietnamese girl naked in the street after a napalm attack (for this reason, the photo is often called "Napalm Girl"). In part because of its graphic nature, the photo was a pivotal piece of journalism during the Vietnam War.[48] But it violated Facebook's Community Standards.[49] Accordingly, Facebook removed the photo and suspended Egeland's account. Because of Egeland's stature, the takedown itself received news coverage. Espen Egil Hansen, the editor-in-chief of the Norwegian newspaper *Aftenposten*, published a letter to Zuckerberg on *Aftenposten*'s front page calling for Facebook to take a stand against censorship. Hours later, Facebook's chief operating officer Sheryl Sandberg admitted that the company had made a mistake and promised that the rules would be rewritten to allow for posting of the photo.[50] Shortly thereafter, Facebook issued a press release underscoring the company's commitment to "allowing more items that people find newsworthy, significant, or important to the public interest—even if they might violate our standards."[51]

The "Terror of War" incident led Facebook to start looking more broadly at how it evaluated newsworthiness outside the context of bullying. "After the 'Terror of War' controversy, we realized that we had to create new rules for imagery that we'd normally want to disallow, but for context reasons that policy doesn't work," says Peter Stern, head of Product Policy Stakeholder Engagement at Facebook. "And that's led us to think about newsworthiness across the board. When we do these things, we have two considerations: safety of individuals on the one hand and voice on the other."[52] But how exactly should "voice" be taken into consideration? Here, again, Facebook has increasingly aligned itself with the Court's public figure doctrine. "When someone enters the public eye," Stern explains, "we want to allow a broader scope of discussion."[53]

THE CURRENT PUBLIC FIGURE AND NEWSWORTHINESS STANDARDS

Over the last several years, Facebook's content moderation policies have continued to evolve and to become somewhat less mechanical and more context-sensitive. For example, in recent months Facebook has modified its rules on bullying and harassment of public figures. "Our new policy does not allow certain high-intensity attacks, like calls for death, directed at a certain public figure," members of the Facebook policy team told me on a recent call.[54] In the past, they explained, a statement such as "Kim Kardashian is a whore" would never be removed for bullying or harassment (whereas a statement calling a private individual a "whore" would be). But now Facebook allows some speech directed at public figures, when it is posted on their own pages or accounts, to be removed depending on the severity of the language. Under this new regime, public figures are defined as people elected or assigned through a political process to a government position; people with hundreds of thousands of fans or followers on a social media account; people employed by a news or broadcast organization or who speak publicly; or people who are mentioned in multiple news articles within a certain recent time period as determined by a news search.

Facebook's current policies on newsworthy content are somewhat harder to pin down. Unlike the term "public figures," which is primarily used by Facebook for purposes of its bullying standards, "newsworthiness" is now a possible exception to all of the company's general guidelines for removing offensive content. And unlike the public figure determinations made in the bullying context, determinations of newsworthiness do not rely on news aggregators. Instead, every suggestion of possible newsworthy content is made by a person and evaluated by Facebook employees on a case-by-case basis.

In deciding whether to keep up otherwise removable content on the basis of its newsworthiness, Facebook officials stress that they weigh the value of "voice" against the risk of harm. Assessments of harm are informed by the nature as well as the substance of the objectionable content. Hateful speech on its own, for instance, might be seen as less harmful than a direct call to violence. Facebook officials maintain, however, that most of the newsworthiness decisions are around nudity. Difficult decisions include what to do about nudity in public protests. "Just a few years ago, we took that down," states David Caragliano, a policy manager at Facebook. "But it's really important to leave this up consistent with our principles of voice. That's led to a policy change that's now at scale for the platform."[55] The non-hateful, nonviolent expressive conduct of public protesters, it seems, will today almost always be considered newsworthy and therefore will not be taken down.

FACEBOOK VERSUS *SULLIVAN*

As the foregoing discussion reflects, the two systems in the United States for adjudicating claims of harmful speech—through tort lawsuits and through private online speech platforms like Facebook—share a number of similarities. Both have developed rules to weigh individual harms against a baseline commitment to enabling as much speech as possible. In the courts, defamation law gives plaintiffs recourse for untruthful speech against them, except that plaintiffs who are public figures have a substantially higher burden to meet. On Facebook, an anti-bullying policy gives users who have been harassed the ability to have the harassing speech removed, except that users who are public figures can rarely avail themselves of this option. In the courts, privacy law allows plaintiffs to hold defendants liable for certain invasions of privacy, except when the underlying information is deemed to be of sufficient public interest. On Facebook, users can request that disturbing content such as graphically violent or hateful speech be taken down, except when the underlying information is deemed to be of sufficient public interest. Federal judges and Facebook executives justify these exceptions in similar terms, citing the importance of preserving public discourse and the special capacities of people who are powerful, famous, or at the forefront of a particular public controversy to rebut speech against them. Even though Facebook is not generally bound by the First Amendment, its content moderation policies were largely developed by U.S. lawyers trained and acculturated in U.S. free speech norms, and this cultural background has invariably affected their thinking.

The observation that First Amendment principles like "public figures" and "newsworthiness" have wended their way into Facebook's content moderation policies is interesting in its own right. But it also suggests several broader lessons about the structure of digital discourse. First, Facebook's use of Google News for its public figure determinations underscores the dangers of reducing such judgments to mechanical calculations. Second, Facebook and other digital speech platforms have helped bring into being the elusive "involuntary public figure" imagined in *Gertz*, even as they undermine the access-to-counterspeech justification for keeping up more speech about public figures. Finally, Facebook's struggle to create principled exceptions for newsworthy content underscores how the company straddles the roles of regulator, adjudicator, and publisher in controlling access to speech for both speakers and listeners.

THE PROBLEMS WITH DEFINING "PUBLIC FIGURE" ALGORITHMICALLY

Facebook's use of Google News to determine whether a person is a public figure provides a vivid illustration of the problems that may be raised when such definitions are outsourced to the media marketplace.

Although it has been suggested to me that this policy may be changing, Facebook's method for ascertaining public figure status has traditionally turned in part on the presence or absence of an individual's name in news search results, which are effectively an averaging algorithm of media outlets' publication decisions. (Facebook's newsworthiness determinations, in contrast, involve multiple layers of human review.) This runs straight into the threat of what Clay Shirky has called "algorithmic authority," insofar as "an unmanaged process of extracting value from diverse, untrustworthy sources" is treated as authoritative without any human second-guessing or vouching for the validity of the outcome.[56]

As commentators have pointed out for over fifty years in a closely related context, if newsworthiness is defined solely in terms of news outlets' publication decisions, then granting a special legal privilege for newsworthy content is liable to swallow torts such as invasion of privacy. "The publisher has almost certainly published any given report because he judged it to be of interest to his audience . . . and believed that it would encourage them to purchase his publications in anticipation of more of the same," a student comment observed in 1963. "A plaintiff in a privacy action would thus have lost almost before he started."[57] Partly for this reason, courts making these determinations have considered a range of factors[58] and, especially in recent years, have been unwilling to defer entirely to the media.[59]

Outsourcing public figure determinations to Google News may well result both in too much harmful speech being kept up *and* in too much benign speech being taken down. As for the former, consider the case of an involuntary public figure. Although a rare phenomenon in the physical world, the involuntary public figure is far from an unusual occurrence in the online realm (more on this below). Countless stories exist of relatively unknown individuals being filmed or photographed and then finding themselves subject to widespread online shaming and related news coverage.[60] Should such an individual report any particularly offensive posts to Facebook for violating the company's anti-bullying rules, the Google News search results would indicate that the individual is a public figure at the center of a newsworthy event and—at least until recently—the posts would stay up. Google News is unequipped to distinguish between situations where people have voluntarily "thrust themselves to the forefront of particular public controversies"[61] and situations where speech platforms have themselves facilitated the creation of "news."

As for the problem of taking down too much benign speech, consider that the vast majority of content that gets flagged for Facebook moderators, according to many different Facebook employees with whom I have spoken over the years, is not speech that amounts to bullying, defamation, or a privacy violation but rather content that certain users simply don't like. Moreover, a great number of virtual communities and groups have formed on Facebook, many of which have their own distinctive cultures and social structures. Provocative content flagged in these communities may not seem to involve any "public figures" when judged against a global Google News search and therefore may be removed even it involves a matter of intense interest within that local community.

In short, relying exclusively on algorithmic news aggregators to determine who is and who is not a public figure is an invitation to over- and under-removal of content. Whereas the Supreme Court has essentially folded the determination of whether a tort plaintiff is a public figure into a larger inquiry into whether the speech in question is sufficiently a matter of public concern, Facebook seems to have done the opposite by using newsworthiness as an element of defining public figures. It may be impossible to define either of these concepts in an entirely satisfying way. At the very least, however, both courts and platforms should start to rethink the treatment of people involuntarily thrust into the spotlight, as the next section describes.

THE RISE OF THE INVOLUNTARY PUBLIC FIGURE

In attempting to define the concept of public figures, the *Gertz* Court expressly included not only individuals who "have assumed roles of especial prominence in the affairs of society" but also individuals who have "thrust [themselves] into the vortex of [a] public issue."[62] Both of these formulations seemed to assume that public figure status is something voluntarily attained. But could there be an involuntary public figure? The Court gave a vague and dismissive answer: "Hypothetically, it may be possible for someone to become a public figure through no purposeful action of his own, but the instances of truly involuntary public figures must be exceedingly rare."[63]

Cases since *Gertz* have done little to clear up this vagueness. As a general matter, these cases require that a person who is not in a role of especial prominence "take voluntary, affirmative steps to thrust himself or herself into the limelight," and "they make it difficult for anyone to be found an involuntary public figure."[64] The *Restatement (Second) of Torts* defines involuntary public figures as "individuals who have not sought publicity or consented to it, but through their own conduct or otherwise have become a legitimate subject of public interest. They have, in other words, become 'news.'"[65] The only examples given by the *Restatement* of such figures are "victims of crime" and "those who commit crime or are accused of it."[66]

For the first time since the Court imagined them in *Gertz*, the democratization of publishing platforms on the internet has created a generation of truly involuntary public figures. Some of these public figures are more compellingly "involuntary" than others.[67] One of the clearest examples in recent internet history is that of "Alex from Target." On November 2, 2014, an anonymous Twitter user "tweeted a picture of a Target employee wearing the name tag 'Alex' and bagging items behind the cashier. In the following 24 hours, the tweet gained over 1,000 retweets and 2,000 favorites."[68] Over the next day, "the hashtag #AlexFromTarget was mentioned more than one million times on Twitter while the keyword 'Alex From Target' was searched over 200,000 times on Google."[69] Shortly thereafter, Twitter users started an effort to identify the "Alex" in the photo, which resulted in the publication of his Twitter handle, @acl163, at which time he amassed more than 250,000 followers.[70] Two days later, he appeared on the television talk show *Ellen*. Death threats, denigrating posts, and "fabricate[d] stories" soon followed.[71]

It is hard to argue that Alex from Target, a "global celebrity" with hundreds of thousands of social media followers,[72] is merely a private figure. Similarly, it is hard to argue that Alex from Target is a *voluntary* public figure who thrust himself into the vortex of a public issue by bagging groceries at his part-time job. Moreover, Alex from Target does not fall into the one category of involuntary public figures that has been clearly established in the case law thus far: people who have been victims of crimes or accused of committing crimes. Because of the strong public interest in crime and criminal justice, courts have been very reluctant to allow liability for harmful speech about such individuals, even when their stories are highly sympathetic.[73]

How should First Amendment law treat an involuntary public figure such as Alex from Target in whom the public interest arguably has less relevance to democratic deliberation? One option is to decide that this collection of facts makes such a person more like a private figure than a public one and therefore to give lower constitutional protection to harmful speech about her. This approach recognizes the importance of not allowing the actions of others to extinguish ordinary people's privacy rights. A second option would be to treat Alex from Target like a crime victim. Under this approach, judges would not have to make controversial judgments about the degree to which speech about Alex from Target does or does not contribute to public debate; all the memes, posts, and cultural engagement generated by his celebrity would be enough to trigger First Amendment protection for anything that is said about him. For better or worse, the privacy and reputational interests of "Alex the Person" would give way to the public interest in Alex from Target.

Perhaps most persuasively, however, the Alex from Target episode might be seen as a reason to dispatch with the "voluntary" and "involuntary" concepts altogether. The Court's original rationale for granting special First Amendment protection to speech about public figures, as discussed above, emphasized that such figures had greater access to means of rebuttal and had assumed the risk of unwanted publicity through their own actions. Yet in both systems of speech regulation discussed in this essay—courts and private platforms—these rationales are becoming increasingly outmoded. The ease of publishing speech online means that virtually every person now has access to means of rebuttal. The powerful and the well-connected may be better equipped to amplify their speech, at least in some cases. But for everyone who feels victimized by the expression of others, projecting one's counterspeech has never been easier, even as raising one's voice above the fray has never been harder.[74] Moreover, the enormous volume of hateful and harassing speech that circulates online has raised the stakes for victims of such speech. To require the targets of this speech to surrender their privacy rights whenever they speak out in response risks "blaming the victim"[75] and chilling their expression. The growing number of truly involuntary public figures, meanwhile, means that there will be more and more victims who have not so much thrust themselves into the vortex of a public controversy as have been consumed by it.

In recent months, as discussed above, Facebook appears to have adopted several new criteria for identifying public figures and to have moved away from its prior position that public figures receive no protection from bullying or harassment. Even if speech concerns public figures, the company's content moderators will now consider whether it is directed toward an individual on a personal page or group page, rather than in general conversation elsewhere on the site, as well as whether the language rises to the level of an attack.[76] This new policy continues to permit involuntary public figures to be subject to more bullying and harassment than nonpublic figures. Given that platforms like Facebook must make millions of content moderation decisions a day, there is no way for the company to analyze every case of arguable involuntariness in a rigorous manner. The new policy does, however, allow for more sensitive judgments about speech concerning the full range of public figures. Going forward, both Kim Kardashian and Alex from Target should have an easier time convincing Facebook to remove the most abusive posts made directly against them.

STRADDLING THE ROLE OF GOVERNOR AND PUBLISHER

In a long line of cases, U.S. courts have developed the public figure and newsworthiness doctrines to help balance promotion of uninhibited speech with protection from harmful speech. Newspapers and, later, other types of media companies were given substantial deference in deciding what to publish. Platforms like Facebook do not map neatly onto this traditional model. They are both the governors, setting speech policies and adjudicating speech disputes, and the publishers, controlling access to speech on behalf of speakers and listeners. They are the *Sullivan* Court, and they are the *New York Times*.

As a "new governor" of the public sphere, Facebook has created intricate rules and systems to weigh individuals' rights to control what is said about them against the values of free expression.[77] These rules reflect the strong pro-speech orientation of modern First Amendment theory, and some of the key concepts they use—including public figures and newsworthiness—originated in First Amendment law. Unlike the courts, however, Facebook does not adjudicate legal claims for monetary damages based on factual scenarios in which it has no direct stake. It adjudicates extralegal claims about whether allegedly harmful speech should be kept up or taken down *on its own platform*. In this sense, Facebook is more like a newspaper, deciding what is or isn't published within its pages.

The courts and the press have sought to preserve robust public debate on matters of public concern. Facebook seems to have this same goal, but it must also satisfy shareholders and take into account the interests, expectations, and concerns of billions of users worldwide. Facebook's mission statement is interestingly ambiguous in this regard. "Giv[ing] people the power to build community and bring the world closer together"[78] could be seen as a mandate either for vigorous suppression of antisocial content or for free speech absolutism.

It is not clear what Facebook itself makes of this ambiguity. A few weeks before the 2016 presidential election, the company's founder and chief executive Mark Zuckerberg held a closed-door "town hall" in Menlo Park, California. The meeting came in response to weeks of agitation by employees charged with creating and enforcing the company's content moderation policies. Some of these employees were upset that even though then-candidate Donald Trump's posts about a Muslim ban appeared to violate Facebook's policies on hate speech, the posts were not taken down. Over the course of the two-hour meeting, Zuckerberg justified this decision on the ground that Trump's status as a "public figure" made the posts "newsworthy or in the public interest."[79] "In the weeks ahead," Facebook announced shortly afterward, "we're going to begin allowing more items that people find newsworthy, significant, or important to the public interest—even if they might otherwise violate our standards."[80]

A little less than two years later, on July 26, 2018, Facebook removed four videos from pages belonging to Alex Jones, the controversial radio host, conspiracy theorist, and founder of the fake news site Infowars. The removed videos were found to have violated Facebook's Community Standards by encouraging physical harm (bullying) and attacking "someone based on their religious affiliation or gender identity" (hate speech).[81] A few weeks later, more content was removed, triggering all of Jones's pages to be unpublished on Facebook. In a statement made after the decision, Facebook explained that "upon review, we have taken [Jones's pages] down for glorifying violence, which violates our graphic violence policy, and using dehumanizing language to describe people who are transgender, Muslims and immigrants, which violates our hate speech policies."[82]

Both the Trump and the Jones decisions concern high-profile figures with massive followings who made statements that violate Facebook's policies against hate speech, yet one was blocked and the other not. Facebook's explanation of its policies suggests that the two decisions can be reconciled through a simple test that balances "the public interest value of the content against the risk of real-world harm."[83] Jones's speech was bullying, hateful, and low-value, on this view, and it was specifically harmful to other users on the site. To many at Facebook, blocking Jones may have appeared a relatively easy call. But it seems equally easy to argue that Trump's anti-Muslim rhetoric, which led more or less directly to a travel ban once he became president, did much more significant "real-world harm" than Jones's conspiracy theories. Similarly, it is unclear whether Jones's Facebook pages would have stayed up had he simply run for political office and thereby *amplified* his offending messages and their potential negative impact on society.

There are no easy answers to the question of how Facebook should strike the balance between protecting users and protecting free expression. Debates like the ones raised by these examples—whether to publish inflammatory content and what factors to weigh in that decision— are usually thought to be the province of newsrooms. Today, alongside the adjudication of individual speech grievances, they are also the province of platforms.

CONCLUSION

The realization that Facebook is playing the part of the *Sullivan* Court and the *New York Times* not only is descriptively illuminating but also provides tools for more nuanced normative assessments of how Facebook should develop its speech policies going forward. These two roles, of governor and publisher, can supply guiding values. Facebook should be somewhat less concerned with avoiding the suppression of speech when it finds itself acting like a court and evaluating claims that specific content has harmed a specific individual, and more concerned with avoiding suppression when it finds itself acting like the press in evaluating general newsworthiness.

Under its existing policies, Facebook acts most like a court when making "public figure" determinations for purposes of deciding whether content that violates the site's anti-bullying rules will nevertheless stay up. In this role, Facebook should maintain a robust commitment to free expression but also recognize that features of the internet—including the dynamics of online virality, shaming, and involuntary notoriety—can amplify the harms of abusive remarks directed at particular public figures. In contrast, when Facebook acts like the press in balancing considerations of newsworthiness against more generalized concerns of social harm, the company should be guided by a strong preference for keeping up as much human speech as possible consistent with its users' safety and security—perhaps more so than a traditional media outlet that doesn't also double as a public forum. And across each of these domains, Facebook must continue to develop more consistent and transparent protocols for content removal. It should not take so many hours of academic sleuthing to figure out basic facts about what these protocols look like and how they are being administered.

Meet the New Governors, Same as the Old Governors

Enrique Armijo

IT IS A CATEGORY ERROR to assume that an old paradigm is obsolete simply because of the emergence, or even the dominance, of a new one. Although the title of Kate Klonick's thoughtful essay sets Facebook and *New York Times Co. v. Sullivan* against each other by inserting a "v." in between them, one upshot of her piece, and indeed of much of her other important work in this area,[84] is that the First Amendment continues to play a critical role in resolving disputes about what people should be able to say online. What Klonick describes isn't a face-off between social media content moderation and First Amendment law. It's more like the story of a child who thought herself equipped by her parents to understand the world but then finds herself in a novel setting—a semester abroad, a rave—where some of the rules she was taught don't seem to help.

To unpack some of the free expression-related issues raised by social media, it is useful to separate the content moderation practices Klonick discusses into two related but distinct types: what can be said about whom, and who can say it. With respect to the first type, the influence of the First Amendment still reigns, and for a good reason. It still works. To paraphrase Judge Easterbrook's early critique of the law of cyberspace, general First Amendment rules have proven themselves adaptable to the "specialized endeavors" of social media,[85] even if the role of applying those rules has largely shifted from courts to moderators. The converse is also true. We should be careful not to let that which we perceive as special about the social media context overwhelm the soundness, wisdom, and relevance of the general rules.

With respect to the second type of practice, however, the First Amendment has not been nearly as helpful for resolving content moderation problems. And if social media has largely failed to become the engine for social change and political discourse that many hoped it would, the influence of First Amendment ideology on questions concerning who can speak online—and in particular its valorization of anonymous speech—is one reason why.

LIMITED-PURPOSE PUBLIC FIGURES AND SOCIAL MEDIA

As Klonick writes, in *Gertz v. Robert Welch, Inc.*[86] the U.S. Supreme Court extended its actual malice doctrine to defamation plaintiffs who have come to be known as "limited-purpose public figures"—otherwise private people who have voluntarily inserted themselves into controversies and thus become the subject of public discussion. The Court concluded that these people should, like public officials, have to show actual malice in defamation suits relating to the controversies of which they are a part, because they assume the risk of being talked about negatively and even falsely when they enter public debates "in order to influence the resolution of the issues involved."[87] The Court also responded to a potential unfairness in its ruling, insofar as it might sweep in people who do not *choose* to be a public figure. As Klonick notes, the Court said that "hypothetically, it may be possible for someone to become a public figure through no purposeful action of his own, but the instances of truly involuntary public figures must be exceedingly rare."[88]

Klonick is absolutely correct that the internet has put the lie to the Court's suggestion in *Gertz* that someone can involuntarily enter public debate only in the rarest of cases. By making public so much of day-to-day life that was formerly private, social media has been used to thrust publicity upon many individuals through no fault of their own. As Klonick also notes, there is a significant First Amendment risk in permitting the limited-purpose public figure doctrine to take online notoriety into account. To take proper account of this risk, however, it is helpful to consider the case not of Alex from Target but of a different Alex: Alex Jones.

Recently, several parents of Sandy Hook Elementary School children sued Alex Jones for defamation, pointing to Jones's statements falsely implicating the parents in faking the shooting and deaths of their children.[89] In his response to the suit, Jones has argued that the plaintiff-parents are limited-purpose public figures—that they have been discussed as part of, and have inserted themselves into, the larger controversy around gun rights in the United States—and that under *Gertz* they should therefore have to prove that his statements about them were made with actual malice. It is true that some Sandy Hook parents (though not the plaintiffs who have sued Jones) became vocal participants in the gun-control movement in the wake of the tragedy and that others have organized online to try and prevent future attacks. But Jones and similar defendants should not be able to expand the bounds of the controversies that they themselves create so as to raise the burden of proof for those implicated in the controversies who sue them for reputational harm. Making such individuals prove actual malice in defamation cases gets the First Amendment backward. It will encourage individuals to take the tragedies that happen to them and swallow them silently—to not get active, to not connect with others who have similar purposes, to not share in sorrow and attempt to make change.

No one would have volunteered for the kind of attention that the Sandy Hook parents have received, and no one would argue that the controversy of which they became a part was not widely discussed, particularly online. But if a court were to "dispatch with the 'voluntary' and 'involuntary' concepts altogether," as Klonick proposes, and go on to find that the parents were public figures because of that attention alone, then future parents might not speak out at all, which would do significant harm to the marketplace of ideas that the First Amendment is intended to promote.

Courts should therefore continue to ask whether, consistent with *Gertz*, a plaintiff in a defamation case has acted voluntarily—exercising her will to undertake "a course of action that invites attention."[90] This inquiry should not turn on whether a speech platform has itself facilitated discussion of that person. After all, Alex from Target voluntarily appeared on *Ellen*. But one should not be transformed into a public figure through no affirmative, purposeful act of one's own. The long-standing law of defamation gets this right.

Judicial doctrine has another public figure rule that remains relevant online: a defamation defendant cannot cause a plaintiff to become a public figure by dint of the statements that gave rise to the claim.[91] The relevant controversy, in other words, "must have existed prior to the publication of the defamatory statement."[92] This too provides a useful heuristic for content moderation. Klonick describes a policy in which Facebook uses Google News to determine whether an individual is a public figure when deciding whether to take down bullying speech about or directed at that person. The case law suggests that if the results of that search include only stories about the complained-of bullying itself, then the victim of the bullying is a private person. Looking at the sheer number of Google News hits or at whether an individual is being discussed widely on social media obscures, rather than clarifies, these questions. Good old-fashioned First Amendment law does the job much better.

The same is true with regard to "newsworthy" yet harmful content generally. The "more protection for speech about issues and groups, less protection for speech about specific individuals" decision rule that Klonick appears to recommend (my paraphrase, not her words) loosely tracks the development of legal rules around group libel and hate speech in the years since the Supreme Court's 1952 decision in *Beauharnais v. Illinois*.[93] In recent decades, the federal appellate courts have concluded that cases such as *Sullivan* have "so washed away the foundations of *Beauharnais* that it [cannot] be considered authoritative."[94] Accordingly, First Amendment doctrine already calls for general statements about groups to receive more protection than statements about particular individuals. Both Facebook's Community Standards and Klonick's proposed intervention point content moderation decisions regarding takedowns in the same direction as that doctrine. And even before the First Amendment entered the tort law picture at all, many state courts faced with claims of privacy violations or intentional infliction of emotional distress took into account a public interest- and newsworthiness-based "privilege to interfere"[95] with the legal interests those torts protect—the very same considerations that social media companies take into account when deciding what to take down or keep up.

The challenge for Klonick's decision rule, or for Facebook or Twitter in applying it, is that the hard cases are not those in which offending content is *either* about a specific individual *or* about a matter that is "generally" newsworthy. The hard cases are those in which the offending content is about a specific individual who is herself newsworthy. In such a case, it is perfectly legitimate to ask—again, as current doctrine does—whether the individual is herself a primary source of or reason for that newsworthiness and, if so, to count that fact as relevant with respect to that individual's burden of proof if she sues the source of the content for defamation. This is the question the Supreme Court asked with respect to Elmer Gertz, and it is the question courts should ask with respect to Alex from Target or a Sandy Hook parent.[96] It is also a relevant question with respect to whether content about those individuals should be taken down by a social media moderator.

So, existing law is well equipped to handle public figure questions, even in the age of online oversharing. But content moderation policies concerning who may speak present an entirely different set of challenges. And the problem with these policies is not too little First Amendment, but rather too much.

FOR EVERY ONE MRS. MCINTYRE, A THOUSAND TROLLS

The Supreme Court has forcefully and consistently held that the right to express oneself anonymously is protected by the First Amendment. In the 1995 case *McIntyre v. Ohio Elections Commission*,[97] the Court declared that the right of Margaret McIntyre to express her opposition to a proposed school tax levy without putting her name to that opposition was rooted in a free speech tradition older than the republic. The speaker's "decision in favor of anonymity may be motivated by fear of economic or official retaliation," noted the Court, or "by concern about social ostracism . . . or merely by a desire to preserve as much of one's privacy as possible."[98]

Individuals certainly do use Twitter's ability to speak pseudonymously to express themselves in ways that would cause them harm if the expression was associated with their actual identities.[99] But verbal harassment, hate speech, doxxing, death threats, revenge pornography, and the like have all been turbocharged online by that same functionality. And the targets of that kind of expressive conduct are often the equivalent of the Jehovah's Witnesses in the seminal First Amendment cases of the late 1930s and 1940s, or the socialists in the 1920s: members of politically unpopular, historically subordinated groups.[100] It thus seems clear that social media companies have overlearned the lesson of the benefits of anonymous speech, and the lesson has come at a frightening cost.

Social science research bears out the commonsense conclusion that platforms that permit speech from anonymous, fake-name, and sham accounts are less civil than those that don't. In one study, political scientist Ian Rowe compared reader comments on a *Washington Post* story made on the site itself, which permitted anonymous speech, to those made in response to the article's posting on Facebook, which has a real-name policy. The anonymous comments were more uncivil, more disinhibited, and contained more ad hominem attacks against other commenters.[101] Anonymity, at least as a First Amendment–informed design principle for communications networks, tends to result in a degraded expressive environment, not an improved one.

Although it might be a marginally more civil place for political discourse than Twitter, Facebook is not free from blame. While the platform requires real names, its identity-verification policies are easy to circumvent. As we now know, this can facilitate not only harassing and offensive speech but also election interference by foreign states,[102] the dissemination of false propaganda,[103] and, in the case of Myanmar's Rohingya minority, literal genocide.[104]

Value judgments about forum quality are certainly relative, and each of us decides for ourselves how much ideals such as civility and trustworthiness are worth. But it bears remembering that the First Amendment is itself a significant impediment to government interventions that aim to improve deliberation and mitigate social harms on social media. Many believe that the content moderation policies of social media platforms, however self-serving or misguided, are themselves constitutionally protected speech. The First Amendment, consequently, is both a cause of the infection and an antibody that fights off several possible cures. No one should pretend that the First Amendment lights the path forward for many of the most significant problems facing online content moderation.

If we want to build a better speech space online, either the Governors or the Governed will have to lead the way. And if the Governors won't act, it may be time to withdraw our consent to be governed by them.[105]

Newsworthiness and the Search for Norms

A LITTLE MORE THAN a decade ago, an Oklahoma television news program broadcast 39 seconds of a woman's rape. The news story featured "brief shots of [the woman's] naked feet and calves," and it depicted her naked attacker "moving above and around [her] obscured body."[106]

The woman sued the station for invasion of privacy and lost. The federal trial court explained that the rape itself was newsworthy and that the broadcast of the videotape had news value because it proved to viewers both that the rapist was identifiable and that he had videotaped his crime. Moreover, the court explained that it could not "appropriately engage in after-the-fact judicial 'blue-penciling,'" lest the press be chilled in its freedom to decide what is news.

Horrifying. But as Kate Klonick points out in her essay, courts had for years deferred to the media in privacy cases, fearful of undermining the First Amendment by second-guessing journalism. A pro-press outcome like the one in the Oklahoma case was also made easier by the fact that there was and is no clear definition in the law of what qualifies as newsworthy. Even though the Supreme Court has repeatedly suggested that some sort of line protecting privacy over press freedom is appropriate — explaining that "there *is* a zone of privacy surrounding every individual, a zone within which the State may protect him from intrusion by the press, with all its attendant publicity"[107] — the Court itself has never drawn that line.[108]

The *Restatement (Second) of Torts*, meanwhile, unhelpfully suggests that journalists' publication decisions help to define newsworthiness[109] and that news includes information "of more or less deplorable popular appeal" but not "morbid and sensational prying for its own sake."[110] And the *Restatement* offers such guidance only after suggesting that Supreme

Court precedent may not allow for any balancing against individual privacy interests at all.[111]

All this leaves courts confused and searching for additional guidance. Compare that Oklahoma ruling favoring the press—one that supported a journalist's decision to reveal what another court later called "the most private of matters: namely [the plaintiff's] body being forcibly violated"[112]—to a 2008 ruling favoring privacy, *Conradt v. NBC Universal, Inc.*[113] *Conradt* involved the NBC *Dateline* program *To Catch a Predator*, a show that filmed unsuspecting men as they attempted to meet in person the underage "children"[114] they had engaged with online in graphically sexual language.

One of the men, who turned out to be a county prosecutor and therefore a public official, killed himself as police arrived to arrest him for child sex solicitation. Blaming NBC for her brother's suicide, his sister sued on his behalf, arguing that *Dateline* journalists had intentionally inflicted emotional distress upon him.

The federal trial court sided with the sister. "NBC was in a position of power, both with its ability to disseminate information to the public and with its apparent influence over the police," the court wrote, "and NBC knew or should have known that Conradt was peculiarly susceptible to emotional distress and suicide."[115] The court also found that NBC had arguably violated journalism's ethics codes and that such a violation would further support liability. After reciting the ethics standards of the Society of Professional Journalists (SPJ) that it found relevant,[116] the court suggested how each had been broken:

> A reasonable jury could find that Dateline violated some or all of these standards by failing to take steps to minimize the potential harm to Conradt, by pandering to lurid curiosity, by staging (or overly dramatizing) certain events, by paying [a group of online vigilantes with which it worked] and providing equipment and other consideration to law enforcement, by failing to be judicious about publicizing allegations before the filing of charges, by advocating a cause rather than independently examining a problem, and by manufacturing the news rather than merely reporting it.[117]

This is horrifying in a different way. Read broadly, the court held that the news value of a public official's arrest could be outweighed by that official's interest in privacy, as long as the court found the arrest to involve "lurid curiosity" and inappropriate media–police interaction. Why did news coverage of a prosecutor's arrest on child sex solicitation charges lead to a successful privacy-based claim against the media, when the privacy claim of a crime *victim*—a woman whose rape just happened to be videotaped by the perpetrator—was summarily dismissed?

The answer lies in the absence of clear norms regarding newsworthiness. Not only has the Supreme Court been wary of drawing such lines, there aren't that many relevant lower court cases either. In the past, the journalism profession routinely defined and enforced its own ethics standards—and when journalists pushed the boundaries, courts mostly gave them the benefit of the doubt, concerned more about a chilling effect on the media than on harm to an individual. As long as journalists stuck to the standards of their field, courts treated them with deference.

* * *

Today, however, things have changed. Most online publishers are not journalists who have internalized a widely shared set of professional values and boundaries. These new publishers post on social media and on millions of websites everything from incisive comments on news stories to callously devastating revenge porn. Walter Cronkite has been replaced by *To Catch a Predator*, which in turn has been replaced by websites that extort people with mugshots.

At the same time, the interest in privacy protection has grown, both culturally and in the courts. "Today," the Ohio Supreme Court wrote a few years ago, "thanks to the accessibility of the Internet, the barriers to generating publicity are slight, and the ethical standards regarding the acceptability of certain discourse have been lowered."[118] The Ohio justices then recognized a certain privacy-related tort ("false light") for the first time, explaining that "as the ability to do harm has grown, so must the law's ability to protect the innocent."[119]

Against this backdrop, Facebook's increasingly explicit ambition to assess newsworthiness is both interesting and troubling.

What makes it interesting is that, as the *Restatement* reflects, newsworthiness norms have traditionally been determined by journalists and publishers themselves, and in crafting these norms, journalism codes of ethics strive to balance press rights and privacy rights. The SPJ's Code of Ethics, for example, includes the seemingly conflicting mandates to "Seek Truth and Report It" and to "Minimize Harm," with the suggestion that the two may need to be balanced in any given news story.[120] When courts knew that journalists were guided by professional codes that urged both that individuals be held "accountable" and that they be treated with "compassion,"[121] judges were inclined to stay out of the way.

But this balance now resides in unfamiliar and, therefore, dangerous hands, as the *Conradt* case suggests. The SPJ has become sufficiently concerned about courts' search for newsworthiness norms that it now appends to its ethics code the following warning: "The code should be read as a whole; individual principles should not be taken out of context. It is not, nor can it be under the First Amendment, legally enforceable."[122]

Which is why Facebook's role as an arbiter of newsworthiness is also troubling. As Klonick points out, given the central role Facebook plays as a source of news and information for large swaths of the public, its decisions to restrict information carry obvious significance for the democratic process.

But there is more. If certain judges, upset with today's media excesses, appear willing to use prevailing publishing standards against the media, and if questions of newsworthiness must be decided by someone other than the publishers themselves in order to protect privacy, then Facebook's standards could offer courts guidance and conceivably one day become law. Put another way, if the *Conradt* court decided that the SPJ and its approximately 7,500 members[123] should help guide newsworthiness determinations, why not Facebook, which has more than 200 million users in the United States alone?[124] These users arguably approve of Facebook's assessments of news value to at least some extent, and as the *Restatement* suggests, newsworthiness considerations should include "customs and conventions of the community"[125] and community "mores."[126]

What this means is that Facebook's decisions on what to keep up and what to take down could well do more than establish what we read about and know about on the Facebook platform. Facebook's standards could help establish what we as a society deem newsworthy, ultimately helping courts decide in a legal sense the future of news.

This prospect is deeply troubling on a press-rights front. Klonick's essay does not say much about the background of the Facebook employees who make newsworthiness decisions. Are they trained in journalism? Do they understand that the most important stories are also, at times, the most harmful to particular individuals? Do they consider the same things that journalists do when journalists consider what to publish? Do they believe, in the words of the SPJ code's preamble, "that public enlightenment is the forerunner of justice and the foundation of democracy"?

Facebook's newsworthiness assessments are troubling on a privacy front as well. While there are risks from Facebook being too aggressive in restricting information, there are also risks from Facebook being too permissive in allowing publication of potentially harmful information—risks that seem to be on the rise.

Klonick's essay initially describes Facebook's application of the newsworthiness concept in a way that might well parallel journalism's ethics codes, weighing "the value of 'voice' against the risk of harm." She further notes that "every suggestion of possible newsworthy content is made by a person" at Facebook and evaluated "on a case-by-case basis." That sounds pretty much like what happens in newsrooms every day.

But Klonick then explains that Facebook's newsworthiness assessments might actually tip in favor of "allowing more items that people find newsworthy, significant, or important to the public interest," even if these items violate Facebook's Community Standards. Words like "significant" and "public interest" in this formulation threaten privacy rights. So does the suggestion that newsworthiness determinations may effectively be crowdsourced. Consider, for example, the 17 million people who reportedly looked at a video taken of sportscaster Erin Andrews, naked, surreptitiously recorded through a peephole in her hotel room.[127] A large number of people apparently found that highly invasive footage to be significant and interesting.

* * *

As Klonick rightly warns, there are no easy answers for Facebook about how to strike an appropriate balance between the protection of the individual and the free flow of information. Nonetheless, a more sensitive approach of some sort—one not so focused on Google News search results or on the elusive public figure/private figure distinction—is critical for two main reasons. First, as outlined above, any test has at least some potential to become law and, therefore, must be mindful of both press rights and privacy rights. And second, should Facebook fail to take down privacy-invading posts, it could further irritate an already privacy-interested and media-condemning judiciary, leading to further narrowing of the meaning of news and, just as early courts warned, chilling journalism.

In recent work, I have argued for an updated press-privacy balancing test, suggesting that courts reject newsworthiness protection for things traditionally kept private in the United States, such as gratuitous nudity, gratuitous graphic sexual information, and gratuitous private medical information.[128] At the dawn of the internet age, the Seventh Circuit described information that should be off-limits in more general terms: intimate information that, if revealed, would be considered embarrassing, painful, and "deeply shocking to the average person."[129] Admittedly, even these lines would need to be crossed at times, and there is certainly an element of subjectivity in the word "gratuitous."

But again, there are no easy answers in this area. The Supreme Court has observed that in the "sphere of collision between claims of privacy and those of the free press, the interests on both sides are plainly rooted in the traditions and significant concerns of our society."[130] For the sake of privacy and the press alike, Facebook must strive to minimize the impact of such collisions, and one place to begin is by adopting a clearer test for newsworthiness.

Profits v. Principles

Sarah C. Haan*

IN HER COGENT and insightful essay, Kate Klonick describes how Facebook wears three hats: regulator, adjudicator, and publisher. In these three roles, she explains, Facebook relies on "public figure" and "newsworthiness" concepts that are similar to those developed by U.S. courts, and it endorses some of the judicial reasoning behind them. Yet Facebook's "public figure" and "newsworthiness" concepts are not identical to those concepts as they appear in First Amendment doctrine, and Facebook's use of them continues to drift.

Klonick's work is part of a broader project in which scholars assess the speech regulation of Facebook and other social media companies against principles of First Amendment law. The project is particularly worthwhile, I think, when it excavates the values at the heart of the private ordering these companies do. Among the most important values shaping private companies' speech rules are *business* values, such as the desirability of generating high profits, creating long-term value for investors, and successfully competing against rival businesses. In this commentary, I offer a few modest observations about the influence of Facebook's business model and global ambitions on its regulation of speech.

FACEBOOK'S BUSINESS MODEL

I was struck by the part of Klonick's essay in which she describes how Facebook's former global policy manager, Jud Hoffman, denied that Facebook borrowed its regulatory approach from First Amendment public figure doctrine. Instead, Hoffman told Klonick that Facebook derived its regulatory approach primarily from its corporate mission, which, in Klonick's words, "had to be balanced against competing interests," namely "users' safety and the company's bottom line."

And there it is—a clear acknowledgement that Facebook's decisions about how to regulate speech are being shaped by its profit motive. This is not surprising. In fact, it would be astonishing if a leading public company was regulating its customer platform without attending to the influence of such regulation on its business.

Mark Zuckerberg, Facebook's CEO, has defended Holocaust deniers as unintentionally mistaken, and in the name of free speech Facebook treats Holocaust denial as an idea worthy of distribution on its platform.[131] These choices, too, may be driven by the company's business interests. In its published "News Feed Values," Facebook explains that it won't discriminate among ideas because its "aim is to deliver the types of stories we've gotten feedback that an individual person most wants to see. We do this not only because we believe it's the right thing but also because it's good for our business."[132] What the company means is that it is firmly committed to a customization model, in which it delivers value to users by providing them with the information they demand. If customization is critical to the business model, and customization means delivering content that users want, how can the company criticize its users' content choices? Instead, Facebook prefers to defend those choices and, ultimately, satisfy them.[133]

Facebook must work hard to appear ideologically neutral in order to avoid pushing away users of any particular type—including anti-Semites, white supremacists, and misogynists. Because Facebook and other social media companies are engaged in surveillance capitalism, they need access to *everyone's* data, without exception, to feed their machine learning.[134] In surveillance capitalism, value is created by processing individuals' data, using data analytics, to make predictions about human behavior. Ultimately, what these companies sell are behavioral predictions, not just the attention of their users. If right-wing users quit the platform, Facebook's machine learning will lose some of its data inputs and, as a result, it will produce less accurate predictions about human behavior. So, to produce the highest-value data analytics, the company must play to all sides of the political spectrum. Elsewhere, I have referred to this as "both sides" capitalism.[135] The "both sides" approach is a recurring feature of surveillance capitalism and commercializes our understanding of what free speech means in private, digital spaces.

Tensions exist between Facebook's business interests and its aspiration to create a prosocial expressive environment, and we are about to learn how the company resolves such tensions when it is under market pressure. After Facebook's fourth quarter in 2017, the company began telling investors that its efforts to revamp its News Feed were reducing engagement.[136] The company subsequently experienced the single biggest one-day decline in market value—of any company, ever, in American history—in the summer of 2018, after it issued second-quarter results showing that its revenue growth has slowed.[137] To be clear, Facebook's worldwide revenue is still growing, but its revenue growth rate has fallen off. So demanding is the market in which Facebook operates that slight growth deceleration over two consecutive quarters caused its stock price to plummet. Its stock price has recovered, but its revenue growth continues to slow.

Since the 2016 election, the company has hired thousands of new employees as it has ramped up its speech-regulating regime, all the while noting that its expense growth would begin to exceed its revenue growth in 2019.[138] This proved true in the first quarter.[139] As the bills for these speech-regulating choices come due, we'll see how committed the company is not only to those particular choices but also to transparency about them.

AUTHENTICITY: SPEECH VALUE OR BUSINESS VALUE?

The relationship between social media companies' speech regulation and their business interests is complex. "Authenticity" rules, in which companies require users to present only their "true" selves online—and which empower companies to censor "inauthentic" speakers—offer another example.[140] Facebook presents authenticity as a speech value for users, but its real significance, at least in light of historical American speech commitments, lies in its business value to social media companies. The industry's fixation on authenticity shows how expressive values and business values are deeply intertwined in private companies' speech rule systems.

Authenticity rules lay the groundwork for companies to use data analytics to create predictions, which they sell. In order for companies' machine learning to capitalize on patterns in human behavior, companies must have accurate data inputs about identified, individual users. After all, Facebook cannot tell which age group is most likely to buy widgets unless it has accurate age information about each user. Authenticity rules not only ensure that users submit only accurate data about themselves, which is critical for data analysis, but also provide the basis for key business metrics. They make it possible for companies to offer advertisers a reliable count of ad recipients in order to charge fees, and they provide investors with a measure of the company's user base, user growth, and future cash flows. Authenticity rules make it possible for a company to marry data it has collected on an individual with commercially available data about that person, allowing it to participate in lucrative data markets.

To be sure, authenticity has some value for speech. In digital spaces, where speakers and listeners never meet face to face, listeners might trust speech more when they feel confident that speakers have been honest about their identities and their personal experiences. Speakers might feel more unconstrained if they feel confident they are speaking to people like them. Outside of fraud, of course, there is no question that, under the First Amendment, the state cannot make it illegal to speak or behave in "inauthentic" ways. Facebook and other social media companies are moving in a different direction.

Is it important to know all sorts of true personal information about someone before they speak? Our free speech tradition places a high value on anonymous political speech, which authenticity rules essentially forbid. And who is to say which aspects of your identity are "authentic" or not? For these and other reasons, "authenticity" policing presents a mixed bag for free speech—but, as social media companies know, its *business value* is great. If scholars fail to consider the business motivations underlying companies' speech rules, they miss a critical dimension of the private ordering of speech.

FACEBOOK'S GLOBAL AMBITIONS

Facebook is a global company, and both its user base and its user growth are now largely abroad. Of the company's 1.56 billion daily active users at this writing, roughly 88 percent are outside the United States and Canada and therefore likely unfamiliar with American free speech norms.[141] Although a high proportion of Facebook's worldwide revenue comes from the United States and Canada—over 48 percent in the first quarter of 2019[142]—the fact remains that the vast majority of the people whose speech Facebook regulates live outside the United States. Facebook risks alienating most of its users by adopting American First Amendment law or American free speech values. Accordingly, Facebook has a business reason to develop speech rules that incorporate speech values from the international community and from important markets for the company's advertising.

This is, in fact, what the company is doing. In August 2018, an executive in Facebook's public policy unit for Europe, the Middle East, and Africa wrote in a blog post that Facebook has looked to the International Covenant on Civil and Political Rights (ICCPR) "for guidance" about when it's appropriate to place restrictions on free expression.[143] The post suggests that the main legal influence on Facebook's current approach to this question is not U.S. free speech doctrine—which is not mentioned at all—but international human rights law.[144] The post goes on to offer the company's interpretation of the ICCPR's take on free expression, contending that this international covenant backs up Facebook's emerging principle that speech should be restricted when "necessary to prevent harm."[145] Given Facebook's global ambitions, we should expect the company to continue incorporating international law concepts into its speech rules, and to try to "sell" these concepts to an American audience.

We are at the beginning of a paradigm shift in which private companies are becoming, as Klonick memorably puts it, the New Governors of the public square. One thing this means for speech regulation is that corporate interests and accountability mechanisms will help shape the rules. Klonick's essay describes how Facebook has recently applied the "public figure" concept to users with thousands of followers, while also softening the rules so that it can offer this category of users a bit more protection against direct verbal attack. The company's approach allows it to continue to harness certain users' popular appeal to build engagement, while reducing these users' vulnerability to disparaging speech. It may not be clear where the concern for principle ends and the concern for profits begins. But the line is there somewhere for scholars to find. We won't understand what is really going on—and which values are really shaping the new speech rules and norms—until we find it.

NOTES

1. Kate Klonick, *The New Governors: The People, Rules, and Processes Governing Online Speech*, 131 Harv. L. Rev. 1598 (2018).
2. *Cf.* Frederick Schauer, *Thinking Like a Lawyer: A New Introduction to Legal Reasoning* 105 (2012) ("The common law 'works itself pure,' said Lord Mansfield, in a phrase subsequently made famous by the American legal theorist Lon Fuller,

and these words aptly capture the belief that the common law, in being fluid and always improvable at the hands of common-law judges, gradually approaches a perfection in which the rules almost never generate suboptimal outcomes." (citing Omychund v. Barker, 26 Eng. Rep. 15, 23 (Ch. 1744) (Mansfield, L.J.); and Lon. L. Fuller, *The Law in Quest of Itself* 140 (1940))).

3. Alexander Somek, *Authoritarian Constitutionalism: Austrian Constitutional Doctrine 1933 to 1938 and Its Legacy*, in *Darker Legacies of Law in Europe: The Shadow of National Socialism and Fascism over Europe and Its Legal Traditions* 361, 362 (Christian Joerges & Navraj Singh Ghaleigh, eds., 2003).

4. *Id.*

5. Mark Tushnet, *Authoritarian Constitutionalism*, 100 Cornell L. Rev. 391, 396 (2015).

6. *See* Anupam Chander, *Facebookistan*, 90 N.C. L. Rev. 1807, 1813 (2012) ("These direct relationships with a significant percentage of humanity and the power they give to Facebook have led many to employ the language associated with sovereigns to this company.").

7. *See, e.g.*, *Newsfeed Values*, Facebook, https://newsfeed.fb.com/values (last visited July 18, 2019) ("We don't favor specific kinds of sources—or ideas. Our aim is to deliver the types of stories we've gotten feedback that an individual person most wants to see. We do this not only because we believe it's the right thing but also because it's good for our business.").

8. *See, e.g.*, Jeremy K. Kessler & David E. Pozen, *The Search for an Egalitarian First Amendment*, 118 Colum. L. Rev. 1953 (2018); Genevieve Lakier, *Imagining an Antisubordinating First Amendment*, 118 Colum. L. Rev. 2117 (2018); Jedediah Purdy, *Beyond the Bosses' Constitution: The First Amendment and Class Entrenchment*, 118 Colum. L. Rev. 2161 (2018).

FACEBOOK V. SULLIVAN

The author is grateful to Jack Balkin, Molly Brady, Danielle Citron, Thomas Kadri, Margot Kaminski, David Pozen, and colleagues at the Yale Information Society Project and the Cornell Tech Speed Conference for helpful thoughts and comments on earlier versions of this essay.

9. Julia Angwin, Ariana Tobin & Madeleine Varner, *Have You Experienced Hate Speech on Facebook? We Want to Hear from You.*, ProPublica (Aug. 29, 2017), https://www.propublica.org/article/have-you-experienced-hate-speech-on-facebook-we-want-to-hear-from-you.

10. Casey Newton, *Facebook Is Deleting Links to a Viral Attack on a Charlottesville Victim*, Verge (Aug. 14, 2017), https://www.theverge.com/2017/8/14/16147126/facebook-delete-viral-post-charlottesville-daily-stormer.

11. *Id.*

12. *Gertz v. Robert Welch, Inc.*, 418 U.S. 323, 345 (1974).

13. 376 U.S. 254 (1964). The suit also included four African American clergymen.

14. *Id.* at 279–80.

15. *Id.* at 268–83. For an excellent overview of the history of the public figure doctrine, see Catherine Hancock, *Origins of the Public Figure Doctrine in First Amendment Defamation Law*, 50 N.Y.L. Sch. L. Rev. 81 (2005).

16. *Sullivan*, 376 U.S. at 270.

17. In a footnote mid-decision, the *Sullivan* Court brushed away the question of defining public officials, stating: "We have no occasion here to determine how far down into the lower ranks of government employees the 'public official' designation would extend for purposes of this rule, or otherwise to specify categories of persons who would or would not be included." *Id.* at 283 n.23.

18. 385 U.S. 374, 390 (1967); *see also* Hancock, *supra* note 15, at 105–12 (discussing the relationship of *Hill* to *Sullivan*).

19. *Hill*, 385 U.S. at 388 (internal quotation marks omitted).

20. *Id.* at 391.

21. *See id.* at 387–88 ("We hold that the constitutional protections for speech and press preclude the application of the New York statute to redress false reports of matters of public interest in the absence of proof that the defendant published the report with knowledge of its falsity or in reckless disregard of the truth.").

22. Samantha Barbas, *When Privacy Almost Won:* Time, Inc. v. Hill, 18 U. Pa. J. Const. L. 505, 508 (2015).

23. On the overlap between inquiries into matters of public concern and newsworthiness, see Richard T. Karcher, *Tort Law and Journalism Ethics*, 40 Loy. U. Chi. L.J. 781, 824–30 (2009); and Mary-Rose Papandrea, *Citizen Journalism and the Reporter's Privilege*, 91 Minn. L. Rev. 515, 578–81 (2007). *See also, e.g.*, Fla. Stat. § 90.5015(1)(b) (2017) ("'News' means information of public concern relating to local, statewide, national, or worldwide issues or events.").

24. 388 U.S. 130 (1967).

25. 403 U.S 29 (1971).

26. *Id.* at 43. "The public's primary interest is in the event," Justice Brennan continued; "the public focus is on the conduct of the participant and the content, effect, and significance of the conduct, not the participant's prior anonymity or notoriety." *Id.*

27. *Id.* at 43–44.

28. 418 U.S. 323, 339–48 (1974).

29. *See* W. Wat Hopkins, *The Involuntary Public Figure: Not So Dead After All*, 21 Cardozo Arts & Ent. L.J. 1, 21 (2003) ("[T]here is disagreement as to whether the Supreme Court identified two or three categories of public figure status.").

30. *Gertz*, 418 U.S. at 345.

31. *Id.*

32. *Id.*

33. The following section borrows from the research and conclusions in my previous work on the history of content moderation, Kate Klonick, *The New Governors: The People, Rules, and Processes Governing Online Speech*, 131 Harv. L. Rev. 1598 (2018).

34. Telephone Interview with Jud Hoffman, former Global Policy Manager, Facebook (Mar. 6, 2018); Telephone Interview with Dave Willner, former Head of Content Policy, Facebook (Mar. 5, 2018). All interview notes are on file with the author.

35. Telephone Interview with Dave Willner, *supra* note 34.

36. *Id.*

37. Telephone Interview with Jud Hoffman, former Global Policy Manager, Facebook (Jan. 22, 2016).
38. Telephone Interview with Jud Hoffman, *supra* note 34.
39. *Id.*
40. *Id.*
41. Telephone Interview with Dave Willner, *supra* note 34.
42. *Id.*
43. Simon Adler, *Post No Evil*, Radiolab (Aug. 17, 2018), https://www.wnycstudios .org/story/post-no-evil.
44. Telephone Interview with former member of Facebook Policy Team (Aug. 28, 2018).
45. *See supra* notes 25–32 and accompanying text.
46. *Gertz v. Robert Welch, Inc.*, 418 U.S. 323, 346 (1974).
47. Telephone Interview with former member of Facebook Policy Team, *supra* note 44.
48. *See* Kate Klonick, *Facebook Under Pressure*, Slate (Sept. 12, 2016), http://www .slate.com/articles/technology/future_tense/2016/09/facebook_erred_by_taking _down_the_napalm_girl_photo_what_happens_next.html.
49. The photo was likely removed because of the nudity, not because it was child pornography. *See* Kjetil Malkenes Hovland & Deepa Seetharaman, *Facebook Backs Down on Censoring "Napalm Girl" Photo*, Wall St. J. (Sept. 9, 2016), http://www .wsj.com/articles/norway-accuses-facebook-of-censorship-over-deleted-photo-of -napalm-girl-1473428032.
50. *See* Claire Zillman, *Sheryl Sandberg Apologizes for Facebook's "Napalm Girl" Incident*, Time (Sept. 13, 2016), http://time.com/4489370/sheryl-sandberg-napalm -girl-apology.
51. Joel Kaplan & Justin Osofsky, *Input from Community and Partners on Our Community Standards*, Facebook Newsroom (Oct. 21, 2016), https://newsroom .fb.com/news/2016/10/input-from-community-and-partners-on-our-community -standards.
52. Telephone Interview with Peter Stern, Head of Product Policy Stakeholder Engagement, Facebook (Mar. 7, 2018).
53. *Id.*
54. Televideo Interview with Idalia Gabrielow and Peter Stern, Policy Risk Team, Facebook (Aug. 15, 2018).
55. Televideo Interview with Ruchika Budhraja, David Caragliano, Idalia Gabrielow, and Peter Stern, Policy Risk Team, Facebook (Oct. 4, 2018).
56. Clay Shirky, *A Speculative Post on the Idea of Algorithmic Authority*, Clay Shirky (Nov. 15, 2009), http://www.shirky.com/weblog/2009/11/a-speculative -post-on-the-idea-of-algorithmic-authority.
57. Comment, *The Right of Privacy: Normative-Descriptive Confusion in the Defense of Newsworthiness*, 30 U. Chi. L. Rev. 722, 725 (1963).
58. *See, e.g.*, *Snyder v. Phelps*, 562 U.S. 443, 453 (2011) ("Deciding whether speech is of public or private concern requires us to examine the content, form, and context of that speech, as revealed by the whole record." (internal quotation marks omitted)).

59. *See, e.g.*, Amy Gadja, *Judging Journalism: The Turn Toward Privacy and Judicial Regulation of the Press*, 97 Calif. L. Rev. 1039, 1041–42 (2009) (explaining that some courts have become less deferential to the media in determining newsworthiness, perhaps on account of "growing anxiety about the loss of personal privacy in contemporary society" or "declining public respect for journalism"); Sydney Ember, *Gawker and Hulk Hogan Reach $31 Million Settlement*, N.Y. Times (Nov. 2, 2016), https://www.nytimes.com/2016/11/03/business/media/gawker-hulk-hogan-settlement.html (describing the groundbreaking jury verdict that awarded former professional wrestler Hulk Hogan $140 million after the gossip news site Gawker.com published a sex tape featuring him). *But cf.* Erin C. Carroll, *Making News: Balancing Newsworthiness and Privacy in the Age of Algorithms*, 106 Geo. L.J. 69, 77–81 (2017) (discussing cases in which the courts have "largely left the role [of determining what is newsworthy or of legitimate public interest] to the press").

60. *See generally* Kate Klonick, *Re-Shaming the Debate: Social Norms, Shame, and Regulation in an Internet Age*, 75 Md. L. Rev. 1029 (2015).

61. *Gertz v. Robert Welch, Inc.*, 418 U.S. 323, 345 (1974).

62. *Gertz*, 418 U.S. at 345, 352.

63. *Id.* at 345.

64. Erwin Chemerinsky, *Constitutional Law* 1474 (3d ed. 2009).

65. *Restatement (Second) of Torts* § 652D cmt. f (Am. Law Inst. 1977).

66. *Id.*

67. *Compare, e.g.*, Jon Ronson, *How One Stupid Tweet Blew Up Justine Sacco's Life*, N.Y. Times Mag. (Feb. 12, 2015), https://www.nytimes.com/2015/02/15/magazine/how-one-stupid-tweet-ruined-justine-saccos-life.html (describing the instant notoriety a thirty-year-old communications executive received after a racist tweet), *with* A.J. Willingham, *Why the Mom of a Child with a Facial Deformity Fought to Take Down Just One Cruel Tweet*, CNN (Feb. 7, 2018), https://www.cnn.com/2018/02/07/health/sophia-weaver-natalie-facial-deformities-advocates-medically-fragile-kids-trnd (describing online abuse directed at a child with a rare genetic disease that causes facial deformities).

68. *Alex from Target/#AlexFromTarget*, Know Your Meme, https://knowyourmeme.com/memes/alex-from-target-alexfromtarget (last visited July 18, 2019).

69. *Id.*

70. *Id.*

71. Nick Bilton, *Alex from Target: The Other Side of Fame*, N.Y. Times (Nov. 12, 2014), https://www.nytimes.com/2014/11/13/style/alex-from-target-the-other-side-of-fame.html.

72. *Id.*

73. *See, e.g.*, *Florida Star v. B.J.F.*, 491 U.S. 524 (1989) (finding that public access to lawfully obtained truthful information outweighed the privacy interests of a rape victim, even where state law barred the press from reporting the names of sexual assault victims and publication had led to the victim's harassment).

74. *Cf.* Wu, this volume ("The most important change in the expressive environment can be boiled down to one idea: it is no longer speech itself that is scarce, but the attention of listeners.").

75. For discussion of this general problem online and in other areas of law, see Danielle Keats Citron, *Hate Crimes in Cyberspace* 77–78 (2014); Heidi M. Hurd, *Blaming the Victim: A Response to the Proposal That Criminal Law Recognize a General Defense of Contributory Responsibility*, 8 Buff. Crim. L. Rev. 503 (2005); Josephine Ross, *Blaming the Victim: "Consent" Within the Fourth Amendment and Rape Law*, 26 Harv. J. Racial & Ethnic Just. 1 (2010); and JoAnne Sweeny, *Gendered Violence and Victim-Blaming: The Law's Troubling Response to Cyber-Harassment and Revenge Pornography* 8 Int'l J. Technoethics 18 (2017).

76. In Facebook's vernacular, "attacks" include calls for death or serious disease or disability, statements of intent or advocacy to engage in sexual activity, claims about sexually transmitted diseases, and terms pertaining to sexual activities used to describe an individual. Email from Ruchika Budhraja, spokesperson, Facebook, to author (Sept. 10, 2018) (on file with author).

77. *See generally* Klonick, *supra* note 33, at 1630–58.

78. *About*, Facebook, https://www.facebook.com/pg/facebook/about (last visited July 18, 2019).

79. Deepa Seetharaman, *Facebook Employees Pushed to Remove Trump's Posts as Hate Speech*, Wall St. J. (Oct. 21, 2016), http://www.wsj.com/articles/facebook -employees-pushed-to-remove-trump-posts-as-hate-speech-1477075392. Although Zuckerberg used the term "public figure," it appears that he did so casually, as a proxy for newsworthiness and not in reference to Facebook's public figure policy, which applies only to bullying and harassment and would not be applicable here.

80. Kaplan & Osofsky, *supra* note 51.

81. Casey Newton, *How Conspiracy Sites Keep Outsmarting Big Tech Companies*, Verge (July 28, 2018), https://www.theverge.com/2018/7/28/17623290/facebook -youtube-infowars-ban-discipline-policies.

82. *Enforcing Our Community Standards*, Facebook Newsroom (Aug. 6, 2018), https://newsroom.fb.com/news/2018/08/enforcing-our-community-standards.

83. *Introduction*, Facebook Community Standards, https://www.facebook.com /communitystandards/introduction (last visited July 18, 2019).

MEET THE NEW GOVERNORS, SAME AS THE OLD GOVERNORS

84. *See, e.g.*, Kate Klonick, *The New Governors: The People, Rules, and Processes Governing Online Speech*, 131 Harv. L. Rev. 1598 (2018).

85. Frank H. Easterbrook, *Cyberspace and the Law of the Horse*, 1996 U. Chi. Legal F. 207, 207. Of course, the *application* of those rules by particular actors is a separate question, which raises its own set of issues of administrability, consistency, and transparency. *See, e.g.*, Jason Koebler & Joseph Cox, *The Impossible Job: Inside Facebook's Struggle to Moderate Two Billion People*, Motherboard (Aug. 23, 2018), https://motherboard.vice.com/en_us/article/xwk9zd/how-facebook -content-moderation-works; Sandra E. Garcia, *Ex-Content Moderator Sues Facebook, Saying Violent Images Caused Her PTSD*, N.Y. Times (Sept. 25, 2018), https://www .nytimes.com/2018/09/25/technology/facebook-moderator-job-ptsd-lawsuit.html.

86. 418 U.S. 323 (1974).

87. *Id.* at 345.

88. *Id.*
89. *See, e.g.,* Elizabeth Williamson, *In Alex Jones Lawsuit, Lawyers Spar over an Online Broadcast on Sandy Hook,* N.Y. Times (Aug. 1, 2018), https://www .nytimes.com/2018/08/01/us/politics/infowars-sandy-hook-alex-jones.html.
90. *McDowell v. Paiewonsky,* 769 F.2d 942, 949 (3d Cir. 1985); *see also, e.g., Schultz v. Reader's Digest Ass'n,* 468 F. Supp. 551, 559 (E.D. Mich. 1979) (concluding there is no such thing as an involuntary public figure, given that the limited public figure category is confined to those who have thrust themselves in the vortex of a controversy); *Chafoulias v. Peterson,* 668 N.W.2d 642, 653 (Minn. 2003) ("'The proper question is not whether the plaintiff volunteered for the publicity but whether the plaintiff volunteered for an activity out of which publicity would foreseeably arise.'" (quoting 1 Rodney A. Smolla, *Law of Defamation* § 2:32 (2d ed. 2002))).
91. *See, e.g.,* Robert D. Sack, *Sack on Defamation* § 5.3.3 (3d ed. 2002).
92. *Wells v. Liddy,* 186 F.3d 505, 534, 541 (4th Cir. 1999).
93. 343 U.S. 250 (1952).
94. *Am. Booksellers Ass'n, Inc. v. Hudnut,* 771 F.2d 323, 331 n.3 (7th Cir. 1985); *see also Dworkin v. Hustler Magazine Inc.,* 867 F.2d 1188, 1200 (9th Cir. 1989).
95. David A. Anderson, *Torts, Speech, and Contracts,* 75 Tex. L. Rev. 1499, 1512 (1997); *see also* Alan E. Garfield, *Promises of Silence: Contract Law and Freedom of Speech,* 83 Cornell L. Rev. 261, 320–21 (1998) ("[E]ven before the First Amendment was invoked in private-facts cases, the common law recognized a First Amendment-like defense to the tort: no liability arises if the information disclosed is of legitimate concern to the public." (internal quotation marks omitted)).
96. Although a court might not ask the same question about Charlottesville victim Heather Heyer based on the long-standing rule that postmortem defamation is not actionable, a social media content moderator could certainly consider these issues when deciding whether to take down the post about Heyer that Klonick describes at the outset of her essay.
97. 514 U.S. 334 (1995).
98. *Id.* at 341–42.
99. *See, e.g.,* Parker Higgins, *Hey Twitter, Killing Anonymity's a Dumb Way to Fight Trolls,* Wired (Mar. 13, 2015), https://www.wired.com/2015/03/hey -twitter-killing-anonymitys-dumb-way-fight-trolls.
100. *See* Tarleton Gillespie, *Custodians of the Internet: Platforms, Content Moderation, and the Hidden Decisions that Shape Social Media* 24 (2018) ("For years Twitter ha[s] been criticized for allowing a culture of harassment to fester largely unchecked on its service, particularly targeting women, but also the LGBTQ community, racial and ethnic minorities, participants of various subcultures, and public figures.").
101. Ian Rowe, *Civility 2.0: A Comparative Analysis of Incivility in Online Political Discussion,* 18 Info., Commc'n & Soc'y 121 (2014).
102. *See* Nancy Scola, *Massive Twitter Data Release Sheds Light on Russia's Trump Strategy,* Politico (Oct. 17, 2018), https://www.politico.com/story/2018/10/17 /twitter-foreign-influence-operations-910005.
103. *See* Matthew Hindman & Vlad Barash, *Disinformation, "Fake News" and Influence Campaigns on Twitter,* Knight Found. (Oct. 2018), https://kf-site -production.s3.amazonaws.com/media_elements/files/000/000/238/original /KF-DisinformationReport-final2.pdf.

104. Paul Mozur, *A Genocide Incited on Facebook, with Posts from Myanmar's Military*, N.Y. Times (Oct. 15, 2018), https://www.nytimes.com/2018/10/15/technology/myanmar-facebook-genocide.html.

105. *See* Dakota Shane, *Research Shows Users Are Leaving Facebook in Droves. Here's What It Means for You.*, Inc. (Sept. 11, 2018), https://www.inc.com/dakota-shane/research-shows-users-are-leaving-facebook-in-droves-heres-what-it-means-for-you.html.

NEWSWORTHINESS AND THE SEARCH FOR NORMS

106. The facts and case description are from *Anderson v. Blake*, No. CIV-05-0729-HE, 2006 WL 314447 (W.D. Okla. Feb. 9, 2006).

107. *Cox Broadcasting Corp. v. Cohn*, 420 U.S. 469, 487 (1975).

108. *See, e.g., Florida Star v. B.J.F.*, 491 U.S. 524, 533 (1989) ("We continue to believe that the sensitivity and significance of the interests presented in clashes between First Amendment and privacy rights counsel relying on limited principles that sweep no more broadly than the appropriate context of the instant case.").

109. *Restatement (Second) of Torts* § 652D cmt. g (1977).

110. *Id.* § 652D cmt. g, h.

111. *Id.* § 652D, Special Note on Relation of § 652D to the First Amendment to the Constitution.

112. *Anderson v. Blake*, 469 F.3d 910, 914 (10th Cir. 2006).

113. 536 F. Supp. 2d 380 (S.D.N.Y. 2008).

114. The "children" were really adults posing as tweens.

115. *Conradt*, 536 F. Supp. 2d at 397.

116. *Id.* at 397–98.

117. *Id.* at 398.

118. *Welling v. Weinfeld*, 866 N.E.2d 1051, 1058–59 (Ohio 2007).

119. *Id.* at 1059.

120. *SPJ Code of Ethics*, Soc'y of Prof. Journalists, https://www.spj.org/ethicscode.asp (last updated Sept. 6, 2014).

121. *Id.*

122. *Id.*

123. *About SPJ*, Soc'y of Prof. Journalists, https://www.spj.org/aboutspj.asp (last visited July 18, 2019).

124. *Number of Facebook Users by Age in the U.S. as of January 2018 (in Millions)*, Statista (2018), https://www.statista.com/statistics/398136/us-facebook-user-age-groups.

125. *Restatement (Second) of Torts* § 652D cmt. h (1977).

126. *Id.* § 652D cmt. g.

127. Emily Kaplan, *The Pain You Can't See*, Sports Illustrated (Jan. 24, 2017), https://www.si.com/mmqb/2017/01/24/erin-andrews-cervical-cancer-diagnosis-hotel-stalker-civil-trial-privacy-laws-fox-dancing-stars.

128. *See, e.g.*, Amy Gajda, *Privacy, Press, and the Right to Be Forgotten in the United States*, 93 Wash. L. Rev. 201, 262 (2018).

129. *Haynes v. Alfred A. Knopf, Inc.*, 8 F.3d 1222, 1234–35 (7th Cir. 1993).

130. *Cox Broadcasting Corp. v. Cohn*, 420 U.S. 469, 491 (1975).

PROFITS V. PRINCIPLES

The author wishes to disclose that she owns a small amount of Facebook stock.

131. *See* Sara Fischer, *Facebook Ignites Free-Speech Debate*, Axios (July 19, 2018), https://www.axios.com/facebook-mark-zuckerberg-free-speech-holocaust-denial-big-tech-bebef4e7-c89e-4607-bf3e-fdf5cac2eb44.html.

132. *News Feed Values*, Facebook, https://newsfeed.fb.com/values (last visited July 18, 2019).

133. *Cf.* Zeynep Tufekci, *YouTube, the Great Radicalizer*, N.Y. Times (Mar. 10, 2018), https://www.nytimes.com/2018/03/10/opinion/sunday/youtube-politics-radical.html.

134. *See generally* Shoshana Zuboff, *The Age of Surveillance Capitalism: The Fight for a Human Future at the New Frontier of Power* (2019).

135. Sarah C. Haan, *Facebook's Alternative Facts*, 105 Va. L. Rev. Online 18, 34–35 (2019).

136. Transcript of Facebook Fourth Quarter and Full Year 2017 Results Conference Call at 2 (Jan. 31, 2018) (remarks of Mark Zuckerberg), https://s21.q4cdn.com/399680738/files/doc_financials/2017/Q4/Q4-17-Earnings-call-transcript.pdf; *see also* Jacob Kastrenakes, *Facebook Usage Falls in the US as It Begins to Tinker with the News Feed*, Verge (Jan. 31, 2018), https://www.theverge.com/2018/1/31/16956818/facebook-q4-2017-earnings-50-million-hours-reduced-usage.

137. *See* Akane Otani & Deepa Seetharaman, *Facebook Suffers Worst-Ever Drop in Market Value*, Wall St. J. (July 26, 2018), https://www.wsj.com/articles/facebook-shares-tumble-at-open-1532612135.

138. Transcript of Facebook Second Quarter 2018 Results Conference Call at 8 (July 25, 2018) (remarks of David Wehner), https://s21.q4cdn.com/399680738/files/doc_financials/2018/Q2/Q218-earnings-call-transcript.pdf.

139. *See* Facebook, Inc., Form 10Q (March 31, 2019) at 25; Transcript of Facebook First Quarter 2019 Results Conference Call at 7–8 (April 24, 2019) (remarks of David Wehner) (revenue increased 26 percent year-over-year while expenses increased 80 percent including a $3 billion accrual anticipating an FTC fine (and 34 percent not including this one-time expense)); *see also* Jeff Horwitz, *Facebook Sets Aside $3 Billion to Cover Expected FTC Fine*, Wall St. J. (Apr. 25, 2019), https://www.wsj.com/articles/facebook-sets-aside-3-billion-to-cover-expected-ftc-fine-11556137113. In July 2019, the FTC voted to fine Facebook $5 billion. *See* Emily Glazer, Ryan Tracy & Jeff Horwitz, *FTC Approves Roughly $5 Billion Facebook Settlement*, Wall St. J. (July 12, 2019), https://www.wsj.com/articles/ftc-approves-roughly-5-billion-facebook-settlement-11562960538.

140. *See* Sarah C. Haan, *Bad Actors*, 22 U. Pa. J. Const. L. (forthcoming 2020).

141. *See* Facebook, Inc., Form 10-Q at 25–26 (Mar. 31, 2019), http://d18rn0p25nwr6d.cloudfront.net/CIK-0001326801/99de879a-f34a-480f-9a13-ea0e6219cabb.pdf.

142. *Id.* at 28.

143. Richard Allan, *Hard Questions: Where Do We Draw the Line on Free Expression?*, Facebook Newsroom (Aug. 9, 2018), https://newsroom.fb.com/news/2018/08/hard-questions-free-expression.

144. *See id.* ("Human rights law extends the same right to expression to those who wish to claim that the world is flat as to those who state that it is round—and so does Facebook.").

145. *Id.*

CONTRIBUTORS

ENRIQUE ARMIJO is a professor of law and the academic affairs dean at the Elon University School of Law and an affiliated fellow of the Yale Law School Information Society Project. He teaches and writes in the areas of First Amendment, torts, administrative law, internet law, and international freedom of expression. He is a member of the American Law Institute.

DANIELLE KEATS CITRON is a professor of law at Boston University School of Law. Her scholarship focuses on privacy, free speech, and civil rights. Her book *Hate Crimes in Cyberspace* (Harvard University Press) was named one of the "20 Best Moments for Women in 2014" by *Cosmopolitan* magazine. Citron is the vice president of the Cyber Civil Rights Initiative.

JELANI COBB is the Ira A. Lipman Professor at Columbia Journalism School. He is also a staff writer at the *New Yorker* and author of *The Substance of Hope: Barack Obama and the Paradox of Progress* (2010).

MATTHEW CONNELLY is a professor of history at Columbia and principal investigator of History Lab, a project to use data science to preserve historical accountability in the age of "big data." He received his BA from Columbia and his PhD from Yale. His next book, to be published by Pantheon, is a history of official secrecy in the United States.

MARK EDMUNDSON teaches English at the University of Virginia. He is the author of *Self and Soul: A Defense of Ideals* (2015) and *The Heart of the Humanities: Reading, Writing, Teaching* (2018). He is working on a book about Walt Whitman and democracy to be published by Harvard University Press.

DAVID S. FERRIERO was confirmed as the tenth Archivist of the United States on November 6, 2009. Previously, he served as the Andrew W. Mellon Director of the New York Public Libraries and, before that, in top positions at two of the nation's major academic libraries, the Massachusetts Institute of Technology and Duke University.

AMY GAJDA, a former award-winning journalist, is the Class of 1937 Professor of Law at Tulane University. Her expertise is in privacy and media law, and she is the author of *The First Amendment Bubble* (2015) and *The Secret History of the Right to Privacy*, to be published in 2021 by Viking.

ELIZABETH GOITEIN codirects the Brennan Center for Justice's Liberty and National Security Program. She previously served as counsel to Senator Russ Feingold on the Senate Judiciary Committee and as a trial attorney in the Federal Programs Branch of the Department of Justice's Civil Division. She is the author of several articles, book chapters, and reports on government secrecy and surveillance practices.

SUZANNE B. GOLDBERG is the Herbert and Doris Wechsler Clinical Professor of Law at Columbia Law School. In 2015, Goldberg was appointed to serve as Columbia University's first executive vice president for university life. In this role, she works with students, faculty, and administrators throughout the university on issues of inclusion, belonging, and ethical leadership.

ERIC GOLDMAN is a professor of law and codirector of the High Tech Law Institute at Santa Clara University School of Law. Before becoming a full-time academic in 2002, Goldman practiced internet law for eight years in Silicon Valley. His research and teaching focuses on internet, intellectual property, and advertising law topics, and he blogs on these topics at blog.ericgoldman.org.

JACK GOLDSMITH is the Henry L. Shattuck Professor at Harvard Law School, a senior fellow at the Hoover Institution, and cofounder of Lawfare. He teaches and writes about national security law, presidential power, cybersecurity, international law, internet law, foreign relations law, and conflict of laws.

JAMES GRIMMELMANN is a law professor at Cornell Tech and Cornell Law School. He studies how laws regulating software affect freedom, wealth, and power. He tries to help lawyers and technologists understand each other by writing about digital copyright, search engines, privacy on social networks, online governance, and other topics in computer and internet law.

SARAH C. HAAN is an associate professor of law at Washington and Lee University School of Law. She teaches business law and writes about corporate governance, corporate speech, and the role of corporations in democracy. Her interdisciplinary scholarship has been published in the *Yale Law Journal, Business Lawyer*, and *University of Pennsylvania Journal of Constitutional Law*, among other venues.

RACHEL A. HARMON is the F.D.G. Ribble Professor of Law at the University of Virginia Law School, where she writes about policing and the law. She previously worked as a prosecutor in the U.S. Department of Justice, Civil Rights Division, and served as a law enforcement expert for the independent review of the 2017 protest events in Charlottesville, Virginia.

NANI JANSEN REVENTLOW is the director of the Digital Freedom Fund, which supports the advancement of digital rights in Europe through strategic litigation. She is a recognized international lawyer responsible for groundbreaking freedom of expression cases around the world, a lawyer at Doughty Street Chambers, and lecturer in law at Columbia Law School.

DAVID KAYE is a clinical professor of law at the University of California, Irvine, and, since 2014, the UN Special Rapporteur on the right to freedom of opinion and expression. His book *Speech Police: The Global Struggle to Govern the Internet* (2019) explores how companies, governments, and activists struggle to define the rules for online expression.

DAPHNE KELLER is the director of intermediary liability at Stanford's Center for Internet and Society. She has published, testified, and lectured extensively on platform regulation and internet users' rights. She was previously associate general counsel to Google, where she led work on the company's search products. She is a graduate of Yale Law School, Brown University, and Head Start.

KATE KLONICK is an assistant professor at St. John's University Law School and an affiliate fellow at Yale Law School's Information Society Project. Her research on networked technologies' effects on social norm enforcement, freedom of expression, and private governance has appeared in the *Harvard Law Review*, *New York Times*, *New Yorker*, *The Atlantic*, *The Guardian*, and numerous other publications.

GENEVIEVE LAKIER is an assistant professor of law at the University of Chicago Law School. An anthropologist as well as a lawyer, she studies the connections between culture and law. Her recent work examines the competing conceptions of freedom of speech in American constitutional discourse and popular culture, and how these competing conceptions play out in specific doctrinal contexts.

JONATHAN McCULLY is legal adviser to the Digital Freedom Fund, an organization that supports strategic litigation to advance digital rights in Europe. He previously held a senior legal role at an international press freedom organization, working on strategic litigation before international, regional, and domestic courts. He has published widely on freedom of expression, privacy, open justice, and intellectual property.

FRANK PASQUALE is the Piper & Marbury Professor of Law at the University of Maryland. He has been recognized as one of the intellectual leaders of a global movement for algorithmic accountability. His work is among the leading research on regulation of algorithmic ranking, scoring, and sorting systems, including the free expression implications of such regulation.

DAVID E. POZEN is the Charles Keller Beekman Professor of Law at Columbia Law School. He teaches and writes about constitutional law, nonprofit law, and information law, among other topics. During the 2017–2018 academic year, he served as the Knight First Amendment Institute's inaugural visiting scholar. In 2019, the American Law Institute awarded Pozen its Early Career Scholars Medal.

FREDERICK SCHAUER is David and Mary Harrison Distinguished Professor of Law at the University of Virginia and Frank Stanton Professor of the First Amendment, Emeritus, at Harvard University. A fellow of the American Academy of Arts and Sciences, his six books include *Free Speech: A Philosophical Enquiry* (1982) and, most recently, *The Force of Law* (2015).

GEOFFREY R. STONE is the Edward H. Levi Distinguished Service Professor of Law at the University of Chicago. He has served as dean of the Law School and as provost of the university, and he is the author or coauthor of many books on constitutional law, including most recently *Sex and the Constitution* (2017) and *The Free Speech Century* (2018).

OLIVIER SYLVAIN is a professor at Fordham Law School. His academic interests lie in information and communications law and policy. He is part of a team of researchers to whom the National Science Foundation awarded a grant to prototype an affordable, community-administered computing network for Harlem residents.

REBECCA TUSHNET is the inaugural Frank Stanton Professor of First Amendment Law at Harvard Law School. Her work focuses on copyright, trademark, and advertising law. Her blog, tushnet.blogspot.com, is one of the top intellectual-property blogs, and her writings may be found at tushnet.com. She is also an expert on the law of engagement rings.

KIRSTEN WELD is professor of history at Harvard University, specializing in the politics of archives, information, and historical knowledge production in the Americas. Her publications include the award-winning *Paper Cadavers: The Archives of Dictatorship in Guatemala* (2014) and articles in venues including *Hispanic American Historical Review, Journal of Latin American Studies, NACLA Report on the Americas,* and *Radical History Review.*

HEATHER WHITNEY is a PhD candidate in philosophy at New York University. She earned a JD from Harvard Law School, *magna cum laude,* and a BA in philosophy from UCLA, *summa cum laude.* She has worked on Google's Global Ethics and Compliance team, clerked for Chief Judge Diane Wood of the Seventh Circuit, and been a Bigelow Fellow at the University of Chicago Law School.

TIM WU is the Julius Silver Professor at Columbia Law School and the author of *The Master Switch: The Rise and Fall of Information Empires* (2011), *The Attention Merchants: The Epic Scramble to Get Inside Our Heads* (2016), and *The Curse of Bigness: Antitrust in the New Gilded Age* (2018). A Silicon Valley veteran, he has also worked in state and federal government.

INDEX

abortion clinics, 109n78
accomplice liability, 35–37
accountability, 306–11
activism, 341, 357, 373n76
adult establishments, 105n44
advertising: algorithmic processes for, 158–59; clickbait, 185; content ads, 217; discriminatory designs and, 184–85; economics of, 194; images for, 215; legal history of, 195; on social media, 157, 208–9; targeted ads, 194–95, 198, 213–16, 235n216
Aftenposten, 341
Ahmadinejad, Mahmoud, 298
Airbnb: discrimination on, 202–3; discriminatory designs on, 226n87; Facebook and, 181–82, 225n74; fair housing laws for, 189, 192–94, 234n201; FHA for, 214–15
Alai, Robert, 266
Alexander, Keith, 245
Alex from Target, 346–48, 353–55
algorithmic processes, 116; for advertising, 158–59; for content, 216; data in, 197, 202–3; of digital companies, 13n29; discriminatory designs and, 225n71; on Facebook, 165n91, 194–95, 227n91; as free speech, 127; legislation for, 132–33; for platforms, 166n96; policy for, 344–45; in publishing, 125–26; for YouTube, 205
Ali, Zine El Abidine Ben, 246
Alito, Samuel, 1

Allow States and Victims to Fight Online Sex Trafficking Act (FOSTA), 210–11
Amalgamated Food Employees Union Local 590 v. Logan Valley Plaza, 139
Amazon.com, 130, 184–85. *See also* tech companies
America Online, 147, 184
analogies, 113–14; competing, 134; for Google, 116; legal history of, 150–55; legislation and, 174nn219–21; social media and, 141–45. *See also* editorial analogy
analog problems, 7, 9
Andrews, Erin, 362
Angwin, Julia, 214, 231n164
anonymous posting, 185, 192, 202–3, 230n145, 370n26
anti-censorship principle, 242
antidiscrimination laws, 214
anti-pornography movement, 109n79
anti-Semitism, 81, 127–28
antitrust concerns, 221n20
antitrust law, 107n62
Apple, 160n7, 172n189, 239
Arab Spring, 246, 250
Arab states, 250–51
archives. *See* National Archives & Records Administration
Asia, 268n19
audiences, 20–21, 39–41, 48–51, 89. *See also* hostile audiences
authenticity, 366–67